THE NUCLEAR MUSE

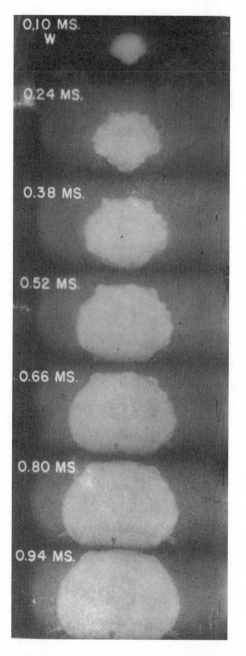

Trinity Nuclear Explosion, July 16, 1945. (Courtesy Los Alamos National Laboratory Archives.)

The Nuclear Muse

LITERATURE, PHYSICS, AND

THE FIRST ATOMIC BOMBS

JOHN CANADAY

THE UNIVERSITY OF WISCONSIN PRESS

The University of Wisconsin Press
2537 Daniels Street
Madison, Wisconsin 53718

3 Henrietta Street
London WC2E 8LU, England

5   4   3   2   1

Printed in the United States of America

A version of Chapter 3 previously appeared in the journal *Social Text* 59 (1999): 67–95, published by Duke University Press.

Library of Congress Cataloging-in-Publication Data
Canaday, John, 1961–
    The nuclear muse: literature, physics, and the first atomic bombs / John Canaday.
    pp.   cm.
    Includes bibliograpical references and index.
    ISBN 0-299-16850-6 (cloth: alk. paper)
    ISBN 0-299-16854-9 (paper: alk. paper)
    1. Nuclear energy—History. 2. Atomic bomb. 3. Nuclear physics in literature.
    I. Title
QC791.96C36   2000
355.8'25119—dc21   99-052229

For my "New Clear" Family

The unleashed power of the atom has changed everything save our modes of thinking, and we thus drift toward unparalleled catastrophe.
—Albert Einstein

. . . art makes nothing happen . . .
—W. H. Auden

CONTENTS

ILLUSTRATIONS

PREFACE

As its title suggests, this book crosses boundaries. It explores realms of experience and action—the literary, scientific, and historical—that we commonly, and with good reason, treat as the provinces of independent disciplines. These disciplines describe a conceptual grid that helps us understand and navigate our world: by dividing the world among them, they render it comprehensible and meaningful. It is no wonder we have enshrined them in academic institutions. And no wonder partisans of these disciplines defend their turf so vigorously. Indeed, past efforts of scholars in the humanities to cross disciplinary boundaries and conduct studies of the sciences have stimulated a sharply defensive response on the part of scientists who (sometimes rightly) perceived these studies as inept or hostile intrusions on their domain. The result has been an ongoing interdisciplinary battle known as the "Science Wars."

I feel great admiration and fascination for the work of my colleagues in other disciplines—perhaps especially those in the sciences. If only out of a desire to avoid alienating them, I believe that a strong and clear purpose is required to justify the trespasses undertaken in this study. That purpose may be simply stated: As separate as literary, scientific, and historical conceptions may seem, they share crucial common ground. That ground is the world of human experiences and actions. As I will demonstrate in this study, despite their tendency to elucidate, disciplinary boundaries also obscure. The conceptual grid they superimpose on the world obscures the continuity of our experiences and actions and, ultimately, misrepresents the explanatory power of these disciplines themselves. Therefore, in order to understand both the tenor and the vehicle of our academic disciplines (for they are metaphorical in nature), it is necessary to explore the boundary lands among them.

This study undertakes one leg of that exploration, focusing on what seem to me the crucial relations between literature and physics in the development of quantum mechanics and the subsequent construction and dissemination of the first atomic bombs. In the history of human actions, few are either so critical to the character and well-being of our society or so in need of elucidation. This study tries to address that need. In doing so, it complements a growing body of work by cultural critics, rhetoricians, sociologists, historians, and literary critics who have turned their analytic attentions to science. Among the various circles of these scholars, boundary crossing has become something of a commonplace (though few would deny that we are only beginning to learn how to do it). To these readers, some of my general observations about the interactions between literature and physics will not seem particularly startling, although many of the details of my explorations will be unfamiliar. But, as I have suggested, many (though not all) scientists still resist this endeavor. Nor have public conceptions of science and art yet caught up with the past several decades of academic scholarship. As a result, there is still need for further study, both to substantiate more fully the observations and arguments already advanced by other scholars and to refine and extend their analyses of these most complex issues.

Writing this book has obviously required that I gain familiarity with a number of disciplines in addition to my home ground of literary criticism. Most obviously, I have engaged in extensive study of the physics of atoms and their constituents as that discipline developed during the first five decades of the twentieth century. In addition, I have delved into the history of science in general and of physics in particular, especially the shift from classical to quantum mechanics. I have also investigated the philosophy of science; cultural studies, both of literature and of science; sociological studies of science; linguistics; rhetorical analysis; and, of course, the history and sociology of the development of the first atomic bombs. I cannot pretend to have mastered each of these disciplines with equal success, but neither could I ignore the insights and points of view peculiar to each. I have, consequently, relied on a range of work by other scholars in each of these fields, as indicated in the notes and bibliography. But I have tried also to make an asset of my outsider status by not taking their arguments for granted. Instead, I have tried to build my own arguments inductively, through the analysis of specific cases and of the larger patterns outlined by those cases.

This book will, I hope, appeal to a wide range of readers, offering theoretical analyses and specific case histories of interest to students and specialists in each of the fields I have mentioned, as well as to the general educated reader curious about these topics. To make this work accessible to such a diverse readership, I have tried throughout to write in the vernacular, avoiding overly technical language wherever possible, regardless of its disciplinary origins, and offering clear explanations where such language proved essential. There will, however, inevitably be passages that strike some readers as mundane, but which at the same time present a challenge to other readers. In these cases, I hope both groups will keep an eye on the larger argument to which such passages contribute. It is not possible to please all readers at every point, particularly when they come from such a wide range of backgrounds as this study engages, but I believe that the larger significance and interest of this book will justify any reader's investment of time and attention, and may even inspire the effort necessary to qualify and extend its observations and conclusions.

ACKNOWLEDGMENTS

The relationships that underlie this book (and not just those between literature and science) are, from its author's perspective, its more rewarding parts.

All writers should be as lucky in their editors as I have been in mine: George Levine followed this project from its beginning and not only offered useful criticisms and suggestions but also constantly reminded me in his own work why scholarly writing can matter (and be fun to read). My copyeditor, Carole Schwager, also deserves thanks: her intelligence and diligence made this book both more consistent and more readable. Among other friends and colleagues, thanks are due those who offered encouragement and/or read the manuscript in one of its various incarnations: Charles Bazerman, Daniel Bosch, Lucinda Damon-Bach, Stephen Donadio, Tom Edwards, Dan Elish, Ben Ferber, Beate Jahn, Myra Jehlen, Paul Mariani, Janet Mazur, John McWilliams, Dick Poirier, May Poovey, Barry Qualls, Warren Reed, Justin Rosenberg, Marian Yee, and Marta Zurad. In addition, several anonymous readers offered constructive comments along the way, and two readers for the University of Wisconsin Press, Robert Frost and Bryan Taylor, gave the manuscript particularly thoughtful reviews: I hope this study has benefited from their kind intelligence. My students, too—especially Stuart Abelson, Sarah Bruner, Alexander Dunn, Ezra Feinberg, Ben Kelley, Matthew Lindberg, Jay Myers, and John Purcell—deserve thanks for listening to my ideas, challenging my assertions, and offering their own insights in our work together over the years.

The friendly, knowledgeable, and patient staff at several institutions made my work easier and more thorough. Thanks especially to Roger Meade and Linda Sandoval at the Los Alamos National Laboratory; Heddy Dunn, Pat Golding, Linda Aldrich, Theresa Strottman, and Rebecca Collinsworth at the Los Alamos Historical Society; Holly Reed at the National Archives and Records Administration; Jean Hrichus at the Niels Bohr Library of the American Institute of Physics; and Felicity Pors at the Niels Bohr Archive in Copenhagen.

No study of the physics and history of nuclear weapons would get very far without the support of the men and women (and their families) who did the work in the first place. In particular, I would like to thank Norris Bradbury, William and Bebe Caldes, Winston Dab-

Acknowledgments

ney, Rachel Fermi, Kenneth Greisen, Sigmund and Florence Harris, William Higginbotham, Fred House, Theodore Jorgensen, Joanna Jorgensen Kaestner, Joseph McKibben, John Mench, William Menker, Philip Morrison, Glenn Price, Robert Porton, Joan Bainbridge Safford, Raemer Schreiber, Florence and Ben Schulkin, Robert Serber, William Spindel, Meyer Steinberg, James and Sally Taub, Edward Teller, Rudy Vergoth, Robert Webster, Jay Wechsler, John Weil, John Wieneke, and Robert Wilson for sharing their memories and perceptions with me, in interviews, conversations, and/or correspondence.

Some debts of gratitude defy words but must be acknowledged anyway. Special thanks go to Timothy Taylor and Sherry Ortner, though I know in advance that nothing I say could match their generosity of spirit and body. Likewise, my "new clear" family (as Riddley Walker would say) has been a constant support and inspiration. Last of all, in the "hart of the wud," come those who deserve to be thanked both first and last. Elizabeth and Thomas have blessed me with their intelligence, humor, and patience throughout my labors. They have made this book possible—and worthwhile. Its very best parts belong to them.

THE NUCLEAR MUSE

View of the Rio Grande Valley from Los Alamos. (Courtesy Los Alamos Historical Museum.)

INTRODUCTION

LITERATURE, PHYSICS, AND

THE FIRST ATOMIC BOMBS

Before they became physical facts, atomic weapons existed as literary fictions. As the Hungarian physicist Leo Szilard recalls:

In 1932, while I was still in Berlin, I read a book by H. G. Wells. It was called *The World Set Free*. This book was written in 1913, one year before the World War, and in it H. G. Wells describes the discovery of artificial radioactivity and puts it in the year of 1933, the year in which it actually occurred. He then proceeds to describe the liberation of atomic energy on a large scale for industrial purposes, the development of atomic bombs, and a world war which was apparently fought by an alliance of England, France, and perhaps including America, against Germany and Austria, the powers located in the central part of Europe.[1]

From our perspective, Wells's "prescience" seems almost miraculous, and even before history had echoed any of the events his novel depicts, it must have "made a very great impression"[2] on readers with some knowledge of the new science of atomic physics, as it did on Szilard. Yet at the time even Szilard, who would be inspired by *The World Set Free* to go on to play a pivotal role in motivating the United States to begin its atomic weapons program, "didn't regard it as anything but fiction."[3] Nuclear power still seemed a fantasy on par with the dreams of alchemists, even to those at the forefront of atomic research. Ernest Rutherford, for example, a Nobel laureate in chemistry for his work in nuclear physics and the man responsible for the first artificial nuclear reaction, addressed the British Association for the Advancement of Science in 1933, warning "those who look for sources of power in atomic transmutations" that "such expectations are the merest moonshine."[4] Yet artificial radioactivity was indeed discovered during that year, just as Wells had predicted. By then, Szilard thought well enough of the novel to send a copy to Sir Hugo Hirst, founder of the British General Electric Company. "Of course, all this is moonshine," he wrote in an accompanying letter, echoing the great Rutherford; but he went on to add, "I have reason to believe that in so far as the industrial applications of the present discoveries in physics are concerned, the forecast of the writers may prove to be more accurate than the forecast of the scientists."[5]

When Szilard first encountered *The World Set Free*, he had not yet done any work in nuclear physics. After reading the novel, however, he began to consider the possibility, and the consequences, of "the unleashed power of the atom," as Albert Einstein would describe it.[6] Rutherford's blank denial of its feasibility did not discourage him—if anything, it spurred him on:

This sort of set me pondering as I was walking the streets of London, and I remember that I stopped for a red light at the intersection of Southampton Row. As I was waiting for the light to change and as the light changed to green and I crossed the street, it suddenly occurred to me that if we could find an element which is split by neutrons and which would emit two neutrons when it absorbed one neutron, such an element, if assembled in sufficiently large mass, could sustain a nuclear chain reaction.[7]

Szilard pursued this line of reasoning and only a few months later was ready to patent his idea. He was deeply concerned, however, over the potential effects of his discovery:

He was oppressed, he was indeed scared, by his sense of the immense consequences of his discovery. He had a vague idea that night that he ought not to publish his results, that they were premature, that some secret association of wise men should take care of his work and hand it on from generation to generation until the world was riper for its practical application. He felt that nobody in all the thousands of people he passed had really awakened to the fact of change; they trusted the world for what it was, not to alter too rapidly, to respect their trusts, their assurances, their habits, their little accustomed traffic and hard-won positions.[8]

Ironically, this description is not of Szilard himself but of the character in *The World Set Free* credited with devising a method of releasing the energy stored in radioactive materials. It might as well have been Szilard, however. In the end, he did not patent his chain-reaction idea in his own name but in the name of the British Admiralty. Once again, Wells's novel had influenced his scientific practices in a direct, concrete way: "Knowing what [the possibility of a chain reaction] would mean—and I knew it because I had read H. G. Wells—I did not want this patent to become public."[9] His concern was somewhat premature, however; he was still a few years ahead of both the scientific and the military establishments. No one else was yet ready to pursue the implications of Szilard's patent; in fact, the British War Department even turned the patent down before Szilard offered it to the Admirality.[10]

In January 1939, Szilard learned of Otto Hahn's discovery of "nuclear fission":

Hahn found that uranium breaks into two parts when it absorbs a neutron. . . . When I heard this I saw immediately that these fragments, being heavier than corresponds to their charge, must emit neutrons, and if enough neutrons are emitted in this fission process, then it should be, of course, possible to sustain a chain reaction. All the things which H. G. Wells predicted appeared suddenly real to me.[11]

At this point, Szilard began to work earnestly in a number of directions to further the Allies' distillation of Wells's "moonshine." He encouraged other physicists to apply their efforts to the problem, despite the initial skepticism he often encountered, even from men like Enrico Fermi, who would go on to produce the world's first self-sustaining nuclear chain reaction.[12] Szilard additionally sought funds and laboratory facilities to explore his own approach to the realization of this fiction. He also lobbied scientists in the Allied nations to censor themselves and withhold publication of research papers that might encourage the Germans to accept Wells's fiction as potentially significant in scientific terms. Finally, Szilard looked for ways to encourage the Allied governments' participation in "the construction of bombs which would be extremely dangerous in general and particularly in the hands of certain governments."[13] His greatest success in this last endeavor took the form of a letter which he drafted for Einstein to send to Franklin Roosevelt, warning of the possible construction, as the result of "the work of Joliot in France as well as Fermi and Szilard in America," of "extremely powerful bombs of a new type."[14] In response to this letter, Roosevelt appointed a committee to look into the issue; this committee recommended the first commitment of funds by the United States government, thus laying the foundation for what would become the Manhattan Project.

Over the course of seven years, Szilard went from a belief that Wells's portrayal of atomic weapons was nothing but "fiction" to a conviction that it was "suddenly real." This change of heart suggests that the boundary between literary discourse and other, more "realistic" forms of discourse, such as science,[15] are not as hard and fast as we generally assume. For instance, it is a central irony of the postwar world that after Wells's literary vision helped make the scientific development of atomic weapons possible, the scientific fact of these new weapons made possible their existence as fictional entities: their physical substance notwithstanding, since World War II nuclear weapons have exercised their power in a purely symbolic form.

This assertion is, of course, highly counterintuitive. It contradicts a number of assumptions that most of us would be eager to defend, and skepticism is an entirely appropriate response to such a pronouncement. Yet we should not make the mistake of dismissing it out of hand. In the next section, I will go on to examine some of the specific assumptions that underlie our skepticism. As an immediate justification of my claim, however, consider this: The nuclear powers have built atomic weapons not because they want to employ them in combat, but they have continued to develop, construct, maintain, and deploy these bombs for symbolic ends. By representing the massive death and destruction they might cause, they are meant to render their physical use superfluous. In effect, atomic weapons are useful because of the stories people tell about them, the fears those stories inspire, and the actions by which people respond to those fears. And if we are wise, we will fervently pray that they continue to act only in this symbolic manner.[16]

Literature and Physics as Tools of Change

In May 1946, within a year of the successful detonation of the first atomic bomb, Einstein published an open telegram in the *New York Times* soliciting contributions on behalf of the Emergency Committee of Atomic Scientists (ECAS). In that telegram, he adopts an oracular tone: "The unleashed power of the atom has changed everything save our modes of thinking, and we thus drift toward unparalleled catastrophe."[17] Although the ECAS had little luck promoting its platform of international control over atomic energy, Einstein's appeal managed to capture the popular imagination, to the extent that his words have become a kind of cultural emblem, quoted again and again in contexts ranging from scholarly works to comic books. This popular impact seems the result of two factors in particular: Einstein's authority as *the* representative figure of twentieth-century science—which had just produced a spectacular example of its command over the natural world in the form of nuclear weapons—and the dexterity of his rhetorical flourish itself, which constructs an apparently inevitable movement from "unleashed power" to "unparalleled catastrophe." In this one line, Einstein crystallized a popular conception of science as a nearly omnipotent force in a world fraught with unprecedented dangers.

In contrast, W. H. Auden makes a very different claim for the affective power of his discipline: "Art makes nothing happen."[18] Almost as if to prove his point, he reached only a small audience with his aphoristic essay based on William Blake's prophetic work of 1793, *The Marriage of Heaven and Hell*. Although Auden wrote his essay in 1939, it remained unpublished until a collected edition of his poems, essays, and dramatic pieces appeared in 1977. Auden must have felt strongly about the point, however, since his elegy for W. B. Yeats, also written in 1939, makes a remarkably similar assertion:

> For poetry makes nothing happen: it survives
> In the valley of its making where executives
> Would never want to tamper, flows on south
> From ranches of isolation and the busy griefs,
> Raw towns that we believe and die in; it survives,
> A way of happening, a mouth.

Although Auden's rhetoric is much less urgent in tone than Einstein's (Auden seems resigned, almost perversely satisfied with the situation he describes), he makes a similarly sweeping claim. Indeed, both the similarities and the differences of these claims are striking, and it is worth bearing in mind that they appeared at opposite ends of the same period of cultural turmoil, for while Einstein's telegram confronts the costs of victory in World War II and the newly assumed burden of social responsibility on the part of the scientists who, like himself, helped bring it about, Auden's poem engages the apparent defeat, with Yeats's death and Europe's second descent into war in twenty years, of his belief that he or his poetry might make a difference in the world.

Auden and Einstein would seem to speak from positions of authority. Their words command our respect, based on each man's superlative accomplishments; so when they comment on the social relevance of their respective disciplines, we are inclined to take them seriously. Nor do their remarks strain our credulity. Indeed, after half a century and countless borrowings, these utterances have become fragmented in the minds of readers, divorced from their original contexts, and remembered more for the rhetorical éclat they offer the narratives that cite them than for the particular meanings their authors hoped to convey. So they affect us less as firsthand accounts from the front lines of physics and literature than as echoes of what we already believe to be true about those disciplines.

These beliefs are relatively easy to summarize. In general, our society harbors deeply ingrained conceptions of science as central, active, objective, true, and influential, and of art (in general) and literature (in particular) as marginal, passive, subjective, fictional, and ineffectual. For example, a 1992 annotated ranking of the hundred most influential people in history placed Shakespeare, almost the only literary figure included, far down the list. The author justified this by saying, "I have ranked Shakespeare this low not because I am unappreciative of his artistic accomplishments, but only because of my belief that, in general, literary and artistic figures have had comparatively little influence on human history."[19] Not surprisingly, many literary critics would disagree with this appraisal, having felt the power of literature themselves and having witnessed it acting on their students, friends, family, and fellow subway passengers. But these observations only confirm the "folklore" conception of literary criticism as "a species of highly elaborated connoisseurship, interesting and valuable, perhaps, but subjective beyond hope of redemption, and thus out of the running in the epistemological sweepstakes."[20] If we accept this appraisal, the animadversions of practitioners of this solipsistic, elitist discipline—if it even deserves the name—would hardly seem worth listening to.

Science is another story: "The rule of thumb has been that the hard scientists produce reliable knowledge, assembled into coherent theories."[21] All around us we see the fruits of the scientific method: television, computers, automobiles, Velcro, contact lenses, this book. Who can doubt the importance and efficacy of the scientific method? Most of us would be inclined to ridicule a literary author for making the kinds of claims that seem to fall easily from the lips of scientists: "Science in being research, may be to the liberal education, not an accident, not an ancillary or secondary or convenient thing to be held in balance— it may be the scripture itself."[22] For obvious and compelling reasons, we tend to view science as an essential foundation and motive force for our society. Even our everyday language can be construed as a function of science: as M. A. K. Halliday and J. R. Martin point out, "The language of science has become the language of literacy."[23] Few people would say as much for literature. My own attitudes have developed in this same context, and as a result I constantly question the value of literature and the usefulness of a life devoted to its study and production. And yet, in attempting to pursue this doubt in a rigorous way, I have found that it leads, ironically, to a greater appreciation for the social power of literature and literary modes of thinking, speaking, and writing.

In the end, antagonistic conceptions of art and science prove compelling largely to the extent that they remain general. It is quite easy to distinguish between scientific and artistic productions or to characterize the activities of "science" or "art" on a stereotypical level. When we look more closely at the specific practices of real individuals, however, the initial clarity of the differences between these disciplines grows somewhat more cloudy. Suppose, for instance, that we find a given individual at a particular moment engaged in crafting an extended metaphor around the conceit of "wandering on new paths." Is this person a literary author or a scientist? Is the metaphor part of an article in a physics journal or a poem in a literary magazine? As it happens, I have taken this phrase from an essay by Niels Bohr, published in *Nature* in 1928, in which he introduces his complementarity principle.[24] But it could as easily have come from a poem by John Donne or from a text outside the conventional boundaries of either art or science, such as Lewis and Clark's journals,[25] or even from a scientist quoting Donne or Lewis and Clark as a way of commenting on a particularly innovative development in physics.[26]

The range of rhetorical contexts in which this metaphor might occur suggests that categories such as "physics" and "literature" describe activities that overlap more than popular conceptions recognize. Numerous studies in recent years have explored this overlap. Many point out the common ground of textual orientation and, accordingly, focus on the rhetorical practices through which science constructs its powerful descriptions of the natural world.[27] Some explore the dependence of science on what are commonly thought of as "literary" practices, such as the use of metaphors, narratives, personification, and dramatic representations.[28] Others examine the thematic contents of literary texts alongside prominent scientific theories, either implicitly or explicitly engaging in comparative analyses.[29]

The quality of studies of this kind is uneven. The relations between literature and physics, for example, are tremendously complex, and studying these relations involves one in a nearly monumental effort to gain sufficient knowledge of both subjects as well as a number of ancillary fields. Obviously, some authors will be more successful at this than others. Even the most responsible and successful studies will, almost inevitably, be flawed. In addition, some scientists react territorially to incursions onto their turf by scholars from other disciplines. Some even respond to these studies as though they presented a threat to the social prestige and the economic well-being of science. As a result, a passionate debate, often referred to as the "Science Wars," has erupted in recent years between competing academic camps generally associated with conservative scientists on the one hand and radical, or "constructivist," cultural critics on the other. Once all the sound and fury dies down, I think we will find some justice on both sides: some studies of this sort undoubtedly deserve the contumely heaped on them by defensive scientists; yet some of these studies have unearthed a wealth of evidence establishing strong connections between the traditions of science and literature and demonstrating the need for further study.[30]

In undertaking a study of this kind, it behooves us to listen carefully to the objections advanced by those who view the enterprise skeptically. In particular, we should never lose sight of the fact that, whatever their similarities, science and literature remain very different in a variety of respects.[31] Additionally, it would be wise to bear firmly in mind the range and value of the contributions to our culture that each has made and continues to make. At the same time, however, we must vigilantly resist the Snow-blinded temptation to assume the absolute solidity and solidarity of these useful categories.[32] The simple fact that "science" and "art" both refer in themselves to large groupings of widely diverse activities—from immunology to quantum mechanics, from poetry to performance art—should alert us to the danger of uncritically accepting the assumption that a given discipline constitutes a unique epistemological realm unto itself.

Consider, for example, the connection between literature and physics as text-based activities. Literature, of course, consists entirely in the production and consumption of texts. Physics manifests a similar emphasis; indeed the two involve a comparable variety of texts: scientific articles and short stories, textbooks and novels, lab reports and poems, memos and memoirs. One might usefully object that physics does not restrict itself to a textual relation to the world, for in the laboratory physicists engage in physical manipulation of natural phenomena. This is a tangible basis of difference. Yet even experimental activities demonstrate a thoroughgoing dependence on textual practices: without lab notebooks, equipment manuals, wiring diagrams, correspondence files, memoranda, Post-it Notes, grant proposals, commentary on photographic plates, and other textual apparatuses, experimental physics could not exist in any meaningful form. And, ultimately, its practices derive from and feed into such textually based activities as publication of experimental results, confirmation or refutation of theoretical texts, and instigation of new theoretical formulations and research proposals.

Furthermore, the degree of physical interaction with the natural world can be as much of a distinguishing feature *within* physics as *between* physics and literature. Physicists routinely define their own practices based on their relative theoretical and experimental emphases. The importance of this distinction is apparent, for instance, in Ian Hacking's influential introductory text on the philosophy of science, in which it is a central organizing principle. More recently, Peter Galison has expanded on Hacking's contention that "the relationships between theory and experiment differ at different stages of development, nor do all the natural sciences go through the same cycles."[33] Galison offers a detailed examination of the discontinuities between experimental and theoretical branches of microphysics, pointing out that they resemble separate cultures closely tied together by regular commerce in well-established "trading zones," such as laboratory colloquia, conferences, and e-mail exchanges. This observation allows Galison to account for the simultaneous continuity and flexibility of the scientific tradition as a product of "intercalated periodization,"[34] in which the branches of physics—theory, experimentation, and instrumentation—go through overlapping and largely autonomous periods of stability and change.

For the purposes of my study, it is helpful to recognize that each of these subdisciplines of physics is itself an intercalation of many distinct but overlapping elements.[35] Indeed, it is ultimately impossible either to draw absolutely distinct boundaries or to assert the complete unity, at any level, among the many individuals and the myriad prejudices, practices, and texts that we collectively call contemporary physics. Wherever we draw our boundaries, we are uniting disparate things and separating connected ones. The same holds, on a larger scale, with art and science. As I have said, there are many differences between the realms of human activity we generally label with these terms. But once we acknowledge the intercalation of all human knowledge, it is hardly surprising that we seem unable to agree just what those differences are in any sort of rigorous or absolute sense—despite authoritative attempts like C. P. Snow's *The Two Cultures* to spell them out. This should remind us of the need to be aware of both the limitations and advantages of the groupings made in this, or any study; although we cannot and should not avoid them altogether, neither should we allow our thinking to stagnate around them.

The consequent terminological difficulties will quickly become obvious. Throughout this study, beginning in its subtitle, I refer to "literature" and "physics." These are useful (indeed unavoidable) terms. Most readers will think they understand immediately what I mean by them. But precisely because of the dynamic I have described, such terms are not as straightforward as they appear. Whether we are contrasting "art" and "science," "literature" and "physics," "fiction" and "nonfiction," "experimental physics" and "theoretical physics," "naturalism" and "magic realism," "the Copenhagen interpretation" and "the Schrödinger interpretation," "Auden's style" and "Yeats's style," or "Bohr's approach" and "Einstein's approach," there are no absolute boundaries between these pairs of terms, despite the many differences between them. Furthermore, each term is schizophrenic in its own right, referring simultaneously to a body of knowledge—a canon or corpus— and a bodiless set of practices. My use of these terms reflects this schism: sometimes I use them to refer to productions, such as particular theories, novels, papers, plays, or formulas; sometimes to practices, such as taxonomy or the use of metaphorical language.

As a result, over the course of this study, some readers will notice inconsistencies in my use of terms like "literature" and "physics." This is not, however, a failure on my part—quite aside from its being an unavoidable characteristic of the terrain I cover. Each of these terms may be either broken apart into distinct subcategories or conjoined with similar terms to form higher level categories. Rather than being a hindrance to our analytic efforts, however, the intercalation of the real-world practices to which these terms refer is what makes such analysis both possible and necessary. Although literature and physics lack the obvious "trading zones" connecting the theoretical, experimental, and instrumental branches of physics, they are linked by a different kind of trading zone consisting of their common involvement in the production of texts, as noted above. Differences in tendency and intention notwithstanding, both disciplines share limited resources of diction, syntax, and figuration, providing the grounds for a wide range of complex interconnections between them, as I will demonstrate in the chapters that follow.

The Prolific and the Devourer

With these considerations and cautions in mind, let us examine Einstein's and Auden's characterizations of their respective disciplines in more detail. As we shall see, there is a great deal more common ground between them than initially appears. Einstein, for his part, describes the contemporary condition of society in terms of a potential catastrophe, and he identifies the source of that catastrophe in the development of atomic weapons. Yet he does not mention atomic weapons directly, preferring instead to allude to them obliquely through a vague phrase, "the unleashed power of the atom." Although his readers, particularly at the time, would invariably understand "atomic bombs" as the referent of this phrase, and despite his apocalyptic tone, Einstein apparently wishes to balance a sense of the scientific achievement and technological benefits that accompany the liberation of atomic power against the unrestrained destructive force of atomic weapons. In part, this search for balance reflects a concern over his personal involvement in the condition he laments: Einstein was well aware that his work on relativity theory and quantum mechanics earlier in the century could be seen as directly preparing the way for the eventual "unleashing" of atomic power.[36] Furthermore, he had signed his name to the 1939 letter, mentioned earlier, warning President Roosevelt that "Germany has actually stopped the sale of uranium from the Czechoslovakian mines" and that one reason for this might be an attempt to construct "extremely powerful bombs of a new type."[37] This letter is generally credited with stimulating the United States to begin its own atomic bomb program.[38]

Not surprisingly, therefore, Einstein's open telegram is also vague on the subject of the agency responsible for unleashing the "power of the atom." The absence of direct attribution engenders a tension between the implicit figure of the scientist, in this case Einstein himself, and the explicit agent of change, the atom. In Einstein's rhetoric, the atom takes on the active role and underscores our own reduction to a passive state in which "we thus drift toward unparalleled catastrophe." So Einstein figures the liberation of atomic energy in terms of an inhuman lack of restraint in which the scientist-liberator disappears into grammatical oblivion. The absence of the scientist figure just where Einstein's authoritative rhetoric would lead us to expect it must complicate our initial reading of the telegram as an implicit claim for the affective power of science. If the scientist does not occupy a position of special power, then perhaps it is possible to avoid questions of individual responsibility. But if this were the case, Einstein would be undermining the basis of his own rhetorical authority. Furthermore, Einstein's reputation suggests he did not lack the courage of his convictions: he might be distressed by the implication that he had contributed to the deaths of hundreds of thousands of Japanese civilians, but he would not attempt to escape the consequences of his actions.

Clearly there is more at work here than an attempt on Einstein's part to deny personal involvement; perhaps even more, his rhetoric reflects a loyalty to the impersonal model of the ideal scientist. Einstein's telegram implicitly asserts that science plays a powerful role in changing the material conditions of human existence, and a large and unspoken part of that claim involves the dissociation of agency from the individual scientist. Einstein's very ability to make such a causal assertion on behalf of science depends on the impersonality of the discipline, on its "transcendence" of the quirks and vagaries of particular scientists. This apparent transcendence dresses the individual productions of specific scientists in the cloak of objectivity. But it also masks the interplay of individual and institutional forms of responsibility and power that underlie an objective consensus. Einstein's telegram, therefore, in packing so much meaning into a single line with an ostensibly straightforward and practical message, exemplifies the ways in which scientists must exercise considerable rhetorical acumen to contain the conflicting meanings and involved power dynamics that seethe under the seemingly placid surface of the scientific tradition as it exists as a real social entity.

Perhaps the greatest irony of Einstein's rhetoric is that ultimately it depends for its authority on the situation it seeks to redress. The unleashing of atomic power, in both civilian and military forms, led to an era in which scientists enjoyed an unprecedented degree of direct influence over their culture, as well as a new level of popular awareness of that influence—as manifest in the assumptions regarding the affective power of science that I have already outlined.[39] Samuel Allison, for example, describes a sudden change in the social status of science following the war: "Suddenly physicists were exhibited as lions at Washington teaparties, were invited to conventions of social scientists, where their opinions on society were respectfully listened to by life-long experts in the field, attended conventions of religious orders and discoursed on theology, were asked to endorse plans for world government, and to give simplified lectures on the nucleus to Congressional committees."[40] The newly lionized physicists produced a flood of lectures, articles, editorials, autobiographies, educational tracts, political proposals, short stories. They even began to publish their own nonscientific journal, the *Bulletin of the Atomic Scientists*. Einstein was among them. His telegram for the ECAS is just one of many similar examples of scientists at this time trying to live up to the sense of social responsibility that accompanied their newfound influence. Thus Einstein's struggle with the twin demons of influence and responsibility, far from being an extraordinary instance, in many ways typified the experience of scientists, particularly physicists, following the war.[41]

Interestingly, their new level of popular influence tended to lead many physicists away from physics, the apparent medium of their achievement, and toward more literary forms of expression. These physicists did not, of course, simply abandon their discipline. But the time and energy they devoted to writing, speaking, petitioning, and editing; to drafting legislation and international treaties; to testifying and to reminiscing—all this could fairly be said to distract many physicists from the active pursuit of physics. So the simple opposition, which at first glance seems to characterize the relations between literature and science, is undermined by the very conditions for which it attempts to account. A more sophisticated understanding is needed.

Auden, for his part, had an admirably subtle and nuanced sense of the relationship between science and literature. To him, the image of a scientist as a socially responsible individual would have offered little novelty. His father, a physician with a well-established practice in York at the time of Wystan's birth, brought up the young poet in a household in which "scientific books stood side by side with works of poetry and fiction."[42] Indeed, practically speaking, Auden felt a deep and abiding connection between the two disciplines; for years he pursued an active interest in the science of mining which, as he wrote, "deceived not only myself but my parents into thinking that it was a genuine scientific interest and that I was gifted to become, what I said I was going to become, a mining engineer."[43] He went so far as to pass the Preliminary Examination in Natural Science at Oxford, successfully completing courses in zoology, botany, and chemistry, before turning in 1926 to read first philosophy, politics, and economics, and then English language and literature.[44] As he later recognized, his initial infatuation with the technical details of mining was "a symbolic one."[45]

Auden, however, never lost his respect for or his general interest in science, and his poetic practice throughout his life reflects this interdisciplinary leaning. We can find evidence of it ranging from his choice of topics to the use of technical diction in his poems. But for my current purposes, a more interesting connection might be drawn between Auden's pronounced sense of the social responsibility of the poet and his father's immediate and powerful embodiment of the figure of the scientist. Not only was George Auden a doctor, and therefore a particularly active and influential manifestation of the scientist as a socially responsible individual, but he gave up his lucrative private practice in York when Auden was a child in order to accept a lower-paying position as "Birmingham's first School Medical Officer, a pioneer job which would chiefly mean inspecting and where necessary improving the sanitary arrangements in the schools controlled by the city's Education Committee."[46] During the 1930s, following his graduation from Oxford until he moved to the United States in 1939, Auden demonstrated a similar commitment to the use of his professional abilities in a socially influential form. In 1937, for instance, he traveled to Spain as a part of the International Brigade, as did so many other European and American intellectuals and artists, in an attempt to combat and document the excesses of Franco's Nazi-backed nationalist forces. Likewise, in 1938, he and Christopher Isherwood toured China and reported their observations in *Journey to a War*.[47]

The pronouncement "art makes nothing happen," therefore, which I initially contrasted to Einstein's view of his own discipline, represents a marked shift in the poet's formerly activist attitude. A closer look at the rhetorical contexts in which Auden makes that shift reveals a further complication of the simple opposition between art and science. In his elegy for Yeats, Auden writes of a poet who was in many ways his mentor, one of a group of influential figures to which his father also belonged. Like Auden's father, Yeats encouraged the view that poetry could be a socially effective medium; as an Irish nationalist, a celebrant and eulogist of revolutionary activists, Yeats strove to make a practical difference with his verse. Evaluation of Yeats's success or failure in this regard is therefore central to Auden's reflection on the elder poet's life and, simultaneously, a commentary on his own efforts in the same direction. In the context, then, of Yeats's death, the apparently endless and stifling internecine struggle in Ireland, the fall of the republican forces in Spain, a decade of Sino-Japanese conflict in China, the emergence and spread of Nazi Germany, and the beginning of World War II, Auden would come to question the efficacy of his discipline to influence the events with which he had been most intimately involved during his entire adult career.

As a result, Auden began to develop a new characterization of poetry. In his elegy for Yeats, for example, Auden portrays the dead man's poetry as a medium of survival on the level of individual expression and specifically denies its ability to function as a vehicle of social reform: despite Yeats's best efforts, "Ireland has her madness and her weather still." In place of an activist view, the first section of "In Memory of W. B. Yeats" asserts that when he died the elder poet "became his admirers"— "The words of a dead man" surviving, though modified, "in the guts of the living." Then, in the brief second section of the poem, Auden repeats this idea of survival three times: "Your gift survived it all. . . . For poetry makes nothing happen: it survives . . . it survives, / A way of happening, a mouth." Auden added this section between the poem's initial publication in March 1939 in the *New Republic* and its subsequent appearance in the *London Mercury* in April, during what seems to have been a period of crisis. As Humphrey Carpenter writes in his biography of Auden, "In these lines, all Auden's attempts during the previous ten years to involve his poetry in politics and society were categorically rejected."[48]

This repudiation of his activist tendencies may also help explain Auden's omission of the poem "Spain, 1937" from post-1945 editions of his *Collected Poems*. The poem was originally published in March 1937 as a pamphlet with a print run of three thousand copies; proceeds from its sale went to support the work of Medical Aid in Spain.[49] In it, Auden portrays "the poet," "the [scientific] investigator," "the poor," and "the nations" in a time of struggle, calling out in doubt and pain to "the life / That shapes the individual belly . . . 'Intervene.' " But "the life" replies:

> "O no, I am not the Mover,
> Not to-day, not to you. To you I'm the
>
> "Yes-man, the bar-companion, the easily-duped:
> I am whatever you do; I am your vow to be
> Good, your humorous story;
> I am your business voice; I am your marriage.
>
> "What's your proposal? To build the Just City? I will.
> I agree. Or is it the suicide pact, the romantic
> Death? Very well, I accept, for
> I am your choice, your decision: yes, I am Spain."[50]

Here Auden's abstract life force insists that human history is the product of human will and human action; it is one of Auden's strongest statements of his belief in the efficacy of individual effort. The poem rather bleakly concludes, "History to the defeated / May say Alas but cannot help or pardon." And yet this voice, whether that of history, God, some vague life force, or simply Auden himself, although it appears indifferent in its refusal to protect or forgive us, is strikingly affirming in that it grants us both the power and the responsibility to take control of history. No doubt Auden's later return to the Church of England and his belief in a beneficent God influenced his repudiation of this uninvolved godlike voice, but such a shift also ironically coincides with the skeptical tone of his elegy for Yeats, which portrays our only real power as deriving from the simple survival of our words.

Despite Auden's apparently pessimistic pronouncements, however, we should be wary of dismissing this power as inconsequential. The survival of particular verbal formulations is, after all, central to the success and endurance of both science and literature. While individual scientists and authors live for a rather brief time, according to almost any scale, the durability of written language gives our utterances a power we lack. As long as our words retain a physical substance, they have the potential to be read and to affect those who read them. It is no coincidence that both literature and science began their phenomenal development in Europe just when the invention of the printing press made the preservation and dissemination of the written word practical.[51] Auden knew this as well as anyone, which accounts, I think, for the paradoxical power of the language with which he describes the powerlessness of poetry. Ultimately, the powerlessness is our own: Regardless of the strength of our convictions or the depth of our desire, we cannot control what people do with our writings. Auden clearly felt this to a profound degree, and, ironically, Einstein's experience also illustrates this situation quite forcefully. Yet just because poetry (or science) will not serve as a medium for the poet (or scientist) to make something particular happen, it does not follow that poetry (or science) itself makes nothing happen.

The Manhattan Project

My analysis of Einstein's and Auden's remarks points out the considerable complexity lurking within even such epigrammatic characterizations of their disciplines. In this book I intend to examine these disciplines in sufficient detail to reveal this complexity more fully and to elucidate its sources. To do so, I have chosen the development of the first nuclear weapons, and the physics behind their construction, as a focus. It is a compelling case, for many reasons. Nuclear weapons present a significant threat to the continued survival of the human species and, indeed, the planet—a threat that, in my view, compels us to strive for a more complete understanding than we have yet attained. At the same time, these weapons embody perhaps the most impressive single creative achievement in our history. Not surprisingly, therefore, they involved physicists in circumstances that challenged cherished assumptions regarding their discipline and required them to strain its resources to the utmost. As a result, the context of their development forces into relative prominence social and representational processes that in more familiar circumstances tend to go unremarked.

For a better sense of this context, let us return to the consideration of the historical development of nuclear weapons with which we began. By the spring of 1943, a little more than three years after Einstein sent his famous letter to Roosevelt, the Manhattan Engineer District consisted of a number of semiautonomous divisions, each with its own director but all subject to supervision by General Leslie Groves of the Army Corps of Engineers.[52] Groves, in turn, reported to James Conant, director of the National Defense Research Council, which was itself overseen by Vannevar Bush of the Office of Scientific Research and Development. In addition, each of the divisions of the Manhattan Project was administered by a corporate or institutional entity, such as DuPont, the University of Chicago, and the Massachusetts Institute of Technology. These divisions included theoretical groups at Columbia University and the Universities of Chicago and California at Berkeley; research and pilot uranium separation facilities at Princeton University and MIT; a fifty thousand–person plutonium production plant located in Hanford, Washington; and an equally large electromagnetic isotope separation and gaseous diffusion works at Oak Ridge, Tennessee. But in many ways the heart of the project was at Site Y, better known as Los Alamos, where J. Robert Oppenheimer directed a majority of the greatest physicists from Europe and the United States in the actual effort to design and build usable atomic bombs.

Despite the discovery of nuclear fission in 1938, the outbreak of war in Europe in the following year, and the warning conveyed in Einstein's August letter, the United States government appears to have been reluctant to commit itself to an atomic bomb project. The gigantic and complex organization outlined above took shape only gradually, beginning with a small group of scientists at Columbia and an initial investment of just a few thousand dollars. But in September 1942, the United States government decided to pursue the possibility of atomic weapons aggressively. Colonel Groves was promoted to brigadier general and put in charge of the effort. By March 1943, the first of over six thousand physicists, chemists, metallurgists, ballistics specialists, engineers, and technicians, along with their wives, children, and the military and civilian personnel necessary to support them, began to arrive at Los Alamos, an isolated mesa at the foot of the Jemez Mountains on the edge of the Rio Grande Valley in central New Mexico. This gathering constituted the largest, most complex, expensive, and ambitious scientific project ever undertaken. Its goal was the manipulation of forces on a scale beyond that of any previous human experience. Its context was the most extensive war in human history, and the physics on which it depended was younger than many of the physicists involved. Furthermore, all this took place in a setting unfamiliar to most of the participants: a landscape of vast proportions and almost unearthly beauty.

In the face of so many unknowns, such disorienting conditions, the Los Alamos scientists searched for ways to organize their experience in a more familiar framework. They looked for a means of describing their new experience that would connect it to the old. Among these efforts, they turned again and again to literature—for its metaphors, for the context and tradition it offered, for a sense of continuity to counterbalance the pervasive strangeness in their lives at Los Alamos, and for its ability to represent the social meanings of their work. They read the Bible and the *Bhagavad Gita*, Thomas Mann's *Magic Mountain* and H. G. Wells's *The World Set Free*; they quoted John Donne's divine poems and the legends of Faust; they cited Columbus's letters and Puritan descriptions of the New World; they produced morality plays and comedies, manifestos and petitions; they wrote and rewrote their own histories. In general, literature provided them with a way of accounting for the strange and threatening aspects of their errand in the wilderness: it named and subdued the unknown. It allowed them to submerge previously incompatible elements of their experience—pacifist convictions and military research, for example—within a wide variety of compelling narratives. Existing works of literature thus enabled the Los Alamites to tell stories of their war that cast its contradictions and drastic consequences in terms of narrative necessity, of tradition, and of social continuity.

The stories the Los Alamites told did more than simply comfort them or explain away inconvenient details. These stories also had a powerful practical effect, helping the scientists to cast their work within a conceptual framework that allowed them to proceed with the work of building the most destructive weapons humanity had ever seen. In addition, literature provided the scientists with a context that helped them bind more than six thousand individuals from a wide variety of national, economic, and ethnic backgrounds into a coherent community. Literature also helped connect their particular experience and work at Los Alamos to the context of society at large. Fitting their experiences to existing narratives tended to lift the Los Alamites out of the isolation imposed on them by their geographical situation and a rigorous military censorship. This helped them to feel connected to society and a part of larger social processes. What is more, the Los Alamites not only told these stories to themselves and to each other; they also published them to the world. In this, we see a primary mechanism of the scientists' social influence: by promulgating these narratives, the Los Alamites employed literature as a powerful medium that helped them to influence the ways in which atomic weapons have been incorporated into the structures of individual, institutional, and international relations.

While these narratives proved useful as vehicles for the Los Alamites' complex experiences and conceptions of their work, they were also extremely difficult to control. Their power and their limitations, in fact, derive from the same sources. The Los Alamites did not invent their narratives; their efficacy as a means of representing the more unfamiliar and threatening aspects of the bomb project depended precisely on their existence as established social artifacts. As such, they offered a kind of prefabricated foundation on which the Los Alamites could construct their experiences as meaningful in ways that would appear coherent within existing forms of social discourse. Likewise, literature served as an effective medium for the scientists' complex and often contradictory perceptions because its rhetorical practices promote multilayered, polysemic representations. Yet both of these characteristics also make literature extremely unreliable in the transmission of unitary, deterministic meanings.

By incorporating their own experiences into existing literary models, the Los Alamites seemed to be simplifying their work of representation; but doing so simultaneously complicated the experiences they meant to convey. In the process, the scientists ceded a great deal of the authority of their direct knowledge of atomic weapons to the narratives themselves. Therefore, it should be no surprise that a majority of vocal scientists has professed dissatisfaction with the attitudes toward nuclear weapons prevalent in the world today, even though those attitudes owe so much to their "own" narratives. Indeed, the more power such narratives have to integrate our experiences into the complex fabric of social meaning, the less we are able to direct them, to reduce their energies to the service of a single, determinate message.[53]

The implications of this dynamic will become clear later in this study when I consider it in more detail in the context of a variety of specific examples. For the moment, however, a general sense must suffice as I round out my narrative of the Manhattan Project with a description of the two different types of bombs it produced. "Little Boy," dropped on Hiroshima, was a "gun-type" bomb. In this weapon, conventional explosives fired two subcritical masses of uranium-235 down a gunlike barrel into one another, causing the split-second formation of a critical mass of fissionable material. In this critical mass, stray neutrons collided with uranium nuclei, splitting each atom into two lighter elements and releasing two or more additional stray neutrons. These neutrons in turn collided with other uranium nuclei, and the process perpetuated itself at an exponential rate. The explosive energy itself resulted from the fact that as each atom fragmented some of its mass converted to energy according to Einstein's famous equation $E = mc^2$: The resultant energy equals the converted mass times the square of the speed of light.

Constructing uranium bombs presented a particularly daunting challenge, however. The most abundant isotope found in natural samples of the element, U-238, has a tendency to absorb stray neutrons without fissioning. But the more highly fissionable U-235 is chemically identical to the more abundant isotope, and therefore efforts to separate out sufficient quantities of bomb-grade uranium involved procedures based on the slight difference in mass between the isotopes, such as electromagnetic separation and gaseous diffusion, which were prohibitively expensive and extremely slow. In response to this difficulty, the Manhattan scientists designed a second bomb using plutonium. But this weapon raised its own problems; in particular, it required exceptionally rapid assembly of a critical mass of plutonium to avoid the possibility of predetonation caused by stray neutrons. To solve this problem, the Los Alamites pioneered implosive techniques using lenses of conventional explosives to create a symmetrical shock wave around a hollow, spherical mass of plutonium. This assembly could force the fissionable material into a critical mass much more quickly than the gun-type method, allowing the use of plutonium. But the methods were so unusual and involved so many untried features that the physicists decided they would have to test the weapon before it could be turned over to the military for use in combat.

A special committee of Los Alamos scientists set up the test, code-named Trinity, during the summer of 1945. They chose a site in the Jornada del Muerto, or Journey of Death, a desert some two hundred miles south of Los Alamos. The military "leased" the MacDonald family ranch (it was, in effect, commandeered) and turned its central buildings into a temporary command center. Some two miles away, workers erected a one hundred–foot tower at the designated ground zero. On the afternoon of July 15, they hoisted the completed bomb, nicknamed "Fat Man," to the top of the tower. Detonation was scheduled for four the next morning to diminish the number of potential witnesses, but persistent rain and lightning forced its postponement until 5:30. Meanwhile the scientists had established an unofficial pool on the probable yield of the bomb. As it happened, almost all the estimates were low; only I. I. Rabi, a friend of Robert Oppenheimer's and an occasional visitor to Los Alamos, guessed close to the actual yield of 18,600 tons of TNT. He later explained that his relatively large estimate "was really only out of politeness. I thought that as a guest I ought to name a flatteringly high figure."[54]

When the detonation finally occurred, it was a spectacular sight. It looked like a giant magnesium flare which kept on for what seemed a whole minute but was actually one or two seconds. The white ball grew and after a few seconds became clouded with dust whipped up by the explosion from the ground and rose and left behind a black trail of dust particles. The rise, though it seemed slow, took place at a velocity of 120 meters per second. After more than half a minute, the flame died down and the ball, which had been a brilliant white, became a dull purple. It continued to rise and spread at the same time, and finally broke through and rose above the clouds which were 15,000 feet above the ground. It could be distinguished from the clouds by its color and could be followed to a height of 40,000 feet above the ground. Windows were shattered in farmhouses fifty miles away. Later that day, the military released a report claiming that an ammunition dump had blown up, in an attempt to quiet speculation. But the explosion had been so large, few people believed the story.

I have described the test blast in some detail, yet my description is not really my own—and how could it be? I was not there and so did not see what I describe. Like everyone else who has not witnessed the test of an atomic bomb or who was not present in Hiroshima or Nagasaki at the beginning of August 1945, I have ultimately had to depend on the narratives of others who have had these authorizing experiences, in this case the account of Hans Bethe, head of the Theoretical Division at Los Alamos, whom I have quoted verbatim.[55] I have done this to stress the extent to which an author must make use of existing texts in reconstructing even the most objective aspects of a historical event. Ironically, as we shall see, eyewitness accounts of Trinity themselves also inevitably reconstruct the events they describe. So the dependence of postwar authors' conceptions of atomic weapons on the Los Alamos scientists' narratives mirrors the Los Alamites' turn to even earlier texts for the models and metaphors on which they based their own conceptions of those weapons.

The Nuclear Muse

The Nuclear Muse to which the title of this study refers may be thought of as the tenth muse—a muse unknown in classical times, a lost child of Zeus and Mnemosyne. This is the muse that inspired Lise Meitner and Niels Bohr, Robert Oppenheimer and Enrico Fermi, Joseph Rotblat and Edward Teller. This is the muse that inspires terror and wonder in us when we think of the forces we have learned to unleash but are not quite certain how to control. This is, like Calliope or Melpomene, a muse who loves literature. Only now, however, are we coming to understand how this can be—how the apparently impersonal, nonaesthetic discipline of physics can harbor such a figure. The melding of literature and physics may be subtle, but it is quite thorough. The Nuclear Muse requires only our willingness to be inspired, to make the effort to seek her out; there is no limit to what she will reveal to the dedicated supplicant.

The Nuclear Muse is, therefore, a study, at one level, of physics and, at another level, of literature. At a third level, it is an experiment designed to test literary criticism—that curious hybrid discipline, born out of a combination of aesthetic obsessions and scientific method. It deals in the stuff of literature: metaphors, narrative, representation, symbolism, imagery, ambiguity, implication, allusion, tone. But it applies a number of assumptions central to science: objectivity, cumulative analysis, consensus, a belief in true and false readings. Literary criticism represents a curious mixture of these disciplines brought to bear on one of them. Can it also be applied to the other? This study is an effort to answer that question in practical terms by applying the tools and techniques of literary criticism to uncover the uses of literature in the development and deployment of nuclear weapons and the physics on which they most overtly depend.

Chapter 1 begins with an overview of physicists' uses of figurative language in the context of the development of the new science of quantum theory. Both classical and quantum physics make use of metaphors and analogies, but each reflects a different attitude toward figurative language on the part of its practitioners. I pay special attention to physicists' attitudes to the tropes of wave and particle as a source of insight into the shift between the classical and quantum paradigms, using as yardsticks both traditional distinctions between literal and metaphorical descriptions and recent scholarly work on tropological language. I also consider the interest many physicists display in self-referential examinations of their own representational practices—an interest reminiscent of attitudes common in the seventeenth and eighteenth centuries when scientists were still overtly in the process of exploring representational strategies. Finally, I suggest that physicists faced a crisis in their use of figurative language when the formalization of quantum mechanics in the mid-1920s forced them to confront their dependence on inconsistent metaphors.

Chapter 2 continues the considerations begun in the first chapter, focusing on a particularly influential attempt to resolve the representational dilemma of quantum mechanics: Niels Bohr's 1927 Como lecture (and subsequent *Nature* article) in which he introduced the complementarity principle. This chapter offers an extended consideration of that paper along two lines: first, an analysis of the ways in which Bohr made use of literary rhetoric to mediate between classical and quantum physics as well as between competing factions within quantum mechanics itself; second, an exploration of its implications for the larger role of figurative language in subatomic physics.

The development of quantum mechanics, from Max Planck's discovery of the quantum of action in 1900 through the beginnings of the

Manhattan Project in 1942, was a particularly fertile period in modern physics. Knowledge of atomic structure was growing at an overwhelming rate, and disagreements over the most productive avenues of inquiry were common. Several times during this period, physicists found themselves confronting crises in their discipline. In 1932, a group of physicists met in Copenhagen to discuss the most recent crisis and debate the future of quantum mechanics. Perhaps the most unusual and suggestive of their activities centered on rewriting and staging Goethe's *Faust* with themselves as the principal characters. Chapter 3 examines the text of the *Blegdamsvej Faust* in detail and considers how such a literary undertaking could be useful to nuclear physicists in the context of a professional gathering.

Ten years later, new arrivals at the Los Alamos Laboratory in New Mexico, the heart of the Manhattan Project, were greeted with a mimeographed booklet summarizing a series of lectures by Robert Serber intended to "get them up to speed" on the laboratory's work. These lectures made use of a variety of literary techniques to indoctrinate the Los Alamos physicists into a particular conceptual perspective necessary to the coherent functioning of the laboratory. Chapter 4 explores the *Los Alamos Primer*'s use of literary devices, with a special emphasis on its use of fiction. My argument suggests that the creation of scientific communities in general may depend in part on the incorporation of the representational flexibility of such literary techniques into the heart of their scientific practices.

Chapter 5 continues the examination of the construction of the Los Alamos community begun in the preceding chapter, focusing particular attention on the role played by the rhetoric of exploration and discovery. For security reasons, the military situated the laboratory in the remote desert highlands of New Mexico in a landscape that remained as striking and nearly as formidable as it had been in the days of the Spanish Conquistadors. The new residents of the Los Alamos mesa found themselves in a challenging situation: *de facto* invaders displacing the indigenous population and then encouraging its dependence on the new economy stimulated by the laboratory, on the one hand, and themselves subject to stifling restrictions and discomforts, on the other. In response, they turned to metaphors of exploration and discovery as a means of encoding their unsettling experiences in a comforting—and transforming—rhetoric.

In addition to its function in the social context of Los Alamos, the rhetoric of exploration and discovery also played a significant role in the scientists' conceptions of their technical work. Chapter 6 looks at this other side of the Los Alamites' use of these metaphors, examining the ways in which such language helped them to balance the competing demands of individual initiative and submission to the tradition that is central to the practice of modern science. The second half of the chapter focuses on the ways in which metaphors of exploration and discovery allowed the Los Alamites to both express and contain the "terror" associated with their work as scientists in general and on nuclear weapons in particular. The chapter concludes with a consideration of the consequences of such representations.

Many of the scientists who joined the Los Alamos Laboratory had long been pacifists and were opposed in principle to the application of science to military ends. How did they reconcile their political convictions with their participation in the Manhattan Project? How did they think and talk about what they were doing? Chapter 7 looks at the Los Alamites' use of religious rhetoric to describe the overwhelming natural forces they were attempting to liberate and their efforts to shape those forces into a practical military weapon. It shows how their language created "the verisimilitude of high moral purpose"— not by means of overt justification, as one might expect, but through a more subtle and far-reaching confrontation with the meaning of their labors. In the process, both their conception of nuclear weapons and their moral beliefs were transformed into a new consistency—but at what price?

Chapter 8 examines in more detail the price of the Los Alamites' literary representations of their work and its products. Among the consequences of their reliance on figurative language and references to preexisting works of literature was a tendency to transform nuclear weapons themselves into literary entities. This chapter further traces what happened once the Manhattan Project had accomplished its mission and its existence was no longer a carefully guarded secret. During this time, the Los Alamites' accounts were in great demand, for they occupied a position of privileged intimacy in relation to nuclear weapons. As a result, they passed on to policymakers and the general public alike their conceptions of the weapons they had made, with powerful and lasting consequences for the social relations underlying our continued use of nuclear weapons.

Finally, Chapter 9 returns to the consideration of the literary origins of "atomic" weapons described in this introduction, bringing it full circle with an examination of two works of fiction written in response to the existence of nuclear weapons. As we have already seen, Leo Szilard's reading of Wells's *The World Set Free* led him to work that helped initiate the Manhattan Project. After the war, Szilard continued to draw inspiration from Wells's novel in his attempts to promote the cause of world government. In particular, he wrote an influential novella,

"The Voice of the Dolphins," which in some important respects closely parallels *The World Set Free*. Novelist Russell Hoban's *Riddley Walker*, on the other hand, offers a very different vision of our nuclear future. Following on the analysis of the literary aspects of subatomic physics and the construction of nuclear weapons that comprises the bulk of this study, these two overtly literary constructions of nuclear weapons provide an axis of reference on which to turn and take a final look at the relations between physics and literature.

Conclusion

It will be immediately apparent that this book does not use the methods of science although my thinking, like that of most people, has been profoundly influenced by its epistemological assumptions. I am writing as a literary critic with some formal background in physics and a good deal of independent study of the field. But my conclusions will not meet standards of rigorous scientific inquiry, even as those standards exist in the social sciences, although I have taken great care to ensure that I do not misrepresent the scientific work I discuss. Please take this as a caution, not an apology. I am writing about topics for which there is as yet no proven means of applying scientific methodology. They involve interpretation and exploration of meanings. Therefore, my analyses will not please all readers. But I am in good company. Even physicists, when they begin to interpret their work, whether in the context of a popularization or of a colloquium, or to talk about the meaning of a principle or theory, find themselves in a realm in which their conventional methods of consensus-building do not quite apply.

This is eloquently demonstrated by Sheldon Goldstein in his contribution to a volume entitled *The Flight from Science and Reason*. Goldstein's intention is, apparently, to pull the rug out from under what we might call "extrascientific" interpretations of quantum mechanics, but his approach backfires. He argues that such interpretations are dependent on the more "philosophical" interpretations of their own work on the part of a number (in fact, the majority) of the original quantum mechanists themselves. This reading is almost certainly correct. But his desire to discredit such interpretations puts Goldstein in the difficult position of having to contradict the likes of Niels Bohr, Werner Heisenberg, John von Neumann, Max Born, and Eugene Wigner, while attempting to disprove the orthodox Copenhagen interpretation of quantum mechanics. Not an enviable task. One would think he would proceed cautiously and deferentially, but he opts instead for a frontal assault: "It is not at all unusual, when it comes to quantum philosophy, to find the very best physicists and mathematicians making sharp emphatic claims, almost of a mathematical character, that are trivially false and profoundly ignorant."[56]

One has to admire his courage, even while doubting his wisdom. Despite his rhetorical pyrotechnics, he fails to build a convincing case against the "profound ignorance" of the Copenhagen interpretation. He enlists Einstein, Erwin Schrödinger, and David Bohm as allies, but their contributions do not always inspire confidence. Goldstein quotes Schrödinger as saying, for example: "With very few exceptions (such as Einstein and Laue) all the rest of the theoretical physicists were unadulterated asses and I was the only sane person left."[57] Nothing Goldstein adduces as evidence of the Copenhagen crowd's intellectual bankruptcy comes so close to sounding like the ravings of an unbalanced mind.

This is unfortunate, for Goldstein is right to argue that Bohm's work offers an important and philosophically relevant alternative to the Copenhagen interpretation. His most serious mistake, to my mind, is his apparent motivating desire to quash any "interpretation" that might provide fodder for scholars (including, apparently, physicists) interested in examining the possible meanings of quantum mechanics. By initiating such a vitriolic attack on his colleagues, present and former, he fatally undermines his larger purpose, demonstrating quite effectively that there is, in fact, a great deal of room for philosophical interpretation and debate even within the ranks of the most eminent physicists themselves. I believe Goldstein is mistaken if he imagines that his display will convince scholars in other disciplines, who have their own motivations and methods that he never addresses, to cease and desist. His argument is, if anything, further evidence of the need for detailed examination of the Copenhagen interpretation—for even if it is "false," as Goldstein contends, it is hardly "trivially" so.

If we are ever to come to an adequate understanding of literature and science as independent disciplines, I believe a piece of that understanding must involve an examination of their interrelations. Of course, we must be constantly attentive to the nuances and details of both disciplines. We must not give in to the temptation to twist either one to produce the meanings we hope to find. Whatever we can say about the larger categories of literature and science will necessarily be tied to the accuracy with which we grasp the details of their specific manifestations. But we must also have the courage to overcome both the defensive fears of those who may feel threatened by our sometimes bumbling efforts to understand and the fanatic enthusiasm of those who wish to urge us beyond the bounds of reason. I hope to be equally true to literature and science in this study, for I could not have sustained the effort it required if I did not have a profound respect for both. I know at first hand something of the dedication and energy each calls for; I have also felt and hope to share the wonder and the aesthetic pleasure that inspire men and women to search for those necessary qualities in themselves.

Niels Bohr and Max Planck. (Courtesy AIP Emilio Segrè Visual Archives, Margrethe Bohr Collection.)

1

"WHAT WE CAN SAY

ABOUT NATURE"

METAPHOR, ANALOGY, AND THE

BIRTH OF SUBATOMIC PHYSICS

Toward the end of 1938, Otto Frisch traveled from the Institute of Theoretical Physics in Copenhagen to Kungälv, Sweden, to visit his aunt. Lise Meitner, "a pioneer in radioactivity"[1] and longtime collaborator with the renowned German chemist Otto Hahn, had recently fled Nazi Germany, part of a growing exodus of Jewish scientists. As Frisch recalls: "I had always kept the habit of celebrating Christmas with her in Berlin; this time she was invited to spend Christmas with Swedish friends in the small town of Kungälv (near Gothenburg), and she asked me to join her there. That was the most momentous visit of my whole life."[2] Frisch does not overstate the significance of this meeting with Meitner. On their first day together in Kungälv, Meinter received a letter from Hahn describing the results of an experiment in which he and Fritz Strassmann had analyzed the substances formed by bombarding uranium with neutrons. Much to their surprise, they had identified isotopes of barium, an element of about half the atomic weight of uranium, among the end products of this reaction. During a long walk through snowy woods, Frisch and Meitner sought a way to explain these results. After lengthy discussion and hasty calculations on scraps of paper, they concluded that a uranium nucleus might resemble "a wobbly, unstable drop, ready to divide itself at the slightest provocation, such as the impact of a single neutron."[3] Soon thereafter, having assured himself that this model accounted for all the empirical data, Frisch published an account of "fission," so named because of its resemblance to the division of cells in living organisms.[4]

Twenty-six years later, this scientific article led to another opportunity for Frisch to display his flair for explicating atomic structures. In 1965,

31

"What We Can Say about Nature"

the editors of a series of books on "Science and Discovery" asked him to write a volume called *Working with Atoms*, believing that "As the scientist who first understood and proved to the world what takes place when the uranium atom is split, Dr. Frisch is uniquely qualified to present this account."[5] Frisch obliged with a narrative of "how we have come to unlock that treasure-house of energy deep down in the atom."[6] As this choice of words suggests, the book was a popularization, intended for a general audience with no prior knowledge of atoms or even of scientific practices. Yet this does not mean that its rhetorical strategies were simplistic. Frisch demonstrates an acute sense of his audience, of its expectations, and of his role as the representative of a scientific tradition. He gives his readers what they want, or perhaps what he wants them to want: a particular thread in the history of science woven into a story of treasure and triumph, exploration and discovery.

Implicit in his use of the fairy-tale phrase "unlock that treasure-house" and the spatial metaphor "deep down in the atom" is the strategy of rendering science as a fictional narrative. This strategy becomes explicit when Frisch characterizes his book as "quite an exciting sort of detective story" and one, furthermore, in which he "had a small part to play."[7] His choice of metaphors overtly links the scientific tradition with the fictional tradition of detective narratives and presents Frisch himself as a particular kind of protagonist: the detective-scientist. It is a powerful conceptual move, though it might at first seem curiously self-defeating. Why would he encourage an identification between scientific history and fictional narrative when practicing scientists have traditionally insisted on an absolute distinction between these two discursive forms?

This question raises a number of complex issues that will continue to surface at various points throughout this book. In broadest terms, it involves us in a consideration of the relation between fictional narratives, such as Wells's *The World Set Free*, and narratives of the historical development of physics, which would include the development of nuclear weapons. For the moment, however, I will continue to focus more narrowly on the apparent conjunction of these two types of narrative in *Working with Atoms*. In particular, there are two important motivations behind the narrative stance adopted by Frisch, one obvious and the other less so, and both are of interest in the context of this study.

Watching the Detective

Because Frisch intends his narrative for a popular audience, he feels obliged to render it in a form that will prove accessible to readers who lack a scientific background. On the most basic level, this means that he must avoid mathematical expressions. Anyone who has acquired more than a nodding familiarity with modern science will recognize the challenge this presents: Science from Newton on makes extensive use of mathematics both on the level of observation and in generalizing from observation to abstract laws. And while a nonmathematical component inevitably plays an indispensable role in scientific descriptions, and frequently prefigures the mathematical component, there are instances in which pure mathematical manipulation has generated a description that only later receives an empirical interpretation. The upshot is that popularizations of science rely entirely on a language that cannot be purged of features commonly used in the expression of subjective experience—and they lack the antidote of the abstract, impersonal, mathematical formulations on which scientific descriptions lean so heavily. Scientific popularization, therefore, cannot help but exaggerate the role that metaphors, analogies, and other tropes play in science, and consequently such writing tends to read more like a work of fiction than some of its authors might like.

Frisch seems to feel little compunction on this point, however. In fact, as we have seen, he emphasizes the fictional character of his narrative. This emphasis, above and beyond the inevitable fictive aspects of scientific popularizations, would seem to be an obvious attempt to engage the general reader. As such, it represents a conscious choice on Frisch's part between pandering to a nonscientific audience and maintaining that aloof, objective stance of an initiate. He chooses to cross a line here—though whether that line exists in some absolute epistemological sense or merely in the eyes of its beholders remains to be debated—between the ivory tower of scientific discourse and the crude and approximate province of the popular.[8] Yet even now that it appears well-established, many scientists continue to cross the line that demarcates their discipline, all the while treating the texts produced by such crossings (especially those of their counterparts in the humanities who foray the realm of science to bring back tales of their adventures) with skepticism, often rejecting or disowning even their own texts as, well, not really science, though perhaps the best that can be done in a popular context.[9]

Quite apart from its appeal to a nonscientific audience, Frisch's fictional treatment stems from a second, less obvious motive: It allows him to finesse a troublesome aspect of any effort to discuss a particular piece of scientific knowledge. On the one hand, scientists labor to form scientific knowledge into a stable edifice that attains to Truth. On the other

"What We Can Say about Nature"

hand, that very labor subjects the edifice to daily additions, challenges, and revisions by fallible, subjective individuals. How should we weigh the contributions of the individual and the discipline, the subjective and the objective, the provisional and the absolute? The most common expedient adopted by scientists is to emphasize the subservience of individuals to the tradition, as Frisch does. Yet this emphasis is problematic, given the fact that in practical application subservience to a tradition tends to reduce individual performance to a least common denominator. The scientific tradition has, of course, prospered by virtue of the decidedly individual talents of its practitioners, involving a large measure of intuition, inspiration, and good fortune. The relationship between individual and tradition is, therefore, a dynamic one in which a scientist's need for individual autonomy competes with her dependence on the authority granted by membership in a specialized, almost priestly caste.[10]

This competition becomes most pronounced in contexts which involve a focus on the contributions of specific individuals, such as *Working with Atoms*. Frisch's approach helps him to balance the opposing claims of the individual and tradition in two ways. First, it constitutes scientists not as real individuals but as fictional characters—as individuals but not *real* individuals. Second, Frisch evokes a character who belongs to a tradition of stock types. This allows him to represent individual scientists as powerful figures without threatening the authority of the tradition. Indeed, the more powerful the character—a Sam Spade, say—the more thoroughly the tradition absorbs and reproduces him as a stereotype.

Frisch begins his detective story with an account of the adoption by modern scientists of an atomic model of matter:

Almost two hundred years ago the chemists found that they could explain a lot by assuming that all things are made from a few dozen different kinds of tiny bits called atoms, just as the content of a book is made from about two dozen different letters. Chemists are particularly interested in pure substances, and these are rather like a book in which the same word is repeated over and over again. A book that reads HOH HOH HOH HOH would make dull reading, but that is just what pure water is like.[11]

This passage exemplifies the clarity and economy of the best scientific popularization, and at first glance it may seem to require little comment. Yet in these few sentences, Frisch recounts one of the most significant developments in the longstanding efforts of scientists to describe nature, and it is worth noting some of what he leaves out in order to achieve this compression—as well as why he might do so. For instance, contrary to the expectations he has raised, the action of this portion of his "detective story," which we might expect to include the work of particular scientists over the past "two hundred years," consists of a single verb: "found." Frisch's narrative, therefore, elides the countless observations, experimental manipulations, detailed hypotheses, and outright guesses that actually constituted the introduction of atomic theory in modern science. The result is a narrative that deemphasizes people doing things in favor of an account of what was discovered. The actors here are not people so much as ideas.

Frisch's presentation does not simply reflect an idiosyncratic take on history. It is, rather, predicated on two analogies that have played a pivotal role in the development of the scientific tradition. First, Frisch presents the activity of the chemists as an implicit narrative of discovery—the chemists "found" that matter is constructed of atoms—which suggests that an atomic model existed as a natural fact prior to the chemists' specific formulation of it. This analogy is a central assumption underlying the practices of physics.[12] Like the model of the fictional detective story, the narrative of discovery serves to undercut the dependence of the scientific tradition on individual scientists and, in doing so, implies that scientific descriptions are not the creations of fallible individuals but discoveries of objective truth. This same claim is made by Frisch's second analogy—the comparison of water to a book. Once again, a scientist is not the source of the descriptions she formulates; instead, she finds in the very molecules before her an inscription of the natural order.

Frisch would not, of course, deny the agency of the scientist. Quite the contrary—his narrative acknowledges the chemists' subjective involvement in their work: "The chemists found *that they could explain a lot by assuming* that all things are made from a few dozen different kinds of tiny bits called atoms." The phrase in italics neatly encapsulates the activity of the scientist: to test the explanatory value of various assumptions about the structure of particular natural phenomena in the context of experimental observations of those phenomena. My paraphrase is somewhat more formal than Frisch's original—and may therefore sound more impressive, as though I attribute to science a more rigorous epistemological basis than Frisch. In practice, the truth is somewhere in between: scientists are generally quite rigorous in their pursuit of stable, widely applicable formulations, and they are supported in this endeavor by their training in the use of thoroughly tested heuristic tools; yet there is also a considerable element of chance—of intuition, guesswork, and even luck—involved in the work of a productive scientist, as Frisch's breezy language implies.

Despite his obvious awareness of the role of the scientist as an intermediary between the natural world and the edifice of received scientific knowledge, Frisch constructs his narrative as though the two ends of the scientific process were firmly joined. Nature and scientific descriptions, in his view, retain a basic equality. I added the emphasis to the phrase examined in the last paragraph, not Frisch. Indeed, he structured his sentence so that the phrase in question is grammatically unnecessary: one could remove it with no essential loss to the overall meaning of the sentence. What does Frisch most want his reader to know? That the chemists found that all things are made of atoms. We are not meant to feel any sense of distance between the description and the phenomenon; in Frisch's mind they are equivalent, and in this regard his perspective is that of science. Although no self-aware scientist would deny her own involvement in the formulation of scientific descriptions of nature, the discipline routinely assumes that such descriptions are finally independent of any given author and offer a literal representation of nature.

Frisch's rhetorical minimization of the scientist's individuality is not, therefore, a denial of its importance. Instead, it reflects a deep-seated and largely automatic disciplinary bias manifest to a much greater extent in public texts than in the laboratory. This bias has been useful to scientists in promoting the truth value of their claims. Portraying the chemists' adoption of an atomic model as a "finding," for instance, rather than a "making," asserts their passive attentiveness to nature: their models spring from nature and therefore embody the authority of nature. Likewise, precisely the qualities that distinguish the scientist as a worthy protagonist in Frisch's narrative also serve to minimize their presence as individuals: the chemists' ability to "find" is neither accidental nor easy to obtain but derives from their particular identity as "chemists." Ultimately, it is their participation in the institution of science that grants them the intimate relationship to nature necessary to make such findings. Their specialized training allows them to read nature like a book, as Frisch's analogy between water and "a book that reads HOH HOH HOH HOH" implies.

It should be clear by now that Frisch's "detective story" does not offer an easy read—in fact it requires considerable detective work on the reader's part. This is true even in the case of the historical facts he claims to be elucidating. Although he does hint at his compression of the past two hundred years, for example, he omits any mention of the true pedigree of the atomic model. In fact, it has been kicking around for closer to two thousand than two hundred years. Classical philosophers introduced the idea of tiny elemental particles as the basis of matter, and medieval European scientists debated the merits of such a model. Yet it was not until the period Frisch describes that the idea achieved widespread acceptance. These details might have enhanced the narrative power of *Working with Atoms*, for the centuries-long search for a productive description of the constitution of the material world could be seen as offering considerable dramatic material. But Frisch, in the end, is interested not in that drama but in the descriptive system that has been abstracted from it.

Of course, one might argue that Frisch does not intend to recount the whole history of the idea. But if so, this intention is revealing in itself, for it shows him straddling two alternative treatments of his subject. For one, he clearly feels the need to say *something* about the historical context of the atomic model. But, at the same time, his concern centers on the ways in which the model is useful today rather than on its evolution. This leads him, aside from this token acknowledgment of the past, to treat the atomic model as an eternally present concept. Therefore, the chemists are interesting not for their unusual ideas, for the blind alleys or alternative approaches they explored, but because they were the first scientists to participate in the atomic model's current uses. Frisch's brief historical note turns out to be a placebo: it serves less as a source of information than as a marker for his real interests, the promulgation of scientific truths that stand outside time.

What's in a Name? Metaphor in Science

In my account of *Working with Atoms*, Frisch's ability to produce so robust yet nuanced an engagement with his discipline, to represent the atomic description of nature so succinctly and with such an air of authority, depends largely on his use of metaphors like "detective story," "letters," and "book." Where do these metaphors come from? There is no single answer. In part, Frisch's metaphors express his individual rhetorical practices. His rhetoric earns a reader's respect by marking him as an eloquent individual—a writer who has mastered the conventions of his medium. But what is his medium? I have called it a "popularization of science." Does this mean it is not science itself? Surely it is closely related, for it purports to convey information about science, and Frisch's primary interests are those of a scientist. Indeed, a significant degree of his mastery of metaphorical discourse derives from science, for it was his ability to render empirical observations into metaphorical models, as in the case of "nuclear fission," that established his scientific eminence and attracted the attention of his editors in the first place. By setting up analogies between the history of science and a detective story, atoms and letters, physical substances and books, Frisch demonstrates once again the discursive prowess that allowed him to play a "small part" in formulating the atomic description of nature itself. The rhetorical use of metaphors in *Working with Atoms*, therefore, also reflects his training in the institutional practices of science.

This training occurs on two levels: how to do science and how to talk (or think) about what a scientist does. The bulk of a scientist's training centers on internalizing a binary knowledge of existing scientific "facts" and the methodology necessary to produce more of them. What all of this *means* does not generally constitute a formal component of a scientist's training, but a semiotic dimension is nonetheless implicit in everything she does. This dimension becomes manifest most clearly in scientists' use of a number of long-lived metaphors to characterize the work of science, such as the process of exploration and discovery or the comparison of nature to a book. Interestingly, while the facts and the methods of science are subject to change over time, the metaphors that give social meaning to the tradition demonstrate considerable stability—probably because of their connotative flexibility.

A glance at the tenure of Frisch's book metaphor in scientists' discourse about science offers a case in point. As early as the late Middle Ages, clear precedents had come into common use. William of Conches, for example, wrote that elements were like letters: the smallest units of language out of which all larger units, including syllables, words, sentences, and books, were made. From 1454 on, of course, books were in the air, so to speak; theologians, philosophers, natural philosophers, and intellectuals of any ilk, could hardly ignore the growing importance of the printed words as *the* medium of intellectual exchange. Though the situation may now be changing, as electronic media offer more condensed storage capacity and faster transfer of information, for the past five hundred years the printed word has defined the character of our scholarly disciplines. Without the availability of inexpensive, mass-produced books, modern science would have been at best impracticable and perhaps even unthinkable. It should be no surprise, therefore, that modern scientists, from William of Conches through Otto Frisch, turn to this representational medium for a metaphor with which to describe their interpretations of the natural world it allows them to represent.

Metaphor is useful not simply in talking about science, however; it is also an integral part of practicing science. To apply this to the case at hand, we might note that Frisch's use of metaphorical language to represent the *history* of the atomic model in modern science effectively reenacts its *practices* as well. His reduction of the chemists' complex and manifold experience in adopting an atomic model parallels the atomic model's own representation of a wide variety of disparate natural phenomena in the form of a coherent representational structure. In science, such structures often take the form of collections of mathematical equations. But they are inevitably accompanied by extended verbal equations: statements in vernacular language that translate between the mathematical expression and the world of natural phenomena. Examples of such statements include comparing electricity to a fluid, the interactions of particles to the collisions of billiard balls, or light to waves or to particles. In each case, the link centers on an implicit or explicit use of the phrase "is like." This reliance on metaphor commonly generates multilevel rhetorical structures at the heart of scientific representations.[13] Thus Frisch's use of the metaphor "two dozen different letters" to describe atoms should not strike us as an "unscientific" popularization; it is, in fact, typical of scientific representations, stripped of their mathematical apparatuses, and parallels, for example, the innovation of the chemists' in describing nature as "made from a few dozen different kinds of tiny bits."

One might object at this point that no self-respecting chemist would use the phrase "tiny bits" in a scientific discussion or publication. Although "tiny bits" may strike a reader as verging on the equivalent of scientific baby talk—a painfully clear instance of a specialist "talking down" to noninitiates—we should beware of differentiating this phrase too strictly from the colorful terminology studding contemporary discussions of subatomic phenomena, such as "strangeness," "handedness," or "charm"—or even from more apparently prosaic words like "atoms," "waves," "particles," or "neutrons." Scientists choose these terms from the lexicons of Greek, Latin, and the modern languages, particularly English, or coin them in much the way Lewis Carroll constructed the language of "Jabberwocky." In doing so, they attempt to lay claim to natural facts, on their own behalf as well as that of science, as Frisch did in applying the word "fission" to nuclear division.[14] At times, these labels are bitterly contested, and they inevitably come freighted with established connotations and allusions. Part of the difficulty of analyzing the function of such language in science is that scientists use these terms in a variety of ways—sometimes as catachresis, "the use of metaphor to remedy gaps in vocabulary,"[15] and sometimes to exploit the very messiness of their associations. As we shall see, metaphorical language allowed classical physicists to assert a general conceptual frame for their work without committing them too closely to any single interpretation of it.[16] They were then able to proceed with their work by filtering out what they came to regard as their terminology's extraneous meanings, gradually emphasizing a more literal use of language, which characterizes traditional scientific discourse.[17]

The word "atoms," for example, to which "tiny bits" directs us, depends for its descriptive power on its metaphorical character. A glance at any history of science (other than Frisch's, perhaps) will reveal that the English word does not conduct us straight to the chemists' "tiny bits"; instead it leads us by way of its Greek origin in a word meaning "indivisible," which Democritus first yoked into service as a label for the hypothetical particles he believed to be the most elementary constituents of matter. The eighteenth-century chemists' use of this term, therefore, describes the existence in nature of elementary substances— which we would now call "elements"—indirectly, by comparison to Democritus' conception of indivisible particles. This rhetorical move is metaphorical in two senses. First, it splits our attention between the natural phenomenon it describes and the classical model from which it borrows. This double referent holds two objects in suspension, physical particle and physical theory, and claims their equality.[18] Even today, after experimental manipulations have revealed the term to be a misnomer in the classical sense, since "atoms" turn out to be all too divisible, scientists retain it. Thus the word is metaphorical in a second sense, for it has acquired a use that tropes its literal meaning. It should be apparent that the descriptive longevity of the term derives in large measure not from any literal representational truth, but from its metaphorical flexibility. I will develop this important point in more detail as we go along.

It is useful to note here that in addition to their importance in constructing stable yet flexible scientific descriptions of natural phenomena, following out the implications of such metaphors provides an essential impetus for the scientific tradition. In fact, a scientist's understanding of a natural phenomenon frequently derives from, as well as calls for, the verbal equations generated by these metaphors. In the case of light, for example, the debate between the wave and particle models has provided a focal point for scientific investigations of electromagnetic radiation for the last three hundred years. In 1672, Newton published his first and only journal article, "A New Theory of Light and Colours," in the *Philosophical Transactions of the Royal Society of London*, in which he developed a description of the refractive properties of light based on a corpuscular model.[19] Newton continued to expand on the consequences of this conception of light, refining and extending his analysis, until in 1704 he published his monumental *Opticks*, in which he directly compared light to "very small Bodies."[20] In 1690, meanwhile, Christian Huygens, in his *Traité de la Lumière (Treatise on Light)*, suggested a different analogy:

Now there is no doubt at all that light also comes from the luminous body to our eyes by some movement impressed on the matter which is between the two; since, as we have already seen, it cannot be by the transport of a body which passes from one to the other. If, in addition, light takes time for its passage—which we are now going to examine—it will follow that this movement, impressed on the intervening matter, is successive; and consequently it spreads, as Sound does, by spherical surfaces and waves: for I call them waves from their resemblance to those which are seen to be formed in water when a stone is thrown into it, and which present a successive spreading as circles, though these arise from another cause, and are only in a flat surface.[21]

Each model seemed to offer a useful basis for explaining particular features of the behavior of visible light. But by the end of the seventeenth century, Newton's authority was so great that his model carried the day. For the next hundred years, the wave theory took a back seat to the corpuscular.

In the early nineteenth century, however, the wave model enjoyed a sudden reversal of its fortunes. Thomas Young, an English physician, applied it in his successful interpretation of the interference patterns produced by light after it passes through a diffraction grating. Soon after, Augustin Fresnel, a French civil engineer, produced a compelling mathematical quantification of Young's interpretation. In the second half of the century, James Clerk Maxwell developed a wave-based electromagnetic theory of light that unified much of the preceding fifty years of work in optics, electricity, and magnetism. At this point, there seemed to be little doubt that the wave metaphor had rendered the particle model obsolete. Yet some difficulties remained, and in the late nineteenth century inconsistencies between the wave model and increasingly precise

"What We Can Say about Nature"

observations—for example, the Michelson–Morley measurements of the speed of light—reasserted the need for a corpuscular model just as physics was about to plunge into its greatest crisis since the introduction of Newtonian mechanics.

The quantum revolution began in such a modest way that it took some physicists nearly twenty years to acknowledge that they had been in the midst of a radical break with classical mechanics. On December 14, 1900, Max Planck finished working on a paper that historians of science generally cite as "the birth of quantum physics."[22] In it, Planck introduced the basis of what has come to be known as quantum theory. The heart of the paper,[23] and of the theory, consists of a simple assertion of proportionality: "Das Energieelement ϵ proportional der Schwingungszahl ν sein muss, also: $\epsilon = h \cdot \nu$"—the elemental energy ϵ must be proportional to the vibration frequency ν, thus $\epsilon = h \cdot \nu$. Thus, with a magisterial "thus," Planck turned the world of physics on its ear, introducing what he called a "universal constant," h, with a half-casual, half-oracular "hereby"—"Hierbei sind h and k universelle Constante"—but doing so, it seemed, only as a step toward deriving a more ambitious formula for the density of blackbody radiation μ as a function of frequency ν and temperature ϑ:

$$\mu = \frac{8\pi h\nu^3}{c^3} \frac{1}{e^{h\nu/k\vartheta} - 1}$$

Ironically, Planck did not seem to recognize the revolutionary implications of his own assertion, and, indeed, his formula drew heavily on the work of his predecessors, including Wilhelm Wien's earlier description of short wavelength radiation and the Rayleigh–Jeans formula for long wavelengths. Yet before this, no one had managed to derive a single expression capable of giving consistent results across the entire spectrum; even more important, no one had found a way to explain an increasingly troublesome discrepancy between the causal descriptions of classical mechanics and an instance of apparently arbitrary behavior on the part of nature. In the years leading up to Planck's paper, spectral analysis of blackbody radiation had made it clear that, contrary to classical assumptions, material bodies do not emit light over a continuous spectrum. Instead, heated matter produces electromagnetic radiation only at particular frequencies. This inconsistency between theory and observation had frustrated scientists, including Planck himself, for years before his introduction of a theoretical model which simultaneously explained the puzzling observations and cast doubt on the edifice of classical mechanics.

Planck's innovation consisted of elevating the results of these spectroscopic observations to the level of a general principle, in much the same way Einstein would soon treat the surprising fact that the velocity of light has a constant magnitude, regardless of an observer's frame of reference, as a basic assumption in his formulation of the Theory of Special Relativity. So Planck writes:

Es kommt nun darauf an, die Wahrscheinlichkeit W dafür zu finden, dass die N Resonatoren insgesamt die Schwingungsenergie U_n besitzen. Hierzu ist es notwendig, U_n nicht als eine stetige, unbeschränkt teilbare, sondern als eine discrete, aus einer ganzen Zahl von endlichen gleichen Teilen zusammengesetzte Grösse aufzufassen. Nennen wir einen solchen Teil ein Energieelement ϵ, so ist mithin zu setzen:

$$U_n = P \cdot \epsilon,$$

wobei P eine ganze, im allgemeinen grosse Zahl bedeutet.

[It now comes to find instead the probability W that the N resonators in total have the vibrational energy U_n. For this it is necessary to understand U_n not as continuous and divisible without limitation but as made up of discrete and finite equal integer parts. Let us call such a part an energy element ϵ, placed so that

$$U_n = P \cdot \epsilon$$

whereby P means a whole, in general large number.][24]

Planck's "whole number" P (which later in the paper gives way to the universal constant h mentioned above), contradicted one of the fundamental assumptions of classical physics: a belief in the continuity of natural phenomena, summarized by the Latin phrase *natura non saltum est*, "Nature does not make leaps." In its place, Planck expounded a different assumption: that nature did make leaps—from one energy level to another. Yet he did not seem to recognize that this assumption presented any difficulties within the existing conventions of physics, and his article portrays his work as a contribution rather than a challenge to the mainstream.

Planck's work received an enthusiastic reception, for it offered a precise description of the troubling spectroscopic results. Furthermore, perhaps because of Planck's failure to emphasize the essential discontinuity between his model and classical assumptions, as well as his continuing reliance on a classical frame of reference in propounding those ideas, most scientists, like Planck himself, seem not to have recognized or to have been reluctant to acknowledge the radical consequences of his revolutionary integer. Five years passed before anyone took up the challenge presented by Planck's constant. Then, in 1905, Einstein began to publish the results of the first rigorous analysis of the quantum of action. This work pushed the implications of Planck's formula further to demonstrate that, in its absorption and emission by matter, electromagnetic radiation behaves as if it were made up of particles each having a definite momentum. In this way, Einstein resuscitated Newton's particle model of light. On the face of it, this would hardly seem to be a radical act; but as I suggested earlier, the work of Young, Fresnel, and Maxwell was thought to have resolved the particle–wave debate in favor of the wave model by proving that only the latter could explain certain features of the behavior of electromagnetic radiation. Einstein's work demonstrated that Planck's formula required the scientific community to accept the simultaneous validity of the particle model as well, without resolving its contradiction of the wave model, and this seemed to many physicists to undermine their deeply held belief that it is possible to describe natural phenomena according to the principle of causation.

Here, at last, physicists began to recognize the subtle but revolutionary character of Planck's quantum of action. I use the words "subtle" and "revolutionary" in conjunction here because the radical consequences of the quantum theory did not derive from its dramatic overthrow of the wave model of light. The triumph of one metaphorical model over another has occurred repeatedly throughout the history of science; indeed, such competition constitutes a primary means by which the scientific description of nature expands to incorporate new phenomena. The quantum theory, however, introduced a radical challenge to science in a rather different way, by insisting that a second, contradictory model was necessary for a complete description of a particular set of physical phenomena. In effect, Planck's formula undermined a basic premise of science—the assumption that it is possible to construct an entirely consistent description of nature—by proving that a complete description of electromagnetic radiation equally requires two models, based respectively on the metaphors of waves and particles, despite their unresolvable contradictions.

Consistency vs. Completeness

Gradually over the next twenty years scientists struggled to come to terms with the consequences of Planck's formula. Einstein, for his part, argued that the quantum theory "set science a fresh task: that of finding a new conceptual basis for all of physics."[25] Niels Bohr, likewise, believed that "A new epoch was inaugurated in physical science by Planck's discovery of the quantum of action."[26] Such praise sounds comfortably celebratory from our retrospective position; but to understand the impact of Planck's work, we must bear in mind how threatening terms like "new conceptual basis" and "new epoch" sound to practitioners of a discipline like physics, which depends on its ability to incorporate new observations and new phenomena into a stable representational system.

In an interview in which he discusses the history of the quantum revolution, Werner Heisenberg repeatedly stresses the need for continuity in the production of scientific knowledge:

> I remember that at that time we frequently quoted this sentence from Hilbert who had studied the inconsistencies of mathematical axioms and who had proved that if the mathematical system of axioms does contain an inconsistency—B equal to non A—then you can prove everything from this scheme. That we applied, of course, with great pleasure to physics. As soon as you came into a real inconsistency, then you could go anywhere. That, of course, is nowhere.[27]

In the context of normal science, the need for consistency is such a deep-seated assumption as to be practically invisible. The crisis that gradually grew out of Planck's quantum of action, however, made it virtually impossible for physicists to be unaware of their dependence on the continuity of the scientific tradition and the very real possibility that such continuity could be lost. Furthermore, the quantum revolution was only a part of a more widespread reevaluation of classical conventions in mathematics and the sciences. The introduction of Riemannian geometry in the middle of the nineteenth century, for example, had emphasized the arbitrary character of mathematical axioms, ended the long monopoly of Euclidean geometry, and led, in part, to the work of David Hilbert that Heisenberg cites. Thus, while early twentieth-century physicists addressed the implications of Planck's constant for specific problems of their research, mathematicians at the time were engaged in a similar reappraisal of the axiomatic systems they had inherited.

Because of its abstract nature, mathematics allows a more systematic approach to such considerations. As a result, a number of mathematicians became involved in attempts to resolve whether logical consistency, of the kind exhibited by Euclidean geometry or that sought by classical physicists, inevitably prevented any symbolic system from completely describing all possible phenomena. In their *Principia Mathematica*, for example, Bertrand Russell and Alfred North Whitehead sought to prove that "it is possible to construct a mathematical logic which does not lead to contradictions."[28] To do so, they needed to demonstrate that a mathematical system might contain all true statements about its field of reference and at the same time avoid any internal contradictions, such as stem from attempts to merge existing systems, like Riemannian and Euclidean geometries, based on incompatible primary assumptions. By examining the special case of axiomatic mathematics, Russell and Whitehead believed they had chosen a closed system of sufficient abstraction to put the dual goals of consistency and completeness within reach, and that it was possible to construct a mathematical logic which does not lead to contradictions.

Hilbert, to whom Heisenberg's reference directs us, supported the aim of the *Principia*, but he remained uncertain that the work, despite its impressive bulk, included all true statements involving numbers or, notwithstanding the great intelligence of its authors, succeeded in avoiding internal contradictions. Like many of his colleagues, Hilbert turned his own energies toward proving that an essentially unbounded and therefore all-inclusive system of this type could, in principle, be derived from a finite and therefore demonstrably consistent set of rules. To do so, he needed to prove that a complete system—that is, a system containing all possible true statements derivable from its axiomatic elements—might also be consistent in the sense that it would not also contain any statements which could not be proven either true or false. Although a project of this kind may strike us as abstract to the point of being purely academic, Heisenberg's interest in Hilbert's work speaks for its relevance outside the realm of pure mathematics. Indeed, the possibility of a proof of the type Hilbert sought, even in principle and even in the abstract case of mathematics, led Heisenberg and his colleagues to hope that quantum theory's contradictions of classical physics represented only a temporary obstacle in their search for a complete and consistent understanding of the natural world. Einstein, for one, clung to this hope until his death, long after most physicists had given it up.

In 1931, however, Kurt Gödel published a paper entitled "Über Formal Unentscheidbare Sätze der Principia Mathematica und Verwandter Systeme, I," in which he laid to rest the dream of an all-inclusive and completely consistent symbolic system, even one made up of pure abstract numbers.[29] Gödel argued that any system claiming to contain all true statements based on its axioms must also contain some statements regarding its own axioms which cannot be proven either true or false using statements based only on those axioms.[30] Therefore, such a system will contain inconsistencies; or, if it proves all such statments about its own axioms by reference to other statements not contained within it in order to avoid inconsistencies, then it must be incomplete. In this way, Gödel's "Incompleteness Theorem" invokes the idea of self-referentiality to prove that no system can exist which is at once complete and consistent. This proof effectively destroyed the belief, widespread since the Renaissance, that science might hope to resolve all inconsistencies while including all natural phenomena in its descriptive domain.

Interestingly, the physicists grappling with quantum theory had already tacitly accepted much the same conclusion. In fact, one of the chief difficulties confronting them provides an excellent illustration of the self-referentiality problem invoked by Gödel. In their efforts to construct a model of subatomic processes, of which Einstein's quantum theory of photon emission and absorption was a part, these physicists at first tried to follow the dictates of classical mechanics, which suggested that in order to fully describe the behavior of an electron (for example) it was necessary to derive a means of determining both its momentum and its position at any given time. Yet it quickly became apparent that electrons showed a definite reluctance to cooperate in this endeavor. In fact, the more precisely one measured an electron's momentum, the less idea one had as to where it actually *was*. And conversely, the better idea one had of its exact position, the less one could say about where it was going, or how quickly.

The problem sprang from the fact that in order to "see" an electron, an observer must interact with it—must, for example, bounce a photon off it and observe the electron by observing the photon. But electrons are small compared with the wavelength of light required to determine their momentum with any degree of accuracy, which makes it impossible to determine just where they are. Likewise, decreasing the wavelength to get a better sense of the electron's position increases the frequency of the light, which means that a higher energy photon collides with the electron and changes its momentum. To take the interference of the photon into account, it would be necessary to determine the momentum of the photon or, in effect, observe the instrument of observation. Aage Petersen quotes Bohr's description of this problem: "For instance, when we observe an object in a microscope, we consider the light used to localize the object as a part of the measuring tool. But there is nothing to prevent us from making this light an object of investigation by introducing new measuring tools to define and obtain the information we want about the new system."[31] But where do we stop? Why not investigate the tool doing the investigation of the investigating tool? There is no necessary end to our self-referentiality. And this is precisely the dilemma that Gödel describes as an inevitable part of any system which attempts to extend its consistency to ever-increasing levels of inclusiveness.

Practically, physicists dealt with this situation by developing and refining the unsettling findings of quantum theory into a full-blown system in its own right: quantum mechanics. This development, however, was neither easy nor peaceful. The new system was based on a number of assumptions about the world and the possibilities of describing it that were incompatible with the classical view. Some scientists, like Einstein, despite their seminal role in its development, resisted with all of their considerable intellects the elevation of quantum theory to the status of an equal but separate system. But quantum mechanics provided answers where classical mechanics never could. In the case at hand, for instance, classical mechanics could only insist that at some future time it would be possible to know both the position and the momentum of any subatomic particle with an arbitrary degree of precision. Quantum mechanics, on the other hand, dealt with this ambiguity by elevating it to the level of a basic assumption. This assumption is manifest in physics in a variety of forms, including Heisenberg's and Bohr's respective principles of uncertainty and complementarity, the latter of which concludes, in Petersen's words, that "Two phenomena obtained by observing the same system with two different types of instruments are mutually exclusive."[32] In the next chapter, I will consider these principles, especially complementarity, in more detail.

It will be useful at this point to pause for a moment and consider why Gödel's Incompleteness Theorem, in refuting one of the motivating assumptions of science, did not more seriously disrupt its practices. Like all scientists, the Los Alamites continued to rely on the assumption that science could produce—in fact, had to produce—a description of nature that was both consistent and increasingly inclusive, and they went to great lengths to maintain this conception of their discipline. Of course, science had acquired considerable institutional momentum over the three centuries since it had emerged in its modern form; but inertia in itself provides no guarantee of an institution's continuing viability. What particular characteristics of the science practiced by Planck, Einstein, Heisenberg, and Bohr allowed them to weather the challenges presented by quantum theory and hand on to the Los Alamites a robust though revised tradition?[33]

During the first three decades of this century, science withstood the disruption of the causal paradigm of classical mechanics, along with the loss of a motivating belief in the possibility of producing a complete and consistent description of nature. I would argue that the scientific tradition survived this challenge in part because of its messy reliance on metaphorical as well as literal modes of representation. In this chapter, I have broadly traced the dynamic through which uses of wave and particle metaphors played an important role in shaping the practices of physicists from Newton's day to Planck's. In particular, I have discussed the physicists' inability to synthesize the competing representations of the wave and particle metaphors into a continuous causal narrative, and I have identified this as a threat to their confidence in the edifice of classical physics. In other words, classical physicists were suspicious of their own metaphors *as metaphors* and sought to reduce their multivalent meanings to a literal consistency. Yet the very metaphors that distressed them have enabled physicists to resolve such crises and continue in their pursuit of a literal description which they know to be tremendously productive, even if illusory in absolute terms.

In their use of the literal mode of representation, scientists strive for fixed referentiality in their discourse. The payoff for successfully fixing the relationship between the representational structures of science and the physical phenomena of nature remains clear and straightforward: A consistent description of nature is a powerful description, as nuclear weapons demonstrate. Metaphorical representation, on the other hand, offers scientists something different: both a practical means of discussing abstract subjects, such as "the causal structure of the world,"[34] and an impetus for ongoing theory development and experimentation. The drawback is, of course, that they remain a slippery—polysemic— vehicle for describing physical phenomena. It is difficult to control their allusiveness, for they function by extending associations. Yet this drawback is precisely the source of their peculiar power in literary and scientific applications alike. Where literal language asserts consistency by constraining representation, at least in ideal terms, to one-to-one correspondences, metaphorical language casts the representational net more widely. Literal language, at its most extreme, limits representation to a kind of taxonomic function, and metaphors offer scientists a means of broadening the inclusiveness of their representations. Describing light in terms of waves or particles, for example, not only assists scientists in "making possible socially coordinated epistemic access to a particular sort of thing or natural phenomenon"[35]—translating what they have figured out into English—but, as we have seen, fuels and directs the scientific investigation of nature by allowing scientists to structure a mixture of hypothesis and uncertainty into their representations of electromagnetic phenomena. Such work calls for the active extension of scientific hypotheses from territories laid out and described by literal representation, and by metaphors rendered "static" in particular uses, into the otherwise unfamiliar and perhaps inaccessible realms represented by dynamic metaphors.[36]

In general, the course of scientific practice leads toward the "circumscription" of any given metaphor over time—its transformation from dynamic to static—as subsequent experimentation defines its applicability with increasing precision and renders its original dynamic reach part of a carefully maintained literal consistency. In some circumstances, however, a scientific metaphor is found to be inconsistent with the scientific tradition's larger literal description of nature, and that metaphor, though perhaps of considerable tenure, must be abandoned and a new metaphorical cast of the net attempted. Thomas Kuhn describes this process as a scientific revolution based on a shift from one metaphorical paradigm to another.[37] But the development of quantum mechanics involved a rather different situation.[38] In this case, scientists failed to resolve the competition between the dynamic aspects of the wave and particle metaphors in favor of one or the other; instead, each proved equally valid and, what is more, contradictory of the literal truth of the other.

The quantum revolution, therefore, raised questions about the ability of science to resolve dynamic metaphors into static ones. And in doing so, it highlighted the physicists' dependence on metaphorical modes of representation. While this did not inspire physicists to abandon their discipline or to reject its claims, it did cause them an extended period of methodological anxiety, during which they questioned the role of language in their daily practices. We do not generally associate science with an examination of linguistic issues, yet Bohr, for one, expressed a view that became widely influential among his contemporaries when he said: "It is wrong to think that the task of physics is to find out how nature *is*. Physics concerns what we can *say* about nature."[39]

This view accords well with the age-old assumption that nature itself is a kind of *saying*: "And God said, Let there be light: and there was light." To the natural philosopher in the Middle Ages, struggling to find a new way to talk about God's creation, no human saying could aspire to imitate the Word of God except in a pale Platonic manner; physics could never attain the status of the great I AM or proclaim with finality what nature *is*. Physics would always remain fallen talk about divine processes. Yet over the following centuries, the power of this fallen talk frequently allowed modern scientists to ignore its representational dynamic and to proceed on the assumption that science would eventually provide an exact pattern of nature, complete and entirely consistent. The descriptive instabilities exposed by the quantum revolution shocked modern physicists back into an immediate awareness of the provisional character of their pronouncements.

Conclusion

Feynman, in the course of describing the behavior of electrons, exemplifies this renewed awareness when he pauses to reflect on his own representational method:

How they behave, therefore, takes a great deal of imagination to appreciate, because we are going to describe something which is different from anything you know about. . . . It will be difficult. But the difficulty really is psychological and exists in the perpetual torment that results from your saying to yourself, "But how can it be like that?" which is a reflection of uncontrolled but utterly vain desire to see it in terms of something familiar. I *will not* describe it in terms of something familiar; I will simply describe it. . . . So do not take the lecture too seriously, feeling that you really have to understand in terms of some model what I am going to describe, but just relax and enjoy it. I am going to tell you what nature behaves like. If you will simply admit that maybe she does behave like this, you will find her a delightful, entrancing thing. Do not keep saying to yourself, if you can possibly avoid it, "But how can it be like that?" because you will get "down the drain," into a blind alley from which nobody has yet escaped. Nobody knows how it can be like that.[40]

Electrons, like light, display a kind of dual behavior: At times they behave like particles and at other times they behave like waves. Sometimes they even appear to choose consciously between these behaviors. Feynman's claim, "I *will not* describe it in terms of something familiar; I will simply describe it," therefore, reflects a common discomfort with the metaphorical language of, for example, waves and particles that played such a prominent role in bringing on the quantum revolution. At first, this claim may seem a rather willful assertion of a scientist's ability to engage in a purely literal discourse. But by interrupting a lecture on the behavior of electrons to discuss the behavior of his own language, Feynman calls attention to the complexities which he initially appears to gloss over.

Indeed, for an account which claims to avoid comparative language, this passage contains a striking number of occurrences of the word "like." Similarly, the wonderfully mixed metaphor with which he concludes his abjuration of metaphorical language cannot help but remind us of his dependence on the very rhetorical mode he seems to reject. In fact, Feynman does not reject metaphor, but he does approach it in a typical quantum manner. Rather than offering a description of electron behavior in terms of a single, consistent metaphor and assuming its fixed referentiality, he openly questions the ability of such language to represent the phenomena he wishes to describe. Then, having alerted his audience to the dangers of metaphorical description, he goes on to use that very mode and, more specifically, its most suspect terms:

So then, let me describe to you the behaviour of electrons or of photons in their typical quantum mechanical way. I am going to do this by a mixture of analogy and contrast. If I made it pure analogy we would fail; it must be by analogy and contrast with things which are familiar to you. So I make it by analogy and contrast, first to the behaviour of particles, for which I will use bullets, and second to the behaviour of waves, for which I will use water waves.[41]

It might well strike a reader as strange that Feynman should invoke metaphors of waves and particles, the very terms that played such a prominent role in the quantum crisis, as an example of the resulting orthodoxy: the "typical quantum mechanical way" of describing electrons and photons. But this reflects the extent of the scientific tradition's dependence on metaphorical language, as well as the extent to which that crisis was eventually resolved by a new willingness to accept metaphorical language on its own terms and not, therefore, as requiring literal circumscription. Even after such terms led to an apparent impasse, from which only a revolutionary reevaluation of the underlying assumptions of physics could extricate it, they continued to play a central role in scientific discourse.

The continuity of these particular metaphors in science, or indeed of metaphorical language in general, was neither inevitable nor easy to maintain. The process by which the challenges of quantum theory became the new orthodoxy of quantum mechanics involved the efforts (and established the reputations) of the greatest physicists over a period of decades. Perhaps chief among these was Bohr, whose complementarity principle, examined in the next chapter, played a decisive role in resolving the uncertainty over the role of metaphorical language in quantum mechanical descriptions of subatomic phenomena, in laying to rest the apparent conflict between the wave and particle metaphors, and, thereby, in helping to prepare the way for the development of atomic weapons.

Niels Bohr, Werner Heisenberg, and Wolfgang Pauli. (Courtesy AIP Emilio Segrè Visual Archives, Niels Bohr Archive.)

2 "WANDERING ON NEW PATHS"

NIELS BOHR'S

COMPLEMENTARITY PRINCIPLE

In the years following Max Planck's discovery of the quantum of action in 1900, quantum theory matured into the powerful mathematical formalism of quantum mechanics, as expressed in 1925 by Werner Heisenberg's particle-based matrix approach and in 1926 by Erwin Schrödinger's wave method. At first, these two formulations appeared to be as incompatible as Newton's and Huygens's classical conceptions of light, similarly based on the contradictory models of particle and wave. If anything, they seemed even more radically opposed, for Heisenberg's mechanics eschewed classical visualization, while Schrödinger's tantalized physicists with the possibility of a reconciliation with the classical descriptions of Maxwell's electromagnetic field theory. Schrödinger soon demonstrated, however, that the two descriptions were mathematically identical. After twenty-five years, physicists had at last developed a quantum analysis capable of treating subatomic phenomena in both their particle and wave manifestations— though they still had not managed to reconcile these two metaphorical conceptions within a single formalism.

Indeed, a profound incompatibility between Heisenberg's and Schrödinger's methods persisted at the level of interpretation. As Niels Bohr remarked, "A divergence of opinion had arisen with regard to the physical interpretation of the methods, and this had led to much discussion."[1] There was no clear way of translating the mathematical descriptions provided by these quantum mechanical methods into a language capable of connecting what was going on at the subatomic level with our sensory experience of the world—which, to most physicists, was synonymous with the descriptive modes of classical physics. Over the centuries leading up to 1900, the wide-ranging successes of classical physics had seemed to establish it as *the* medium of a true understanding of natural phenomena. But the necessity of rethinking the fundamental assumptions of classical physics within a quantum context had shaken physicists' confidence. Had the time truly come, as Heisenberg and his followers contended, to abandon the classical effort to integrate quantitative and qualitative conceptions in a causal, space–time description of the natural world?

At stake for quantum theorists in this discussion was the status of their work within the larger framework of physics. Some physicists, Einstein perhaps most famously, saw quantum mechanics as a stopgap measure based on a hodgepodge of ideas—ranging from Einstein's own theory of photons (1905) and Bohr's model of the hydrogen atom (1913) to Heisenberg's matrix and Schrödinger's wave mechanics.[2] In 1927, no one would have denied that quantum mechanics offered useful mathematical descriptions of atomic phenomena, yet it had so far failed to integrate these abstract formulations into a description consistent with the conventions of classical mechanics. And rather than bringing them closer together, the passing years only seemed to make a reconciliation between the two branches of physics less and less likely.

This was an intensely stressful period in the lives of many physicists, and for none more than for Heisenberg and Bohr. Both men had well-established careers based on their respective contributions to quantum theory; both had, therefore, staked out particular conceptual territories in the course of their past work—territories they were motivated to defend in the face of the inevitable shifts that occur during the development of a new discipline.[3] Bohr was the senior man, the director of the Institute for Theoretical Physics in Copenhagen, where Heisenberg was a visiting *lektor* from May 1926 to June 1927.[4] They therefore had the opportunity to engage in an intense, ongoing dialogue that focused on the most productive way to integrate the mathematical tools of the new quantum mechanics into the existing conventions of physics. Their conversations were often heated, sometimes leaving the younger Heisenberg in tears, and for months they seemed to be going nowhere. Then in February 1927, Bohr went to Norway on a skiing vacation, leaving Heisenberg on his own in Copenhagen for a month. Free of the pressures exerted by his host, it took Heisenberg only a few days to lay out the groundwork for a new paper in which he formulated his response to the issues he had been debating with Bohr.[5] By the time Bohr returned in mid-March, Heisenberg had finished a draft of the paper he would shortly send to the *Zeitschrift für Physik*.[6]

This paper introduced what Heisenberg's biographer has described as his "most famous and far-reaching achievement in physics"—the uncertainty principle.[7] As Oskar Klein recalled years later, "Bohr read the paper and was at first very taken with it but when he began to look more closely he became very disappointed."[8] Bohr's disappointment centered on two issues, both of which coincided in a thought experiment proposed by Heisenberg involving observation of an electron through a gamma-ray microscope. The first issue concerned an error in Heisenberg's analysis of the experimental situation.[9] The second, more far-reaching issue reflected Bohr's deep epistemological dissatisfaction with Heisenberg's representation of the electron as a particle. Whereas Heisenberg was prepared to abandon the search for a vernacular description of subatomic phenomena in favor of a workable mathematical formalism, Bohr, for a variety of reasons that I will explore as we go on, remained more firmly committed to the conventions of visualization he had internalized during his training in classical mechanics. Such visualization required some sort of reconciliation of the wave and particle metaphors, rather than a retreat into an abstract mathematical apparatus, such as Heisenberg's, based on only one of these metahpors.[10]

Bohr was not an impartial judge of Heisenberg's work, for he had not been idle during his trip to Norway; as Heisenberg was drafting his uncertainty article, Bohr was struggling to articulate his own response to the difficulties of interpreting the quantum mechanical formalism. Later commentators, including Heisenberg himself,[11] have described Bohr's ultimate response as a broader and more comprehensive expression of the ideas implicit in Heisenberg's uncertainty principle. Given the scope and intensity of their exchange during this period, it is hardly surprising that both men were thinking along similar lines. But in a discipline in which precedence is all-important, it should not surprise us either that both men would feel a strong degree of professional competitiveness. This would certainly help explain both Heisenberg's eagerness to publish his article quickly and the energy with which Bohr urged him to wait and undertake a number of revisions first, including direct acknowledgment of the precedence of some of Bohr's own work.

None of this suggests that either man behaved in a particularly *un*professional manner. Although their exchanges were disagreeable enough to warrant tears on Heisenberg's part, and even to involve "gross personal misunderstandings"[12] on at least one occasion, we should expect that such revolutionary episodes as this—in any human enterprise, even science—must require a great deal more of their participants than cool-headed objectivity. At any rate, the two men soon made an apparently successful effort to heal any lingering wounds, and their friendship continued. Even in the midst of their sharp exchanges, Heisenberg appended a postscript to his article acknowledging both his debt to Bohr's earlier work and his mentor's criticisms. For his part, despite his reservations, Bohr continued publicly to praise Heisenberg's article, writing to Einstein, for instance, that it "probably marks a very momen-

"Wandering on New Paths"

tous contribution to the discussion of the general problems of quantum theory," and sharing prepublication proofs with his colleagues.[13]

It took six months of intense work following his return from Norway before Bohr felt ready to make a formal presentation of his own ideas. Finally, on September 16, 1927, he addressed an international congress of physicists assembled in the Italian city of Como and, in a lecture entitled "The Quantum Postulate and the Recent Development of Atomic Theory," introduced his principle of complementarity.[14] A month later he repeated more or less the same lecture at the Solvay conference in Brussels. Then in April 1928, he published a revised version of the paper in *Nature*. Indeed, he continued to work on his complementarity principle in one form or another for the rest of his life, gradually attempting to extend its application well beyond its original quantum mechanical confines.[15] It represents a major investment of time and effort on the part of one of the preeminent minds of this century, and it has received a comparable return in the attention lavished on it by subsequent commentators. There is as yet, however, no broad consensus on the meaning, or even the importance, of Bohr's principle. Despite Bohr's extensive elaboration and the critical analysis of physicists, historians, and philosophers, complementarity remains, as Mara Beller noted, "a challenge and a puzzle," thought by some to be "the most profound intellectual insight of the twentieth century" and by others to be "an obscure 'double-think.' "[16]

Wherein does the difficulty lie? Bohr's own remarks introducing his presentation would seem to belie any great complexity:

I shall try by making use only of simple consideration[s] and without going into any details of technical mathematical character to describe to you a certain general point of view which I believe is suited to give an impression of the general trend of the development of the [quantum] theory from its very beginning and which I hope will be helpful in order to harmonize the apparently conflicting views taken by different scientists.[17]

The difficulty can hardly be a technical one. Although the paper does involve some mathematical transformations, they are just technical enough to challenge a reader with a working knowledge of a standard high school curriculum and would certainly have presented no difficulty to his audience. Bohr himself asserts that in his audience there were "several who, due to their participation in the remarkable recent development, will surely be more conversant with details of the highly developed formalism than I am."[18]

Indeed, between the Como and Solvay conferences, his audience consisted of the major figures in the discipline, including Planck, Einstein,

Heisenberg, Schrödinger, Ehrenfest, de Broglie, Dirac, Born, Jordan, Fermi, Segrè, and Wigner. These individuals brought a stunning intellectual power and a wide array of views to bear on Bohr's presentation. Some considered it revolutionary—a "theory that Dirac said 'led to a drastic change in the physicist's view of the world, perhaps the biggest that has yet taken place'; that Oppenheimer called 'the inauguration of a new phase in the evolution of human thinking'; and that John Wheeler, professor of physics at Princeton University, described as 'the most revolutionary scientific concept of this century.' "[19] Others found it almost boring; Eugene Wigner, for instance, commented to Léon Rosenfeld that "This lecture will not induce any one of us to change his own meaning about quantum mechanics."[20] But regardless of the flavor of any given individual response, the talk seems to have lit a fire under the assembled physicists, drawing them into an immediate and ongoing debate. At the Solvay conference, for example, "So great was the noise and the commotion that Ehrenfest slipped up to the blackboard, erased some of the figures that filled it, and wrote: 'The Lord did there confound the language of all the earth.' "[21] How could Bohr's "simple considerations" have led so many brilliant minds into a state of Babel, in which each seemed to be speaking a private language?

The existing commentary suggests that the complementarity principle is itself a confluence of an almost Babel-like variety of scientific, philosophical, and literary sources. Gerald Holton, for example, describes the breadth of influences, in addition to the obvious scientific precursors, that fed Bohr's complementarity principle, including a "light story, *The Adventures of a Danish Student*," by the nineteenth-century Danish poet and philosopher Poul Martin Møller; William James's *Principles of Psychology*, particularly the chapter on "The Stream of Thought"; various writings by Harald Høffding, a professor of philosophy at the University of Copenhagen; and, through Høffding, the work of Søren Kierkegaard.[22] Taking a different tack, Beller examines Bohr's dialectical habit of thought as it manifests itself in dialogues embedded in "The Quantum Postulate" between Bohr and several of his contemporaries. And Pais, obviously, comes at complementarity from yet another angle in writing Bohr's biography. Each of these approaches, along with others cited elsewhere in this chapter,[23] adds significantly to our understanding of the complementarity principle; but none of them resolves the questions that continue to revolve around Bohr's presentation of a "general point of view."

In what follows, I will employ the tools of literary analysis in an effort to extend and complement the insights of previous readers, paying close attention to the language in which Bohr presents his complementarity principle. I believe that this is a particularly useful approach because Bohr's awareness of every physicist's inescapable reliance on language functions as a central pillar of complementarity. More specifically, he focuses on the possibilities of observing and describing physical phenomena and, in doing so, points to an underlying dependence on metaphor in both classical and quantum physics—a dependence that grows inevitably out of their common use of the symbolic tools of language in their efforts to cross the gulf between the objective world and our subjective experience of it. By tracing this dependence, and playing upon it at every level of his own work, from the rhetorical to the conceptual, Bohr offers a reconception of the symbolic methods of modern physics that strives to maintain their continuity and flexibility.

"To Escape from the Pitfalls": Bohr Prepares His Rhetorical Ground

In an introduction written in 1929 to a volume reprinting "The Quantum Postulate," Bohr summarizes his project in these terms:

It is maintained in the article that the fundamental postulate of the indivisibility of the quantum of action is itself, from the classical point of view, an irrational element which inevitably requires us to forego a causal mode of description and which, because of the coupling between phenomena and their observation, forces us to adopt a new mode of description designated as complementary in the sense that any given application of classical concepts precludes the simultaneous use of other classical concepts which in a different connection are equally necessary for the elucidation of the phenomena.[24]

Bohr refers to the quantum of action's contradiction of sensory experience as an "irrational element." But he does not reject it on this basis. Instead, he contextualizes that irrationality in a particular conceptual stance—"the classical point of view"—and then goes on, rather disconcertingly, to suggest that in this case the rationality of the classical perspective must yield to the irrationality of the quantum of action: We must "forego a causal mode of description and . . . adopt a new mode of description designated as complementary." This assertion may well strike a lay reader as part of a radical argument, and statements of this sort have, indeed, tempted some cultural critics to explore twentieth-century physics for analogies to their own postmodern theories—an activity other critics have viewed as a left-wing effort to undermine the traditional authority of science.[25] Even some of Bohr's colleagues, like

Max Von Laue and Erwin Schrödinger, felt that he was advocating an unacceptably radical break with classical physics.[26] In fact, Bohr had been perceived as radical, even fanciful, since the time of his earliest contributions to quantum theory, as the introduction to his *Nature* article suggests: "To some of the more conservative physicists the account of Bohr's atom reads like a fairy tale."[27] Yet his position in 1927 was actually more conservative than that of others of his colleagues, like Max Born, who in a paper published in June 1926 had argued, "It is necessary to drop completely the physical pictures of Schrödinger which aim at a revitalization of the classical continuum theory."[28] Bohr remained interested in mediating between the classical and the quantum perspectives, searching out possible continuities, and maintaining the importance and utility of descriptive modes associated with classical mechanics.

In another sense, however, Bohr's argument would probably have appeared quite radical to all of his colleagues. A few early drafts of his talk were entitled "The Philosophical Foundations of the Quantum Theory,"[29] and the philosophical orientation that this suggests is fully evident in the final paper itself. This orientation, I would argue, was an important cause of the varied responses of Bohr's colleagues—as well as the continuing interpretive difficulties experienced by later readers. His presentation of the complementarity principle strays well outside the normal scientific purview, indulging in a highly self-referential examination of the conditions pertaining to the production of scientific knowledge. Although Bohr's argument has a very direct bearing on the practice of quantum mechanics, its mode challenges the conventions of scientific discourse by taking such discourse as a central subject. As I will attempt to demonstrate, Bohr's own discourse shows the strains inherent in this project, as he tries, on the one hand, to construct a rhetorical vehicle capable of representing an extravagant conception of his discipline and, on the other hand, to keep his rhetoric within the bounds of that discipline.

There is evidence of this strain, for example, in the passage I quoted from his "Introductory Survey." Even two years after his initial presentation, Bohr continued to feel the need to stack his rhetorical deck: he employs the passive voice and the conventions of scientific impersonality to elide his own subjective agency and depict his thesis as though it were a natural and therefore inevitable conclusion. At the same time, however, he is struggling to establish the authority of his argument that focuses on the role of subjective observation and rationality in physics. Ironically, Bohr uses his evocation of human subjectivity confronting a concatenation of natural and logical forces as the foundation of his own rhetorical authority in two ways. First, he deftly aligns himself with the reader by portraying himself as a member of a community—"us"—predicated on a direct and unflinching examination of these forces, whether irrational or not. Second, he uses his submission to the dictates of nature as a means of underscoring the power of his argument by implying that it is ultimately an argument made by nature. Both rhetorical stances are typical of scientific discourse, as many historians of science have pointed out. By playing on the rhetorical conventions of his discipline, therefore, he downplays the unconventionality of his argument even as he asserts it. But the reader should not be lulled into a false sense that this is just so much science as usual,[30] for the convoluted conventionality of his prose masks an unconventional message. Bohr contends that the work of quantum theory necessitates not merely a suspension of disbelief— no brief period of indeterminacy before the return of reason with the causal mode of description—but an abdication of the "classical point of view" in favor of an open acceptance of a new "irrational element."[31]

Even granting the need for such rhetorical gymnastics, it is striking that nowhere in "The Quantum Postulate" does Bohr provide such a succinct statement of his intention. The absence of such a statement reflects Bohr's sense of the need for a politically expedient approach. He had taken on a difficult, perhaps professionally dangerous task: "to harmonize the apparently conflicting views taken by different scientists." Precisely because he was attempting to "harmonize" the incompatible views of opposing camps (note that he does not say "reconcile"—his argument is not about reducing opposing views to unity), he would have expected to meet with antagonistic reactions on all sides. In forwarding an argument that quantum mechanics "inevitably requires us to forego a causal model of description," he was contradicting his colleagues who wished to maintain the continuity of quantum and classical physics. Yet he himself remained convinced of the deep continuity underlying the radical revisions he advocated. Indeed, he was well aware of the possibility that his quantum colleagues would view his efforts as selling out: an established, middle-aged director of a prominent institution dropping the standard of the radical discipline he had championed in his youth in order to preach conservation of the tradition. Bohr had set out to walk a tightrope between quantum and classical mechanics in order to convince the physics community that it was possible to bridge the two.

It should come as no surprise, therefore, that in writing the talk in which he formally staked out his position, Bohr's revisions nearly overshot the occasion, and his subsequent efforts to turn the talk into a printed article threatened the patience of his editors at _Nature_.[32] His meticulous attention to the rhetorical foundation of his paper is evident from the opening paragraph, in which he writes: "No subject indeed may be better suited than the quantum theory to mark the development of physics in the century passed since the death of the great genius, whom we are here assembled to commemorate."[33] Bohr begins with a common rhetorical flourish, reminding his audience of the context of his talk: the anniversary of the death of Alessandro Volta, a great figure of classical physics. But there is a good deal going on underneath this apparently simple gesture, for he is playing not only to the different factions in his audience, but in fact to more than one audience. As Moore points out, the Como meeting was "planned as 'one of the realizations of the Fascist regime,' of which Mussolini and the newspapers were constantly talking. It was also to put Italy into the running in the suddenly important new area of theoretical physics."[34] Bohr's acknowledgment of Volta, therefore, attempts simultaneously to soothe the political tensions surrounding the conference and to introduce a theme that will play a central role in his effort to speak to all the disparate perspectives in his immediate audience. On the one hand, his remarks are to be commemorative, a celebration and a tribute to the work of a "great genius"—a representative of the classical tradition. Bohr intends to express his admiration for this tradition; he was trained in classical physics and was well aware of its achievements. On the other hand, however, these remarks point out that Volta has been dead for a hundred years and that physics has continued to develop during that time. So the essay begins with an implicit assertion that the most appropriate tribute to the achievements of the past may be an examination of how the tradition to which they contributed has developed beyond them.

Bohr then goes on to introduce a metaphor that will frame his presentation: "At the same time, just in a field like this where we are wandering on new paths and have to rely upon our own judgment in order to escape from the pitfalls surrounding us on all sides, we have perhaps more occasion than ever at every step to be remindful of the work of the old masters who have prepared the ground and furnished us with our tools."[35] Here Bohr turns to the rhetoric of exploration and discovery. Such metaphors have for hundreds of years allowed physicists to describe their discipline as capable of incorporating new facts and phenomena—of "wandering on new paths"—while maintaining its continuity and extending its traditional domain.[36] But where such assertions might seem natural in the context of *discussions* of science, Bohr's remarks occur in the presentation of a new principle to a highly specialized audience; they therefore form part of his active *practice* of his discipline. In part, this passage points out Bohr's exploitation of the blurry boundary between discussion and practice, for in "The Quantum Postulate" he makes talk about science an essential component of its practice. Of course, the work of science never stops at the laboratory door. As a social institution, science must reproduce itself continuously, both within the scientific community, as established scientists initiate new members, and in the society at large. In this context, one of the practices of science *is* talking about science: recruiting new members, soliciting public funding, forging alliances, and indoctrinating neophytes in the reigning paradigms of the discipline. Bohr's presentation is out of the ordinary only in the sense that it is rare to see open self-referentiality at the heart of a paper aimed at such a specialized audience.

In another important sense, therefore, the conflation of talk and practice reflects the particular task Bohr takes on. He means to direct the scientific tradition onto "new paths," to extend its applicability, to render it more inclusive. Yet, as I have suggested, he also demonstrates a strong awareness of the need to maintain the consistency of that tradition. In "The Quantum Postulate," he engages in precisely the kind of self-referential examination of physics that Kurt Gödel identified with the inevitable inconsistency of any symbolic system.[37] In this way, Bohr's article represents the exigencies of his historical moment. In the eighteenth and nineteenth centuries, the metaphors of wave and particle allowed physicists to stake out a vast conceptual terrain; by the early part of this century, these metaphors had led the discipline to so literal a mastery of that terrain that their internal contradictions in themselves became the necessary focus of scientific inquiry. Bohr's reflexivity, therefore, represents a special case stemming from the use of metaphors in the discipline as a whole.

Bohr's article can, as a result, be seen as an effort to defend the tradition of physics against the inconsistencies of its unavoidable dependence on metaphorical language. It does so by challenging the descriptive model of classical physics that had involved the tradition in such a dependence on those metaphors. Ironically, however, this descriptive model, now a source of inconsistency and weakness, was also the means by which physics had proven itself so widely applicable and so strong. In effect, Bohr sought to save his discipline by knocking away one of its foundation stones. His argument involved reducing the causal assumptions of classical mechanics from the level of guiding principles to that of special cases. To do this he had to convince his audience that quantum mechanics offered a more comprehensive description of natural phenomena, one that could include the classical assumptions. Many physicists felt that this amounted to drawing battle lines between classical and quantum mechanics. Yet Bohr's point was far more subtle and balanced. Heisenberg, for instance, like many of the younger physicists of the time, was more willing to accept the incompatibility of the classical and quantum models.[38] But Bohr saw in the quantum challenge to the classical view an opportunity to reconcile the two models. Accordingly, his complementarity paper repeated well-known proofs of the inconsistency of causal description; but at the same time, he sought to turn that weakness into a new strength by remaking inconsistency itself into the basic principle—complementarity—of a new, overarching system.

Clearly, Bohr took on an immense task, and his rhetoric is correspondingly strained. An inconsistency in his use of the geographical metaphor, for example, demonstrates the complex purpose I have described. In the passage quoted above, Bohr portrays physicists of his day as "in a field . . . wandering on new paths." Yet in the same sentence, he invokes "the work of the old masters who have prepared the ground." He means to have it both ways. He intends to go his own way, "wandering on new paths" of quantum mechanics, but at the same time sticking to the prepared ground of classical mechanics. The metaphor does not quite hold together in a literal sense, which is how physicists prior to Bohr sought to apply their metaphors. Scientists in the classical tradition turned to metaphorical language as a means of succinctly representing phenomena at a high level of abstraction; but in the interests of continuity they also demanded a more literal coherence from their metaphors. Importantly, it was a literal contradiction between the wave and particle metaphors, rather than a failure of either metaphor to describe a significant range of phenomena, which contributed to the quantum crisis. So Bohr's use of contradictory geographical metaphors not only describes the state of contemporary physics but also invokes one of its central dilemmas.

To resolve that dilemma, Bohr sets out to find a new way of using the wave and particle metaphors. Where Heisenberg or Born might be willing to abandon such metaphorical description in favor of purely mathematical expressions, Bohr maintained a conviction that such language reflects a necessary element of human experience.[39] In "The Quantum Postulate," he puts it this way:

In the discussion of these questions, it must be kept in mind that, according to the view taken above, radiation in free space as well as isolated material particles are abstractions, their properties on the quantum theory being definable and observable only through their interaction with other systems. Nevertheless, these abstractions are, as we shall see, indispensable for a description of experience in connexion with our ordinary space–time view. (581)

Here we can see that despite his partisan role as a spokesman for quantum mechanics, Bohr remains firmly convinced of the value of the classical mode of description, or "our ordinary space-time view." To reconcile the two, he seeks a way of incorporating the "abstractions" of "radiation in free space" and "isolated material particles" into quantum theory's increasingly statistical description of nature. This requires, in his opinion, not so much a defense of the usefulness of either metaphor, which he takes to be "well-known,"[40] as a challenge to the classical way of looking at metaphorical language in the first place. In his words, "we are not dealing with contradictory but with complementary pictures of the phenomena, which only together offer a natural generalisation of the classical mode of description" (581). This effort to redefine the classically unacceptable contradiction of the wave and particle metaphors as an orthodox quantum "complementarity" stands at the heart of Bohr's essay and of an enormous textual output during the rest of his life. As a result of this effort, the complementarity principle occupies a prominent place in the history of quantum mechanics—despite its unsettling ability to elude all efforts to render it in straightforward, literal language, and despite the fact that, as Ehrenfest put it in a letter to several colleagues, complementarity consists of "the awful Bohr incantation terminology. Impossible for anybody else to summarize."[41]

Mathematics and Metaphors: The Substance of Bohr's Strategy

Bohr divided his presentation of complementarity into seven sections. In the first, he offers a detailed consideration of the contradictory dynamic he hopes to address. As he sees it, this dynamic centers on an interlocking struggle between two sets of oppositions: classical versus quantum mechanics on the one hand, and the wave versus the particle model on the other. Each opposition involves the other, and it soon becomes nearly impossible to maintain clear distinctions between them. Bohr plays on this mutual interdependency, and in particular on the cast of mind required to appreciate it, in illustrating his notion of complementarity, much as he uses the internal contradiction of his opening geographical metaphor to foreshadow his subtle conception of a complementary use of scientific metaphors.

Bohr begins with the classical–quantum opposition. Of the former he says, "Our usual description of physical phenomena is based entirely on the idea that the phenomena concerned may be observed without disturbing them appreciably" (580). In contrast, "The quantum postulate implies that any observation of atomic phenomena will involve an interaction with the agency of observation not to be neglected" (580). For Bohr, this distinction constitutes one of the "well-known" reference points by which he guides his essay in its wandering along new paths. But he does not linger on this point. Instead, he hastens through the well-rehearsed implications of these opposed conceptions and on to his own daring attempt to reconcile them:

This situation has far-reaching consequences. On one hand, the definition of the state of a physical system, as ordinarily understood, claims the elimination of all external disturbances. But in that case, according to the quantum postulate, any observation will be impossible, and, above all, the concepts of space and time lose their immediate sense. On the other hand, if in order to make observation possible we permit certain interactions with suitable agencies of measurement, not belonging to the system, an unambiguous definition of the state of the system is naturally no longer possible, and there can be no question of causality in the ordinary sense of the word. The very nature of the quantum theory thus forces us to regard the space–time co-ordination and the claim of causality, the union of which characterises the classical theories, as complementary but exclusive features of the description, symbolising the idealisation of observation and definition respectively. (580)

Once again, Bohr implicitly claims solidarity with his audience, portraying himself as "forced" into complementarity by the "nature" of the quantum postulate. The problem seems clear in his portrayal of it, and indeed quantum theory's insistence on the contradiction between our need to observe natural phenomena and to avoid disturbing them were all too familiar to everyone in Bohr's audience. The failure of quantum theory to suggest a solution to this contradiction led classically oriented physicists, such as Einstein or Schrödinger, to view it as incomplete. For quantum mechanists, however, this contradiction spelled the obsolescence of classical mechanics. Bohr chose neither of these options, but instead tried to portray his own complementarity principle as the inevitable conclusion to the debate: a conception that developed out of the quantum postulate but that allowed the preservation of classical assumptions in the form of mutually exclusive and yet interdependent idealizations of physical experience.

Implicit in this description of the opposition between the classical and quantum descriptions is the second opposition mentioned above, between the two conceptions of electromagnetic radiation employed by classical mechanics. When Bohr writes of "the space–time coordination," he is generally read as referring to the particle model, which conceives of the existence of "tiny bits" of matter or energy occupying specific locations in space and time; and when he mentions "the claim of causality," he invokes the wave model, which depicts electromagnetic and material interactions in terms of a continuum.[42] But there is a problem with this characterization: although one might argue that it is often *possible* to read Bohr's presentation in this way, it is not *necessary* at every point. Indeed, such a reading is at some points, at least, a misleading oversimplification of what Bohr is struggling to represent as a complex relationship between the wave–particle duality, on the one hand, and the classical–quantum frameworks, on the other. I would argue that Bohr's use of the terms "space–time" and "causality" constitutes a third binary that mediates between the two primary pairings. In the passage quoted above, for instance, in which Bohr argues that quantum theory requires a different conception of the relationship between "the space–time co-ordination and the claim of causality, the union of which characterises the classical theories, as complementary but exclusive features of the description," if we substitute "particle model" and "wave model" in the appropriate places, we create an absurd assertion. Classical physics was clearly *not* characterized by the union of wave and particle models—rather, these models were considered mutually exclusive—while it *was* characterized by a belief that physical phenomena could be located in a precise spatiotemporal coordinate system that would allow for a detailed causal description. Therefore, I would suggest that the terms "space–time" and "causality" should be considered distinct from "particle" and "wave" models, respectively, though in many instances Bohr does evoke this conflation in the service of his larger project. In particular, by using these terms to relate the wave–particle and the classical–quantum oppositions, Bohr makes each contingent on the other, which allows him to define the controversy over the relative status of classical and quantum theories as a function of the status of the two classical metaphors, or vice versa, at his convenience.

In the second section of his essay, Bohr simultaneously shifts his focus to the wave and particle metaphors and his approach to that of mathematical analysis. The following extended passage demonstrates the way he interweaves mathematical and verbal argumentation to build slowly to a key moment of reflexive revelation:

The fundamental contrast between the quantum of action and the classical concepts is immediately apparent from the simple formulae which form the common foundation of the theory of light quanta and of the wave theory of material particles. If Planck's constant be denoted by h, as is well known,

$$E\tau = I\lambda = h, \tag{1}$$

where E and I are energy and momentum respectively, τ and λ the corresponding period of vibration and wave-length. In these formulae the two notions of light and also of matter enter in sharp contrast. While energy and momentum are associated with the concept of particles, and hence may be characterised according to the classical point of view by definite space–time co-ordinates, the period of vibration and wave-length refer to a plane harmonic wave train of unlimited extent in space and time. Only with the aid of the superposition principle does it become possible to attain a connexion with the ordinary mode of description. Indeed, a limitation of the extent of the wave-fields in space and time can always be regarded as resulting from the interference of a group of elementary harmonic waves. As shown by de Broglie (Thèse, Paris, 1924), the translational velocity of the individuals associated with the waves can be represented by just the so-called group-velocity. Let us denote a plane elementary wave by

$$A \cos 2\pi (vt - x\sigma_x - y\sigma_y - z\sigma_z + \delta),$$

where A and δ are constants determining respectively the amplitude and the phase. The quantity $v = 1/\tau$ is the frequency, $\sigma_x, \sigma_y, \sigma_z$ the wave numbers in the direction of the co-ordinate axes, which may be regarded as vector components of the wave number $\sigma = 1/\lambda$ in the direction of propagation. While the wave or phase velocity is given by v/σ, the group-velocity is defined by $dv/d\sigma$. Now according to the relativity theory we have for a particle with the velocity v:

$$I = (v/c^2)E \quad \text{and} \quad vdI = dE,$$

where c denotes the velocity of light. Hence by equation (1) the phase velocity is c^2/v and the group velocity v. The circumstance that the former is in general greater than the velocity of light emphasises the symbolic character of these considerations. At the same time, the possibility of identifying the velocity of the particle with the group-velocity indicates the field of application of space–time pictures in the quantum theory. Here the complementary character of the description appears, since the use of wave-groups is necessarily accompanied by a lack of sharpness in the definition of period and wave-length, and hence also in the definition of the corresponding energy and momentum as given by relation (1). (581)[43]

Bohr's argument in this passage is driven largely by mathematical conventions, meaning that it does not engage in overt interpretation of natural phenomena. Although it does rely on past interpretations— from which it takes the concepts of energy, momentum, wavelength frequency, period, and velocity—in itself the line of reasoning presented above simply follows the abstract rules of mathematics. Yet these rules lead Bohr to a crucial interpretive moment in which his argument reflects back on itself: "The circumstance that the [phase velocity] is in general greater than the velocity of light emphasises the symbolic character of these considerations." His first equation (1) describes the behavior of electromagnetic radiation as including both energy and momentum, as if it were made up of particles, as well as period and wavelength, as if it were composed of waves. By following out the mathematical implications of this dual description, he arrives at an expression for the relationship between the velocity v of the radiation as a particle and the velocity c^2/v of the radiation as a wave. But despite his rigorous application of the rules of mathematical reasoning, this final relationship does not make sense if we apply it in a literal interpretation of nature. As Bohr points out, his result makes sense only if we interpret it symbolically.[44]

By acknowledging "the symbolic character of these considerations," Bohr invokes the conventional distinction between symbolic and literal modes of scientific discourse that I discussed in the last chapter. Most contemporary studies of the history of science recognize, whether implicitly or explicitly, that scientific discourse employs both modes. But there is a clear prejudice in the scientific community itself in favor of literal representation over symbolic. Traditional physics has struggled for centuries to maintain an unambiguous relationship between its laws and the natural world. The conventions of mathematical analysis lose their force and physics begins to break down if relations at opposite ends of a series of purely mathematical transformations do not represent the phenomena to which they refer with the same degree of literal accuracy. And yet, as Bohr's example demonstrates, this is precisely the position in which physicists found their discipline during the first three decades of the twentieth century, when the wave and particle metaphors became equally necessary and the contradiction between them grew so marked that their symbolic character could no longer be subsumed under a literal framework.

In this difficult position, Bohr chose neither to abandon the metaphors of classical mechanics nor to reject the mathematical formalism of quantum mechanics. He saw that these metaphors played a crucial role in the interpretation of natural phenomena; abandoning them would weaken the foundations of a tradition that was the basis of his own quantum mechanical work. As equation (1) suggests, for example, the wave and particle metaphors remained central elements even in the "irrational," or nonsensory, quantum description of nature. Indeed, where classical theory was at a loss to reconcile these two central metaphors, quantum theory insisted on their mathematical relationship. Yet, at the same time, Bohr recognized how fruitful and indeed necessary the quantum theory's contradictions of sensory experience and common "sense" were to the growth of his discipline. In this context, his reference to the "symbolic character" of the passage quoted above is meant not to dismiss the metaphors in question, as it might at first seem, but in fact to insist on the prominence and necessity of the symbolic mode.

Exploring the "Field of Application"

As the preceding remarks suggest, a central theme of Bohr's presentation may be expressed in these terms: What is "the field of application of space–time pictures in the quantum theory" (581)?[45] Here "space–time pictures" includes both the wave and particle models; in fact, it refers to the metaphors of classical mechanics in general. His approach to this question parallels Planck's formulation of quantum theory and Einstein's development of relativity theory. While the former treated the troubling spectroscopic observations of blackbody radiation as an essential given in his investigations, and the latter accepted the absolute constancy of the speed of light, Bohr affirmed the simultaneous necessity and inadequacy of the "space–time pictures" as the center of the classical–quantum debate and the key to its resolution. In effect, he argues that physicists should acknowledge the metaphorical character of these descriptive models and employ them accordingly rather than attempt to force them into a literal mold for which they remain poorly suited.

Bohr labels the descriptive character of such metaphors "complementary." Complementarity, therefore, centers on a recognition of the metaphorical character of scientific metaphors. As previously suggested, physicists were traditionally accustomed to emphasizing "literalized" or static applications of metaphors; here Bohr insists on their dynamic role. In doing so, he manages to preserve the use of such metaphors, along with the classical tradition that depended on them, by redefining their "field of application." Rather than attempting to minimize or deny the contradictions inherent in a metaphorical use of language, he elevates these contradictions to the level of a general principle.

This apparently simple move actually required great courage and painstaking elaboration, for it went against the grain of the tradition to that point. From a classical point of view, it appeared vague and incomplete, another step on the road to a purely statistical description of nature and a rejection of the ideal of certainty that had been a central tenet of the tradition; from a quantum perspective, it seemed to cling to outmoded views and to emphasize a dangerous reliance on a sensory conception of the world. Yet Bohr's presentation of complementarity

"Wandering on New Paths"

suggested that classical metaphors, when viewed as metaphors, actually required, in themselves, the irrational effects that had seemed to be the sole domain of quantum theory. In other words, from the point of view of the complementarity principle, the contradictions inherent in a use of the wave and particle models do not represent a failure of these metaphors, as it had seemed to both classical and quantum physicists, but in fact provide further proof of their usefulness by predicting uncertainties that do exist in nature, such as our inability to determine both the position and momentum of an electron to an arbitrary degree of precision. So Bohr seeks to reconcile classical and quantum physics by the ingenious device of acknowledging the metaphorical character of the language on which his discipline depends.

Bohr develops this point by introducing a second fundamental equation:

From equation (1) we find thus:

$$\Delta t \Delta E = \Delta x \Delta I_x = \Delta y \Delta I_y = \Delta z \Delta I_z = h \tag{2}$$

as determining the highest possible accuracy in the definition of the energy and momentum of the individuals associated with the wave-field. (582)

Like equation (1), this relation (Bohr's own derivation of the uncertainty relations) stresses the central role of the quantum of action in the application of classical concepts to the subatomic realm. But unlike (1), (2) includes quantities that may all be considered as representations of the particle model alone. Therefore, we might suspect that the contradictions involved in a simultaneous use of the wave and particle metaphors might be avoided in this case and an unambiguous description of the phenomenon in question achieved. But whereas on the macroscopic level the quantum of action is small enough that it disappears when compared with the magnitude of common experimental error, effectively allowing both the position and the momentum of any macroscopic object to be known to any practical degree of precision, at the microscopic level the size of the particles being observed becomes small relative to the quantum of action, and therefore the proportion of uncertainty that exists in all measurements of position and momentum becomes considerable. As a result, consideration of subatomic phenomena revealed the uncertainty in measurements that had previously been concealed by their size. At the same time, the limitations within the particle metaphor—and by extension within any similar classical metaphor of sensory experience—become apparent: the quantities that it assumes must be measurable in an absolute sense actually exist only in the act of measurement and may be determined at best to a degree of accuracy dictated by the quantum of action.

Equation (2) could be read, therefore, as a demonstration of the unreliability of sensory metaphors in general. Such a reading echoes a current of thought favored by some physicists beginning in the 1920s, such as Heisenberg, who viewed the classical reliance on visualization and its attendant metaphors with suspicion. Since Heisenberg's 1925 matrix mechanics paper provided a successful mathematical model divorced from sensory description, these physicists had argued that such descriptions were inappropriate at the subatomic level because they were inevitably inconsistent attempts to describe what came into existence only through the act of observation. In citing this paper of Heisenberg's, however, Bohr countered this argument with a caution against the temptation to dismiss classical metaphors because of their inconsistencies:

As is known, the new development was commenced in a fundamental paper by Heisenberg, where he succeeded in emancipating himself completely from the classical concept of motion by replacing from the very start the ordinary kinematical and mechanical quantities by symbols, which refer directly to the individual processes demanded by the quantum postulate. . . . This ingenious attack on the dynamical problem of atomic theory proved itself from the beginning to be an exceedingly powerful and fertile method for interpreting quantitatively the experimental results. . . . It must be remembered, however, that the procedure described is limited just to those problems, in which in applying the quantum postulate the space–time description may largely be disregarded, and the question of observation in the proper sense therefore placed in the background. (585)

Ironically, Heisenberg's "ingenious attack on the dynamical problem of atomic theory," which threatens "the classical concept of motion" by rejecting its dependence on sensory metaphors, may be seen as an endorsement of the central classical insistence on literal representation. That is, Heisenberg may dismiss "the ordinary kinematical and mechanical quantities" of classical physics that derive from sensory metaphors like waves and particles, but by substituting his own "symbols which refer directly to the individual processes" he reveals a continuing reliance on the underlying classical belief in the possibility of maintaining a literal relationship between the abstract symbols of physics and the material objects and processes of the physical world.

In effect, therefore, Heisenberg "attacked" the metaphorical strategies of classical mechanics and affirmed its literal ideals. Bohr applauds the positive power of this affirmation and makes use of its mathematical fruits, but he also cautions his audience to remember the limitations inherent in such a one-sided approach. However "powerful and fertile" Heisenberg's method may be, it applies only in physical situations in which "the question of observation" may be "placed in the background."[46] Since "observation" represents the connection between the human mind and its physical surroundings, it is essential in any literal relationship to the world. Yet, as both Bohr and Heisenberg insist, observation inevitably involves an appreciable degree of uncertainty: by focusing on some details, an observer misses others; by poking and prodding at a physical situation, an observer alters it in ways that cannot be precisely known. One might go so far as to say that observation imposes an inherently metaphorical behavior on phenomena. Heisenberg responded to this situation by retreating from the question of observation and the messy metaphorical approximations of sensory experience it entails into the abstract mathematical relations that he hoped would allow him to maintain a literal correspondence between his descriptions and the natural world. Bohr, however, recognized that in the long run a stable, literal representation of the world cannot exist without a slippery, metaphorical immersion in it.

These issues are by no means simple or clear-cut. Bohr recognized that in relation to the "reality" of subatomic phenomena, metaphorical descriptions are just as abstract as mathematical formulas. He therefore acknowledges the justice of the suspicion with which many theorists regarded them. Yet he continues to grapple with what he sees as their inevitability:

On the whole, it would scarcely seem justifiable, in the case of the interaction problem, to demand a visualisation by means of ordinary space–time pictures. In fact, all our knowledge concerning the internal properties of atoms is derived from experiments on their radiation or collision reactions, such that the interpretation of experimental facts ultimately depends on the abstractions of radiation in free space, and free material particles. Hence, our whole space–time view of physical phenomena, as well as the definition of energy and momentum, depends ultimately upon these abstractions. (586)

The key, for Bohr, lay in the centrality of observation in physics. Perhaps he had a more highly developed sense of the experimental basis of his discipline than many of his theoretical colleagues. As Heisenberg recalls, "His insight into the structure of the theory was not a result of a mathematical analysis of the basic assumptions, but rather of an intense occupation with the actual phenomena, such that it was possible for him to sense the relationship [sic] intuitively rather than derive them formally."[47] Accordingly, Bohr insists that "all our knowledge concerning the internal properties of atoms" depends on experimental observation. At the same time, his theoretical knowledge of observation leads him to conclude that "the interpretation of experimental facts ultimately depends on the abstractions of radiation in free space, and free material particles." Therefore, Heisenberg's "powerful and fertile method" offers at best only a quantitative abstraction; ultimately, a complete and satisfactory description of nature requires the complementary qualitative abstractions of the classical view.

In the conception of the scientific discipline for which Bohr argues, both the classical and the quantum methods demonstrate an inescapable dependence on metaphorical language. While classical mechanics makes use of "the abstractions of radiation in free space, and free material particles," quantum theory reduces to its "symbolical methods" (*passim*). Both branches of the discipline rest on the production of symbolic descriptions of nature, of which, for example, "It might be said that the concepts of stationary states and individual transition processes within their proper field of application possess just as much or as little 'reality' as the very idea of individual particles" (589). This mention of stationary states suggests an underlying motivation for Bohr's extended efforts to harmonize the competing claims of the metaphors of classical visualization and the abstract mathematical description required by the quantum postulate.[48] His first major contribution to quantum theory hinged on just such a complementary use of metaphors, though in 1913 he had not yet constructed the theoretical framework of complementarity. His model of the hydrogen atom made simultaneous use of classical space–time metaphors—the Rutherford comparison of atoms to tiny solar systems—and abstract quantum metaphors—stationary states. He had been repeatedly criticized for these mixed metaphors, and for many years he could not answer these criticisms. But with complementarity he finally had what he believed was a sound theoretical justification.

Bohr offers a powerful example of the practical consequences of a complementary use of metaphors:

In a judgment of the well-known paradoxes which this assumption [of stationary states] entails for the description of collision and radiation reactions, it is essential to consider the limitations of the possibilities of definition of the reacting free individuals, which is expressed by relation (2). In fact, if the definition of the energy of the reacting individuals is to be accurate to such a degree as to entitle us to speak of conservation of energy during the reaction, it is necessary, according to this relation, to co-ordinate to the reaction a time interval long compared to the vibration period associated with the transition process, and connected with the energy difference between the stationary states according to relation (1). This is particularly to be remembered when considering the passage of swiftly moving particles through an atom.

"Wandering on New Paths"

According to the ordinary kinematics, the effective duration of such a passage would be very small as compared with the natural periods of the atom, and it seemed impossible to reconcile the principle of conservation of energy with the assumption of the stability of stationary states (cf. *Zeits. f. Phys.*, **34**, 142; 1925). In the wave representation, however, the time of reaction is immediately connected with the accuracy of the knowledge of the energy of the colliding particle, and hence there can never be the possibility of a contradiction with the law of conservation. (587–588)

In this passage, Bohr deals with a particularly awkward contradiction between the classical and the quantum descriptions of collisions among subatomic particles. On the one hand, the conservation of energy is a hallowed classical concept that requires the total energy of a system to remain constant so that energy is neither created nor destroyed. Practically, this had always been applied by means of metaphorical space–time descriptions, in which when two particles collide, the sum of their energies before the collision must equal the sum of their energies after the collision: Any energy lost by one particle in the collision must immediately be transferred to the other particle. On the other hand, the quantum metaphor of stationary states describes electrons as existing in certain stable configurations between which they move in sudden, instantaneous leaps. Therefore, when a particle from outside the atom collides with an electron, the electron does not respond like a billiard ball moving through space to a new position but rather reappears in a new orbit without moving through the "space" in between. Furthermore, this leap does not happen instantaneously, but according to "the natural periods of the atom." If the intrusive particle is moving "swiftly" through the atom, relative to its "natural periods," the particle will leave the collision with its reduced energy before the electron has jumped to its higher energy state. This would seem to result in a direct contradiction, suggesting that either the quantum metaphor of stationary states or the metaphors of the classical space–time description must be abandoned.

To resolve this dilemma, Bohr uses the two equations we examined above, (1) and (2), to demonstrate that the principle of complementarity precisely reconciles the classical and quantum metaphors describing such phenomena. According to his argument, either the particle or wave model on its own will always offer only an incomplete picture of the phenomenon in question. So, while "ordinary kinematics" insists on a literal application of one or the other metaphorical model, which in this case would lead to a classical contradiction within the metaphor of stationary states, Bohr suggests that quantum physics allows us to resolve this contradiction by applying the models of wave and particle in a complementary fashion. In particular, by applying the wave model to a particle interaction, we find that according to the relation $E\tau = h$ either the energy of the interacting particles E or the period of their interaction τ cannot be defined precisely enough to contradict the law of conservation of energy.

In this way, Bohr uses the contradiction between the wave and particle models as a powerful tool in resolving an incompatability between the classical space–time description of particle interactions and his own quantum metaphor of stationary states. It should be clear that this practical resolution derives in large part from his general desire to relate the abstract methods of quantum mechanics with the visualization inherent in a classical approach. Where a Heisenberg might be satisfied with a purely mathematical description of nature and an Einstein might reject a statistical description because it contradicted his sensory conception of the orderliness of nature, Bohr maintains his conviction that both quantum and classical descriptions provided important ways of saying things about nature.

In this context, it should be clear that Bohr's complementarity principle stands or falls as a theoretical explanation of (and prescription for) the role of metaphors in contemporary physics. Unlike Planck's quantum theory or Einstein's relativity theory, the complementarity principle does not attempt to account for any new or troubling physical phenomena. It does not, for instance, allow us to explain anything in the electron collision situation considered above that had not already been explained; instead, it provides a theoretical justification for the inconsistency of the existing description and transforms that inconsistency from a liability into an asset by using it to resolve the apparent violation of the energy conservation law. Put most simply, Bohr's principle concerns itself with the apparently abstract question of "what we can say about nature." But as Bohr strives to demonstrate, in his consideration of stationary states, for example, this self-referential examination has direct consequences for the practical ways in which scientists try to describe natural phenomena.

This reading of the complementarity principle also helps to explain why, in the years following 1927, Bohr argued for its application in domains far removed from quantum mechanics. As a metaphorical conception of the interwoven possibilities of observation and expression, it could be applied to any situation involving these activities—which is to say, everywhere. No wonder some physicists in Bohr's audience greeted his presentation as far-reaching and universally significant, while others dismissed it as lacking focus and clarity. Each characterization is accurate—in the context of the mind set that articulates it. For a physicist who wants only a mathematical formalism capable of calculating the necessary values, complementarity has little to offer. But for anyone interested in the relationship between the observer and the observed, as well as the epistemological status of the descriptive formalism produced by that relationship, Bohr's complementarity principle will have a deep and lasting significance.

Conclusion

Bohr concludes his essay by returning to the geographical metaphor with which he began:

Indeed, we find ourselves here on the very path taken by Einstein of adapting our modes of perception borrowed from the sensations to the gradually deepening knowledge of the laws of Nature. The hindrances met with on this path originate above all in the fact that, so to say, every word in the language refers to our ordinary perception. In the quantum theory we meet this difficulty at once in the question of the inevitability of the feature of irrationality characterizing the quantum postulate. I hope, however, that the idea of complementarity is suited to characterise the situation, which bears a deep-going analogy to the general difficulty in the formation of human ideas, inherent in the distinction between subject and object. (590)

So, after an extensive period of "wandering on new paths," at the end "we find ourselves here on the very path taken by Einstein." The apparent circularity of this route might remind us of the circular process of scientific inquiry itself: from the observation of nature scientists abstract data, manipulate them into mathematical laws and general principles, and then reapply them to the further observation of nature. So the circularity of Bohr's concluding metaphor, by means of which he constructs his essay as itself circular, echoes his opening metaphor in another way as well, by offering us a rhetorical embodiment of the conceptual dynamic that he believes to be characteristic of his subject.

Bohr's rhetoric tries to contain and control the many disruptive elements he encounters in the course of his wanderings, over both old and new terrain. As we have seen, one of the primary ways in which he attempts to do this is by incorporating the viewpoints of anticipated critics within his argument. Perhaps the most potentially damaging of these critics was Einstein, whose absence at the Como meeting only increased the tense expectation of his response at the Solvay congress: "Until the master was heard from, no one could be wholly certain in his own position. The question all over Europe was "What will Einstein say?' Would he demolish Bohr?"[49] This overstates the case in the interests of narrative drama. But the fact remains that Einstein was a formidable opponent—even if in an increasingly symbolic way—and therefore it should not surprise us that Bohr ends with a rhetorical assertion of the continuity of their work. Yet this was not a mere pose on Bohr's part; rather, it reflects his belief in the continuity of physics, which we have seen throughout his essay. Indeed, in large measure, his essay constitutes an effort to maintain this continuity—in the face not only of "the apparently conflicting views taken by different scientists"[50] but also of the contradictions inherent in the very metaphors that had widened the domain of his discipline to the point that their discontinuities became a topic of primary interest.

Bohr finally turns his recognition of the metaphorical character of much scientific description into an assertion of a troubled discipline's ability to conquer the new territory of subatomic physics without giving up its old ground, despite the contradictions that had plagued it through the first three decades of the twentieth century. His conclusion, therefore, constitutes his essay's closure as an act of expansion; the analogy between his own work and that of Einstein, based on the metaphor of the path, sets him up directly for this final analogy. While his purpose in writing "The Quantum Postulate" is in an important sense radical—an eccentric wandering—it is also conservative: recovering the ground prepared by the old masters and maintained by Einstein and others. So his final sentence reflects the same apparent contradiction between the traditional and the revolutionary expressed in his opening metaphor of the "new paths" on "prepared ground." His last words on complementarity sum up his hope "that the idea of complementarity is suited to characterize the situation," by extending it beyond the scope of his essay "to the general difficulty in the formation of human ideas, inherent in the distinction between subject and object." In this way, Bohr's conclusion exemplifies his belief in the power and pervasiveness of metaphorical language by repeating his opening metaphor as a means of casting his net wider at the end, claiming an even greater relevance for his insight than could be contained in the scope of a single presentation—or even a series of presentations in a wide variety of forms.

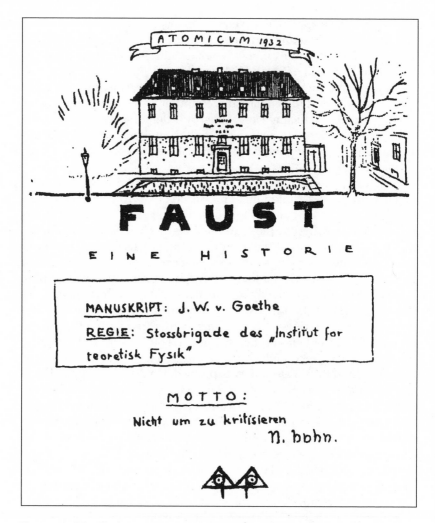

First page of the *Blegdamsvej Faust* script. (Courtesy Niels Bohr Archive, Copenhagen.)

3

"THE SENSE OF OPTION

IN KNOWLEDGE"

THE *BLEGDAMSVEJ FAUST* AND

QUANTUM MECHANICS

*In this way quantum theory reminds us, as Bohr has put it,
of the old wisdom that when searching for harmony in life
one must never forget that in the drama of existence we are
ourselves both players and spectators.*
—*Werner Heisenberg,* Physics and Philosophy

From April 3 to April 13, 1932, one hundred years after
the death of Johann Wolfgang von Goethe, Niels Bohr's Institute of
Theoretical Physics hosted its annual working conference on quantum
mechanics. Housed in a small, unassuming building on Blegdamsvej
Street in Copenhagen, it was perhaps the most important center of
theoretical physics at that time in the world. As Russian physicist George
Gamow put it, "During that era the roads of theoreticians of all na-
tionalities led, not to Rome, but to Copenhagen."[1] Accordingly, the
institute's spring conference had become a magnet for the world's
leading theoretical physicists, a place where the latest, most controversial developments in physics were discussed and debated, day after
day. Carl Friedrich von Weizsäcker, a participant in the conference,
recalls: "There were no prepared manuscripts, and everything had the
highest degree of topicality; and because the conference in those good
early years had twice as many hours as participants there was time
to discuss every worthwhile problem."[2] Thirty-five physicists, most
of whom knew one another, many of whom were friends, gathered
in an effort to create a sense of coherent order out of their disparate
explorations in isolated universities and laboratories.[3] Bohr led them
through a vigorous, sometimes heated exchange of ideas, beginning
with is own "fundamental report on the current difficulties of atomic

theory,"[4] as the audience struggled to follow his nearly unintelligible mumbling in English, German, and Danish. Other notables followed, with reports on their own groundbreaking work: Werner Heisenberg, Paul Ehrenfest, Wolfgang Pauli, P. A. M. Dirac, and others. The gathering offered a precious opportunity for the assembled physicists to consult with one another, talk, speculate, and argue face to face. No one wanted to waste any time.

At the heart of their work, these physicists were struggling to build a powerful new understanding of the foundation of the natural world: the subatomic realm of electrons, protons, and neutrons. The work was both exciting and groundbreaking. Indeed, James Chadwick had reported his discovery of the neutron only three months before, and Pauli had not yet published his own hypothesis regarding another particle that he, too, in private correspondence had been calling a "neutron." As Stalin tightened his grip over the Soviet Union, as the Nazis consolidated their power in the Reichstag, and as the Western world struggled through the Great Depression, these physicists were confronting their own "difficulties." As we saw in the first two chapters, their discipline was in the midst of an unsettling transformation, as fundamental discoveries and radical revisions of existing theory competed for the physicists' attention.

In an eloquent passage from his 1960 essay "Tradition and Discovery," Robert Oppenheimer describes his sense of the conceptual upheaval at this time:

> The great discovery was that you cannot attribute such properties as position and velocity and energy to such a system, unless you have taken the trouble to make an experiment in which you are prepared to measure what this quantity is. It is not that you do not know it; it is that you cannot assume that it exists. The attempt to objectify this, and say, it is there, but I am not clear just what it is, leads to disaster. This, which is the heart of quantum theory, the theory of complementarity, still further reinforces the sense of option in knowledge, the sense that you have a choice as to which study you make; the sense that having made that option, there is a kind of indivisible whole to the affair. You cannot go back on your bargain without spoiling everything.[5]

Oppenheimer remarks that chief among the unsettling consequences of the new physics was an emphasis on "the sense of option in knowledge." This sense follows directly from an increasing awareness of the role of the observer in physics. Quantum mechanics inspired a new emphasis on the shaping power of the scientist, in everything from the influence of observation on the phenomena observed to the power of metaphorical language in constructing representations of those phenomena. This dynamic relation between observer and observed phenomenon required a sometimes radical conceptual adjustment, as in the new awareness that "unless you have taken the trouble to make an experiment . . . you cannot assume" the physical property you wish to measure even "exists." Suddenly, scientists found themselves forced out of the objective shadows into an unfamiliar role as actors on the stage of nature.

Likewise, as the phenomena on which they were taking the trouble to experiment grew more exotic and powerful, the social consequences of the quantum physicists' work became more dramatic. The construction of nuclear weapons during World War II is a particularly dramatic instance of these consequences, but the groundwork for that development (among others) was being laid in the years leading up to the war. Not surprisingly, the quantum physicists displayed an increasingly pronounced sense of themselves as actors on a public stage even during the early 1930s. Self-reflection became a standard feature of these physicists' explorations of the phenomenal world, for with their growing power came a new sense of responsibility. It had become clear that the choices they made, even the "choice as to which study to make," had significant repercussions both within the physics community and, increasingly, in the world at large. In both spheres, physicists were discovering that, having exercised the option of their knowledge, they became committed to its consequences: "You cannot go back on your bargain without spoiling everything."

These bargains were being made at a rapid pace. Physics was changing so quickly that at times it seemed ready to tear loose from its traditional moorings. It had become difficult simply to stay abreast of all the latest developments. Even renowned physicists were not immune to the unsettled state of their discipline. Paul Ehrenfest, for example, a younger protégé of Bohr's and a rising star in the discipline, committed suicide in the fall of 1933, in despair over what he felt to be his inability to keep up with the changing quantum view of the natural world: "In recent years it has become ever more difficult for me to follow developments [in physics] with understanding. After trying, ever more enervated and torn, I have finally given up in DESPERATION."[6] Less dramatically but with more widespread consequences, disagreements over which theoretical and experimental directions to follow among the many conflicting options threatened the crucial consensus-building efforts of the scientific community. Even longtime friends and legendary figures like Einstein and Bohr found their structural assumptions growing increasingly irreconcilable.

Chadwick's neutron was a particularly hot topic of discussion at the Copenhagen Conference that spring, as was Pauli's "neutrino," or "little neutron," as Enrico Fermi suggested it be called.[7] The confusion over names was only a minor issue, though Pauli's notoriously blunt disposition may have made it a touchy one. The real issue focused on whether Pauli's purely theoretical justification constituted a sufficient proof of the neutrino's existence. Some physicists were uncomfortable with the increasingly radical departures from classical physics advocated by a growing number of quantum theorists who, following Heisenberg, were impatient with what they saw as the more plodding pace of their tradition-bound colleagues. Pauli's neutrino served as a touchstone for both camps. Here was a theoretical claim that a material particle could exist without any associated mass or charge, an assertion that simultaneously violated the classical definition of matter and challenged the traditional role of experiment in the construction of scientific knowledge.

The debate on this occasion was inconclusive, but it had a curious upshot. "It had become customary," as Gamow reports, "at the end of each spring conference . . . to produce a stunt pertaining to recent developments in physics."[8] Perhaps the dramatic changes in physics during those years suggested that a dramatic "stunt" constituted the most appropriate way to comment on the discipline. Certainly, the rapid developments in quantum mechanics lent themselves to theatrical interpretation—and that spring the vehicle was particularly potent. In honor of the hundredth anniversary of Goethe's death, several of the younger participants in the conference hastily rewrote his *Faust* with the most famous of the conferees as the play's main characters.[9]

The resulting play, now known as the *Blegdamsvej Faust*, was written largely in German, the language of Goethe's original and a common language for the polyglot physicists who gathered at Bohr's institute.[10] Max Delbrück is generally credited with being the play's principal author, although he and his associates sought to remain anonymous.[11] It was acted by the more junior members of the conference, using masks, with the persons represented in the play watching among the audience.[12] The characters include Pauli in the role of Mephistopheles, disgruntled, disparaging of the current state of physics, and intent on selling his colleagues on the existence of the neutrino as part of his more radical quantum program. Bohr, on the other hand, was cast in the role of God—standing at the pinnacle of the discipline, an embodiment of order and continuity, yet wielding a power derived from his leadership in the new physics. Paul Ehrenfest, Pauli's most stubborn opponent, stood in for Faust, beloved of God and the focus of Mephistopheles's efforts to bargain for his belief. Other characters included Chadwick as Wagner, Robert Millikan as Ariel, and Dirac and Oppenheimer as themselves.

The *Blegdamsvej Faust* offers a glimpse into the ways these physicists viewed both their discipline and one another during this unsettled time. Though its tone is humorous, the play centers on representations of discomfort and conflict. No one was safe from its critical barbs—even Bohr and Einstein, the most illustrious physicists of the day, are subject to ridicule on both personal and professional levels. The irony is multilayered and ubiquitous, and it will not let the audience hold on to any single point of view. Everything seems to be in a state of confusion and flux. Even though the play was written by adherents of quantum mechanics and, in broad terms, explores the tension between classical and quantum mechanics, this opposition offers little by way of stable conceptual ground. Despite its portrayal of classical mechanics as a moribund discipline, quantum mechanics itself comes across as acrimonious and muddled. Furthermore, embedded in the classical–quantum opposition lies an additional conflict within quantum mechanics itself, between what might be called its neoclassical and its more radical practitioners. Even their choice of an original to parody is a powerful commentary on their sense of what they had gotten themselves into. The "bargain" of which Oppenheimer speaks reflects a new power in the physicists' efforts to circumscribe the natural world by means of a theoretical structure of symbolic representations; but with this power came a sense of unease. The seriousness of that unease underlies even the comedy that is ostensibly the main point of the *Blegdamsvej Faust*. During a meeting at which every hour was precious, the fact that the participants took the time to write, stage, and watch a parody of themselves in a Faustian context suggests that it offered them something of considerable importance.

Some readers will object that I make too much of the *Blegdamsvej Faust*'s representation of unease and conflict within the physics community. They will accuse my literary-critical approach of overemphasizing the play's significance, of granting too great a privilege to its literary devices and its literary model. These readers will also be likely to assert a great divide between the social realms of literature and science, suggesting that each contains little of relevance to the other. Perhaps so. Yet I feel justified in my application of a literary-critical perspective to the *Blegdamsvej Faust* precisely because its creation and performance in the context of a highly specialized scientific conference suggests that the Copenhagen conferees themselves felt a strong sense of the relevance of literature to their work as physicists. In the first two chapters, I explored the quantum physicists' shifting attitudes toward metaphor within their own work. Their increasing recognition of the metaphorical character of their work, and of the complexities of subject–

object relations implicit in it, seem to me to lead to the kind of overtly literary self-exploration we see in the *Blegdamsvej Faust*. I am interested in exploring the relevance of this literary vehicle, in terms both of what the *Blegdamsvej Faust* allowed them to say about themselves and their work and of how this turn to literature might even have contributed something to that work.

Burying Their Noses in Rubbish: Images of the State of Physics

The *Blegdamsvej Faust* opens with a prologue in which Arthur Eddington, James Jeans, and E. A. Milne as "die drei Erzengel," or "the three Archangels," boast about the recent advances of physics to an audience made up of "der Herr, der Heerscharen"—"the Lord and the Heavenly Hosts":

Prof. Eddington: [Die Sonne] strahlt bekannter [Weise]
In polytroper [Sphären] Glanz,
[Und ihre vorgeschrieb'ne Reise]
Bestätigt *meine Formeln* ganz.
[*Ihr* Anblick gibt] Lemaitre [Stärke,
Wenn keiner sie ergründen mag.
Die unbegreiflich hohen Werke
Sind herrlich wie am ersten Tag.] (2)[13]

Prof. Eddington: [The sun] shines its well-known [song]
In the brilliance of polytropic [spheres],
[and its prescribed journey]
Confirms *my formulas* entirely.
[*Its* aspect gives] Lemaître [strength,
When no one can get to the bottom of it.
The incomprehensible high works
Are splendid as on the first day.]

The tone here is celebratory, and appropriately so given the recent emergence of a highly successful quantum mechanical formalism: "confirms *my formulas* entirely," "*Its* aspect gives Lemaître strength . . . splendid as on the first day." Eddington speaks out of a firm conviction of the orderliness of the natural world: "The sun shines" while it travels on "its prescribed journey." He also speaks out of a conviction that scientific theories directly correspond to the natural phenomena they describe. The *Blegdamsvej Faust* betrays this common assumption in its neat elision of the author of "Die unbegreiflich hohen Werke"; this leaves "the incomprehensible high works" representing with equal ease either the canon of physics or God's Creation itself. Each of the other grand old men of physics echoes in turn their colleague's self-congratulatory opening.

Even here in the very first lines of the play, however, an underlying sense of discomfort and insecurity appears. Despite the successes of modern physics in extending the reach of the scientific tradition into formerly inaccessible nooks and crannies of nature, unexplained mysteries still taunt the presumptuous physicist: "The splendid works" of nature remain "incomprehensible." Even theories elucidating phenomena that the physicists do claim to have mastered can remain impenetrable in themselves: So the physicists echo Goethe's original, "Da keiner dich ergründen mag"—"But no one can get to the bottom of it"[14]—in admitting that they lack a complete understanding of Lemaître's theory of the expanding universe.[15] Furthermore, these three "Archangels" represent the classical point of view in physics; their celebration of the achievements of the classical tradition, therefore, would strike a comic, even ironic note in the ears of the quantum physicists gathered at Bohr's institute.

Into these cracks in the celebration of the discipline springs Mephisto:[16]

[Von] Stern' [und Welten weiss ich nichts zu sagen,	[Of] Stars [and Planets I have nothing to say,
Ich sehe nur, wie sich die Menschen plagen.]	I only see how Mankind plagues itself.]
Und ist die ganze Theorie auch Mist,	And even though your Theory is shit,
Du bist doch immer wieder in Extase,	Yet you are again and again in ecstasy,
Beschwigtigst, wo nichts mehr zu retten ist;	Appeasing, where nothing can be rescued;
[In jedem Quark begräbst] du deine [Nase.] (3)[17]	You [bury] your [nose in all kinds of rubbish.]

In his first appearance, Mephisto is angry, barely able to disguise his contempt for the Archangels' naïve celebration of astronomical wonders. His focus is down to earth and clearly centered on the human social world: "I only see how Mankind plagues itself." The first two lines echo Goethe word for word, and where the *Blegdamsvej* character departs from his predecessor, it is to be even more openly contemptuous of abstract, theoretical maundering: "And even though your Theory is shit. . . ."

The joke is double-edged. On the one hand, it pokes fun at Pauli himself by alluding to the fact, well known among members of the *Blegdamsvej* audience, that he could be quite rude even in the formal arena of scientific debate. But on the other hand, this in-joke veils a deeper tension. The *Blegdamsvej Faust* was performed a mere five years after Bohr introduced his complementarity principle in an effort to bridge the uncertain and increasingly bitter division between the neoclassical and radical branches of quantum physics. In 1932, significant tensions remained between them, and the conflicts Bohr addressed were far from resolved. Therefore, Pauli's outburst in response to the Archangels' classical platitudes also gives voice to an undercurrent of disdain for their classical apologist colleagues on the part of the more radical quantum theorists, among whom we should probably count the young authors of the *Blegdamsvej Faust*.

Comedy is often a vehicle for social commentary that would be threatening or inappropriate in other contexts. Noncomedic literature has also often functioned in this way: Shakespeare comes immediately to mind. The *Blegdamsvej Faust* makes use of both these strategies. Through its explicit identification as a "stunt," it claims a status similar to that of a court jester; its anonymous authors are free to say or do anything: Bohr is a mumbling, humbuggish God; Pauli a snarling misanthrope. The barbs are wrapped in the cloak of comedy, as if they did not reflect anyone's serious opinion; and, indeed, Bohr was adored by most of his colleagues, and Pauli was deeply respected. But these lines work as comedy precisely because the audience recognizes both the barb and its target—they get the jokes. Furthermore, the lines I have quoted bracket Mephisto's harshest words between lines taken directly from Goethe. By rewriting Goethe, the authors of the *Blegdamsvej Faust* use the established associations of their literary original as a safe opportunity to express in their harshest form the potentially disruptive opinions that were circulating throughout the scientific community. While it would have been unprofessional for a proponent of quantum mechanics to confront a more classically inclined colleague and proclaim "Your theory is shit," the literary medium of *Faust* allows Pauli to do just that. So Mephistopheles' claim that he is interested in the social realm in which men torment one another proves to be a particularly useful context for the authors of the *Blegdamsvej Faust*. Their stunt was itself a highly complex symbolic act focused on the social dynamics surrounding the development of abstract scientific theories.

At this point, Bohr appears in the play in the role he assumed in the physics community as the champion of complementarity. He is the peacemaker between the rival camps of quantum physicists: those who wish to preserve classical assumptions alongside quantum mechanics and those who advocate a more radical break. Bohr begins by trying to quiet Pauli, but to no avail:

Der Herr: [Hast du mir weiter nichts
    zu sagen?
Kommst du nur immer anzuklagen?
Ist] die Physik dir niemals [recht?]

Mephisto: [Nein,] Quatsch! [ich finde]
    sie, [wie immer, herzlich schlecht.]
Bekümmert sie mich auch [in]
    meinen [Jammertagen,]
Muss ich die Physiker doch immer
    weiter [plagen.] (4)

The Lord: [Have you nothing further
    to say to me?
Do you always come only to accuse?
Is] Physics to you never [right?]

Mephisto: [No,] rubbish! [I find] it, [as
    always, thoroughly bad.]
Though it troubles me [on] my [bad
    days,]
I still must continue to [plague] the
    Physicists.

Mephisto interrupts the heavenly revels to contend that modern physics
remains far from the success the grand old men claim. This sounds a surprisingly sour note, and, in effect, the play seconds Mephisto here, but
in more subtle, sophisticated terms, by using him as a vehicle to express,
in the guise of parody, doubt in the community its characters represent.
But the doubt was real, and the problems Pauli raises would have been
fresh in the minds of the audience from the ongoing discussions of the
conference itself. The debate between Bohr and Pauli continues:

H: <Oh, it is dreadful! In this situation
we must remember the essential fail-
ure of classical concepts> .... Muss
ich sagen .... <Just a little remark:>
Was willst du mit der Masse tun?
M: Wieso? die Masse? Die schafft man
ab!
H: Das ist ja sehr, sehr interessant!
.... aber, aber ....
M: Nein, schweig! Halt, Quatsch!
H: Aber, aber ....
M: Ich verbiete dir zu sprechen!
H: Aber Pauli, Pauli, wir sind ja viel
mehr einig als du denkst! <Of course
I quite agree; only> .... Man kann
natürlich die Masse abschaffen, aber
die Ladung <we must uphold> .....
M: Wieso, warum? Nein, nein, das ist
Stimmungsmalerei! Warum soll ich
die Ladung nicht auch abschaffen?
H: Muss ich fragen .... Ich verstehe
ja völlig, <but, but> ....
M: Schweig!

H: <Oh, it is dreadful! In this situation
we must remember the essential
failure of classical concepts> I
must say .... <Just a little remark:>
What do you want to do with Mass?>
M: Why? Mass? One abolishes it!

H: This is very, very interesting! ....
but, but ....
M: No, silence! Stop, rubbish!
H: But, but ....
M: I forbid you to speak!
H: But Pauli, Pauli, we are so much
more in agreement than you think!
<Of course I quite agree; only> ....
One can abolish Mass, naturally, but
Charge <we must uphold> .....
M: Why, what for? No, no that is
sentimental! Why should I not also
abolish Charge?
H: I must ask .... I do understand,
completely, <but, but> ....
M: Silence!

H: Aber Pauli, du musst mich doch ausreden lassen! Wenn man die Masse und die Ladung abschafft, was bleibt denn da noch übrig?
M: Das ist doch ganz einfach! Was dann noch übrig bleibt? Das *Neutron*! (5)[18]

H: But Pauli, you have to let me finish speaking, after all! If one abolishes Mass and Charge, what would be left?
M: That is simple, really! What would be left? The *Neutron*![19]

To an audience that knew Bohr well, these lines would have been tremendously funny: They present him in his typical mumbling manner, trying to argue without arguing, to take issue without overtly disagreeing. These were hallmarks of Bohr's character and were so well known, and Bohr himself such a representative figure in the discipline, that on the title page the play takes as its epigraph one of his trademark phrases: "*MOTTO*: Nicht um zu kritisieren"—"Not to criticize" (1). But the mixture of humor and tribute here proves effective precisely because it cuts so near the bone. In poking fun at Bohr, the *Blegdamsvej Faust* takes some of his most notable characteristics and frames them in a context in which it is permissible to be critical. In this way, the play undercuts its own epigraph, using Bohr's very words, "Not to criticize," as an effective basis for its ironic criticisms. The play's parodic tone invites its viewers to acknowledge, in a safe context, the discipline's current state of imbalance in which the mumblings of an elder statesman of physics can be portrayed as the words of God. And in its laughter, the audience confirms the justice of the representation.

In this context, Pauli's harsh retorts ring with a keener edge: "No, silence! Stop, rubbish!" This tone would not be countenanced in a scientific debate. But the challenge it voices in the play simply exaggerates the threat already implicit in Pauli's neutrino, which requires that physicists confront the question, "If one abolishes Mass and Charge, what would be left?" To accept Pauli's claims would indeed seem to imply an "essential failure of classical concepts," as Bohr opines. So how important are these concepts and the claims made by the Archangels at the beginning of the play? Are they truly based on outmoded paradigms? How far should the new physics be allowed to go in challenging or even contradicting them? These questions constituted a dilemma for physicists at this time; and so the *Bledgamsvej Faust* constructs its humorous parody on a foundation of serious uncertainty. In accepting the destabilizing power of quantum mechanics, what kind of a bargain were these physicists making?

An "Erring Faust": Ehrenfest and the Physicists' Bargain

The terms of the bargain emerge as the play progresses.[20] The "First Part" of the *Blegdamsvej Faust* proper begins with Ehrenfest's entrance in the title role. His first words echo those of Goethe's Faust almost line for line:

[Habe nun, ach,] Valenzchemie, Elektrodynamik und Gruppenpest, [Und leider auch] Transformationstheorie [Durchaus studiert mit heissem Bemühn; Da steh' ich nun, ich armer] Wicht: Nichts gewisses weiss ich nicht! Heisse Magister, heisse] Professor [gar, Und ziehe schon an die] dreissig Jahr, Herauf, herab, und quer und krumm, Meine Schüler an der Nase herum.] (6)	[I have now, alas,] Valence Chemistry, Electrodynamics and Group Theory, [And to my sorrow] Transformation Theory, [Indeed studied with all my might; Here I stand now, a poor] creature: I know nothing for sure! [I am called Master, I am even called] Professor, [And for nearly thirty years, Up, down, crosswise and crooked, I've led my students by the nose.]

The Faust legend proves an effective medium for representing these scientists as servants of a driving desire to master the secrets of the natural world: at once proud of and yet dissatisfied with their attainments, and, consequently, caught between competing avenues, each of which might lead to the longed-for mastery. Yet, curiously, the very efficacy of the play in representing the dilemma of modern physics threatens its dramatic continuity. Like Faust, Ehrenfest represents the epitome of the adept: a man who has mastered the intricacies of the most sophisticated of human disciplines. And, like Faust, he has found them lacking. The similarity of the two figures, however, threatens to unravel the conflict between Ehrenfest and Pauli on which the *Blegdamsvej Faust* is predicated, for Ehrenfest enters the play with a reading of the state of contemporary physics that is remarkably close to Pauli's in the prologue.

In what sense, then, will Ehrenfest offer Pauli a challenge as Bohr's "knight"?[21] Even as it provides a powerful vehicle for confronting and parodying the physicists' sense of the recent turmoil within their discipline, Goethe's *Faust* resists their efforts to draw the lines of conflict where they wish. This resistance highlights an essential difference between the two *Faust*s. In Goethe's version, Mephistopheles and Faust are different kinds of beings, with different motivations. Faust's willingness to engage Mephistopheles on his own terms, to invite him into his house, to play at magic with him, to accept the Devil's current service in exchange for his own future enslavement, reflects his tragic hubris. But in the *Blegdamsvej Faust*, both characters compete as equals, and the aim of both is, presumably, the same: the furtherance of contemporary physics. They would seem to be essential allies, rather than beings from different orders altogether who hate and mistrust one another at every step.

The authors of the *Blegdamsvej Faust* have written themselves into a difficult situation here. Their joint goal—to parody the neutron–neutrino debate by parodying *Faust*—has reached a point at which internal tensions threaten the play's coherence. The requirements of each side of their double parody pull in different directions, and to go in either would destroy their work as a whole. They must find a way to incorporate the antagonism between Faust and Mephistopheles and yet do so within the generally constructive and cooperative framework of modern physics, in which disagreements take place according to the social conventions of the discipline and contribute to the eventual growth of its canon and unanimity of its practitioners.

To achieve this delicate balance, the authors of the *Blegdamsvej Faust* play on the relatively minor difference between Pauli and Ehrenfest as scientists by magnifying their contrasting approaches to the field of quantum mechanics. They begin cleverly, by making a small but significant departure from their model:

Faust (Goethe)

Zwar bin ich gescheiter als alle die Laffen,	Granted I am smarter than all those fops,
Doktoren, Magister, Schreiber und Pfaffen;	doctors, masters, scribes, and preachers;
Mich plagen *keine* Skrupel noch Zweifel . . .	I am *not* afflicted by scruples and doubts . . .
Drum hab' ich mich der *Magie* ergeben.[22]	Therefore I have turned to *magic*.[23]

Faust (Blegdamsvej)

Zwar bin ich gescheiter als die Laffen,	Granted I am smarter than the fops,
Doktoren, Bonzen und anderen Affen.	Doctors, big shots, and other asses.

Mich plagen *alle* Skrupel und Zweifel	I am afflicted by *every* doubt and
. . .	scruple . . .
Drum hab' ich mich der *Kritik*	Therefore I have turned to *criticism*.[25]
ergeben. (6)[24]	

"Doubt" is the source of Ehrenfest's strength and his central identifying characteristic. Unlike Faust, he dedicates himself not to "magic" but to skepticism. This departure from Goethe's model actually helps the *Blegdamsvej Faust* to remain more generally faithful to it. Where Mephistopheles plays on the shared discipline of magic to ensnare Faust into a seemingly equitable pact, Pauli approaches Ehrenfest through their common dedication to quantum mechanics. Within that shared context, then, the struggle between the two men hinges on what would without it be almost meaningless differences. Because they have a common goal as scientists, their different ways of approaching it come to the fore: While Pauli postulates and theorizes, Ehrenfest plays the role of wet blanket, criticizing and resisting Pauli's advances.

When Pauli enters "as a traveling salesman," therefore, he faces the task of unloading his wares on an uncooperative Ehrenfest. These wares it turns out are, in general, the theories of quantum mechanics, and Pauli's pitch for them consists at first of a "Canon, von Allen gesungen" (a "Canon, sung by all"):

> Born Heisenberg
> Heisenberg Pauli
> Pauli Jordan
> Jordan Wigner
> Wigner Weisskopf
> Weisskopf Born
> Born Heisenberg
> u.s.w.   and so on

M: Das sind die Kleinen	These are the little ones
Von den Meinen:	Of my people:
Höre, wie zu Lust und Taten	Hear how they precociously
Altklug sie raten. (7)	Counsel desire and actions.

Mephisto claims as his "little ones" the greatest names among the more radical quantum mechanists, and Bohr's absence, along with Planck, Einstein, and Schrödinger, suggests the subtle lines along which the authors mean to construct the Faust–Mephisto conflict. It will center not on the obvious classical–quantum split—for the limitations of classical mechanics would have been taken for granted by the conferees—but on a more troubling though less precise schism within quantum mechanics, between those who advocated the relevance of classical assumptions even within a quantum approach and those who believed that the effort to maintain a causal rationale in quantum mechanics was not only unnecessary but misleading. Bohr was a well-known proponent of the former position, and in this context Ehrenfest would indeed prove to be his "knight."

The *Blegdamsvej Faust* symbolizes the differences between Ehrenfest and Pauli, and their associated movements, in Faustian terms by linking them with "reason" and "witchcraft," respectively. When Ehrenfest rejects all of Pauli's attempts to sell his quantum mechanical goods, the latter warns:

Verachte nur Vernunft und Wissenschaft,	Despise only reason and science,
Des Menschen allerhöchste Kraft!	Mankind's highest power!
Du lässest doch von Blend- und Zauberwerken	You allow deception and witchcraft
Dich in dem Quantengeist bestärken!	To confirm you in the quantum-mind!
Pass auf, wie jetzt die Schwierigkeiten schwinden,	See how now the difficulties dwindle,
Und wunderbar wirst du das *Neutron* finden! (8)	And, Wonderful!, you will find the *Neutron*!

Here we can see the play's authors pushed into a revealing exaggeration by the effort to maintain their vision of Ehrenfest's and Pauli's methodological differences within the context of the Faust legend. By characterizing the former as based on "reason" and skepticism, the latter on "witchcraft," seduction, and temptation, the *Blegdamsvej Faust* presents the tensions within quantum mechanics not in terms of alternative theories competing within an overarching framework of scientific rationality but rather as two incompatible and antagonistic ways of apprehending the world.

While this representation clearly exaggerates the situation within modern physics in the 1930s, it does so in a meaningful way. The tensions during this period were real, as the *Blegdamsvej* authors seem almost to insist, for the Ehrenfest–Pauli antagonism echoes the classical–quantum conflict with which the play began. Indeed, it goes even further to suggest a struggle within the quantum framework over what underlying assumptions should define acceptable theory. We begin to see this in Ehrenfest's identification with the familiar rational terms of scientific representation and his claim that holding on to such doubt and scruple will help him prevail over "the fops, / . . . big shots, and other asses" who have taken advantage of the recent turmoil in the discipline to claim exaggerated status for their exotic ideas. The *Blegdamsvej* authors are careful to emphasize that Ehrenfest still believes "the tested gospel" of the tradition. But he faces a challenge, in the form of Pauli and his tribe, whom the play portrays as devils seeking to undermine the gospel by seducing away its last adherents.

All of this should suggest how important questions of human perception are to the *Blegdamsvej Faust*. Quantum mechanics was in the process of transforming the ways in which scientists see the world around them. Nature could no longer be thought of as made up of gradual and continuous processes; instead, it now appeared to leap from one state to another. Likewise, our very ability to observe natural processes had to be rethought. It was becoming increasingly apparent that the phenomena one observes (at least on the subatomic level) did not even exist in any meaningful way until the act of observation itself imposed a particular state on them. The kind of shift in mental attitude this required could hardly have been less troubling to physicists in the 1930s than it is to us today, having grown up in a quantum world. And here we find another link between the two *Fausts* in their shared emphasis on the power and instability of human perception. Goethe's drama, for instance, follows Mephistopheles' efforts to ensnare Faust in an acceptance of the infernal art of magic as the basis of true knowledge—to, in effect, "see" the world through the Devil's eyes. The symbol of his triumph will be to lure Faust into saying "Verweile doch! du bist so schön!"—"Oh stay! You are so beautiful!"[26] Likewise, the *Blegdamsvej Faust* centers on Pauli's attempt to sell Ehrenfest a radical version of quantum mechanics, one that delights in upsetting classical notions of causality and destabilizing conventional perceptions of the world—as was characterized in Pauli's exchange with Lord Bohr.

In both plays, Faust's seduction involves a young maiden, Gretchen. In neither play, however, is Gretchen what she seems. In Goethe, Mephistopheles takes Faust to the Witch's Kitchen and convinces him to drink a potion that alters his perception: "Du siehst, mit diesem Trank im Leibe, / Bald Helenen in jedem Weibe"—"With that potion in your belly / you'll soon see Helena in every wench."[27] As a result, Faust sees a plain, working-class woman named Margaret and perceives her as Gretchen, a "schönes Fräulein"—a "fair lady"—when in fact she is "weder Fräulein, weder schön"—"neither lady, nor fair."[28] The *Blegdamsvej* Gretchen might say the same of herself, for she is not a human being at all but a personification of Pauli's neutron.

Gretchen tritt auf und singt:	*Gretchen* enters and sings:
Meine Ladung ist hin,	My charge is gone;
Statistik ist schwer,	Statistics is tricky,
Ich finde sie nimmer	I find them never
Und nimmermehr.	And nevermore.
Wo du mich nicht hast,	Where you do not have me,
Keine Formel passt.	No formula fits.
Die ganze Welt	The whole world
Ist dir vergällt.	Is spoiled for you.
Nur mit mir allein	Only with me alone
Kann der Betastrahl sein.	Can the Beta-rays be.
Auch der Stickstoffkern	Also the nitrogen nucleus
Steht mir nicht ganz fern.	Is not far from me.
Meine Ladung ist hin,	My charge is gone;
Statistik ist schwer,	Statistics is tricky,
Ich finde sie nimmer	I find them never
Und nimmermehr. (8–9)[29]	And nevermore.

The casting of Pauli's neutron in the role of Gretchen is the play's most elaborate joke. It is also one of the play's most complex themes, and it stretches the ingenuity of the *Blegdamsvej* authors in their efforts to maintain the continuity between their "stunt" and its literary model. For example, although Ehrenfest seems to be the target of Gretchen's seductive powers, it is Pauli who turns out to be truly in love with her. Furthermore, as the play continues, it becomes clear that Pauli does not tempt Ehrenfest with the charms of his neutrino in order to fool him into a false perception but, rather, to convince him to accept a perception that Pauli himself believes to be true. Indeed, a crucial piece of the *Blegdamsvej Faust* is, finally, what it fails to copy from Goethe: the magical alteration of Faust's perception. Precisely because Ehrenfest sees Gretchen for what she is, his acceptance of her would involve a real change in the way he perceives the world rather than a temporary, artificially induced aberration. The threat of this change constitutes the underlying dynamic of the entire play.

Although the play presents Ehrenfest's acceptance of Gretchen as a local matter involving, other than the two of them, only Pauli, local actions imply universal consequences in the *Blegdamsvej Faust*, as in Goethe's play. So Bohr and his Archangels watch Pauli's temptation of Ehrenfest as if it represented a struggle between archetypal forces. And, in some ways, to the audience of physicists who also sat and watched, it would have: a struggle between two ways of looking at and representing the world. Nor was it clear what the outcome of this struggle would or should be. Even the staunchest supporters of a given camp felt the destabilizing tremors of uncertainty: Was their approach "right"? Would it stand the test of time?

So in the next scene, set in "Mrs. Ann Arbor's Speak Easy (sonst Auerbachs Keller genannt)" (10),[30] after introducing Gretchen to the "Amerikanische Physiker" who "sitzen traurig an der Bar" (10)— "American physicists" who "sit unhappily at the bar"—Gretchen launches into a parody of Mephistopheles' fable of the flea:

Gretchen singt:	*Gretchen* sings:
[Es war] einmal [ein König],	Once upon a time, [there was a King]
Der hatt' einen grossen Floh.	who had an enormous flea.
Den liebt' er gar nicht wenig	He loved it quite a bit,
Als wie Gravitation.	Just like gravitation.
Der König rief den Mayer	The King called for Mayer;
Der Mayer kam heran	Mayer came
Und mass dem Junker Krümmung	And measured the junker curve
Und Feldtensoren an.	And field tensors.
In invarianter Weise	Without any further ado
Ward er nun durchgeführt.	Matters were set in motion.
Er nahm ihn auf die Reise	He took him on the journey
Und jeder blieb gerührt.	And everyone was touched.
Der Floh, der kam zu Jahren	The flea, it grew in years
Und hatte einen Sohn.	And had a son.
Der Sohn verstiess den Vater,	The son expelled the father,
Doch hatt' er nichts davon.	But gained nothing by it.
Und Floh auf Floh entsprangen	And flea upon flea sprang out
Der Berliner Akademie	Of the Berlin Academy.
Die Physiker besangen	The physicists sang of
Die "neue Feldtheorie." (11)	The "New Field Theory."

The butt of Gretchen's joke is Einstein and his Unified Field Theory (the flea's progeny), in which he attempted to extend his General theory of Relativity (the flea) into an overarching structure capable of reconciling the discontinuities in modern physics' treatment of phenomena on the subatomic, everyday, and cosmic levels. Einstein died in 1955, still pursuing this elusive goal. But even in 1932, his search had become emblematic of efforts to bind quantum mechanics together with its classical predecessor. Gretchen's song, therefore, offers a partisan spoof of Einstein's efforts. Yet it also reflects back on Pauli's own "pet flea," the neutrino, which many physicists, even some of those who shared his general epistemological orientation toward quantum mechanics, would have considered every bit as half-baked as Einstein's Unified Field Theory.

Quantum Witchcraft

The play shifts its focus back to the classical–quantum mechanics conflict in the second act, in which a "Conferencier," or master of ceremonies, presents two "Walpurgis Nights" to Goethe's one. Walpurgis Night falls on the eve of the feast day of St. Walpurga, an English missionary who was celebrated in the Middle Ages as a protectress against magic. It was a night when witches were believed to ride freely through the land. The two Walpurgis Nights offered here are "klassische" and "quantentheoretische"—classical and quantum theoretical. This draws the play's conflict along the same lines as the first act, only with bolder strokes. Likewise, the association of the more radical quantum mechanists with witchcraft continues here, and the Walpurgis Night setting suggests a clear resolution to the conflict. Yet despite the fact that the play seems to meet these expectations in broad terms, it constantly undercuts them along the way—just as Walpurgis Night inevitably leads to the day of St. Walpurga's feast.

First, the M. C. "kündigt den Beginn der klassischen Walpurgisnacht an"—"signals the beginning of the Classical Walpurgis Night":

Faust setzt sich erwartungsvoll zurecht. Es geschieht nichts. Faust beschwert sich darüber beim Conferencier. Dieser ermuntert ihn, genau aufzupassen. Wieder geschieht nichts. Faust protestiert. Conferencier erklärt, man müsse bedenken, dass im klassischen Fall natürlich keine Rückwirkung der Walpurgisnacht auf das Publikum stattfinden könne. (14–15)	Faust sits and attends with great expectation. Nothing happens. Faust complains about this to the M.C. The latter encourages him to pay close attention. Again nothing happens. Faust protests. The M.C. explains, one must expect that with the classical case naturally no effect of the Walpurgis Night on the audience is able to take place.

The audience should have seen this joke coming: of course the Classical will produce no special effects on a Walpurgis Night, since it has been identified as the antithesis of witchcraft throughout the play. The scene, therefore, implicitly criticizes classical mechanics as a dull approach to the natural world, devoid of spectacle or show. So far, the expected dominance of the quantum viewpoint seems to be confirmed. But the long, dead pauses of the Classical Walpurgis Night also set up a contrast through which what follows suggests an equally pointed criticism of quantum mechanics as a chaotic indulgence in flashy, sleight-of-hand theorizing in which the ability to dazzle counts more than a solid applicability to real phenomena.

There is also a more subtle joke here: An important difference between the classical and quantum mechanical approaches centers on the different ways in which they treat an observer. Classical mechanics tends to ignore the observer, assuming that a person exerts little or no influence on whatever is being observed. Quantum mechanics, on the other hand, emphasizes the disruptive role of the observer and argues from this perspective that there are limits to what can be known about any given system being observed.[31] In this context, the Classical Walpurgis Night's failure to affect the audience spoofs the classical insistence on an objective, impersonal observer—a spoof the *Blegdamsvej* audience would have felt all the more strongly through the joke's effect on them. But again the play does not parody classical mechanics in isolation, and by contrast the Quantum Theoretical Walpurgis Night offers little sense of boundary between the observer and the observed, as members of the audience are portrayed on stage side by side with personifications of quantum mechanical effects and even mathematical errors. Who are the actors? Who manipulates whom?

In the course of the Quantum Theoretical Walpurgis Night, in fact, the play threatens to fall apart. The audience witnesses a dizzying sequence of miniature spoofs of the various offspring of quantum mechanics. These include characters repeatedly falling into or narrowly avoiding a number of Dirac holes in the stage; a monopole singing of the love of two monopoles for one another; a dead "Group Dragon," representing group theory, being dragged in; a False Sign dancing around the stage, frustrating efforts to produce new theories; Darwin and Fowler illustrating Heisenberg's exchange relation by leapfrogging all over the stage, until they fall into a Dirac hole; the Spin of the Photon rushing across the stage wearing an Indian sari; the arrival of Four Gray Women, representing perplexing physical phenomena, to the dismay of all the scientists, especially Dirac, who is pursued offstage by one of them: "Ab, verfolgt von der Singularität"—"Exit, chased by a Singularity" (18). The authors throw in everything but the kitchen sink, including this reference to Shakespeare's *Winter's Tale*.[32] Modern physics seems to be every bit as jumbled and incoherent as Pauli claimed when he first appeared in the prologue.

"The Sense of Option in Knowledge"

Just before he goes, Dirac's frustration with the mess of quantum mechanics leads him to cry out:

Ein Vogel krächzt, was krächzt er?	A bird croaks; what does it croak?
Missgeschick!	Misfortune!
Zum Jahre '26 müssen wir zurück,	To 1926 we must return,
Denn alles, was seither besteht,	For all that exists since then
Ist wert, dass es zugrundegeht. (18)	Is worthy of withering away.

Dirac refers here to the mathematical unification of Heisenberg's matrix mechanics with Schrödinger's wave mechanics in 1926, which marked the birth of a powerful quantum mechanical formalism and the elevation of quantum theory to the level of a practical successor to classical theory. Therefore, it marks a point at which the rift between the classical and quantum viewpoints seemed irreconcilable and the more radical quantum mechanists began to feel free to abandon classical assumptions. In effect, Dirac suggests that everything done since 1926 in this more radical quantum vein, including his own prominent efforts, had resulted in an incoherent, jumbled mess and should be discarded.[33] Yet it is too late—they have already gone too far, even if in a haphazard fashion. The anomalous facts of nature that had by then been uncovered by quantum mechanics refuse to cooperate. Nature itself in the play seems to push the physicists further and further away from their classical roots and into a world in which the laws that govern natural phenomena appear ever more removed from the dictates of common sense, to the point that the mastery of those laws amounts to the practice of witchcraft. So Singularity will not "entferne dich, verschwinde!" (18)—"remove yourself! disappear!"—as Dirac commands her, but instead makes even the most accomplished physicists subject to the chaotic drama of the Walpurgis Night.

Ehrenfest, of course, has been the holdout—he has occupied the role of observer rather than participant and has stubbornly resisted Mephisto's radical quantum perspective. But suddenly all that changes, and the Devil seems to have won:

Faust: höchst entzückt, stellt sich für den Pressephotographen in Positur:	*Faust*: very excited, poses for the press photographers:
Zum Augenblicke möcht' ich sagen:	To this moment I want to say:
Verweile doch, du bist so schön!	Do stay, you are so beautiful!
Es bleibt die Spur von meinen Erdentagen	A trace of my days on earth does remain
Doch in den Zeitungen bestehn! (19)	In the newspapers!

Here Ehrenfest utters the words that were supposed to signal Mephisto's triumph. But instead of having been beguiled by the bewitching charms of Gretchen the neutrino, he says them in response to having his picture taken by the press photographers. This is a clever troping of Goethe's scene in the Witch's Kitchen, in which Faust spends a good deal of time staring into a magic mirror at a vision of ideal feminine beauty. There, Faust is beguiled by a reflection of his own desire brought to apparent life by means of the witch's infernal art. In the *Blegdamsvej Faust's*, likewise, the camera uses lights, mirrors, and lenses to produce a technological reflection of its subject that will linger, offering a kind of immortality. This is what Ehrenfest falls for: his own desire for fame and, implicitly, for a stable, lasting form of quantum theory. It is an apt comment on both Goethe's Faust, whose obsession with knowledge has at its root a restless vanity, and the quantum mechanists as well, whose success discovering, ordering, and naming leads both to the Quantum Theoretical Walpurgis Night's instability and their own growing fame.

Ehrenfest's sudden death at this moment sounds a harsh note in what bills itself as a comic stunt. Perhaps it is no more than a note: The moment comes and goes in the midst of a scene of frantic farce, and the play ends shortly thereafter. One could easily dismiss it as a cartoon death, an instance of the manic energy of the quantum mechanical Walpurgis Night scene run amuck. The audience might well have laughed at its very senselessness. But even if the audience were able to take it entirely in stride at the time—and all must have reflected on it more somberly on hearing the news of Ehrenfest's suicide a year and a half later—the moment seems so unnecessary to the themes and drama of the play that I believe it signals something important at stake for the physicists. This would be in keeping with the seriousness I have pointed out underlying the *Blegdamsvej Faust's* comic antics. What is behind Ehrenfest's apparently gratuitous death?

Even in 1932, physicists were getting a taste of the social recognition and status that would bring them billions of dollars during World War II for projects ranging from radar to the construction of nuclear weapons. In part, this recognition depended on the increasingly dramatic character of the phenomena dealt with in their theories: the atomic basis of matter, the relativistic nature of time and space, the wave behavior of physical bodies, the transmutation of elements, the conversion of mass to energy. These alchemical manifestations of the physicists' direct confrontation with the elemental forces of nature increasingly captured the public's imagination, helped along by a growing number of literary treatments of science, from the works of Jules Verne and H. G. Wells to the futuristic visions of Aldous Huxley and George Orwell, to the popular science fiction novels and short stories that began to appear in bulk in the 1930s.

Another part of the scientists' social status depended on the shifting character of their rhetoric. While this rhetoric grew more specialized and opaque to the general public—gone were the days of the dilettante scientist—its philosophical implications only seemed to increase. Einstein's thought experiments, the metaphors of particle and wave, the shifting role of the observer, and the embrace of metaphor on the part of quantum physicists in general, all seemed to attest to the relevance of the physicists' work. The assertion of the far-reaching implications of their theories by some scientists, notably Bohr in his efforts to spread the gospel of complementarity, only encouraged this attitude. Not surprisingly, popular treatments of relativity, "atomic" power, and other suggestively named phenomena such as Charm and Strangeness, often miss the point, reading these metaphors in a loose, general sense rather than according to their more strictly defined scientific meanings. Yet physicists' use of metaphorical language and their perception of its purpose did change with the Quantum Revolution, as I argue in the first two chapters; and the public's interest and curiosity—and, frequently, alarm—about this newly suggestive language was justified. It portended dramatic transformations, both conceptual and practical, and even the physics community itself felt uneasy, as the *Blegdamsvej Faust* demonstrates.

To the public at large and sometimes even to the scientists themselves, both the growing body of technological wonders and the descriptions of increasingly marvelous phenomena produced by physics lent the discipline an aura more in keeping with a witches' sabbath than a dry academic discipline. Its disciples seemed to possess superhuman knowledge, and this drew the public's interest. Now physicists had to begin to confront the consequences of an unfamiliar fame. In this context, the *Blegdamsvej Faust* may be read as an embodiment of a press photographer's camera. It placed the scientific community's best-known figures on stage and had them act out their intellectual struggles in a social forum, under a spotlight and in front of an audience. Its flashbulb captures the physicists' fame for posterity, and even though its authors originally intended to limit their audience and remain anonymous themselves, they have been unable to do so. The symbolic power of this play reflects the magnitude of the physicists' social fame. The *Blegdamsvej Faust* is not read today for its dramatic merit—though it has worthy moments—but because it offers a fascinating glimpse of an episode in our collective social history that matters to us.

For physicists, this fame cuts two ways. On the one hand, of course, public recognition is flattering. It enhances their sense of performing worthwhile work. Eventually, it can lead to increased social support for that work, as it did during and after World War II. But like the physicists' own observations of subatomic phenomena, the public's interest in the work of science interrupts and hampers it. So the M.C. directs his final words to the photographer's camera as an emblem of the audience beyond Blegdamsvej Street and of the fame its attention bestowed:

Blitzlicht, due Blendendes	Flashbulb, you dazzler,
Magnesium spendendes,	Magnesium spender,
Wolken versendendes,	Cloud dispenser,
Viel Zeit verschwendendes,	Much time squanderer,
Stinkendes,	Stinker,
Blinkendes,	Blinker,
Stör' uns nicht mehr! (19)	Disturb us no more!

Ehrenfest fell victim to this "blitzlicht," causing the M.C. to end the play almost immediately with the plea that it "disturb us no more!" It is a waster of time and matter; but it is also dazzling. There is a hint of ambivalence in this depiction similar to the ambivalence toward the state of quantum mechanics expressed throughout the play: it is both exciting and unsettling. Indeed, it seems to me there is a fundamental connection between the dazzle of fame and the infernal science of quantum mechanics that both dazzles in its own right, as we see in the Quantum Mechancial Walpurgis Night, and leads to the dazzle of public recognition. Is there any way for the scientists to choose one and reject the other? Their thirst for knowledge and power pushes them toward quantum mechanics, and the success of that discipline pushes them onto the public stage where the struggles and tensions that underlie their achievements can be seen by all. In this glare of public scrutiny, how is any work to get done? The physicists, having exercised the option of knowledge, seem to be stuck with the consequences of a bargain they never meant to make.

Conclusion

In its "FINALE: APOTHEOSE DES WAHREN NEUTRONS"— its "Apotheosis of the True Neutrons"—the *Blegdamsvej Faust* reaches toward a happy ending to its drama, despite the complexity of the issues that arise in the play and culminate in the death of Ehrenfest. Curiously, it may be that the death of Ehrenfest actually facilitates the play's upbeat resolution. With Erenfest gone, the Mephisto–Faust conflict that ostensibly fueled the play vanishes also. By this time, Goethe's _Faust_ has receded far into the background. When Ehrenfest dies, the _Blegdamsvej Faust_ abandons its literary model entirely and, in this departure, ironically highlights an earlier divergence that may have gone unremarked until now: Ehrenfest, unlike Faust, never makes an explicit bargain with the Devil. Instead, with Ehrenfest gone at the end of the play, Mephisto is himself called upon to agree to a bargain—with Wagner, a figure of academic conservatism in Goethe's _Faust_ and in the _Blegdamsvej_ version none other than Pauli's rival, Chadwick:

Wagner, die Personifikation des idealen Experimentators, erscheint, eine schwarze Kugel balancierend:	_Wagner_, the personification of the ideal experimentalist, appears, balancing a black sphere:
Neutron, es schwankt heran,	The neutron sways right here,
Masse, sie lastet dran,	Mass weighs it down,
Ladung, sie ist vertan,	Charge is gone,
Pauli, er gleubt daran!	Pauli, believe it!
Mephisto:	_Mephisto:_
Gerettet ist das edle Glied	The noble part of the spirit world
Der Geisterwelt vom Bösen.	Is rescued from the malicious.
Wer experimentierend sich bemüht,	Those who try hard through experimenting
Den können wir erlösen.	Know how to reclaim it.
Und hat an ihm die Rechnung gar	And though the calculation
Doch heimlich teilgenommen,	Was secretly partaken in,
Begegnet ihm die edle Schar	The noble band meets him
Mit herzlichem Willkommen! (20)[34]	With a hearty welcome!

Pauli's bargain implicitly involves giving up his particle's claim to the name "neutron" and acknowledging the existence of Chadwick's particle by that name. In the process, the play reaffirms the need to ground quantum mechanics in experimentation. By insisting on a manipulation of the physical world as the basis for the truth claims of science, the play resolves the particular dispute on which it was based: the neutron–neutrino controversy. But its implications are much broader. The dramatic climax of the _Blegdamsvej Faust_ turns on what might in other circumstances seem an abstract epistemological premise: that experimentation has greater authority than any individual theorist, regardless of his orientation, whether infernal, like Pauli, or divine, like Bohr. The play began with a direct confrontation between these men, and at that point Pauli ran verbal circles around Bohr; but here he is obliged to submit to the authority of the experimental tradition of physics. This shift is represented as a climactic moment in the drama, for it answers his opening complaint that "nichts mehr zu retten ist"; now "Gerettet ist das edle Glied/Der Geisterwelt." And so the discipline itself is rescued from its Walpurgis Night chaos, the extremity of abstract theory, and the death of Ehrenfest, by a return to the traditional authority of experiment.

What does Pauli get out of this bargain? In effect, he receives the ability to make the bargain. This may seem a poor deal at first, but it is actually quite advantageous. Entering into this bargain grants him membership in the scientific community for which Chadwick speaks, pro tem. Ultimately, all scientists engage in a comparable bargain in expressing their willingness to submit to the moderating will of the larger community, to abide by its rules, and to use its rhetoric. Indeed, it is this "bargain" that creates the scientific community in the first place, uniting the disparate ideas and persons of its members in a coherent social order.[35] This order in turn provides a context capable of moderating and resolving disputes in the service of a larger conceptual structure: a body of theory that claims to describe the mystery and magnitude of God's creation. By forcing Pauli to submit to the authority of experiment, the *Blegdamsvej Faust* reasserts the authority of physics— including Pauli's own contributions to it—in the face of the disruptions that characterize the historical moment.[36]

In the end, however, even the Devil's submission to the dictates of scientific reason cannot completely contain the disruptive energies embodied in the play. In the final lines, the authors acknowledge the persistence of these tensions and turn to a literary device to explain them away:

Chorus mysticus:	*Mystical Chorus:*
Alles Geladene	All this charge
Ist nur ein Gleichnis!	Is only a parable!
Das oft Missratene,	What frequently fails
Hier wird's Ereignis!	Here becomes an event!
Das Phänomenale,	What is phenomenal,
Hier ist's getan!	Here is it put!
Das Ewig–Neutrale	Eternal Neutrality
Zieht uns hinan! (20)	Pulls us along!

Asserting the fictional character of a text's representations is, of course, a common political move in literary works: "All this . . . /Is only a parable!" Yet it is surprising that the authors of the *Blegdamsvej Faust* feel the need to employ this device, given the fact that their play is obviously an absurd "stunt," a comic exaggeration. Parody or no, it hits home, engaging sensitive issues in the guise of fiction, as literature has so often done throughout its history. Even in the act of disclaiming the seriousness of their enterprise, they assert it, for although a parable is a fictional narrative, it is intended to illustrate a serious message.

What is that message? The final lines require delicate reading. The "Eternal-Neutral" to which they refer is, of course, the neutrality of both the neutron and the neutrino whose conflict powers the play. These newly recognized particles represented a huge leap in the physicists' understanding of subatomic phenomena, and therefore they may well be said to "raise them up" in their work. But the significant position of these lines at the end of the play invites further conjecture, particularly since they echo the motto with which the play began: Bohr's famous "Not to criticize." Ehrenfest is the play's Critic, and the centrality of his role reflects the centrality of critical intelligence in the discipline of physics itself. But a literary form requires closure, and scientific debates proceed in the understanding that their participants are striving for a communally acceptable resolution. For either kind of closure to occur, the critical antagonist must fall silently. Dramatically, this entails Ehrenfest's death. Symbolically, it amounts to the end of the critically charged exchanges that fill much of the play, from Mephisto's opening lines on. Practically, of course, the play's motto was not meant to silence potential critics but rather to serve as a means of fostering constructive criticism: "Not to criticize your theory, but. . . ." The play fills out the ellipsis, and its last words are meant to bring to an end a dispute that Bohr's appearance of neutrality made possible in the first place.

In the end, the *Blegdamsvej Faust* exposes the complex bargains into which each physicist entered willy-nilly on joining the community of quantum mechanists in the early 1930s. Such bargains and the social relations that underlie them have probably always characterized the world of science; yet in this century, exercising the sense of option in knowledge seems to entail scientists in increasingly dramatic consequences, as technological developments as diverse as nuclear weapons, personal computers, and cloning make all too apparent. These consequences challenge the assumption that scientific practices exist in a value-free, objective context; yet the success of modern science has depended on the creation of a community capable of approximating such a context. In an effort to release the tensions that resulted from their efforts to maintain this community during the turbulent changes imposed on the discipline by the development of quantum mechanics, the participants in the 1932

Conference at the Institute of Theoretical Physics turned to literature. By rewriting the Faust legend to represent their own experiences, these physicists found the metaphorical tools with which both to explore and to contain the disruptions involved in this dramatic leap in their search for a deep knowledge of nature. Fortunately for our knowledge of them and their work, in doing so they also put themselves and their bargains center stage.

THE LOS ALAMOS PRIMER

The following notes are based on a set of five
lectures given by R. Serber during the first two
weeks of April 1943, as an "indoctrination course"
in connection with the starting of the Los Alamos
Project. The notes were written up by E. U. Condon.

Bob Serber

1. Object

The object of the project is to produce a <u>practical</u>
<u>military weapon</u> in the form of a bomb in which the energy is re-
leased by a fast neutron chain reaction in one or more of the
materials known to show nuclear fission.

2. Energy of Fission Process

The direct energy release in the fission process is
of the order of 170 MEV per atom. This is considerably more than
10^7 times the heat of reaction per atom in ordinary combustion processes.

This is $170 \cdot 10^6 \cdot 4.8 \cdot 10^{-10}/300 = 2.7 \cdot 10^{-4}$ erg/nucleus.
Since the weight of 1 nucleus of 25 is $3.88 \cdot 10^{-22}$ gram/nucleus the
energy release is

$$7 \cdot 10^{17} \text{ erg/gram}$$

The energy release in TNT is $4 \cdot 10^{10}$ erg/gram or $3.6 \cdot 10^{16}$ erg/ton.
Hence

$$1 \text{ kg of } 25 \approx 20000 \text{ tons of TNT}$$

3. Fast Neutron Chain Reaction

Release of this energy in a large scale way is a
possibility because of the fact that in each fission process, which
requires a neutron to produce it, two neutrons are released. Consider a very great mass of active material, so great that no neutrons
are lost through the surface and assume the material so pure that
no neutrons are lost in other ways than by fission. One neutron
released in the mass would become 2 after the first fission, each
of these would produce 2 after they each had produced fission so
in the nth generation of neutrons there would be 2^n neutrons available.

Since in 1 kg. of 25 there are $5 \cdot 10^{25}$ nuclei it would
require about $n = 80$ generations ($2^{80} \approx 5 \cdot 10^{25}$) to fish the whole
kilogram.

While this is going on the energy release is making
the material very hot, developing great pressure and hence tending to cause an exposion.

In an actual finite setup, some neutrons are lost by
diffusion out through the surface. There will be therefore a certain
size of say a sphere for which the surface losses of neutrons are

4

THE LOS ALAMOS PRIMER

THE USES OF FICTION IN

FOUNDING A LABORATORY

> *Whether the emergence of an argumentative community necessitated a conventional genre in which to carry on that argument or whether the clarification of forms of argument allowed a coherent community to coalesce in discussion is an unanswerable dialectical conundrum. A more exact formulation might be that a community constitutes itself in developing its modes of regular discourse.*
> —*Charles Bazerman,* Shaping Written Knowledge

In October 1942, Major John Dudley of the United States Army Corps of Engineers was dispatched on what he describes as an epic search:

I was borrowed from my district to travel around the West to locate a site for a mysterious installation. . . . I traveled by air, rail and auto. Perhaps a thousand miles were covered on two-lane roads—one lane for the left wheels and one lane for the right wheels. When the going got tough, I switched to a jeep, and when it got even tougher, I rode a horse.[1]

Dudley had been given a long list of criteria for this "mysterious installation." It should be more than two hundred miles inland, remote from any large cities, yet accessible by rail and air, with a pleasant winter climate; some facilities should already exist on the site, to speed its transformation into a viable community; and it should be surrounded by hills, in a kind of natural bowl, to protect it and—ominously—to help contain major explosions. Dudley's theatrical portrayal of his mission is not inappropriate. Its result would be the creation of a new kind of social entity: an enormous, isolated scientific community devoted to the construction of new weapons of unprecedented destructive power—a place now called the Los Alamos National Laboratory, but known then as Site Y of the Manhattan Project.

Despite having been handed a detailed list of site requirements, Dudley was meant to know nothing of the new community he was helping to create. As he recalls:

Officially, I was able to maintain this fiction of ignorance throughout my association with the Manhattan Project. However, as soon as I started talking to scientists, say within a matter of a half hour or forty-five minutes, I knew what they were doing quite thoroughly. I tried to turn them off, but within two minutes they would again be leaking information.[2]

Dudley's description mixes two parts exasperation with one part amusement at the scatterbrained antics of the "longhairs."[3] And who can blame him? His job required balancing the expertise that landed him the assignment with an official "fiction of ignorance." Interestingly, it is difficult to judge whether he is more annoyed with the necessity of maintaining this fiction or with the obstacles to doing so posed by the scientists' blabbermouth tendencies. For their part, the scientists were equally frustrated by this unfamiliar conjunction of military secrecy and the scientific tradition of open exchange. Yet, although the "fiction of ignorance" was imposed on Dudley and the Los Alamos scientists by the military leaders of the Manhattan Project, the scientists themselves also made use of what we might call "fictions of knowledge" in constructing their new laboratory, as this chapter will show.

The tension between the military and scientific needs of the Manhattan Project was just one of many challenges confronting the builders of this new laboratory. On the scientific side, perhaps the most central challenge was the daunting task of bringing together individuals from a wide variety of specializations and different parts of the world and joining them into a coherent and effective scientific community. At the end of 1942 the project leaders chose a site for the new laboratory on a narrow finger of the Pajarito Plateau that jutted out from the Jemez Mountains into the Rio Grande Valley and that was known as the Los Alamos (or "cottonwood") mesa—not, incidentally, one of the locations proposed by Dudley. The Los Alamos mesa was at that time the home of the Los Alamos Ranch School, a private school for boys founded on the premise that living in a magnificent and unspoiled natural setting was the best complement to intense intellectual work. Ironically, the fact that at least one of the Manhattan Project officials who chose the site—the laboratory's new director, Robert Oppenheimer—shared this belief ultimately doomed the school. At the end of the fall term the government seized the land, and in March of 1943 construction began on the new laboratory.

By the end of that month the first scientists began to arrive at Los Alamos. Conditions were, however, still quite primitive. Aside from the few who could be accommodated in existing Ranch School buildings, the scientists were housed on dude ranches in the surrounding countryside. Every day they faced a long and harrowing trek over the Rio Grande and up a switchback road carved out of the mesa's tufa cliff face. Their work consisted of overseeing the installation of laboratory equipment, planning new facilities, and preparing for the arrival of the main body of their colleagues, projected at that time to be about one hundred people. The work was grueling, the hours long, communication awkward (Los Alamos had only one telephone, an antiquated Forest Service line), and both the scientists and the military personnel quickly became convinced of each other's stubbornness and incompetence. Yet within a few weeks some thirty scientists had arrived and construction had proceeded far enough to allow them to begin their research in earnest.

To inaugurate this new community, Oppenheimer arranged for Robert Serber, a friend and former student, to deliver a series of lectures summarizing the state of relevant knowledge in the various branches of the bomb project. An atmosphere of excitement prevailed as the scientists gathered in the classrooms of the former Ranch School.[4] As Serber remembers it,

Everyone had just arrived. Buildings were still under construction. All the apparatus was in crates. People were unpacking it and putting it together and working twelve to sixteen hours a day. Pulling them away from what they were doing and getting them together for a series of lectures wasn't the easiest thing in the world. . . . But within those limitations the [lectures were] essentially a summary of everything we knew in April 1943 about how to make an atomic bomb.[5]

Though it may not have been "the easiest thing in the world," it was a crucial step in the transformation of the Los Alamos mesa into a working scientific community. As the scientists listened to Serber spell out the technical parameters of their mission, they began to come alive with what Richard Rhodes describes as "euphoria at finally learning in detail what they had only previously guessed or heard hinted."[6]

Many of the scientists, of course, already knew something about the project; but Serber's lectures filled in many gaps and laid everything out on the table. The lectures were "news as well as confirmation."[7] Perhaps even more important, they represented the first time that these scientists could discuss what they knew openly and without restraint, in the traditional manner of their profession. Previously, the need for secrecy had kept even those in the know in a kind of intellectual vacuum, such as Dudley describes. Now the lectures officially broke down that restraint, and small groups quickly formed and began animated discussions as the scientists entered into a practical community of intellectual exchange.

The work of constructing the Los Alamos community did not end with the lectures, however. Even as Serber's final words were ringing in the Los Alamites' ears, new colleagues were arriving on the mesa, and they kept on coming until the detonation of Little Boy and Fat Man over Hiroshima and Nagasaki signaled the completion of their work with the end of the war. Between April 1943 and August 1945, the community grew from thirty to six thousand members. Never before had a scientific community existed on this scale, and its existence introduced a host of practical difficulties involving organization, communication, and administration, as well as issues of supply, housing, education, recreation, and security. To meet these challenges, the Manhattan Project involved an unusual collaboration between military and scientific personnel, and this also required a great deal of adjustment of methods and priorities on both sides.[8]

Not surprisingly, Los Alamos was a community in constant flux. Yet stability was essential to the successful coordination of the efforts of its numerous and diverse personnel, and this required some way of integrating the steady stream of new arrivals into the existing community. In an effort to meet this need, Serber and a colleague transcribed his lectures into print for distribution to incoming scientists as an introduction to the laboratory's conceptual foundations. Serber describes the process: "The theoretical physicist Ed Condon served as secretary. . . . He took notes, and then the same afternoon or the next morning he'd write them up and bring them over and we'd discuss them back and forth, edit them a little."[9] The result was "twenty-four mimeographed pages dense with formulas, graphs, and crude drawings,"[10] providing an overview of the current knowledge about fission processes in uranium and plutonium—including sections on such topics as "Energy of Fission Process," "Fast Neutron Chain Reaction," and "Fission Cross-sections." In addition, the text offered a wide-ranging account of the technical considerations involved in transforming this theoretical understanding of fission into a practical weapon, ranging from sections on "Why Ordinary U Is Safe" and "Effect of Tamper on Efficiency" to a consideration of the danger of "Fizzles."

As its title suggests, *The Los Alamos Primer* was something of an odd duck: an attempt to do many things simultaneously. Most obviously, it served as a condensed review of the existing knowledge in nuclear physics relevant to building a weapon. Yet even this function is hardly as straightforward as it might at first appear. It is worth noting that a significant amount of relevant information from other scientific disciplines was omitted. Indeed, Los Alamos was generally treated as a nuclear physicists' gig.[11] This attitude would seem to be the result of a variety of specific actions—including the *Primer*'s particular construction of the epistemological foundation of the project in a way that privileged nuclear physics over any other discipline. One might argue that it would have been impossible to build the bomb without nuclear physics, and so the privilege accorded it is only appropriate. It is true that the idea of nuclear weapons comes from the insights of nuclear physics, and nuclear physicists were the first to advocate the practical possibility of their construction. But these bombs would have been equally impossible without the participation of chemists, ballistics experts, explosives specialists, metallurgists, and others. Indeed, the majority of the scientists employed by the Manhattan Project came from these other disciplines. Yet the *Primer* treats the project as though it were a problem in nuclear physics.

On a less obvious level, the *Primer* was also concerned with what the nuclear physicists did *not* know. It pointed out to the assembled scientists great gaps in the knowledge needed to construct a working bomb. To fill those gaps, it proposed a number of specific lines of research. Some of these proposals were straightforward: "We need to do X and Y." But many were implicit in the *Primer*'s presentation of what was known: By foregrounding certain issues and establishing a particular perspective on them, some ways of proceeding were rendered more likely without any need to advocate for them directly. To complicate matters further, some lines of research that the *Primer* seemed to recommend were not in fact meant as serious proposals at all. Their purpose involved mediating potential conflicts among competing research programs and the individual egos of the scientists behind them. I will consider an example of this in some detail later in this chapter.

This last point introduces a third central function of the *Primer*. I have already mentioned the variety of the personnel gathered at Los Alamos. Conflicts among such a diverse population were inevitable. But the *Primer*'s job was to initiate conversation among these scientists and to frame that conversation along productive lines, which is not to say that it was meant to promote unanimous accord. Such agreement would have been counterproductive—a stifling of the creative, divergent thinking essential in any discipline of human knowledge—and it was impossible, in any event. Rather, the *Primer* was meant to introduce particular lines of thought judged by a small inner circle of scientists to be most likely to lead to valuable results.[12] But while the *Primer* was intended to be a persuasive document, its authors did not want to suggest that its pronouncements were absolute. They tried to walk a fine line between being too persuasive and too permissive. We can see this effort reflected throughout the *Primer*. The dominant voice is that of traditional scientific discourse;[13] but mixed into almost every passage is a healthy dose of the vernacular. The *Primer* is, in effect, a combination of formal presentation and speculative shoptalk, meant to stimulate open conversation, but within a carefully delimited framework.

I have tried so far to offer a sense of the layered context and the various purposes behind the composition of the *Los Alamos Primer*. It is worth noting that while I believe these purposes were central to the construction of the Los Alamos laboratory, I do not mean to assert that the *Primer* singlehandedly constituted the modes of discourse of its community and thereby the community itself. Such an assertion would be absurd. Charles Bazerman's language in the epigraph to this chapter is far less causal and more nuanced than that: "A community constitutes itself in developing its regular modes of discourse." The community does not spring into being in response to a text or conversation; but its discourse, shaped by individuals coming together in a community, helps to shape that community and its subsequent discourse.[14] I have become convinced over the course of my research that the *Primer* manifests a number of important dynamics at work in the construction of Los Alamos as a successful scientific community. To substantiate this claim, I will turn shortly to a close examination of some specific passages from the *Primer*. First, however, it is worth considering what the *Primer*'s name itself suggests about its complex role in the constitution of the Los Alamos laboratory.

What's in a Name?

In putting together this hybrid technical document in the midst of the frantic construction of the largest and most advanced scientific laboratory in the world, in what seemed the middle of a wilderness, and in wartime, Serber and Condon permitted themselves a moment of levity in their choice of a title. Perhaps seeking the release of tension that humor can provide, perhaps in recognition of the oddity of their circumstances,[15] they called their text a "primer," in mock reference to its educational function. The phrase is at once apt and surprising. On the one hand, it expresses the humor inherent in the authors' taking on the role of schoolmasters to the most illustrious collaboration of physicists in history. On the other hand, the title suggests a startling connection between elementary instructional manuals and the construction of nuclear weapons. Indeed, both of the word's primary meanings—a devotional manual for laymen and an elementary reading manual—seem at first glance to lead away from the construction of nuclear weapons or a scientific community altogether.

What could either meaning have to do with a nuclear weapons laboratory? The new arrivals at Los Alamos were, of course, neither laymen nor small children. If we try to pursue the relevance of these connotations, rather than drawing new scientists into the Los Alamos community they seem at first actively to exclude them by casting them in the role of outsiders and beginners. Yet considered more carefully, these apparently extraneous meanings actually serve as a powerful metaphor for the complex social work to which the *Primer* contributed. By casting the newcomers as outsiders, the primer metaphor suggests the existence of an inside to which they may gain admittance through devoted study—of the *Primer* itself. The two meanings of "primer" I have cited characterize this inside in terms of heaven and a social elite based on the principle of literacy. Both of these meanings turn out to be quite significant to the practical, day-to-day work of the scientists who turned to the *Primer* to learn how to read the natural processes of atoms and how they could be shaped into a bomb.

Considered in this way, the *Primer* suggests a complex set of external, social connotations at the heart of the bomb project. Although I will argue for the propriety of these connotations, they will at first strike many readers as strange or extraneous. Such metaphorical connections might well have been equally surprising to the original readers of the *Primer*, for they evoke the deep, usually suppressed relations between the scientific community and the larger, surrounding society. On the surface, science generally seeks out a distanced, objective relation to the turmoil of social interactions—to the extent that many people believe science actually constitutes a separate international society ruled by reason, dedicated to dispassionate intellectual exchange, and free from competition and discord. This utopian conception of science has a long history and has influenced diverse efforts to transform science from an individual activity to a communal one, beginning in the seventeenth century.[16] Of course, few would deny that science always exists in a larger social context; yet its practitioners generally strive to maintain the appearance of rising above or sidestepping overt entanglements with the world around them, and the rhetoric characteristic of most scientific texts has traditionally played an important role in bringing this about.

At Los Alamos, however, the social context was the *sine qua non*. Few scientists would have accepted Oppenheimer's initial invitation to join the project if they had not believed that the very existence of

The Los Alamos Primer

their society depended on it, for many held strong convictions regarding the immorality of war work. But in the context of World War II, the possibility of mobilizing the resources of science in the defense of their society made many scientists not only willing to acknowledge the social consequences of science but determined to explore its furthest potential. The foundation of Los Alamos, therefore, emphasized the inevitable but commonly invisible relations between science and its social context.

These relations are manifest throughout the project, even in unexpected forms such as Serber's and Condon's little joke about their educational mission in the *Primer*. In fact, this joke is merely the tip of a rhetorical iceberg. Although Serber and Condon modeled the body of the *Primer* on the traditional conventions of scientific rhetoric, as I will show in the following pages, the text is also punctuated by intrusions of rhetoric we might most usefully identify as literary. These intrusions reflect the disruptive stresses associated with the unusual prominence of the social implications of the new laboratory's mission. But at the same time, these rhetorical intrusions manifest an effort, perhaps unconscious, on the part of the authors of the *Primer* to contain and control the social implications of their work by, for example, employing metaphors that cast it in terms of an instructive not a destructive enterprise, a morally upright undertaking, even a holy mission.

At this point, differences in the disciplinary leanings of various readers requires some delicate negotiation. On the one hand, scientists and sociologists may object that I am "reading too much into" the language of the *Primer*—that its authors never intended the sorts of implications I am finding in it. On the other hand, readers with a background in literary studies are more likely to understand that the meaning of a text is not dependent on its author's conscious intentions. Although authors exercise a great deal of control in shaping their texts, other factors—including established usage, common symbols, cultural myths, the literary canon, conventional diction, grammatical rules, social conditioning, subconscious desires—also play major roles in determining the semiotic content of any given text, to the point that some of the most significant features of a text often have little or nothing to do with the author's intentions. Furthermore, we must beware of treating scientific texts as a special case, exempt from this principle. Although the dynamics I have described may generally be so deeply submerged in a scientific text that they are inconsequential, special circumstances—such as those surrounding the *Los Alamos Primer*—bring them to the fore and make them more significant aspects of a text.

The title of the *Primer*, therefore, represents the rhetorical and epistemological tensions inherent in the work that text was meant to do, work that significantly parallels the purpose of the original primers. Those texts, too, particularly in their American incarnations in Puritan society, functioned in a dialectical fashion. On the one hand, they purported to teach the arts of reading and writing; on the other hand, they used that immediate purpose to further a larger goal: the creation and maintenance of a community devoted to a particular religious mission. The *Los Alamos Primer* mirrors this process: Its overt purpose was to teach newcomers the fundamental physics of nuclear weapons; but this purpose was in the service of a larger mission—incorporating its readers into a community devoted to the actual construction of those weapons. Furthermore, invoking the primer model calls attention to the moral dimension of its mission and contains that acknowledgment within the metaphorical suggestion that Los Alamos, too, will be a community devoted to the singleminded furtherance of *worthy* goals, a kind of City upon a Hill. This conception helps reflexively to authorize the instructional mission of the *Primer*—to teach the residents of "the Hill," as the Los Alamites called their new home, how to build atomic bombs. Each connotation reinforces the other: the tenor of the primer metaphor channels the social implications of the project toward an association with a community founded upon a holy mission; the instructional vehicle of the *Primer* embodies that mission, giving it substance and direction. In the *Primer*, Serber and Condon drafted a document that combined rhetorics from disparate spheres and that through this combination played an instrumental role in creating a remarkable community. In short, they devised a document that lived up to its name in a final, very practical sense, by serving as the material means of initiating an explosion: a primer.

As these remarks suggest, I believe the *Primer* was much more than simply a technical summary or informational vehicle. It played an important role in helping to construct Los Alamos as a community capable of meeting the scientific challenges of building the first atomic weapons in the context of the social ramifications of that project. To do so, it had to reflect and shape its audience's conception of their work in complex and particular ways. In effect, the *Primer* needed to indoctrinate incoming scientists in a party-line view of the bomb project in order to promote their active participation in maintaining the Los Alamos community and furthering its peculiar goals. Serber and Condon were quite aware of this necessity and, in fact, they preface their work by openly referring to it as an "indoctrination course":

The Los Alamos Primer

The following notes are based on a set of five lectures given by R. Serber during the first two weeks of April 1943, as an "indoctrination course" in connection with the starting of the Los Alamos Project. The notes were written up by E. U. Condon. (3)

The effectiveness of this indoctrination course seems inescapable: the ruins of Hiroshima and Nagasaki attest to it. But why was it effective? How did it achieve its effects? These difficult questions require us to look first at a more immediate one: Why did Serber and Condon assume that the Los Alamos scientists would not object to being indoctrinated?[17]

To address this last point, we must step back and consider science as a disciplinary form of knowledge. As a number of historians of science have demonstrated, the teleological character of the discipline requires its members to engage in elaborately structured social relations.[18] The specific forms of these relations involve scientists in communities capable of evaluating individual knowledge claims and ordering them within an evolving hierarchy of scientific "facts." But scholars also point out that particular scientific communities require constant maintenance and adjustment. Therefore, like any modern discipline, physics requires its adherents to submit to an extended period of initiation as a prerequisite for the conferral of professional credentials. Such initiation involves the acquisition of particular skills and conceptual schema. In the case of physics, these would include—to varying degrees, depending on the individual's intended area of specialization within physics—knowledge of experimental practices, command of a specialized vocabulary, mastery of advanced mathematics, familiarity with specific rhetorical techniques and textual forms (lab reports, grant proposals, scientific articles), and an understanding of the complex conceptual structures of classical and quantum mechanics.

In the process of her training, the neophyte physicist inevitably acquires a great deal of particularized knowledge at the expense of other particular knowledge. It is a bargain that we have already seen enacted in the text and context of the *Blegdamsvej Faust*. Becoming a physicist involves exercising the options of knowledge, for the discipline demands commitment to highly specific ways of looking at the world, and these ways can conflict with other ways of seeing and understanding. This dynamic occurs, in a small way, even within each particular specialization of physics itself, depending on the graduate program in which the novice receives her training. According to the faculty's biases, a graduate student will be indoctrinated in specific attitudes and assumptions regarding unresolved research questions within the discipline. Such assumptions are essential to the successful functioning of a given community of scientists, for it depends on the intricate coordination of its members' individual efforts as they go through the long process of choosing specific topics of inquiry, writing grant proposals, designing and conducting particular experimental procedures, interpreting the data produced by those procedures, and preparing papers for publication. Therefore, just as the large differences between disciplinary ways of conceiving of the world help us distinguish each discipline as a distinct social entity, so the smaller differences between competing assumptions and orientations within a discipline, even in something as apparently simple as the choice of which line of research will prove most fruitful, define separate intellectual communities.[19] As a result, the acquisition of disciplinary knowledge effectively constitutes the acolyte as a member of a particular community.

In this context, the Los Alamites' self-conscious desire to "indoctrinate" new arrivals in a particular knowledge about the nuclear processes involved in building a bomb should not surprise us. Although their tone seems to be lighthearted, the authors' use of the term suggests an awareness of their responsibility in helping to put together a coherent community. This responsibility was not unique to the *Primer*, of course, and the *Primer* does not present its subject as extravagant or unusual— rather, it consistently seeks to contain the extraordinary nature of the bomb project within the conventions of the mainstream of the scientific tradition and the current military context and, in so doing, to construct Los Alamos as a working scientific laboratory in which all the familiar ground rules and procedures remain in force.

The *Primer*'s Rhetorical Constructions

We can see these conventions at work beginning in the first section of the *Primer*:

1. Object
The object of the project is to produce a <u>practical military weapon</u> in the form of a bomb in which the energy is released by a fast neutron chain reaction in one or more of the materials known to show nuclear fission. (3)

Serber and Condon begin in good lab report form, by stating the purpose of the work at Los Alamos as though it were a gigantic experiment. Yet the write-up that follows this bland statement lays the groundwork for an experiment that would ultimately yield rather dramatic results. In this context, it is noteworthy that their language remains so flat and detached from its social consequences, hewing instead to the conventions of scientific rhetoric: abstract, relational verbs ("is," "to produce," "known," "to show"); passive voice ("is released," "known"); avoidance of direct attribution of agency; complex noun groups. It is almost as if its authors were attempting to hide behind these conventions to avoid confronting the horrifying consequences implied by the experiment they are proposing.

If my tone here seems somewhat confrontational, remember that the moral implications of atomic weapons almost inevitably charge discussions of their development with judgmental language or a notable lack of it. It is very hard to strike the right balance here. Should the Los Alamites be held accountable for the products of their labors, even though few individuals had much direct control over them? Was the development of nuclear weapons morally questionable from the beginning? Could their existence, in fact, be a good thing? My concern in the pages that follow is not with finding answers to these important questions but with exploring the ways in which the rhetoric on which Los Alamos was founded combined elements that would commonly be identified as scientific and literary in a context that would seem to have been purely scientific. In the course of this exploration, however, I will suggest a partial answer to a question closely related to those above: Why, as many Los Alamites have noted, was there so little discussion of these issues at Los Alamos itself? I will contend that the combined rhetorics of science and literature provided a medium that diffused these tensions and, in fact, even made it difficult to pursue them. None of what follows should be construed as an indictment of the individuals involved. I am not at all sure that what they did was "bad," or even that it was worse than the alternatives. Though it is difficult, we should beware of confusing a discussion of moral issues with rendering moral judgment.

Far from trying to avoid confronting the consequences of their actions, the language of the *Primer* suggests that even the Los Alamites' scientific rhetoric engaged the social implications of their work. The phrase "in the form of a bomb," for instance, sounds a discordant note in the context of the otherwise technical diction of the passage. The phrasing itself seems reluctant: "in the form of" qualifies the word "bomb" before it is uttered. Furthermore, in scientific prose the phrase "in the form of a bomb" is a somewhat unusual grammatical construction that reflects its being out of place; scientific prose tends to favor compact adjectival forms like "a practical military weapon" or "a fast neutron chain reaction."[20] In fact, the phrase was so out of place that Serber was almost immediately instructed to avoid it.[21] He was to use "gadget" instead. Obviously, the

Los Alamites were obliged to work through a number of rhetorical issues as they proceeded. No project of this kind had ever been attempted before, and even much of the science was new, as another phrase in the opening section suggests: according to the conventions of scientific language, "materials known to show nuclear fission" would soon be further nominalized as "fissile materials."

Despite the newness of the discipline and the stresses involved in being part of a military project, however, the rhetorical conventions of science largely dominate the *Primer*, and the effect is to cast the work it describes in acceptable terms. So in the midst of a radically disruptive undertaking—the creation of terrible and terrifying new weapons; the physical and emotional dislocation from family and home to a military base in an unfamiliar land; the blurring of boundaries that had previously defined science as an objective, academic discipline separate from the world of politics and war—the word "Object" and its placement in the text offer a soothing continuity. In effect, it promises firm footing on familiar ground, a rhetorical stability in the midst of rapidly shifting experience. As such, it makes a striking claim for the social power—as opposed to the purely conceptual utility— of scientific rhetoric. The familiarity of the *Primer*'s rhetoric helps to transform the strange and threatening business of building weapons of mass destruction into the morally unobjectionable terms of science as usual.

The *Primer*, therefore, engages the social implications of its work in a way that partially anaesthetizes the reader to their full import. It manages to include an extended section on "Damage," for example, including considerations of its "severe pathological effects" (33) and the likelihood of the bomb "rendering the locality" in which it is used "uninhabitable" (34) without giving the reader any visceral sense of what this damage might mean in human terms. In part, one might argue, this results from the fact that the Los Alamites did not yet have any direct knowledge of the damage their weapons might cause. Estimates of the bombs' destructive force varied widely right up until the Trinity test, and gathering accurate data on the bombs' effects was a primary concern of the first Allied scientists to visit Hiroshima and Nagasaki. (It is telling that there is still no true consensus of the damage they did even in their actual use on those cities.) But the fact remains that the *Primer*'s rhetoric acts to render these details in a form that dissociates them from the world of human feeling and moral judgment. So in the opening section, the bomb is not simply a bomb but "a <u>practical military weapon</u> in the form of a bomb."

The Los Alamos Primer

The insistence on precision here has a curious dual effect. On the one hand, it insists on calling a spade a spade: its recognition of the "Object" of the Los Alamos laboratory seems unflinching. But on the other hand, the precision of the rhetoric serves to transform the bomb from an instrument of destruction into an object of study. Grammatically, particularly according to the standard model of scientific prose, the sentence was already complete by the end of the first line: "The object of the project is to produce a practical military weapon." "In the form of a bomb" is itself couched in the secondary form of a qualification of the primary clause, and it is further qualified and requalified by a series of four additional elements: "[1] in which the energy is released [2] by a fast neutron chain reaction [3] in one or more of the materials [4] known to show nuclear fission." By the end of the passage, the bomb has lost its power to appall and become an abstracted thing, a subject more suited to inspire mathematical analysis than protest marches.

This, of course, facilitated the work on which the Los Alamos community was predicated. Here we may begin to understand why so many scientists who were morally opposed to war work were able to live day to day with their roles in the construction of the most destructive weapons in history—even after Nazi Germany had been defeated. The *Primer* paved the way by defining Los Alamos as a peculiar kind of human community whose involvement in the production of weapons of mass destruction was subsumed under the language and ethos of the objective practices of science. It is tempting from these observations to identify scientific rhetoric as an agent of objectification and therefore as morally suspect, a view often taken by those who seek to valorize literary representations over scientific ones. But as I suggested in my consideration of its title, the *Primer*'s effectiveness depends on its use of a wide range of rhetorics, including the literary.

Indeed, it is not possible (if we value accuracy) to maintain a rigid distinction between literary and scientific rhetorics in the *Primer*. While we may identify certain uses of language as typical of one or the other discipline in the abstract, the practical context of the *Primer* exhibits a thorough mixture of the two. Let's consider a typical passage:

3. Fast Neutron Chain Reaction
Release of this energy in a large scale way is a possibility because of the fact that in each fission process, which requires a neutron to produce it, two neutrons are released. Consider a very great mass of active material, so great that no neutrons are lost through the surface and assume the material so pure

that no neutrons are lost in other ways than by fission. One neutron released in the mass would become 2 after the first fission, each of these would produce 2 after they each had produced fission so in the nth generation of neutrons there would be 2^n neutrons available.

Since in 1 kg. of 25 there are $5 \cdot 10^{25}$ nuclei it would require about n = 80 generations ($2^{80} \approx 5 \cdot 10^{25}$) to fish the whole kilogram.

While this is going on the energy release is making the material very hot, developing great pressure and hence tending to cause an explosion. (9–10)

At first glance the passage offers nothing out of the ordinary. It seems to be a straightforward example of scientific prose, in which Serber and Condon extend the objectification of the bomb, reducing it to its constituent pieces for clear, unemotional analysis. As such, the passage represents what I have described as the governing mission of the *Primer*—the indoctrination of its readers in a particular set of scientific "facts"—and in fulfilling that mission it employs a rhetoric that seems simply and wholly that of science: impersonal, objective, factual.

The only obvious oddity in the passage is its use of the verb "to fish." Serber alludes, retrospectively, to the formative condition of his facts when he comments in his "Notes":

In the *Primer* we used the verb "to fish." That's some indication of how new our work was. Otto Frisch and Lise Meitner named the new nuclear reaction they confirmed in 1939 "fission," borrowing the word from biology. We hadn't settled on a verb form of the noun yet. "To fish" didn't stick. Today we say "to fission," but we kept the pronunciation: it's *"fishin'*," not *"fizj-un."*[22]

Serber's comments confirm our sense that the verb "to fish" is out of place in the technical prose of Section 3. Significantly, however, it is not out of place because it does not have an appropriately technical meaning but rather because at the time of the *Primer*'s composition that meaning remained too new for its associated terminology to have stabilized. Indeed, "to fish" is a linguistic tip of the iceberg. As scientists gathered at Los Alamos, many of the "facts" reported in Section 3 were of such recent date that they were known only tentatively or incompletely. As the first three chapters of this study indicate, the branch of physics from which they came was in a state of rapid flux. The neutron, which is referred to so authoritatively, was discovered only ten years earlier, and physicists had not yet realized that it was, in fact, composed of a variety of even smaller particles. Likewise, the fission of nuclei in collisions with neutrons was not known until a mere four years before the founding of Los Alamos. Furthermore, the central assumption of this section of the *Primer*—"the fact that in each fission process, which requires a neutron to produce it, two neutrons are released"—had only been experimentally confirmed four months earlier. The physicists still did not know enough about the relative behaviors of slow and fast neutron collisions with nuclei to be able to predict whether plutonium was a viable material for the construction of a nuclear bomb. Thus the confidence with which the *Primer*'s rhetoric dissects and names the phenomena in question glosses over a great deal of uncertainty, claiming an authority for its representations that remained fictional to a significant extent.

The Fictions of Physics

In this context, it may be less of a surprise to learn that the entirety of Section 3 was, in an important respect, fictional. I will, of course, examine the specific evidence for this assertion in some detail. But it may be useful first to offer a few general words here to clarify my use of the word "fiction" in the following argument. I mean the term to indicate an imaginary structure made of words and intended to represent objects or actions that do not exist in the "real" world in the particular form in which the fiction depicts them. This should not be taken to imply any intent to deceive the reader or propagate falsehood. When we read *The Scarlet Letter*, for instance, it is clear that Hawthorne does not intend for us to believe that the particular events he describes ever took place, or even that Hester Prynne and Arthur Dimmesdale were real people. Yet it is equally important that fictions represent objects and actions with a significant resemblance to our experience of reality. Even in the case of Gothic tales, magic realism, fantasies, or science fiction novels, in which the fictional world differs widely from our experience, there must be some substantial relevance to our experience. When we sense that relevance, we are willing to suspend our disbelief (which is not the same thing as believing) and entertain the fiction so that it may entertain or instruct us. So, although Hester and Arthur never existed, the kind of emotions Hawthorne attributes to them, the clothing he has them wear, even the vegetation he surrounds them with are all recognizable to us from our own experience.

I would also distinguish the scientific fictions I will be discussing from hypotheses and theories. Theories are symbolic structures that their sponsors believe to be true, while hypotheses are more tentative structures that, nevertheless, are thought likely to be true. In general, the passages in the *Primer* I will identify as "fictional" are known to be untrue (indeed, they are often openly acknowledged to be so), but they are indulged in because they are thought to have some relevance to the world of real physical phenomena. But I would question those who argue that scientific fictions have more relevance to our experience in the world than literary fictions. In fact, I find the two remarkably consistent, even to the point of their availability for experimental verification. Consider, for instance, Einstein's thought experiments, which were clearly central to his development of relativity theory. They narrate situations that could never exist, as when he imagines himself traveling through space at the speed of light next to a light wave. At the same time, it is possible through historical research to determine with a fair degree of precision which aspects of *The Scarlet Letter* represent people, places, and objects that actually existed in Puritan New England. The point of fictions, unlike hypotheses, therefore, is not to assert potentially factual arguments in a tentative way, but to construct overtly fictional situations in order to shape our perceptions of the real world and isolate specific aspects of it (like Hester's love or Dimmesdale's guilt or a "very great mass of active material, so great that no neutrons are lost through the surface" or a "material so pure that no neutrons are lost in other ways than by fission") in order to further our understanding of them.

In one sense, of course, the *Primer*'s general façade could with some justice be called fictional, for it is constructed of a rhetoric that, as we have seen, refuses to acknowledge any tentativeness or historical contingency. But this particular passage also exhibits a more overt dependence on fictions, in the sense I have just outlined. When Serber urges his audience to "consider a very great mass of active material, so great that no neutrons are lost through the surface and assume the material so pure that no neutrons are lost in other ways than by fission," he is asking them to indulge in such a fiction. The material "25" to which the passage refers did not exist at the time except in microgram quantities.[23] As he points out later in the *Primer*, "Ordinary uranium as it occurs in nature contains about 1/140 of 25, the rest being 28 except for a very small amount of 24" (13). The effort to do anything factual with "a very great mass of active material," therefore, would require

a very great effort of human enterprise. In order to make an atomic bomb with uranium the United States had to separate the 1/140th part of U235 from the

The Los Alamos Primer

139 parts of U238 in natural uranium when the only difference between the two for purposes of separating them was their mass. Most of the two billion dollars that the wartime program to develop the atomic bomb—the Manhattan Project—spent was invested in building the vast machinery necessary to separate uranium.[24]

Even by the end of the war, the best purity achieved was 89 percent—a far cry from the assumption of a "material so pure that no neutrons are lost in other ways than by fission." Furthermore, no matter how great a quantity of uranium might eventually be available, no amount would be "so great that no neutrons are lost through the surface." In fact, the bigger the sample of uranium, the more neutrons were bound to be lost in this way (though the percentage of neutrons lost relative to the total number of neutrons in the sample would decline with increasing size). So Serber's instructions to his readers remained, even after atomic weapons themselves became fact, an indulgence in fiction.[25]

Serber's use of fictions in this passage should not be considered a quirky intrusion on the objective rhetoric of science. On the contrary, his method exemplifies a central technique of the scientific method, without which he and the discipline would be hard pressed to construct their descriptions of nature.[26] By indulging in fictions where physical facts are lacking or inaccessible to the senses, science traditionally extends its ability to delimit and describe the chaotic mish-mash of the experiential world, in something very like what Robert Frost describes as "a momentary stay against confusion." From these initial fictions, scientific communities, unlike their literary counterparts, go on to produce consistent, narrowly defined, and experimentally verifiable descriptions of nature. Yet in the process of piecing together these descriptions, such fictions employ creative agency and thereby introduce a subjective and potentially contentious voice into the uniform objectivity of scientific prose. Scientists can evaluate factual claims against repeatable experimental manipulations of the physical world (with varying degrees of success); but this method does not apply to judging the propriety of fictions. Disagreements over which fictions to pursue can expose underlying personal opinions and sometimes lead to open controversies among larger groups of scientists. Therefore, in constructing a scientific community such as Los Alamos, it was particularly important to define its dominant fictions from the start.

Serber and Condon return repeatedly throughout the *Primer* to the words "consider" and "suppose," in every context from the interpretation of existing experimental results to proposals for potential lines of research:

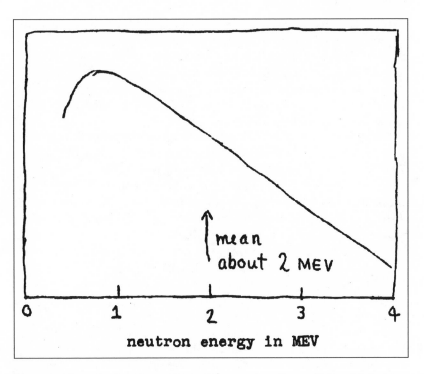

neutron energy in MEV

Illustration from the *Los Alamos Primer*. (Courtesy Los Alamos National Laboratory Archives.) The extract that follows is part of the text that originally accompanied the illustration in the *Primer*:

One can give a quite satisfactory interpretation of the energy distribution in [the figure] by supposing it to result from evaporation of neutrons from the fission product nuclei with a temperature of about ½ Mev. (19)

In this passage, for example, they structure their reading of the experimentally determined distribution of neutron energy illustrated in the figure by organizing it around the metaphor of "evaporation." The "quite satisfactory interpretation" that this reading provides is, in itself, fictional, but it performs a crucial function in helping to define the basic assumptions upon which the work at Los Alamos will be based. In this case, Serber derives his fiction directly from an existing fiction previously employed by Frisch and Meitner in their interpretation of the experimental evidence of fission. The latter explained the process of a heavy nucleus dividing into lighter elements by imagining atomic nuclei as unstable drops of liquid which could be made to fluctuate so wildly that they split in two. Serber extends this implicit narrative in his own passage, hypothesizing that these pieces of the split nuclei could be thought of as giving off neutrons in the same way a drop of water releases vapor molecules through evaporation. In this way, he uses his fictional explanation not only to indoctrinate his readers in a particular conceptual model, but also to establish further its authority by linking it with those of the established tradition of subatomic research represented by the work of Frisch and Meitner.

The fictional character of this passage is not limited to its ideational level but extends to the level of the grammar itself. Consider the phrases: "One can give a quite satisfactory interpretation . . . by supposing it to result from evaporation of neutrons." It is unusual for scientific prose to call attention to the agency involved in its descriptions, even in the abstract third person form we see here. Likewise, "give" stands out because formal scientific prose usually favors passive constructions rather than active ones. So this sentence would most commonly be expressed more along these lines: "A satisfactory interpretation may be derived. . . ." But a grammatical avoidance of agency is pointless here: The source of the "satisfactory interpretation" is clearly the individual human imagination and its ability to produce fictions. Consequently, Serber turns to the more informal rhetoric of shoptalk, echoing the way two scientists might discuss a conceptual problem in the laboratory.

In other passages, Serber also uses fictional narratives to suggest specific lines of research:

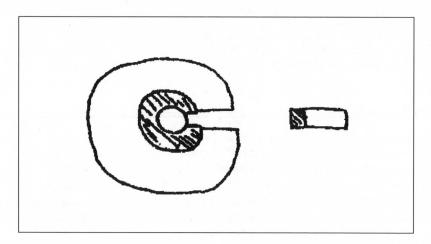

Illustration from the *Los Alamos Primer*. (Courtesy Los Alamos National Laboratory Archives.) The extract that follows is part of the text that originally accompanied the illustration in the *Primer*:

Suppose we had an arrangement in which for example ν' would increase of its own accord from a low value like 0.01 up to a value 10 to 50 times greater. The firing problem would be simplified by the low initial value of ν', and the efficiency would be maintained by the tendency to develop a high value of ν' as the reaction proceeds. It may be that a method of this kind will be absolutely essential for utilization of 49 owing to the difficulties of high neutron background from (α, n) reactions with the impurities as already discussed. The simplest scheme which might be autocatalytic is indicated in the sketch [see figure] where the active material is disposed in a hollow shell. Suppose that when the firing plug is in place one has just the critical mass for this configuration. If as the reaction proceeds the expansion were to proceed only inward, it is easy to see from diffusion theory that ν' would increase. Of course in actual fact it will proceed outward (tending to decrease ν') as well as inward and outward expansion would in reality give the dominant effect. (61)

In this passage, Serber ventures outside the realm of "reality" and "actual fact." Even more than in Section 3, his supposings here have little basis in experimental fact. Yet he apparently feels these speculations are sufficiently important to take up the time of his colleagues, though he has already reminded us of the many pressing demands on their attention. In effect, this passage demonstrates the *Primer*'s assumption that the dissemination of a fictional narrative capable of directing the course of their labors—"suppose we had an arrangement in which . . ."—was as important as the construction of a laboratory in which to engage in those labors.

The fictional character of this passage does not end there, however. In his preface to the commercial edition of the *Primer*, Serber reveals what the text itself only hints at: the inclusion of the autocatalytic hypothesis was in part an intentional red herring designed to defuse tensions within the project by convincing a senior scientist, who had originated the idea, that it was being considered seriously. Serber describes the genesis of the idea at a summer conference in 1942:

Edward Teller is a disaster to any organization. Later, at Los Alamos, he would exasperate Charlotte [Serber's wife and the Los Alamos librarian], because he would start a project—a school for the bright young guys the Army supplied us, for example, the Special Engineering Detachment people—and when it was established, he would walk away and someone else would have to do it. Edward wasn't a villain at the time of the summer conference; he was one of our friends, but he started bringing in all kinds of wild ideas. Edward was always full of ideas. One, for example, was the idea of having absorbers built into the nuclear material of the bomb, so as to have one big core with absorbers that the explosion would compress, which would progressively reduce their effectiveness and make the nuclear material more and more critical—what the *Primer* calls autocatalytic schemes.[27]

The Los Alamos Primer

So why did Serber include such a "wild idea" in the highly compressed text of the *Primer*? In part, the limited information available to the Los Alamites required them to pursue many fantastic lines of research in their rush to find the quickest possible route to a working bomb, so that the distinction between potentially viable hypotheses and overt fictions was at times difficult to maintain. But at least as important was Serber's desire to placate Teller, "one of our friends" and an important ally to have in the struggle to lure other talented physicists to Los Alamos.

By including Teller's scheme in the final "Autocatalytic Methods" section of the *Primer*, Serber promoted an overt fiction in order to pass off a second, implicit fiction as fact—to make Teller believe that his idea constituted an important, and respected, contribution to the bomb effort. Nor was this the only occasion on which Teller would be handled in this way: his insistence on interjecting his ideas for a "Super" fusion bomb into meetings on the simpler fission bomb finally led Oppenheimer to appoint Teller the leader of a separate research group at Los Alamos devoted to this pet project. In doing so, Oppenheimer had no illusion of Teller's work being directly useful to the Manhattan Project, but it helped the project indirectly by getting Teller out from under his colleagues' feet.[28]

This situation illustrates the difficulty involved in distinguishing between fictions and hypotheses in certain circumstances. To Teller, the autocatalytic method and the hydrogen bomb represented important hypotheses; but as far as the Manhattan Project was concerned, they remained pure fiction. Indeed, they forced Teller's colleagues into further fictions designed to placate him and prevent him from unduly disrupting work on the Hill. But, at the same time, Oppenheimer, for example, had to be careful not to make his fictional belief in the Super too convincing in order not to tempt other key scientists into joining Teller. So Serber, likewise, had to incorporate sufficient qualifiers into the *Primer* text to prevent anyone from taking its "wild ideas" too seriously: "Of course *in actual fact* it will proceed outward (tending to decrease v') as well as inward and outward expansion would *in reality* give the dominant effect."

As this suggests, the Los Alamites were well aware of their dependence on fictions. Indeed, Serber and Condon frequently admit the implausibility of their fictions yet continue to pursue them:

10. Simplest Estimate of Minimum Size of Bomb
Let us consider a homogenous material in which the neutron number is v and the mean-time between fissions is τ. In Sec. 3 we estimated $\tau = 10^{-8}$ sec. for uranium. Then if N is the number of neutrons in unit volume we have

$$\dot{N} + \operatorname{div} j = \frac{\nu - 1}{\tau} N$$

. . . Assume a solution whose time dependence is of the form

$$\Delta N_1 + \frac{-\nu' + \nu - 1}{D_\tau} N_1 = 0$$

. . . In the simple case in which we are dealing with a sphere of radius R, we may suppose that N_1 is spherically symmetric.

At $r = R$ we would have, on simple theory $N_1 = 0$. (In point of fact $N_1 > 0$ due to the effect of the mean free path's not being small compared with R, but this will not be considered here.) (25–26)

"In point of fact," the "facts" of the case are not as important here as the speculative model that Serber and Condon choose to "consider." Their goal is simplicity and their medium mathematics. But their rhetorical stance is overtly that of fiction because they believe that this approach offers them the best hope of orienting the Los Alamos community toward the achievement of its particular goals. In this context, it becomes clear that the scientific "facts" being pursued by the Los Alamites were not necessarily hard and fast natural phenomena. Of course, real facts remained central to the project: the average number of neutrons emitted in the fissioning of each isotope of uranium and plutonium; the speed with which a chain reaction blows apart the active material once it becomes critical. All science attempts as direct a confrontation with natural phenomena as possible; all good scientists are rigorous in their efforts to test their descriptions against the phenomena they describe. So the Los Alamites' "satisfactory interpretations" betray their fictional elements to a greater degree than most scientific descriptions.

As this passage indicates, "satisfactory" in the *Primer* does not mean "factual." Due to the limitations of our senses, subatomic physicists deal with natural facts tangentially, through the dense media of experimental apparatuses and symbolic constructions. Similarly, due to the exigencies of military research, scientists do not always have the leisure to work through the fictional elements of their descriptions to a fully realized theoretical formalism. When they describe atomic nuclei as tiny drops of liquid matter, therefore, physicists engage with a factual world, but they do so through the imaginative creation of "satisfactory" fictions. Nuclei are not, "in point of fact," drops at all. Yet this does not negate the utility of the description: by consciously indulging in this fiction, physicists are able to conceive of nuclear phenomena in a way that leads them to a practical manipulative and predictive power over them in a timely fashion. So Serber and Condon feel secure in acknowledging the fictional character of their neutron density model because they believe it offers a "satisfactory interpretation" in the circumstances.

The Physics of Fiction

One might well ask at this point why scholars have not made more of the use of fictions in physics, if it is as well-established a procedure as I have suggested. I will offer two related answers. First, fictions generally play a role in the formative stages of a scientific theory, prior to the completion of its formal structures, and this means that fictions appear in sources that rarely reach a wide audience, such as notebooks, laboratory discussions, and correspondence. In contrast with published articles and textbooks that tend to present highly polished accounts of fully developed theories and their correspondence to empirical data, sources in which the mediating role of fiction is visible are only beginning to receive the attention they deserve. Second, the traditional emphasis of science on the representation of empirical data, and the close correlation between those data and our sensory experience, tended to allow scientists to ignore or discount the fictional element of their own thinking—until the period immediately preceding the Manhattan Project itself. In an effort to elaborate on these points, and to provide further substantiation of my claim regarding this fictional aspect of physics, I will now turn to a brief consideration of the remarks of a prominent physicist on the subject.

In the Herbert Spencer lecture at Oxford, on June 10, 1933, Einstein devoted some time to a consideration of "the purely fictitious character of the fundamentals of scientific theory."[29] Not surprisingly, he suggests that this characterization contradicts notions regarding the factual authority of science that we inherited from the eighteenth and nineteenth centuries. So "Newton, the first creator of a comprehensive, workable system of theoretical physics, still believed that the basic concepts and laws of his system could be derived from experience."[30] Einstein goes on to suggest that Newton's confidence seemed justified, by and large: "Actually the concepts of time and space appeared at that time to present no difficulties. The concepts of mass, inertia, and force, and the laws connecting them, seemed to be drawn directly from experience."[31] Yet even then there were aspects of this assumption that troubled Newton:

We can indeed see from Newton's formulation of it that the concept of absolute space, which comprised that of absolute rest, made him feel uncomfortable; he realized that there seemed to be nothing in experience corresponding to this last concept. He was also not quite comfortable about the introduction of forces operating at a distance. But the tremendous practical success of his doctrines may well have prevented him and the physicists of the eighteenth and nineteenth centuries from recognizing the fictitious character of the foundations of his system.[32]

By the time Einstein addressed his Oxford audience, however, he felt there could be no doubt: "The fictitious character of fundamental principles is perfectly evident from the fact that we can point to two essentially different principles, both of which correspond with experience to a large extent; this proves at the same time that every attempt at a logical deduction of the basic concepts and postulates of mechanics from elementary experiences is doomed to failure."[33]

In arguing against the possibility of deriving "the basic concepts and postulates of mechanics" by means of rational extrapolation from empirical facts, Einstein refers to Bohr's complementarity principle that "two essentially different principles," such as waves and particles, can both "correspond with experience." As I suggested in Chapter 2, Bohr's principle called for a recognition and exploitation of the metaphorical character of much scientific description. Even though Einstein disagreed with Bohr's use of complementarity to justify the existing quantum mechanical formalism, he recognized the essential truth of Bohr's basic observation; in his Oxford lecture he took it even further, contending that the underpinnings of our mechanical theories are not only metaphorical, but fictional:

The structure of the system is the work of reason; the empirical contents and their mutual relations must find their representation in the conclusions of the theory. In the possibility of such a representation lie [sic] the sole value and justification of the whole system, and especially of the concepts and fundamental principles which underlie it. Apart from that, these latter are free inventions of the human intellect, which cannot be justified either by the nature of that intellect or in any other fashion a priori."[34]

Einstein is not suggesting that science does not correspond to empirical fact; rather, "The empirical contents and their mutual relations *must* find their representation in the conclusions of the theory." When this is not the case, there is no science, for this is "the sole value and justification of the whole system" of science. But he does insist that "the concepts and fundamental principles which underlie" a scientific theory are "free inventions of the human intellect" that need maintain no regular relation to empirical fact. These fictions perform a mediating function between empirical facts—which often bear no resemblance to our sensory experience and therefore make no "sense"—and rational thought—on which scientific theories are constructed and which bears no *a priori* relation to the empirical level, despite the classical illusion that such a relation exists.

What then are the consequences of the insight that fiction plays a significant role in the construction of scientific theories? Most immediately, it forces us to acknowledge that physics and literature are in closer conceptual proximity than we are used to granting. The existence of fictions in both disciplines creates a point of contact between them, an interface that might lead us to expect some slippage between them. Neither exists in a social vacuum. If both make use of the conceptual mode of fiction, we should not be surprised to find some degree of interaction, despite the extensive and ongoing efforts of practitioners of both disciplines to claim a unique social and conceptual space for their creations. And, indeed, such interaction exists—at least in the case of the Manhattan Project.

Recall, for example, Leo Szilard's response to H. G. Wells's novel *The World Set Free*, described in the Introduction.[35] Wells's fiction of "atomic bombs" managed a crossing between Snow's Two Cultures, transforming its original appearance in a novel to the status of a scientific fiction capable of directing the efforts of thousands of scientists and the expenditure of billions of dollars. This transformation was possible, I would argue, in large part because fictions are already an active part of the practices of science. No new conceptual space was required: Wells's basic fiction was a conceptual model ready-made to serve Szilard as a means of organizing the empirical phenomena of radioactivity and nuclear fission when they finally became manifest as scientific "facts." Did Wells's fiction play an important role in the construction of nuclear weapons? Yes. Was it necessary for their construction? No. Szilard was not the only scientist convinced of the practical possibility of exploiting fission in the construction of a weapon; many scientists conceived of this possibility without the benefit of having read Wells's novel. But in doing so they too, no less than Szilard, were making use of a fiction. The issue is not where the fiction originated, for it originated in many parallel sites. But *The World Set Free* and its influence on Szilard demonstrate that a given fiction is not solely the property of either literature or physics. A single fiction may perform an integral function in *both* disciplines.

Conclusion

While it has proven convenient in the past to conceive of physics as a world unto itself, a discipline devoted wholly to facts and deriving its principles more or less independently, without regard for its social context, as Bacon and many others since have claimed, such a discipline is impossible in practical terms, as the construction of Los Alamos demonstrates. The physics of nuclear weapons, as described in the *Primer*, relies on a range of rhetorical techniques, including those of fiction; and as it calls upon resources from an array of social circumstances, it cannot claim detachment from those circumstances, though it often attempts to do just that. Our understanding of physics, and its social consequences, will benefit from a recognition of these facts and the ongoing exploration to which such a recognition must lead us.

A better understanding need not threaten physicists or their practice of the discipline. Physicists have amply demonstrated the power and utility of their practices; nothing I have said diminishes the importance of physics in the least. Indeed, it is precisely because of the power of physics in our lives that "we"—both the general public and physicists themselves—need to understand it more thoroughly. Failure to understand has real consequences. Not, perhaps, in the production of scientific knowledge and artifacts, but certainly in their adoption into society and their use. Nuclear weapons would have been developed with or without *The World Set Free*, but would the Los Alamites have been able to play a more productive role in determining their use if they had better understood the fictions that were driving their development? There is no way to answer this question, of course—but the fact that we can propose it introduces intriguing possibilities for the future, possibilities that depend on our understanding of the past.

Consider, for example, the effects of a passage from the *Primer* like this one:

12. Damage
Several kinds of damage will be caused by the bomb. . . .
This points roughly to the kind of results which may be expected from a device of the kind we hope to make. Since the one factor that determines the damage is the energy release, our aim is simply to get as much energy from the explosion as we can. And since the materials we use are very precious, we are constrained to do this with as high an efficiency as possible. (35–36)

The language in this selection exhibits the stress of its different rhetorical approaches. On the one hand, it engages in stunning acts of understatement: "destruction" and "death" appear only in muted and transmuted forms as "damage," "results," and "efficiency." Likewise, the passive voice elides agency—"damage will be caused" and "results . . . may be expected"—and the authors portray themselves as "constrained to do this" by the inescapable fact of its possibility. Yet, on the other hand, the authors use a highly subjective language, speaking of "hope" and "precious" materials. They put themselves center stage and refer actively to "our aim" and "the materials we use." In the end, as its focus shifts back and forth between a "bomb" and a "device," in and out of impersonal scientific prose, the passage strains to contain the various pressures acting on the scientists in the Manhattan Project, from the need for military effectiveness, to the conventions of scientific objectivity, to each individual scientist's sense of moral involvement in the work at hand.

The ambiguity entailed in this rhetorical mix allows two good individuals to engage in a rather ruthless chain of reasoning. The phrase "our aim is simply," for example, quickly and easily glosses over a vastly complex moral decision. In fact, most of the scientists at Los Alamos never had the opportunity to make a decision regarding the use of the bomb. Their decision consisted of a determination to join an effort to ensure that the Allies had atomic weapons before Hitler. Until their work on the bomb was completed, only a few scientists at Los Alamos sought any opportunity to influence the use to which the fruits of their labor would be put. On meeting with apparent indifference, even these few quickly abandoned their efforts. Yet in most circumstances, these individuals would have been far from indifferent. After this work was done, many of these scientists became active in efforts to change the ways in which these weapons were being used in our society. But the genie was already out of the bottle, and changing existing social practices proved much harder than it might have been to shape them before they had gotten properly going.

What in the context of Los Alamos prevented these powerful and conscientious individuals from acting while they were involved in constructing these weapons? One factor, I would suggest, was their lack of understanding of the character and effects of the rhetoric on which their enterprise was founded. As we have seen, the *Primer* defines the Los Alamites' aim strictly in terms of optimal energy release. In this context, certain arguments seem to make indisputable sense: "Since the materials we use are very precious, we are constrained to do this with as high an efficiency as possible." But the violence of the logic becomes clear when we remember that this line hinges on the implicit assumption that "materials" are more "precious" than human lives. In effect, what this passage asserts, without ever saying it in so many words, is that nature itself requires the Los Alamites to be the most effective killers possible. Can rhetoric play a role in shaping the actions of human beings? Countless episodes in history suggest that it can. Could the construction of the Los Alamos laboratory be another such instance?

My point is not to portray the Los Alamites as monsters—indeed, my experience suggests that the majority (including the authors of the *Primer*) were exemplary human beings. I do mean to point out, however, that a particular, complex rhetorical dynamic was central to their ability to do their work *without* being monsters. Their role as agents of destruction is far from their minds. Yet causing the damage described in the *Primer* remains at the heart of their intentions. How can they be simultaneously aware and seemingly oblivious? As I have demonstrated, the *Primer* mixes rhetorics associated with vastly different social contexts, and in doing so it creates a remarkably flexible vehicle for organizing and shaping the Los Alamites' conceptual engagement with their work. The language that enjoins us to "suppose the lifetime of a neutron in the tamper is α/τ" (30) is at once literary and scientific. It asks us to conceive of neutrons in terms of lifetimes in the same document that refuses to depict the lives of the bomb's victims. This mixture, ultimately, allows the construction of a community dedicated to killing human beings and destroying their cities because it transforms these consequences into "the kind of results which may be expected from a device of the kind we hope to make." The key here is not denial, though undoubtedly some Los Alamites have denied the consequences of their work. Rather, the Los Alamos community was founded on the confrontation and containment of disruptive conceptions within the practices of science itself by means of complex rhetorical practices.

"N" Building and typical terrain, Los Alamos Laboratory. (Courtesy Los Alamos National Laboratory Archives.)

5 A CITY ON "THE HILL"

DECODING LIFE AT LOS ALAMOS

The Italian navigator has just landed in the new world.
—Arthur Compton to James Conant

On December 2, 1942, just months before scientists began arriving at Los Alamos, the Manhattan Project celebrated its first major success. After an extended period of theoretical speculation, experimentation, administrative planning, recruitment, requisitioning of equipment, negotiation with university sponsors, and manual labor, the scientists of the Metallurgical Laboratory division, led by the Italian physicist Enrico Fermi, completed construction of the world's first operational nuclear pile in a doubles squash court under the west stands of the University of Chicago's Stagg Field.[1] The pile "contained 771,000 pounds of graphite, 80,590 pounds of uranium oxide and 12,400 pounds of uranium metal,"[2] all laboriously placed by hand in fifty-seven layers to form a flattened sphere with a diameter of seven and three-quarters meters at its equator. While forty-one people looked on, Fermi directed the slow removal of the last cadmium control rod, half a foot at a time. At 3:50 in the afternoon, "Fermi raised his hand. 'The pile has gone critical,' he announced."[3] Four and a half minutes later, the control rod was replaced and the nuclear chain reaction subsided. The pile had achieved a power output of one-half watt.

The United States government had spent one million dollars and devoted an extraordinary amount of human labor to produce approximately enough energy to lift one of the forty-five thousand 19-pound graphite bricks used in its construction to the top of the pile. The scientists were elated. That afternoon, Arthur Compton, director of the MET Lab, called James Conant, president of Harvard University and chairman of the National Defense Research Council, which oversaw all scientific work with military implications in the United States. As Compton later remembered:

He knew of the critical experiment on which we were engaged, but he had not expected results so soon. We talked as usual in an extemporaneous code:

"The Italian navigator has just landed in the new world," I told him. "The earth was not as large as he had supposed"—meaning that the pile of uranium and graphite needed to bring about the reaction was smaller than anticipated—"so he arrived earlier than expected."

"Were the natives friendly?" Conant asked.

"Everyone landed safe and happy."[4]

Although the ostensible purpose of the "extemporaneous code" that frames this message was to control access to the information it conveys, it hardly needs decoding. Indeed, the only "key" it requires is a knowledge of the pile's existence, perhaps along with an awareness of its creator's nationality and the vaguely earthlike shape of the pile. Given that basic knowledge, the code is so simple that Conant feels able to respond immediately in kind.

We should not, however, be lulled into assuming that Compton's code was therefore a simple communicative act. For instance, it is important to recognize that any use of code involves its users in two contrary activities: Janus-like efforts to communicate information and to prevent its communication. For the moment, let us assume that the means by which Compton's code communicates is as obvious as it appears. But how does this code protect the information it conveys? Compton would have believed his use of the Columbus metaphor to be an appropriate basis for a code precisely because all metaphor represents its tenor—in this case, Compton's message—in terms of a relatively *arbitrary* vehicle— Columbus's landing in the New World. The arbitrariness of this connection would have served as a (limited) defense against the dissemination of Compton's and Conant's meaning to any potential eavesdropper by making it difficult to trace their thinking backwards across the gap from vehicle to tenor.

Two important caveats must be made here, however. First, the use of the Columbus metaphor calls attention to itself as a rhetorical device. Compton could have chosen a less obtrusive metaphor that would have functioned more subtly—and therefore, one would assume, more effectively—as a code. For instance, he could have used Fermi's Manhattan Project alias, Henry Farmer, to construct a less obvious but, to Conant, equally "telling" narrative: "Our friend Farmer just returned from climbing the mountain. He reached the summit more quickly than he had expected. The view was magnificent." Instead, the Columbus vehicle actively advertises its function as a protective armature, alerting even an unsuspicious listener that someone was trying to communicate *and* keep secret something of great significance. Why did Compton, despite his clear desire to protect the news of Fermi's successful experiment, allow himself to indulge in this more "poetic" metaphor at the expense of more certain secrecy?

This question, which I will attempt to answer in what follows, leads to my second caveat. Compton's choice of vehicle was not, after all, entirely arbitrary. Some of the factors determining his choice are obvious: Fermi's nationality, the shape of the pile. Others require greater effort to uncover. Perhaps most significantly, Compton's extemporaneous code was not an isolated use of the rhetoric of exploration and discovery within the context of the Manhattan Project. Instances occur at every level of the project, especially at Los Alamos: from scientists' eyewitness accounts of the Trinity Test to their narratives of daily life, from anecdotes of their work on the bomb to descriptions of the science that made it possible. This rhetoric was so prevalent, in fact, that the official history of the project, sponsored by the United States Atomic Energy Commission, bore the title *The New World*.[5] Yet none of this answers the question—indeed, it only makes the question more pressing: Why did so many Manhattan Project scientists find metaphors and narratives of exploration and discovery so compelling as vehicles in their attempts to describe their own experience?

Although Compton and Conant would have had no way of knowing how prevalent these metaphors would become at Los Alamos, and the Los Alamites, for their part, were unaware of Compton's extemporaneous code, there was far more than coincidence at work here. In both the squash court at Stagg Field and the laboratory in the New Mexican desert, scientists were at work on a project that challenged traditional notions of the purpose and conduct of their discipline. Subatomic physics had been perhaps the most abstract and esoteric branch of science; in the Manhattan Project it was suddenly practical in the extreme, charged with the production of a new technology, a physical "gadget." Physicists had thought of their discipline as a pure search for knowledge; suddenly this purity was compromised by the effort to construct weapons of mass destruction. Science had been academic; here it was military, bending every effort toward the creation of a workable means of killing people. In their efforts to reshape their thought and practices to meet these challenges, Manhattan Project scientists became immersed in a profound transformation of their personal, social, and disciplinary lives.

The sudden reclassification of scientific knowledge as military, requiring a new consciousness of "security" and observation of rules of secrecy, was only one manifestation of this transformation.[6] Its influence, however, was felt far beyond the new security fences that ringed the Manhattan Project laboratories and the ubiquitous "G-2" security

personnel, extending into the most intimate and personal family relationships. Scientists who had once shared the day-to-day details of
their work with their spouses now refused to offer even the most vague
idea of why they were being asked to uproot themselves and move to
an undisclosed location for an unspecified amount of time. As Ruth
Marshak recalls:

I was one of the women thus bound for an unknown and secret place. "I can
tell you nothing about it," my husband said. "We're going away, that's all."
This made me feel a little like the heroine of a melodrama. . . . Where was I
going and why was I going there? I plied my husband with questions which
he steadfastly refused to answer.
    "Be very careful what you say," he warned me over and over again. As if I,
confused and distraught, knew anything which might be of aid and comfort to
the enemy! German agents could probably tell me a thing or two, I reflected
bitterly.[7]

Security concerns were so pervasive and compelling that they overrode the habits and inclinations of the scientists and their loved ones,
threatening (and sometimes destroying) the health of their relationships.
On the one hand, this resulted in a kind of enforced depersonaliza-
tion, expressed by Marshak as a feeling that she was "the heroine of
a melodrama." On the other hand, it is important to note that such
representations of their experience in fictional or metaphorical forms
offered these "confused and distraught" Manhattan Project personnel
(both men and women, scientists and spouses) a significant means of
responding to the disjunctions they experienced and ameliorating their
emotional impact.

Secrecy was, therefore, only part of the story behind the Manhattan
Project personnel's use of the rhetoric of exploration and discovery. The
need that Compton and Conant felt to speak in code is emblematic
of a much larger dynamic within the Manhattan Project: the need its
members felt to exert control over unsettled and frightening circumstances through symbolic forms of language. The twined desires to
communicate and to obfuscate involved the Manhattan Project scientists
in a complex form of representation—one that constantly subverts itself,
censoring its own articulations and emphasizing its purposeful silences.
Ironically, the effort to gain control over the dissemination of their
meanings—inspired in part by the pressures of military secrecy that
led them to feel a need to speak in veiled terms—actually led them
into a revealing use of language, for any attempt to control implies
the existence of elements perceived as disruptive or threatening. To the
extent that an effort to control such disruption is successful, it must

itself manifest the elements it seeks to control, just as an immune system tailors antibodies to a particular antigen.

Most of the Manhattan Project scientists, of course, were not used to laboring to conceal their meanings. Previously, their efforts had been focused in the opposite direction: to express an understanding of natural phenomena as clearly and unambiguously as possible. But this goal was not in itself as unambiguous as might at first appear. Consider, for example, the growth of an elaborate technical vocabulary that constitutes an inevitable feature of every branch of science. The overt function of specialized taxonomic diction in scientific communication is to excise connotative, or metaphorical, elements and to emphasize denotative, or literal, representation: to make language more unambiguous. But a second, implicit effect of a specialized vocabulary is to create a community of speakers based on their knowledge, compared with others' ignorance, of its terms. As a result, clear communication does not necessarily correspond to accessible communication, and prior to World War II, scientists increasingly found themselves in the position of speaking a language foreign to nonspecialists. Their efforts were, therefore, more often directed toward rendering their meanings *more* rather than *less* accessible; the apparent need to censor their own publications, their conversations with friends and family, even their technical exchanges with colleagues, confronted them with an unfamiliar and troubling task.

One of the ways in which individuals in the Manhattan Project responded to this simultaneous need to communicate and conceal was, as Compton's extemporaneous code suggests, by turning to metaphorical language. As I have indicated in previous chapters, this mode of language was familiar to scientists even within the daily practice of their discipline—and, through Bohr's complementarity principle, at an increasingly self-conscious level. It was even more commonly used and accepted, of course, in the context of scientific popularizations, and most familiar in its broader social uses in literature and everyday conversation. Metaphor, therefore, offered these scientists an available and apparently natural means of "encoding" their experiences—one that proved to be particularly effective for several reasons. As I have already suggested, the relationship between tenor and vehicle can be arbitrary, enhancing its usefulness as a code. This arbitrary relationship also permits a large degree of freedom in choosing the vehicle of communication, allowing one to draw on a body of allusions and assumptions—a representational history—common to both speaker and auditor. This assists the speaker in shaping a code that will communicate more effectively, enhancing the intended auditor's efforts to interpret the speaker's meaning and hindering the efforts of any unintended auditor who lacks this shared symbolic base.

Ironically, of course, we do not generally think of metaphorical language—or, more broadly, the language of narrative fiction—as a kind of code. It functions ostensibly to extend meanings, not limit them; to assist our understanding of experience, not hinder it. As Hayden White suggests:

> We can make sense of sets of events in a number of different ways. One of the ways is to subsume the events under the causal laws which may have governed their concatenation in order to produce the particular configuration that the events appear to assume when considered as "effects" of mechanical forces. This is the way of scientific explanation. Another way we make sense of a set of events which appears strange, enigmatic, or mysterious in its immediate manifestations is to encode the set in terms of culturally provided categories, such as metaphysical concepts, religious beliefs, or story forms. The effect of such encodations is to familiarize the unfamiliar. . . . The original strangeness, mystery, or exoticism of the events is dispelled, and they take on a familiar aspect, not in their details, but in their functions as elements of a familiar kind of configuration. They are rendered comprehensible by being subsumed under the categories of the plot structure in which they are encoded as a story of a particular kind.[8]

Compton's extemporaneous decision "to encode" the events of Fermi's successful creation of a nuclear chain reaction "in terms of culturally provided categories" can, therefore, usefully be thought of as an extension of what White identifies as a common human response to the "strange, enigmatic, or mysterious"—for certainly these and other, similar terms have often been applied to the work of the Manhattan Project, by scientists and laymen alike.

I would, however, qualify White's assertion that "the original strangeness, mystery, or exoticism of the events is dispelled." I agree that the sensation of such an exorcism (or normalization) is one of the effects that encourages our use of metaphor and narrative in "making sense of events." But Compton's literal "code" suggests that we should take White's metaphorical use of the term "to encode" more seriously than perhaps he did himself. In particular, I would argue that the disruptive elements of our experience are not "dispelled" by metaphor, but encoded: inscribed in a system of symbolic relations that grants us a measure of control over their interpretation, both on the part of our auditors and ourselves, as White describes. The control we gain in this way is mediated by "culturally provided categories" over which we have little or no direct control. Therefore, just as a literary author cannot determine all of the meanings inherent in the use of a particular metaphor or narrative, we should not assume that anyone—including the Los Alamites—can completely control the interpretation of their experiences. In particular, the elements we most wish to control are not dispelled; rather, they remain encoded in our symbolic structures and thereby potentially accessible to subsequent analysis and interpretation.

In this chapter, I will attempt to apply this principle to the Los Alamites' use of metaphors and narratives of exploration and discovery. Like Frisch's detective-scientist, the figure of the explorer-scientist points to a complex interplay between personal and social forms of agency. This dialectic assumes two forms that are especially important to my study: the relation between the individual scientist and his immediate social circumstances, on the one hand, and between the individual and the scientific tradition, on the other. In this and the following chapter, I will examine each of these relationships in some detail, for I believe that in this context it is possible to learn a great deal not only about the ways in which the Los Alamites conceived of their work but also about the ways in which they *did not* conceive of it. Finally, in this and the next two chapters, I will argue that the discursive practices through which the Los Alamites encoded their experiences are of particular importance for two reasons. First, they provide our most direct access to those experiences; and second, they have played a central role in shaping our social interpretations of the Los Alamites and their work, and of nuclear weapons themselves.

The Social Space of Los Alamos

One could argue that the Los Alamos scientists realized the age-old dream of a scientific community removed from its social context. Indeed, the Los Alamos laboratory *was* truly distinct from the surrounding society—a distinction purposely sought in the choice of its isolated setting and rigorously maintained by miles of fences, armed guards, attack dogs, and a system of color-coded IDs, each of which granted a different level of clearance and access to different parts of the laboratory. Even the Los Alamites' more distant social connections (via telephone and mail) were limited and constantly monitored by censors. From a certain perspective, at least, Site Y looked a great deal like Bacon's fiction of a scientific New Atlantis.

A complementary reading, however, reminds us that despite its artificial physical separation from the rest of society, Los Alamos was one of the most glaring intersections of science with its larger social context in history. The laboratory's isolation was, in fact, a direct product of its immediate social significance: without a general awareness of this significance, the elaborate measures that separated it from society would never have been contemplated; and without active ties to other social entities (government, military, university), no such measures would have been possible. Indeed, the means by which this community was constructed involved its scientific members in a bargain with the military as consequential as anything represented in the _Blegdamsvej Faust_. And just as its authors turned in that play to literary language to represent, enact, and contain the conflicts and disruptions they were experiencing in the development of quantum mechanics, the Los Alamites also reached beyond the conventional boundaries of scientific rhetoric for language to represent the "new world" in which they found themselves.

The bargain through which the Los Alamos scientists agreed to collaborate with the military had a profound impact on military and scientific practices alike, both at Los Alamos and afterward, as well as on popular conceptions of each "discipline." In the ten years from the founding of Los Alamos in 1943 to the first test of an American hydrogen bomb, for example, physics went through a transformation at least as dramatic as it had during the quantum revolution. Oppenheimer's experience, to take an emblematic example, demonstrates many aspects of that transformation. His role as scientific director of Los Alamos inaugurated a new breed of scientist: the scientist-administrator.[9] Through this role, he gained tremendous power and prestige: he was pictured on the covers of numerous national magazines; he was instrumental in the formation of national policy; he was given countless honors and awards; he was even invited to be Einstein's boss at the Institute for Advanced Study in Princeton.

At the same time, there was another side to the bargain: his work became increasingly "social" and he no longer engaged directly in scientific work (unless we allow our notion of "scientific" to include the variety of social activities—policy-making, administration, education— on which science in our normal sense directly depends). He was also enmeshed in political conflict: vilified by his political opponents as a communist sympathizer, he was eventually removed from his advisory positions, stripped of his security clearance, and denied access to any technical information related to nuclear weapons—including many of his own writings—largely as a result of his opposition to the development of hydrogen bombs.[10] In this context, Oppenheimer's remarks on "the sense of option in knowledge" that frame my examination of the _Blegdamsvej Faust_ take on an additional significance. Published in 1960, they reflect his intimate and painful experience of the bargains, with their intricate exchange of power and vulnerability, that accompany socially successful knowledge structures such as quantum mechanics.

Oppenheimer's experience manifests some of the consequences of the bargain into which the Los Alamites began to enter in the spring of 1943. But what did it look like to them at the time? The dominant concern was, of course, their belief that subatomic physics offered an important means—perhaps the only means—of defeating imperial fascism. The point of common ground on which their alliance with the military was founded was this sense of purpose that overrode other considerations and created a willingness to place the social good above the personal or even the disciplinary. And there *were* other considerations: Neither the scientists nor the soldiers involved in the collaboration were enthusiastic about the partnership. Many soldiers assigned to the project felt that they had been forced into a backwater that offered them no opportunity to contribute meaningfully to the war effort. The scientists, for their part, were often contemptuous of any military involvement in scientific activity and eager to pounce on any instance of military bungling—of which there were enough to confirm the scientists' worst suspicions. Each group felt a deep-seated mistrust for the other; and each group struggled (with some self-righteousness) to bring the collaboration closer to its own expectations and procedures.

For a considerable period, for example, the military expected the scientists to accept commissions as officers in the army. As Leslie Groves, the military commander of the Manhattan Project, recalls: "This provision was based on the practice that had been followed successfully in World War I with the development of certain chemical warfare products. Conant had participated in one of these projects, and had found the system satisfactory."[11] The scientists, however, saw things differently and strongly resisted this and other military dictates, such as the army's efforts to impose strict compartmentalization within the Los Alamos laboratory: "Groves would have preferred each scientist to know only about the work on which he was directly involved."[12] But even when Groves did give in to the *"prima donnas,"* it was more or less a pyrrhic victory: "General Groves may not have gotten his way in militarizing the personnel of the site; but the environment within which they would work would be military with a vengeance: military-designed, military-built, as quickly, and violently, and cheaply as could possibly be."[13]

Nor did the practical submission of the Los Alamites to the military end there. The military retained control over all of the documents they produced—including lab reports, memoranda, correspondence, minutes of meetings, and the *Los Alamos Primer*—through the tactic of classification. Between 1947 and 1961, for instance, Los Alamite David

Hawkins was denied access to the official "technical, administrative, and policy-making history of the wartime Laboratory" that he had himself written.[14] Even an isotope chart complied by Emilio Segrè and his wife Elfriede was classified, and when it was declassified after the war, "More than fifty thousand copies were sold without our getting any royalties."[15] The military also tried to control what sort of documents *could* be written; personal diaries, for example, were forbidden. Indeed, military influence extended even to the level of what scientific work could and could not be done on the site; the Los Alamites were obliged to abandon many promising leads that appeared in the course of their extensive research because, no matter how worthwhile they may have appeared from the scientists' perspective, they were tangential to the military concerns of the project.

The idealism with which the Los Alamites had plunged, willy-nilly, into this strange project was, therefore, strained by the actions of their military partners and the exigencies of war. "These residents were intelligent people, and they had been asked to relinquish their independence of mind to a higher authority. Now everyday matters made them less and less sure of their bargain, more and more suspicious of the authority to whom they had deferred."[16] Here "everyday matters" refers to the conditions in which both scientific work and everyday life at Los Alamos operated. The Tech Area, for example, was "incredibly dirty, overcrowded, and badly equipped [and] in a state of continuous crisis."[17] Even when the scientists and military agreed on what needed to be done, there was often a great deal of confusion over how (and where and when) to do it. John Manley retained vivid memories of his efforts to set up Van de Graaff and Cockcroft–Walton accelerators:

The Van de Graaffs were very heavy instruments and the accelerator from Illinois was a vertical machine which required a basement, so we'd specified that a basement be excavated for that machine and that there must be a good foundation under the Van de Graaff accelerators. Cost and construction time could obviously be saved if they selected the terrain properly. . . . There are enough jokes about the way of the Army so you can guess what I saw [when I later arrived at Los Alamos]. The basement for the Illinois Cockcroft–Walton had been dug out of solid rock and that rock debris taken over to the other end of the building and used for fill under the Van de Graaffs, where there was supposed to be a good foundation. This was my introduction to the Army Engineers.[18]

Added to these frustrations within the Tech Area were the endless difficulties of what the residents thought of as a "frontier life." These ranged from minor inconveniences to severe discomforts, bordering at times on life-threatening situations. "On the furniture and on the floor, everywhere, was a continuous heavy layer of dust, and here and there were piles like miniature sand dunes."[19] The boilers in each apartment block were too big to work properly, and the plumbing was makeshift, so there were constant problems with "overheated water, hot water in cold water taps, hot water even in the toilets."[20] Water, in fact, was probably the chief source of trouble:

Our water, squeezed from suspect and distant sources, could not be considered pure and undefiled. Even when the town was small, typhoid shots were strongly recommended. Sometimes it seemed a formalism to call the fluid water, for our pipes apparently yielded unadulterated chlorine. The soldier entrusted with the task of purification set about his job with so much enthusiasm that he was soon in bed with chlorine poisoning.

Nor did the problems end there: "Our electric power was uncertain. Our water supply ran out," when, one winter, the main supply pipe froze solid and could not be thawed for several months: "Crisis succeeded crisis. Everything went wrong."[21]

In the face of these social pressures, and the feelings of dislocation and fear that went along with uprooting themselves and moving thousands of miles to found a secret, military community in an unfamiliar landscape, the Los Alamites frequently turned to the language of exploration and discovery, as if only a heightened rhetoric were capable of describing their experiences. Marshak, for instance, "felt akin to the pioneer women accompanying their husbands across the uncharted plains westward, alert to danger, resigned to the fact that they journeyed, for weal or for woe, into the Unknown."[22] Victor Weisskopf, too, sounds like a shipmate of Columbus as he remembers his impression of the Jemez Mountains above the Pajarito Plateau: "Elevations of more than 7,000 feet rose like green islands out of the dry New Mexican desert."[23] Bebe Caldes, the wife of a laboratory group leader, "felt like a pioneer woman."[24] For his part, Hawkins wished that in his history of Los Alamos he could have emulated the style "of a Bernal Díaz in his chronicle of the conquest of Mexico."[25] Carson Mark would also have been glad to be master of such a style, for as they drove up the narrow, cliff-hugging road to the top of the Pajarito Plateau, his wife remembers him asserting, "No doubt this is among the most fantastic of the works of nature."[26] And John Manley, in trying to "convey a correct impression of the beginnings of this new laboratory and its people," suggests: "Perhaps it could be called a new civilization colonizing this Pajarito Plateau of northern New Mexico some 800 years after the first known permanent inhabitants."[27]

The immediate inspiration for the Los Alamites' use of the rhetoric of exploration and discovery is still apparent in the setting of their New

A City on "The Hill"

Mexican laboratory north of Santa Fe. Even today, the approach to Los Alamos tempts visitors to imagine themselves as explorers following the narrow, muddy waters of the Rio Grande as they wind among low, rolling, sun-baked hills dotted with scrub brush. To the west, the sandstone cliffs of the Pajarito Plateau rise toward the volcanic range of the Jemez Mountains and the largest caldera in the world. Some twenty miles to the east, a second line of mountains, the Sangre de Cristos, dominates the eastern edge of the valley. Like many of this region's geographical features, these mountains were named by the Spanish explorers and colonists of the sixteenth and seventeenth centuries, who saw the evening sun shade the slopes a rich, blood red. Not surprisingly, having survived journeys of over five hundred miles through rough, inhospitable terrain to reach this spot, these explorers saw a deep significance in the physical details of this land. So the names they left behind speak of the beauty and the terror they encountered here and of their struggle to contain it with words: Sangre de Cristo, Socorro, Sierra Oscuro, Jornada del Muerto. Three hundred years later, when the first Manhattan Project scientists arrived at Los Alamos in 1943, the area remained a remote, forbidding, even dangerous part of the New World—a place that still inspired extravagant or reverent names: Omega, Satan Pass, Truth or Consequences, Trinity.

What is perhaps most significant is that the Los Alamites found themselves in a landscape radically different from the familiar surroundings they left behind in London, Copenhagen, New York, Rome, Chicago, or Berlin. Many came from academic positions at major research universities with well-equipped labs where they had the freedom to pursue their own research projects. As they rode in army jeeps over the twenty-five miles of rutted dirt roads from Santa Fe up onto the Los Alamos mesa, they entered a wilderness that had changed very little from the days of the Spanish explorers. Many of these scientists were Europeans who had recently arrived in the United States as refugees from Nazi aggression and thus were already acutely aware of their displacement into a New World. Even among the American scientists who journeyed to Los Alamos, few had ever visited the Southwest before. Indeed, in New Mexico, most of the Manhattan Project scientists encountered a world that seemed almost as new to them as it had to the intrepid explorers of the sixteenth century. Here vast distances disoriented those used to the close confines of urban life, imposing new perspectives and unfamiliar meanings on the well-worn phrases and equations of civilized life. Here a day-long trek down to the San Ildefonso Pueblo for the ritual dances of a Native American festival replaced an evening out at the opera or theater. Here the strange scents of piñon and juniper lent even the most conventional debates an odor of new import.

In this context, it may seem natural, even inevitable, that the Los Alamites turned to the language of exploration and discovery to describe their experience of the landscape surrounding the atomic bomb laboratory at Site Y. Like the Spanish explorers and then the North American colonists of the nineteenth century, the Los Alamites entered a world new to them, which they construed as a discovery. Indeed, this vast, beautiful, and intimidating land makes it all too easy to assume that such rhetoric is entirely natural and to examine it no further. But the apparent ease of such a rhetorical move should not distract us from an examination of its surprisingly complex representation of the Los Alamites' reasons for being there and of their relations to the land and its indigenous peoples. This rhetoric did far more than describe in heightened language the grandeur and discomfort of the setting. If we look below the "inevitable" surface of the Los Alamites' language, we will come to a better understanding of the subtle work being performed by their discursive practices.

Individual and Society

In using a descriptive rhetoric that developed during Renaissance voyages of exploration and discovery, the Los Alamites were employing a kind of shorthand—a symbolic medium complete with its own conventions and interpretive orthodoxy. They were, in effect, encoding their experiences in a rhetoric that concealed as much as it communicated. For example, contrary to its metaphorical representations, although the Los Alamites were newcomers to the land, the land itself clearly was not "new," except insofar as their arrival transformed it. And, like each group of newcomers before them, the Los Alamites did not accept the territory as it was; rather, they claimed it with the intent of shaping it to meet their needs. Ultimately, whether they did so intentionally or not (and most did not), their participation in this appropriation of geographical space involved them in a social dynamic that we can, in turn, observe being both played out and concealed in their rhetoric.

When Hugh Richards, a Los Alamos physicist, for instance, playfully reports in a self-published memoir that "Usually there was negligible precipitation until the Indians did their rain dances in June," several layers of meaning are embedded in this code. Most obviously, he is reporting something about the weather. But at the same time, he communicates a layered sense of his own relationship to that weather. First, his reference to Indian society and its customs introduces an exotic element that conveys a sense of how alien the place felt. Second, his remark identifies the Indians as part of the natural landscape, inseparable from the weather itself. Third, it reinforces this sense of alienation by suggesting his own lack of control in contrast to an overt attribution of control to the Indians. Fourth, it undercuts the speaker's alienation by invoking a second, dominant social context in which the reader joins him in laughing at the quaintness of Native American beliefs. Fifth, it establishes the speaker in the privileged position of knowing better than the natives. Sixth, the implicit basis of his privileged knowledge is, of course, science—a primary feature distinguishing his society from that of the Indians.

I have, obviously, oversimplified here—largely by trying to distinguish separate elements of what is properly a unified semiotic fabric—and in the process, I have exaggerated a most subtle dynamic. Overall, however, I have found that Richards's apparently offhand remark is just one instance of a pervasive tendency in the Los Alamites' representations to engage and subdue the disturbing, disruptive aspects of their experience and to incorporate an implicit justification of their activities within even their most casual utterances. The rhetoric of exploration and discovery contributes to this dynamic because, to take only one example, it tends to represents the old inhabitants as a feature of the geography, a natural phenomenon on par with the weather. In contrast to the Los Alamites' scientific work, the indigenous people's beliefs were seen as mildly comic, their customs quaint, and their practices interesting primarily as entertainment. From this point of view, they were comparable to a kind of natural resource and could be treated as such, whether they were employed as maids and janitors, drafted into the army, or simply cleared off the land by the efforts of the Army Corps of Engineers to transform the Los Alamos mesa into a military research facility. Their concerns were, self-evidently, secondary to the scientific and military needs of the newcomers.

There is little evidence of overt prejudice (at least in any virulent form) in the Los Alamites' accounts of their experiences. Indeed, in many of the Los Alamites' accounts, there is a notable sensitivity to the concerns of the "locals." Yet there is, throughout their rhetoric, a tension between what they want to say and what they feel compelled to say, between what their words gloss over and what they reveal regardless of the intentions of the individuals who utter them. In Segrè's autobiography, to offer another example, a photo caption identifies its subject as an "abandoned forester's cabin." Only a careful reader who pauses to wonder about the circumstances of its abandonment will realize that this phrase elides the agency of the forester as surely as the Army

Corps of Engineers that bought out or evicted him prior to Segrè's arrival.

Or consider this larger passage from Marshak:

There are Indian pueblos nearby with civilizations that were old in Coronado's time and have changed but little since. The predominant racial stock in Santa Fe and the country around it is Spanish-American. These people are descendants of the conquistadores [*sic*], have some Indian blood certainly, but still are completely different from the Indians in both appearance and customs. They till the soil much as their ancestors did centuries ago. I was to find both kinds of "natives" working at Los Alamos, and they gave a remarkable flair to the place. There they were, the oldest peoples of America, conservative, unchanged, barely touched by our industrial civilization, working on a project with an object so radical that it would be hailed as initiating a new age. The Indians and Spanish-Americans of New Mexico were the most unlikely of all peoples to be ushers to the atomic epoch.[28]

The perspective in this passage insists on its own distance from its subject—it could almost have been excerpted from a history textbook or from the first-person account of an explorer who wishes to present an "objective" account of what she observes. Its concerns and observations are clearly external to those of the people it describes. But what harm is there in that? None intended, certainly. Yet there are several points worth noting in this passage, and they are made even more significant by the sensitivity and good nature that characterize the author's voice throughout the essay.

A reader cannot suspect Marshak of wishing to assert her own superiority or to denigrate the "natives." And yet her rhetoric relegates them to a role either passive—"unchanged, barely touched"—or confined to providing local "color," when the only thing we are told about their work is that it "gave a remarkable flair to the place." It is not just that these people are treated as an interesting feature of the landscape. Even more telling is that they seem to have been interesting primarily as a function of their usefulness as icons in the Los Alamites' representations of their *own* experience. In Marshak's account, for instance, the "natives" serve as a marker for conservative forces, tradition, continuity. The larger point of the passage is not a consideration of what their lives were really like or what the Manhattan Project meant to them; rather, Marshak uses them as a foil, in contrast to which she constructs a powerful representation of the magnitude of the change brought about by her husband and the other scientists—and not, in the end, by any native ushers.

In this context, it should not surprise us that most accounts of life at Los Alamos during the war devote considerably more energy to describing the coal-burning stoves in the scientists' apartments than to depicting the lives and personalities of the indigenous population. This imbalance is not a result of the scientists' isolation from the locals; busloads of workers came to the site from the surrounding communities each day. As Phyllis Fisher recalls, a "straggling little army of Indian workers continued to appear on our hill daily."[29] Almost every scientist's household employed an Indian maid; the furnaces in every building were stoked by Spanish-American laborers; local men served as machinists, carpenters, electricians, janitors, mess-hall workers. The native population was in evidence wherever one turned. And yet even the most self-aware Los Alamites refer to the mesa as "our hill," while the local workers are "our maids" and "our boiler men."

Such references are not so much possessive as they are a manifestation of the Los Alamites' intense focus on their imported mission. They were not living normal lives: everything was disrupted or transformed; they were cut off from friends and family; they were forbidden to make friends with the locals; they could tell no one where they lived; their driver's licenses bore numbers instead of names; they could not even use words like "bomb," "physicist," or "chemist" among themselves for fear of being overheard by one of the "natives."[30] Their lives were, indeed, narrowly bound by the Manhattan Project within particular strictures of space, acquaintance, and language. And so the lives of those around them, who shared in the work and the hopes and fears of all the Project workers but were not part of the privileged scientific circle, were in their turn encoded and bound within the rhetoric used by the scientists and their families.

As a result, the majority of the Los Alamites' references to the native population are tinged in one way or another by a need to treat the locals as a reflective medium in which to display and examine issues important to the speakers. Weisskopf offers a striking instance of this in describing his "explorations" in the vicinity of Los Alamos:

We also explored the towns of the area. I will never forget our visits to the Indian and Spanish villages. In the adobe churches we discovered masterpieces of sculpture and painting combining Indian artistry with Spanish-Catholic tradition. I am still haunted by one wooden head of Christ, his penetrating eyes and his face mourning the fate of humankind. There was also a wooden chariot steered by Death in the person of an emaciated figure staring into infinite space and time. He aimed arrows at the beholder and touched my deepest roots of fear and awe.[31]

Weisskopf makes no effort to inquire after what these pieces might mean to the locals. Indeed there are no locals in the world of his description; it is a space inhabited by objects waiting, like a natural landscape, to be "discovered." Nor does he reflect on the collision of cultures that might have produced "masterpieces of sculpture and painting combining Indian artistry with Spanish-Catholic tradition." Instead, he describes an anthropomorphic scene in which two sculptures, imbued with the power to "mourn" and "stare" and "aim arrows," serve as powerful symbols for his own readings of them. These readings, in turn, appear to be based on externalizations of his own feelings about his role in building the first nuclear weapons—an account of which is, of course, the context for this little narrative of exploration and discovery.

One might go so far as to call this a kind of imaginative imperialism. Yet is it really so destructive? At best, it was probably no more burdensome to the locals than the various privations resulting from the "frontier conditions" were to the scientific personnel. Each group had to contend with different aspects of the dynamic through which they came in contact. Nor does this dynamic appear to have stood in the way of the largely friendly relations between the two groups. As Charlotte Serber, the Tech Area librarian, recalls, "The Indian girls were not always the cause of discontent and strife. [The Los Alamites were obliged to compete with one another to obtain maid service.] Some of us got to know them a little and found them a charming, friendly group."[32] Some of the Anglo residents waxed more rhapsodic over their Indian maids (and neighbors): "My great, big, beautiful Pascualita. . . . We had known Indians and been to their dances, but because of Pascualita we had the unique experience of going down to the pueblo and having lunch with the Peñas many times."[33] Pascualita, for her part, liked her employers well enough to name her daughter after a mountain she could see from their window. And when the war ended, Bernice Brode remembers that the "grand finale of our association with the Indians took place on a cold December night of 1945 when the square-dance group from the Hill was invited to a party at San Ildefonso."[34] Each group ate food provided by the other and tried to learn a few steps of the other's traditional dances.

What these encouraging tales of cooperation and cultural exchange obscure, however, is the fact that the effects of such interactions were distinctly uneven. While the locals came to Los Alamos to earn a living—sometimes as a result of having been forced out of their former livelihoods by the encroaching lab—their labor, in many cases, represented no more than a luxury to the Anglos who employed them. Furthermore, the travails of the scientists and their families were short-lived—they were, of course, free to return home after the war—and the less pleasant aspects of their experiences could, at any rate, be ameliorated simply by reconceiving of them as unfortunate but unavoidable consequences of their current adventures. The local participants were not, in general, so

A City on "The Hill"

fortunate. Their involvement in the Manhattan Project, even in the case of the locals who did not work at the site but were merely its neighbors, had far longer lasting and more consequential effects. Many locals had been permanently displaced by the laboratory. Unlike their "friends" the scientists, they had no homes to return to. Even their luckier neighbors, whose homes and communities were not absolutely commandeered by the military, had no choice but watch their lives being transformed by the Manhattan Project.

I am referring here to two related effects in particular. First, through their contact with the laboratory and its "civilized" residents, the locals were exposed to unfamiliar patterns and technologies of domestic life. The Los Alamites describe their maids, for example, as initially overwhelmed by modern conveniences such as vacuum cleaners and electric clothes wringers. They recount amusing anecdotes about these women's inability to master such "magical" devices. Yet soon these same devices—especially refrigerators—began to appear in local farm-

Enrico Fermi, physicist, and Maria Martinez, potter. (Courtesy Los Alamos Historical Museum.)

houses and pueblos, along with a wide array of store-bought furniture, machine-woven rugs, mass-produced clothing, and mail-order gizmos. The local population surrounding Los Alamos had gained through their jobs at the lab both exposure *and* access (in the form of income) to a new mode of life. Furthermore, by reaching toward this new life, they unavoidably turned away from parts of the lives they and their ancestors had known for hundreds or thousands of years. As Brode recalls, "We heard tales from Santa Fe people who knew the Indians well, that the influence of Los Alamos was deplorable, that we actually encouraged the Indians to break away from tradition."[35]

Brode goes on to describe a second effect of the lab's presence: "Most of us felt that many Indians were tired of being pressured to remain so traditional for the benefit of tourists and even their well-wishers."[36] Perhaps there was some truth to this rationalization—though it underscores the extent to which Anglos on both sides were speaking for the natives. But it also points out that the aspects of their traditional lives the locals did manage to hold on to tended to be those which were marketable. Richards's "rain dances" are one example. The famous black pottery of the region is another; as one Los Alamite writes,

The best potters of San Ildefonso and Santa Clara (the pueblos nearest Los Alamos) fell weeks and even months behind in the filling of orders. A phenomenal amount of black ware was produced, for the Los Alamos folk had an insatiable appetite for these plain, rich bowls, plates, vases, plaques, and candlesticks which would not shout "regional" too loudly when placed next to Wedgwood or pewter back home. It became almost impossible to buy a new piece not sanctioned by the taste of the Hill or to find a potter with the time to make one.[37]

In short, the native population around Los Alamos became largely dependent on the laboratory and its imported culture for their income, their clothing, their furnishings, their groceries, even what remnants of their own traditional culture they retained.

Conclusion

And is this bad? Surely that is for the individuals concerned to decide. My aim is not to render judgment (like most people, I am unqualified to do so); whether it is good or bad ultimately depends on one's perspective, and we should beware of trying to inhabit the locals' points of view to decide for them, either way. I merely hope to understand better this important but largely ignored dynamic.[38] In

particular, I am concerned with piercing the screen of the Los Alamites'
rhetoric—for, as we have seen, they tended to encode their experiences
in narrative and metaphorical language that promoted certain interpretations and suppressed others. My motivation is, in part, that I see a
danger here. An uncritical acceptance of such language can lead to the
development of blind spots, and these, in turn, can mislead us, as they
misled Segrè, into assuming that such narratives are unexceptional and
unexceptionable:

Once, immediately after the end of the war, when Elfriede was expecting our
second daughter, we went camping near a warm spring in a remote mountain
spot. Next morning we explored the surroundings and found a beautiful hole
of crystal clear warm water. We undressed and were enjoying the water, when
some Indians who had invisibly followed us politely explained, in Spanish,
that the spring was a holy place to them and invited us to decamp. On the
same outing we met a newly wed young Navajo couple on horseback in their
traditional attire. With the groom's permission we took pictures; the bride
objected because she believed that the picture would take away her soul.[39]

Imagine a tourist couple bathing in the baptismal font in Chartres
Cathedral. Would they be politely asked to "decamp"? Then that couple
encounters a pair of newlyweds, and despite the bride's objections, they
make a voodoo effigy of her in her bridal costume. Should we smile
gently at her simple fears?

Of course I'm being heavy-handed here. The point is not to defend
the helpless Indians or to portray Segrè as particularly ignorant or
pushy (though I am surprised that he does not seem more embarrassed
by his faux pas.) But I mean to emphasize my point because I do
believe that the consequences of this sort of analysis are, potentially,
considerable. At worst, such rhetoric can underwrite a habit of reading
the desires or interests of others in terms of one's own—in effect, one
can come to believe one's own code is not a code at all, but a true
and complete representation. In normal circumstances, this is unlikely
to lead to disastrous consequences; but the Manhattan Project hardly
represents normal circumstances. When the first plutonium bomb was
ready for testing in the New Mexican desert, for instance,

An Indian village, Carrizozo, located about sixty miles away, would have been
exposed to dangerous radiation levels if the wind were to shift. Measuring
stations were placed all over the region to monitor the spread of radioactivity
after the blast. For the sake of security we could not warn the village's residents.
Hidden away, out of sight of the population, sixty trucks stood ready to
evacuate them if needed. We could only imagine the turmoil in Carrizozo if it
became necessary to remove all its inhabitants in the early morning hours.[40]

In these circumstances, the ability of the Los Alamites to connect imaginatively with the lives of the "natives" was of extreme importance. As it happened (as far as we know), events turned out well for the residents of Carrizozo. But only a slight shift of the wind could have put the Los Alamites' imaginations to the test, and the consequences would have been measured in lives.

In this context, "We could only imagine" cuts two ways. On the one hand, it expresses a limitation of the speaker's ability (or at least his perception of his ability) to protect the local population from the radioactive fallout from a bomb he had detonated in their neighborhood. On the other hand, even that imaginative power is denied the locals. These circumstances, it seems to me, make it very important that we understand our stories and metaphors, the codes we use, and distinguish clearly what are real limitations and what are products of the language with which we express and conceal what we know. I will continue this task in the next chapter.

Robert Oppenheimer and Major Lex Stevens, scouting possible sites for the Trinity test. (Photo by Kenneth Bainbridge, courtesy AIP Emilio Segrè Visual Archives.)

6

NEW WORLDS, OLD WORDS

THE EXPLORATION AND

DISCOVERY OF NUCLEAR PHYSICS

In the preceding chapter, I argued for the significance of the Los Alamites' use of geographical rhetoric to encode their individual experiences of the new community they had constructed. Like all of us, they felt the need to understand and control the meaning of their experiences—and the drama, the uncertainties, and the hardship of their wartime lives gave them perhaps an even greater motivation. In part, they turned to metaphorical language to write their experiences—to externalize and reify them in a particular form. I have used the term "code" to describe this activity in order to emphasize several of its more important aspects: that it was motivated in part by wartime habits of secrecy, censorship, and coded language; that it conveys information in a form that requires interpretation; that this interpretation is guided by conventions associated with specific, preexisting uses of the "code" in particular cultural contexts (a kind of "key"); and, finally, that such metaphorical expressions also yield to careful analytic "cracking"—as I have tried to demonstrate. Yet I cannot claim the credit due a real code-breaker, for the "cracks" in the Los Alamites' uses of metaphors of exploration and discovery are inherent in the medium. Simply by observing the Los Alamites' rhetorical struggles with the unavoidable ambiguities of their descriptions, it is possible in effect to see inside their hopes and fears as they attempt to determine the meanings of their experiences.

Chapter 5 looked at a specific case of this dynamic, in the application of metaphors of exploration and discovery to the social space of Los Alamos. But the Los Alamites also invoked such rhetoric to make particular sense of the intellectual realm of physics on which their work in that social space depended. In the words of the Los Alamos physicists, their intellectual work, like its physical settings, constituted a conceptual landscape that had not yet been fully explored and that still held surprises for the scientists who had come to occupy it. Edward Teller, for example, refers to the time when "quantum mechanics was discovered"—

some twenty-five years before Los Alamos became a going concern—as the opening up of "a whole new world."[1] Similarly, Elsie McMillan remembers her husband on his way to the Trinity test confessing that "in spite of calculations, we are going into the unknown."[2]

These metaphors reveal a tendency to treat an intellectual landscape as if it existed in the same physical terms as a geographical territory. As careful analysis of their representational "codes" will reveal, this way of conceiving of their discipline involves the Los Alamites in an externalization of the intellectual structures of their science, and it therefore plays a significant role in their relationship to their work. In particular, it allows them to represent their discipline in ways that finesse the complex and shifting relationship between individual scientists and the scientific tradition, on the one hand, and between the scientific tradition and the natural world it is meant to describe, on the other. As I will show in detail in this chapter, the Los Alamites' metaphorical accounts of their experience balance claims for the power conferred on individual scientists by their participation in the scientific tradition with an emphasis on the independence of their discipline from the individuals who happened to make it their home at any given time; at the same time, these accounts also support an assumption central to the social authority of the sciences: scientific description is itself commensurate with the physical phenomena it describes.

The odd conjunction we saw in the last chapter, between the Los Alamites' disorienting encounter with new social phenomena and their imposition of an established order on those phenomena, illustrates the complexity of the dynamic with which their metaphors of exploration and discovery were engaged. This dynamic was no less complex in the scientific than in the social sphere, for, of course, these two spheres are closely related. Metaphorical language offered the Los Alamites a means of expressing their sense of dislocation while at the same time rationalizing their exercise of power in both its scientific and social dimensions. The Los Alamites' use of metaphors of exploration and discovery located them within a network of social meanings that extended in time and space far beyond the security fence ringing the top of the Los Alamos mesa. In doing so, it facilitated the scientists' practical engagement in their work by maintaining a traditional ideological foundation for their scientific activities. As in the preceding chapter, most of the examples here are drawn from narratives written for the general public, and it is important to our understanding of the ideological component of these narratives to bear in mind that they had a wide and varied audience: the educated lay reader, the authors' colleagues and family, potential critics, politicians and policymakers, and the Los Alamites themselves.

Old Novelty and Other Oxymorons

Like many of his colleagues, Robert Oppenheimer turned to metaphors of a new world to describe his complex response to the successful detonation of the first atomic bomb in the Jornada del Muerto desert. "When it went off, in the New Mexican dawn, that first atomic bomb . . . we knew that it was a new world, but even more we knew that novelty itself was a very old thing in human life, that all our ways are rooted in it."[3] Oppenheimer's words reflect the striking tensions inherent in the Los Alamites' attempts to describe the "extremely powerful bombs of a new type"[4] that they had built. These tensions center on a peculiar combination of radical and conservative elements which seem almost invariably to characterize their conceptions of these weapons. Many of the Los Alamites shared with Einstein, though they did not often express it as starkly, a sense that the advent of atomic weapons introduced a radical change in the conditions of human social existence.[5] Yet these same scientists maintained an equally strong belief in the continuity and benevolence of the scientific tradition that had produced these bombs.

For his part, Oppenheimer clearly wishes to convey an impression of the test's drama; his rhetoric suggests that we should interpret the construction of these weapons as a seminal event in human history comparable to Columbus's encounter with the New World's unexpected continents. The periodic rhythm of his phrasing builds from the understatement of "went off," through the specific details of "the New Mexican dawn" and "that atomic bomb"—as if his audience might have dozed off and forgotten which bomb he was discussing—to sweeping claims of a "new world," "human life," and "all our ways." Oppenheimer impresses his listeners with the significance of atomic weapons not by providing a detailed narrative of their effects but by invoking an existing rhetoric of geographical discovery.

Yet, at the same time, Oppenheimer's rhetoric also manifests a marked restraint. Indeed, he appears intentionally to undercut and mute the import of his own claims even as he puts them forward. For example, although he portrays his interpretation of the Trinity test in the authoritative terms of a collective knowledge shared by each of the witnesses—"we knew that it was a new world"—he subordinates that knowledge to a second, greater certainty: "but even more we knew that novelty itself was a very old thing in human life . . . ." In this way, Oppenheimer downplays the radical character of atomic weapons even as he asserts it with the phrase "new world." Likewise, his selection of tenses in this passage sets his declaration that the atomic bomb has engendered a new world comfortably in the past—"we *knew* that it *was* a new world"—where it can be examined as a historical fact in much the same way Columbus's discovery of the Americas is discussed at gatherings of professional historians. Oppenheimer's use of the new world metaphor itself locates his audience at a safe distance from the events he describes. Some three and a half centuries after Columbus's voyage, the "new world" had come to stand for a series of events of the greatest historical importance; but the disruptive consequences and the profound reshaping of the social fabric to which these events led had become known quantities, historical platitudes, and an essential part of the established order.[6]

Oppenheimer's description of his response to the Trinity test, therefore, involves an interplay of tensions between the new and the old, the radical and the conservative. Nor does Oppenheimer attempt to come down on one side or the other; he is neither sensationalistic nor dismissive regarding the implications of the Los Alamites' work. Instead, he leaves his audience with a perspective on atomic weapons that includes a curious mixture of novelty and tradition: "we *knew* that novelty itself *was* a very old thing in human life, that all our ways *are* rooted in it." Here novelty itself becomes the basis of an ongoing order. And while most of his utterance is in the past tense of historical reminiscence, Oppenheimer carefully brings home the implications of his interpretation by creating a present moment characterized simultaneously by the existence of radical, new forces—embodied in the destructive power of atomic weapons—and by the maintenance of a longstanding normality.

At stake here is the Los Alamites' conception of the scientific tradition and the place of individual agency—their own—within it. These two issues ultimately form two halves of a single concern: how the Los Alamites should evaluate their participation as scientists and as individuals in the development of a technology that would, at least potentially, transform the world. The responses of Oppenheimer and his colleagues to the Trinity test, their attempts to conceptualize the "foul and awesome display"[7] to which they had been witnesses, cannot be separated from their awareness of themselves as the agents of that discovery. On the one hand, the destruction of Hiroshima and Nagasaki inspired in them a new sense of their responsibility as individuals for the results of their work. On the other hand, the scale and success of the Manhattan Project forced these scientists to confront the power of the discipline to which they belonged. Never before had a scientific endeavor enlisted the coordinated efforts of so many scientists; never before had so significant a portion of the scientific community been directly involved in the production of military weapons. Should all the scientists who had contributed a cross-section analysis or a theoretical model of neutron absorption hold themselves personally responsible for the deaths of hundreds of thousands of Japanese civilians? Or, if they were not culpable, were they impotent? Had science itself become a new world, unfamiliar to its practitioners who were used to small laboratories and independent research projects, indifferent to their best intentions or their efforts to direct its course? And, perhaps most disturbingly, could it be that the scientific tradition led inevitably to this place? Could it be that the scientific method on which the great advances of the past three hundred years depended was itself a deterministic structure ineluctably directed toward the refinement of humanity's ability to manipulate nature, regardless of the consequences?

In the Manhattan Project, the interaction of these forces, which in general occurs as a subtext of science, occupies a position of relative prominence. As a result, the construction of the first atomic weapons offers an unusual opportunity for scholars interested in the history of science, for the Los Alamites' work involved a dramatic reshaping of the practices that had characterized scientific inquiry more or less since the time of Isaac Newton. Where science had been the province of independent researchers, small laboratories, and even, until the nineteenth century, amateurs, at Los Alamos it became the domain of government contracts, military supervision, and large, specialized professional staffs.

In another sense, however, the Manhattan Project represents a return to "normal" science in the aftermath of a revolution in modern physics. As discussed in the first two chapters, Max Planck's discovery of the quantum of action, Einstein's relativity theory, Heinsenberg's formulation of the uncertainty principle, and Bohr's championing of complementarity—each of these symbolic formulations presented a direct challenge to the existing structure of the scientific tradition and was at the same time an effort to rescue that tradition from the potentially destructive contradictions to which it had led. During the first three decades of the twentieth century, modern physics probed into the subatomic realm and came face to face with phenomena which contradicted the discipline's most fundamental assumptions, forcing a radical reevaluation of many of its founding principles. Out of this reevaluation came an understanding of the subatomic world that made the Manhattan Project possible. So the Los Alamites brought to their work a particularly vivid sense that their discipline involved confrontations with strange, new phenomena and an equally strong conviction that the vitality of the scientific tradition depended on their maintenance of its continuity in the face of such confrontations.

Beyond the immediate military consequences of their work, then, the Los Alamites' encounter with the radically new forces of atomic weapons assumes a second level of significance. When the Manhattan Project scientists speak of their experience in the New Mexican desert, their remarks also have a direct bearing on the scientific tradition that brought them there; and when they discuss the tradition itself, their observations are charged with an intense awareness of what it had led to in the Jornada del Muerto. In the Manhattan Project they found themselves caught between the productive and destructive aspects of their work: practitioners and representatives of a centuries-old scientific tradition and builders of the most terrible weapons in human history. Not surprisingly, the ways in which they describe their participation in the Manhattan Project and the tradition of science in general reflect the force of these concerns. Their rhetorical strategies manifest a consistent effort to seek out a balance among various competing powers: the natural forces they had to manipulate in their work, the creative energies of the scientific tradition, and their own individual agencies within that tradition. Interestingly, however, the Los Alamites do not simply attempt to minimize the negative effects of the tensions discussed above. Instead they shape their expressions of these tensions into a productive dynamic capable of ensuring the flexibility and strength of their discipline as they go about its business, constructing symbolic representations of recalcitrant and contradictory natural phenomena and competing for funding and social prestige among themselves and with other institutional forms of knowledge.

In an address entitled "Tradition and Discovery" delivered at the University of Puerto Rico in 1960, for instance, Oppenheimer engaged these tensions by invoking Columbus's first voyage as a model for more contemporary voyages of scientific discovery. On the most obvious level, Oppenheimer cites Columbus as an analogy for the "voyage of discovery" on which any serious scientist must necessarily embark. Like many of his colleagues, Oppenheimer turns to the travels of Columbus to convey his sense of the extraordinary position occupied by modern scientists. According to this model, scientists stand apart from other individuals as embodiments of the courage and rational acumen required for the exploration of the world around us: manning their laboratory apparatus like Columbus at the helm of the *Santa Maria*, dispelling common fears and preconceptions, leading their assistants (and eventually the rest of us) past the boundaries of the known world, and discovering the wonders that previously lay hidden as if awaiting us there. This conception clearly accords individual scientists a great deal of personal authority: to set out and follow up on a plan of exploration, to direct its course, and to claim the glory of its results.

The analogy between science and geographical exploration balances this vision of individual power, however, with a strong suggestion of individual submission to the tradition. Columbus was, after all, an agent of the Spanish throne. Furthermore, to a scientist, Columbus must also function as a cautionary example, for his inability to put aside preconceptions interfered with his perceptions of the new world he had discovered, leading him to erroneous assertions, ill-conceived actions, and a lonely, impoverished death. Therefore, Columbus serves Oppenheimer and his colleagues not only as an emblem of their authority but also as a reminder of the need to suppress their personal beliefs and opinions in favor of detached observation. The analogy holds in balance a conception of the immediate involvement of scientists in their exploratory activities, of their mastery of the terrain, with an insistence on their distanced relation and essential subservience in the process of exploration.

The flexibility and usefulness of this representation becomes immediately apparent in the vexed context of atomic weapons. Following the bombings of Hiroshima and Nagasaki, many of the Los Alamites experienced considerable distress at the thought that they were responsible for constructing such terrifying weapons. Conceiving of science in terms of a mental geography that exists apart from the scientists who practice it, and which they therefore encounter as an explorer might, offers a clear advantage in responding to these concerns, for it allows Joseph McKibben among others, to assert:

Nature left us very little choice. Very few of us were hoping that we could do it. Rather, we were hoping that we could not do it. But if it could be done, we wanted to get there first. We just have to accept science; we have to accept what we find in science, just as we accept the geography we live in.[8]

McKibben plays upon an objective characterization of the scientist's role to claim that the Los Alamites simply took their directions from the natural order; in fact, he insists that they went against their own inclinations in doing so: contrary to what they hoped to find, they found what was there. As a result, nature itself effectively exonerates the Los Alamites from moral culpability in their construction of atomic weapons.

Yet neither do the scientists wish to relinquish their authority entirely. Nature "left us very little choice," perhaps, but not "no choice." Within their larger submission to nature, the scientists remained volitional agents. "But if it could be done, we *wanted to* get there first." The expression of desire seems particularly pointed in the context of an otherwise frustrated wish to avoid the possible existence of atomic weapons. Furthermore, McKibben asserts the Los Alamites' agency in the process of "getting there first." Here we can see in action the complex interplay between the agency of individual scientists and the authority of the natural phenomena they examine, between "what they half create, /

And what perceive,"[9] that Oppenheimer and others established through their references to Columbus, new worlds, and great discoveries.

Also worth noting is McKibben's conflation of the terms "nature" and "science." He begins, "Nature left us very little choice"; just three lines later this becomes, "We just have to accept science . . . ." Metaphors of exploration and discovery represent a flexible power relationship between individuals and the natural world, but they also encourage belief in a direct correspondence between the symbolic structures of science and the phenomena those structures claim to represent. Indeed, the latter correspondence exists as a direct function of this particular relationship between scientists and their objects of study, for these metaphors position individual scientists as a medium between the natural and scientific orders. According to the exploration model, scientists are at once immersed in the natural world—braving the wide ocean sea, confronting the savage islander in his native home—and aloof from it, dispassionately observing everything in their surroundings. Immersion grants the scientists' descriptions immediacy and therefore authority; removal lends them objectivity and thus accuracy. The combination inspires McKibben's general equation of science and nature.

Despite McKibben's synonymous use of the terms, however, few scientists would resist acknowledging that they remain distinct. The natural order preceded the scientific, and science exists primarily as an attempt to describe nature. In the case of a contradiction between the natural and scientific orders, the link between them may be maintained only if one of them bends, and that one must be science. In the course of their inquiries, therefore, if we follow out the implications of the Columbus analogy, scientists inevitably carry the known structures of scientific knowledge into conflict with the unknown structures of the natural world. And so long as the scientific tradition acknowledges the priority of the natural order, it finds itself in a threatened position. Therefore, Oppenheimer's reference to Columbus quickly leads him to a rather startling assertion: "Terror attaches to new knowledge. . . . Even in discoveries which affect our ideas and even in abstract discoveries, there is this same sense of terror. I have found it among my colleagues and have recognized it in myself."[10] Surely this overstates the case. Can the work of a scientist at the microscope or blackboard fairly be described as involving actual "terror"? Of course, certain scientific undertakings do involve an overt and indisputable terror, the development of atomic weapons being a case in point. But Oppenheimer does not mean to restrict our attention to such extreme instances. The "terror" he refers to is far more widespread and resides in the word "new," being ostensibly the same emotion as that felt by Columbus's crew as they sailed beyond the limits of the known world and off into the unknown.[11] This terror results from a disruption of order, a destabilization of existing frames of reference, and it is an unavoidable part of the ongoing effort to construct scientific description as a consistent symbolic treatment of an effectively unbounded set of natural phenomena.

At this point, Oppenheimer has become entangled in the implications of his own metaphors and must struggle to control how they are interpreted. Portraying the work of scientists as a brave confrontation with the unknown necessarily implies the danger of making terrible discoveries, as in McKibben's reading of the discovery of atomic weapons. This serves as an important basis for Oppenheimer's construction of the authority of the scientist: an individual prepared to face the terrors of the natural world on behalf of humanity demands our respect just as any hero in the literature of great adventures.[12] But, at the same time, an assertion that the "terror" of new knowledge is an inevitable product of the scientific tradition, if we take it seriously, must make us question the costs associated with the discipline and, ultimately, it social worth. So Oppenheimer sets out to subdue this terror before it subverts the authority of the scientific tradition in support of which he introduced it in the first place.

In doing so, Oppenheimer calls upon the example of Columbus in a second, apparently contradictory manner reminiscent of his use of the phrase "the new world." In comparing contemporary scientific research to Columbus's voyage, Oppenheimer not only emphasizes the drama of modern science but also historicizes the terror of its search for new knowledge, partially defusing the threat of the unknown by associating it with the well-known. Put another way, he uses the historical figure of Columbus to remind us of the long tradition that serves as a secure foundation for the extravagant wanderings of contemporary scientists: although their journeys bring them face to face with terrifying unknowns, the long tradition of such encounters gives us confidence that eventually they will return safely to their "normal" lives. Thus Oppenheimer strives both to express his sense of the serious consequences of scientific inquiry—a sense that we should not trivialize, as the example of the atomic bomb reminds us—and at the same time to inspire our confidence in the ingenuity and historical pedigree of the scientific explorer.

Oppenheimer's attempt to balance the competing agencies of scientist, scientific artifact, and science itself forces him to confront the more subtle but equally troublesome conflict between apparently competing claims for the stability of the scientific tradition and for its ability to incorporate new information and account for new phenomena. To constitute a balance between these two essential facets of the tradition, he portrays the "terror" of new knowledge as both a consequence of and a stimulus to science. As we have seen, he implicitly uses the Columbus analogy to support his characterization of the "discovery" of new scientific knowledge as a potentially dangerous activity. Yet scientific inquiry does not in general pose a threat to the individual scientist so much as to its own structure of received knowledge. And precisely because he describes it as a tradition predicated, as the Columbus analogy suggests, on confrontations with the unknown, he constitutes science as a discipline not only capable of overcoming the threat of new knowledge but actually dependent on that threat. Thus the "terror" he invokes performs an essential role in the tradition it threatens in two senses. First, its existence supports his contention that science coincides with the physical exploration of the world. Second, it allows him to define the significance of science as a function of its ability to counteract the terror of the unknown.

Like the analogy between scientific inquiry and voyages of exploration and discovery, Oppenheimer's conception of the ways in which science overcomes the terror of new knowledge depends on a complex dynamic. As he explains: "[Scientific] knowledge is not just a collection of miscellaneous, unrelated things. It is not without order; order is what it is about. Its purpose is to discover, and in order to discover, to create the order which relates things with one another, and to reduce—though it certainly never eliminates—the arbitrary in our experience."[13] Scientific knowledge, in this conception, results from an amassing and ordering of discoveries. But a precondition of such discovery is the creation of "the order which relates things with one another." Which takes precedence? Oppenheimer's rhetoric seems to involve him in a chicken-versus-egg paradox, and so we see him struggling between competing demands of his own complex representation of scientific inquiry as, on the one hand, a plastic process of responding to the dictates of the natural world and, on the other hand, a stable framework that imbues its discoveries with sense and combats all that is arbitrary and terrifying.

The crux of Oppenheimer's representation is that it depends on an implicit conflation between process and system: "in order to discover, to create the order. . . ." The first use of the word "order" involves a process, a goal and motion toward it; the second denotes a static system. These two senses are not separate but cohabit within "the order which relates things." Yet they inherently contradict each other: stability implies fixity; process implies motion. To bind them together, he employs a single term to represent both kinds of "order," repeating the word four times in the space of two sentences and shifting its syntactical role slightly with each occurrence; in this way, he constitutes "order," like "terror," as a term that represents the cyclical process of science in which the product of its inquiries is also the origin of further activity.

The similarity of Oppenheimer's uses of terms like "terror" and "order" reveals an essential relation between them, for the terror of new knowledge arises as the direct result of the order which makes discovery possible, and the order of the scientific tradition develops out of the "arbitrary" terror which science seeks to reduce. He juxtaposes his recognition of the threat involved in new discoveries—that change is inimical to the order on which the scientific enterprise is predicated— with an assertion that science is at the same time the very process of discovery. Out of the combination, he creates a conception of science that is at once constitutive and receptive. As a system it is stable and determinate, directing the efforts of its practitioners; as a process of discovery it is flexible, responding to the contours of the territory it explores. By incorporating the source of change within the order that changes, both needs are balanced, though not, perhaps, finally reconciled, for despite its remarkable accomplishments, science "certainly never eliminates the arbitrary in our experience."

Oppenheimer's rhetorical energy, in engaging the epistemologically vulnerable points of science, helps in the end to assert the discipline's strength. By claiming that science combines a stable system of symbolic representations of nature with the dynamic ability to alter that structure and incorporate new or contradictory observations, he constructs an authoritative connection between scientific discourse and the natural world that most scientists, like McKibben, take for granted. But neither the character of the connection nor its implications should be accepted as inevitable or *a priori* facts. Oppenheimer's words demonstrate the kind of rhetorical activity that underlies such claims; they are, in fact, complex discursive constructs that encode the social assumptions on which much of the practical power of scientific practices rests. Moreover, the uses to which scientists put this power involve them in equally complex discursive activities, as we shall continue to see.

"The Safe Anchorage of Established Doctrine"

On the other side of the Atlantic, Oppenheimer's counterpart, Werner Heisenberg, head of the German effort to build an atomic bomb, described his work by means of the same analogy to Columbus's voyage to the New World. Like the comments of the Los Alamites examined earlier in this chapter, Heisenberg's remarks suggest the pervasiveness of this metaphorical conception within the scientific tradition in general.

New Worlds, Old Words

If I were asked what was Christopher Columbus' greatest achievement in discovering America, my answer would not be that he took advantage of the spherical shape of the earth to get to India by the western route—this idea had occurred to others before him—or that he prepared his expedition meticulously and rigged his ships most expertly—that, too, others could have done equally well. His most remarkable feat was the decision to leave the known regions of the world and sail westward, far beyond the point from which his provisions could have got him back home again.

In science, too, it is impossible to open up new territory unless one is prepared to leave the safe anchorage of established doctrine and run the risk of a hazardous leap forward.[14]

Heisenberg's use of the Columbus analogy, particularly his reference in the last few lines to "the risk of a hazardous leap forward," echoes Oppenheimer's contention that "terror attaches to new knowledge." While both Heisenberg and Oppenheimer remained well aware of the benefits to be derived from science, each had been the leader of a project dedicated to turning the tradition toward more ambiguous ends. Both men confront the darker implications of their discipline, and both use the same metaphors of exploration and discovery to do so.

Clearly, each man remains strongly aware of the hazards as well as the rewards of his discipline. Heisenberg, for instance, argues that reaping the benefits of science, like claiming and clearing a "new territory," inevitably involves a confrontation with real danger. Indeed, both men share a remarkably similar conception of the constitutive role of the "hazardous leap forward" in the progress of science. As we saw in Oppenheimer's account, "terror" may be conceived as driving the engine of science, invigorating its structures and refining its methods. It is important that we bear in mind, however, that this is only an interpretation; such an optimistic view is the product of a particular rhetorical stance rather than an absolute truth about the scientific tradition. Therefore, even among its many complex implications and dramatic consequences, an important but generally neglected feature of the work these men undertook during World War II was their use of metaphorical language to contain and transform potentially disruptive interpretations of their work.

Richard Feynman's claims for the practical power of science, in the last of his Messenger Lectures at Cornell University in 1964, for example, suggest a few of the implications involved in the representation of science by means of metaphors of exploration and discovery:

From experiments and information in a certain range you can guess what is going to happen in a region where no one has ever explored before. It is a little different from regular exploration in that [in scientific exploration] there are enough clues on the land discovered to guess what the land that has not been discovered is going to look like.[15]

Behind Feynman's remarks lies an implicit recognition that the ability to predict the behavior of previously unknown systems represents one of the primary sources of the authority of science. In this ability, science distinguishes itself from literal (one-to-one) description of natural phenomena. While literal description forms a primary basis for the orderly classification of observations, its direct applications are limited to the familiar ground of known experiences. Feynman implicitly asserts on behalf of science the power to transcend this limitation by abstracting catalogued observations into overarching systems of laws and then applying those laws to the formulation of further experimental observations and the manipulation of natural phenomena. In this process, prediction completes the cyclical correspondence between an abstract system of scientific laws and the concrete realm of phenomena to which they correspond. In doing so, prediction stands as proof of that correspondence between the symbolic discourse of science and the natural world it means to represent.

Consequently, scientific theories continue to be judged in large measure by their ability to predict unexpected phenomena. During a solar eclipse in South America in 1919, for example, a team of scientists confirmed Einstein's prediction, in his 1915 General Theory of Relativity, that electromagnetic radiation would interact with a gravitational field. In itself, this observation did little to further our knowledge of the natural world; yet it has become a landmark in the annals of science because of its role in authorizing Einstein's grand revision of the underlying assumptions of physics. Following a period of increasing awareness of the shortcomings of Newtonian mechanics when applied to atomic and electromagnetic phenomena, this revision reasserted the ability of science to formulate symbolic laws which not only describe natural phenomena but allow scientists the almost prophetic power to predict "what is going to happen in a region where no one has ever explored before."

One of the regions that had yet to be explored in 1915 was the subatomic realm in which neutrons collide with large nuclei, splitting them into elements with smaller atomic numbers. Einstein's famous equation, $E = mc^2$, gave scientists like Leo Szilard, Edward Teller, and Einstein himself, in their 1939 letter to Roosevelt, the ability to predict, before any such weapons had even entered a preliminary design stage, that great amounts of energy could be released in an explosive chain reaction of neutron–nucleus collisions. Furthermore, the credibility of such scientific soothsaying had been so well established by 1939 that the governments of several countries initiated development programs that would eventually cost billions of dollars based solely on the predictions of a handful of physicists. The atomic bomb, therefore, may be read as an instance of the power of scientific discourse to organize human observations of the natural world, to construct abstract symbolic representations of those observations, and to reapply such representations in the manipulation of the natural phenomena they describe.

Feynman's choice of an analogy will by now seem almost inevitable. We have already seen its prevalence in the discourse of his colleagues. Furthermore, we have seen its role in rhetorically constructing the equivalence of scientific descriptions and the natural order that is such a central assumption in the practice of science in its modern form. Indeed, the circular relationship between symbolic expression and physical phenomena on which the predictive power of science depends is itself an analogic structure. Feynman's turn to the rhetoric of exploration and discovery is not, therefore, just a cosmetic gesture—an effort to pretty up his lecture for a general audience—for it manifests as well as describes the discursive practices on which scientific knowledge, including its predictive powers, depends.

Interestingly, however, Feynman's analogy threatens the predictive power of science that it is meant to underwrite in the first place. This threat becomes clear in a comparison of Feynman's metaphors of exploration and discovery and McKibben's remarks examined earlier. McKibben, for example, makes his comments in a context that explicitly engages the issue of the Los Alamites' moral responsibility for the bombs they designed and built. As a result, he emphasizes the passivity of the scientific order by asserting its absolute correspondence to nature; in this way he minimizes the scientists' moral responsibility while at the same time maintaining the authority of science. Feynman's remarks, however, occur in a general lecture on the formation of new scientific laws, and he never questions the morality of the activity. Instead, Feynman plays on the power of scientific treatments of the natural world as a way of impressing on his audience the power and utility of his discipline. In this context, he finds the analogy's suggestion of a passive adherence to the contours of an existing geography restrictive, and in order to loosen the restraints he undercuts his analogy, arguing that science "is a little different from regular exploration . . . ."

Feynman, however, does not mean to abandon this proven analogy. So he plays down the tension even as he points it out: "It is *a little* different from regular exploration . . . ." This clearly understates the case, for one might argue that there are worlds of difference between Ernest Lawrence calibrating his cyclotron at Berkeley and Pánfilo de Narváez struggling

up the Gulf Coast of Florida. Yet geographical exploration, like experimental physics, does involve trying to predict the circumstances that
the explorer-scientist will encounter and the ultimate outcome of the
venture. Feynman could, therefore, easily have made far more of the
differences or omitted mentioning them at all. The fact that he refers to
exploration and discovery as he does suggests that he means neither
to accept such metaphors uncritically nor to reject them completely.
Instead, he attempts to negotiate a delicate balance between using and
questioning the exploration and discovery analogy.

In one sense, at least, it can come as no surprise that Feynman
expresses some discomfort with a too-comprehensive reliance on figurative language. His characteristically "lowbrow" locutions offer yet
another example of the undercurrent of skepticism regarding such
metaphorical language that is typical of scientists' attitudes toward their
work. Like many of his colleagues, Feynman felt a discomfort with
his dependence on metaphor and his language displays that feeling.
This discomfort stems from the fact that metaphor depends on the
very discursive complexities he employs it to conceal. Feynman and his
fellow Los Alamites turn to geographical metaphors in an effort to efface
the exegetical practices of their discipline: to suggest a direct correspondence between scientific laws and the phenomena they represent. Unlike
literature, which privileges its representational practices as a primary
attraction in themselves, science attempts to minimize any distinction
between its symbolic structures and the physical relationships they
purport to embody. Of course, few scientists would deny the difference
between the natural world and a symbolic representation of it; in fact,
all scientists struggle with just that disjunction on a daily basis. Yet
their struggle remains an attempt to bridge the gap, to diminish the
distinction, and to perfect the correspondence. In this struggle, they
make use of all the resources available to them, including, ironically, the
metaphorical forms of language they mistrust.

In effect, the representational power of science functions in direct
proportion to its success in effacing its representational practices. At
times, even the mere mention of "science" in an analysis of its proper
workings can serve as an unwelcome reminder of discursive limitations.
So Feynman elides the term. In the three penultimate paragraphs of *The
Character of Physical Law* in which the foregoing quotation occurs, he
does not use the word even once, despite the fact that his subject is the
culmination of the scientific tradition in a complete knowledge of the
natural world. In that culmination, "science" itself disappears, replaced
with an ambiguous "it": "It is a little different from regular exploration
in that there are enough clues on the land discovered to guess what the
land that has not been discovered is going to look like."

This is not to say that Feynman doubts himself or his claims on behalf of science; rather, he mistrusts his own dependence on metaphorical language. So he downplays his own rhetoric across the board, belittling his claims and clothing scientific prediction in the guise of guesswork rather than certainty: "From experiments and information in a certain range you can *guess* what is going to happen . . . ." Through a judicious use of apparently casual, even imprecise language, Feynman parlays his skeptical attitude into an implicit assertion of independence from the very rhetorical forms on which he depends.

Feynman was probably quite conscious of the irony involved in his rhetorical jockeying. His own descriptions of physics make frequent use of metaphorical language; and as a distinguished contributor to his discipline and something of a contrarian, he had to be aware that, as we saw in Chapters 1 and 2, scientific representation itself involves an essential dependence on analogy—in its broadest sense. Indeed, one could argue, as does Ralph Waldo Emerson, that "science is nothing but the finding of analogy."[16] Emerson uses the term "analogy" in a rather straightforward manner, to say that science seeks out the connections between apparently disparate natural facts. On the surface, there would seem to be nothing threatening in this activity. But Feynman's apparent skittishness (as representative of his colleagues mistrust of "rhetoric" in general) suggests that there is, in fact, a deeper terror involved in the metaphorical aspects of physics.

Earlier, I examined Oppenheimer's reference to the "terror" associated with "new knowledge." Now, in the context of Feynman's rhetorical jockeying, it is possible to identify two distinct sources of this terror, which merge in the use of metaphors of exploration and discovery. The first corresponds to the metaphorical vehicle: the physical circumstances of discovery. When we enter a new territory, whether that of the New World or of the subatomic realm, we can experience a disorientation and its resultant terror in much the same way an animal will respond to being removed from its familiar habitat. This terror results from new "knowledge" in the form of unfamiliar sensory input. We "know" what our senses experience by associating it with previous sensory data; but if some new input does not correspond to any pattern in our experience, we cannot process it quickly enough to avoid the fear that it may represent a threat to us. We react fearfully until we are able to "see" something by virtue of having encountered it before.

We can also feel a similar terror, however, to which no other animal is susceptible: the terror of intellectual dislocation. This level of terror is associated not so much with either the vehicle or the tenor of metaphors of exploration and discovery as with the abstract conceptual relationship between them. Most animals make meaning on a somatic level, as they associate various sets of sensory data. But we also experience meaning on an ideational level, and we do so largely through language. Therefore, we are liable to a terror based on our uses of language, and our inability to declare a real independence from our rhetorical practices can, at times, constitute a threat to the stability of our world. This may seem at first like a mild terror, but we should beware of underestimating its potency. Indeed, the metaphors we use to contain the world and make sense of it can easily become liabilities, either tying us to outmoded conceptions of the territory we inhabit or forcing us into unfamiliar, even threatening understandings.

Heisenberg summarizes an illustrative experience of one prominent colleague:

Einstein had devoted his life to probing into that objective world of physical processes which runs its course in space and time, independent of us, according to firm laws. The mathematical symbols of theoretical physics were also symbols of this objective world and as such enabled physicists to make statements about its future behavior. And now it was being asserted that, on the atomic scale, this objective world of time and space did not even exist and that the mathematical symbols of theoretical physics referred to possibilities rather than to facts. Einstein was not prepared to let us do what, to him, amounted to pulling the ground from under his feet.[17]

Despite his reputation as the author of a revolution in modern physics, Einstein worked within a largely traditional conception of the relationship between the "objective world of physical processes" and the verbal descriptions and "mathematical symbols of theoretical physics." As Heisenberg's account suggests, this conception corresponds to the geographical metaphors we examined in this chapter, which assert the potential equivalence of physical processes and our symbolic representations of them—the belief that it is possible for us to clamber out of Plato's cave, to survey the landscape around us, and to compare our shadowy constructions directly to the "objective world" by the light of day.

As Heisenberg points out, however, one of the implications of Einstein's work (on light quanta, one would assume) amounts to a refutation of the assumption of representational correspondences and an assertion that, on the contrary, "on the atomic scale, this objective world of time and space did not even exist." Since the macroscopic world of trains and thunderstorms is itself built up from "possibilities rather than facts," even the simplest, most apparently direct explorations of our physical terrain cannot, at some fundamental level, be relied on as absolute confirmation of the referentiality of our symbolic constructions. No wonder Einstein felt as if his colleagues, in following out the implications of his own writings, were "pulling the ground from under his feet": They were challenging the foundation of Einstein's traditional conception of scientific representation, embodied in the metaphorical description of science as the immediate exploration of an "objective world of time and space." But from this perspective, if no such firm "ground" existed, no "firm laws" could be formulated either, and science would have run into a dead end.

Of course science has done nothing of the kind. In fact, its institutional prestige and practical effect on our society and ourselves continue to flourish. But to many of the scientists who lived through the early years of nuclear physics, and particularly to those actively involved in shaping its practices and underlying assumptions, this was indeed, in Oppenheimer's terms, a "terrifying" time, as they saw the basis of their knowledge become less literal and more metaphorical. The "normal" discourse of science was disrupted, and the greatest scientists were those who acknowledged the necessity of confronting their representational dilemma and of making direct consideration of discursive practices an immediate part of their scientific activities, in much the same way the founders of modern science had done in the late Middle Ages and the Renaissance. Einstein's "thought experiments," Bohr's complementarity, Heisenberg's uncertainty principle, Schrödinger's cat—each of these contributions to early twentieth-century physics depended on an overt reevaluation of scientific representation.

Even Feynman, who downplays his dependence on the complex workings of his rhetoric by adopting a rough-hewn vernacular, ultimately acknowledges, in Bohr's terms, his suspension in language. Indeed, his contributions to physics depended on this acknowledgment: "In physics you have to have an understanding of the connection of words with the real world. It is necessary at the end to translate what you have figured out into English, into the world."[18] Interestingly, although Feynman entered physics after the sweeping transformations of the Quantum Revolution, his assertion that it is possible to work toward an "understanding of the connection of words with the real world" seems to be remarkably consistent with classical conceptions. How can this be? The key lies in a related shift during the first half of this century in physicists' conceptions of *both* the physical world *and* the language through which they described it.

The early quantum physicists inherited a belief that the physical world existed as an objective entity independent of our subjective experience of it, along with the conviction that this world obeyed fixed laws. Furthermore, they assumed that a stable language could be found to mediate between the objective world and their experience of it by expressing those laws. But the growing conviction that the world did not exist in this fixed form led to an increasing disorientation. As a result, some physicists found the language through which their colleagues tried to represent the world imprecise, incomplete, and, therefore, false. In this state of dissatisfaction with their apparent inability to represent this new world in ways that satisfied classical assumptions, the quantum physicists were forced into an overt reconsideration of their modes of representation that paralleled their reevaluation of what in the world they were trying to represent in the first place. By conceiving of the natural world in less objective terms, and by accepting a different set of standards by which to judge their representations, they found a way to incorporate the new, threatening knowledge they had discovered and thereby laid the groundwork for the highly successful work that "culminated" in the development of nuclear power.

The upshot was a new balance between the physicists' representational practices and their understanding of what they were representing. As Feynman's continued belief in the essential referentiality of language and the possibility of relating even the abstract symbols of mathematics to the physical world attests, this new quantum conception bears a striking surface resemblance to the classical balance. Yet there are differences. The "understanding" Feynman offers ultimately assumes the form of a comma, a disjunction: "into English, into the world." That disjunction allows for the maintenance of a sense of common ground shared by the old and new physics and, therefore, of the continuity of the tradition itself. Feynman's ostensible search for a link between "words" and "the real world" results in their equation as "English" and "the world." He engenders this equation by introducing a third term, "what you have figured out," which brings the two original terms together in their common distinction to it. This conjunction between representational system and physical world conforms in its most important aspects to the traditional vision of science as the consummation of a grand exploratory encounter with the geography of all Creation.

Feynman's version of this traditional paradigm, however, achieves a similar representational authority based on a subtly different set of assumptions. For example, classical mechanics was founded on an essentially Adamic vision of language as a stable medium that derived its authority from God and that, therefore, inherently corresponded to the created world. Feynman, on the other hand, assumes a far more flexible relationship between words and the world. Where classical physicists tried to determine whether the wave or the particle metaphor better "fit" the natural phenomena of electromagnetic radiation, Feynman, as a quantum physicist, accepted both metaphors as flawed and incomplete, but useful, descriptions. The main difference between these two practical representations of the physical world stems, in large part, from the ways in which each one uses language to draw, in Bohr's terms, "a partition between the subject which communicates and the object which is the content of the communication."[19] The classical view assumes that this partition, like the language that embodies it, exists as a fixed part of the natural landscape. The quantum view, as articulated by Bohr's complementarity principle, proposes a more arbitrary, contingent set of partitions.

The quantum method of partitioning subject from object allowed physicists to maintain their ideal of impartial observation; but at the same time, the new methods introduced new difficulties. Feynman responds to these difficulties by constructing his partition as a comma, an absence. "What you have figured out," stands, of course, for the system of scientific understanding itself—by most accounts a rather formidable edifice—but Feynman's language once again deflates its magnitude. Through this apparently simple device, he manages a curious but effective assertion of the power of his discipline. He implies that science occupies the ideal space between observer and observed, maintaining the possibility of an objective commerce between them through the medium of its rigorously coherent method. The apparently casual, almost incidental phrase, "what you have figured out," portrays science as a dynamic act of the mind, separate from either language or physical restraint but equally capable of being rendered "into English" or "into the world." This bidirectional ease of translation asserts the representational power of language as insistently as the classical tradition ever did and, in doing so, positions the conceptual system of science as a bridge between language and the natural world.

When the internal contradictions of the classical paradigm erupted in the early twentieth century, physicists found that they had to deal with the terrifying experience of feeling the metaphorical ground shaking under their feet. This led them to develop a new conception of the role of metaphorical language in science capable of containing the contradictions that had threatened the classical model. They managed this in part by developing a dynamic conception built on a metaphorical engagement with those very contradictions. We have seen this dynamic at work in McKibben's reflections on the bombings of Hiroshima and Nagasaki, in Oppenheimer's description of scientific order and the terror of new knowledge, and in Feynman's comments on modern physics. One might argue that these are ways of talking about physics rather than practicing it. But we have also come to see that the way in which the Los Alamites talked about their discipline should not be separated from the ways in which they practiced it. In a very important sense, a central feature of scientific method has been its development of specific rhetorical techniques as well as general attitudes toward its own uses of language.

In the context of Bohr's comments on the nature of physics—"Physics concerns what we can *say* about nature"[20]—the paradigmatic shift represented by quantum mechanics both emphasizes the central role of language in shaping our conception of the world and limits and redefines what that role can be. This transformation leaves physicists in the awkward position of retaining an "uncontrolled but utterly vain desire to see [natural phenomena] in terms of something familiar,"[21] but no longer completely trusting the modes of thinking which once satisfied that desire. The scientists at Los Alamos could not escape the question "But what can I call it?"[22] In this sense, beyond even the upheaval of a world war, the development of the atomic bomb marked a time of crisis, a surfacing of the terror associated with wordlessness, blank spaces on maps, the unknown.

Conclusion

In this chapter, we have seen that the Los Alamites responded to the terror underlying their work in part by turning toward metaphorical language. In particular, I have examined their use of metaphors of exploration and discovery to encode their experience in a form that helped them to control its meanings. I have also shown that this metaphorical vehicle contains rather than eliminates disruptive meanings; indeed, the associative character of metaphors makes it a dynamic form. The Los Alamites' efforts to control this dynamism, therefore, offer us opportunities to understand the ways in which they constructed a viable conception of their work—both for their own consumption and for ours.

In the next chapter, I will broaden my consideration to include a second group of metaphors: those involving a religious or, more broadly, a spiritual apprehension of the world. In particular, I will consider how the Los Alamites attempt to encode their experiences within a rhetoric that controls their moral interpretation. A close examination of both types of rhetoric—of exploration and discovery and of religion—can play a significant role in our understanding not only of the Los Alamites' work as a historical episode, but also of the ongoing development, testing, and deployment of nuclear weapons. Few topics can be of greater significance for the future as well as the past of our society.

Norris Bradbury and an unidentified SED with Trinity bomb. (Courtesy Los Alamos National Laboratory Archives.)

7 "TAKING THE CLOTH"

THE MORAL TEXTURE

OF LOS ALAMOS

On the morning of July 16, in the Jornada del Muerto, or Journey of Death, a desert in New Mexico some two hundred miles south of Santa Fe, the scientists and military personnel of the Manhattan Project detonated the first nuclear bomb in a test code-named Trinity. Detonation was scheduled for 4 A.M. to diminish the number of potential witnesses, but rain and lightning forced its postponement until 5:30. Observation points had been set up for the scientists, military personnel, and a lone, authorized reporter, William Laurence of the *New York Times*, at six-, ten-, and twenty-mile intervals from ground zero. When it finally detonated at 5:29:45, the bomb was so powerful that, even at Los Alamos, persistent watchers were rewarded with a distant vision of their "Fat Man." Closer at hand, but still some hundred miles away, a blind girl named Georgia Green, being driven to an early class at the University of New Mexico, cried out, at the moment of the first flash, "What was that?"[1] How should her companion, gifted with sight, have answered her? What would the scientific witnesses have said? How can we, with the benefit of hindsight, describe it? Later that day, in an attempt to quiet speculation, the military released a report claiming that an ammunition dump had blown up. But the explosion had been so large, few people believed the story.

Many of the scientists who witnessed the test offered their own stories, of course, once the strictures of military secrecy loosened. Robert Oppenheimer, the director of the Los Alamos Laboratory, for instance, recalled:

We waited until the blast had passed, walked out of the shelter and then it was entirely solemn. We knew the world would not be the same. A few people laughed, a few people cried. Most people were silent. I remembered the line from the Hindu scripture, the *Bhagavad Gita*: Vishnu is trying to persuade the Prince that he should do his duty and to impress him he takes on his multi-armed form and says, "Now I am become Death, the destroyer of worlds." I suppose we all thought that, one way or another.[2]

Oppenheimer's words are probably the most famous and frequently quoted response to the Trinity test. They are a powerful evocation of the emotional experience of a witness to the "birth" of nuclear weapons. Yet it would be hard to find an allusion more remote from this feat of twentieth-century technology than a two thousand-year-old Hindu text. The choice is remarkable for two reasons in particular. First is its anachronism: Why does Oppenheimer's quote from the *Bhagavad Gita* strike us as an appropriate means of commenting on events so remote from its original context? Second, why would he turn to *any* work of literature to describe the results of a scientific experiment of which he had firsthand knowledge? Surely he was aware that his audience had no personal experience of nuclear weapons; surely he knew the importance of direct observation and the conventions of simple, literal description of a scientific experiment such as this; surely the situation called for a "direct" representation, without the additional mediation of literary representation and especially not a representation so entirely unrelated to the subject at hand.

Surprisingly, no one who quotes Oppenheimer (so far as I am aware) mentions these oddities. Of course, this may be explained, at least in part, by Oppenheimer's authority as the scientist most responsible for overseeing the construction of the first nuclear bombs. His voice has lent these borrowed words the weight of direct revelation, muting and disguising the anachronism involved in his use of them, and so we have come to accept them as an appropriate comment on the detonation of the first nuclear weapon. Yet why did Oppenheimer choose to quote a literary text at all, instead of simply using his "own" words? The answer to this question—or the beginnings of an answer that I shall propose here—requires a continuation of our examination of the subtle ways in which the Los Alamos scientists employed literary rhetoric and allusion: in particular, how they used it to construct narratives capable of expressing and containing the moral ambiguities of their involvement with nuclear weapons. This exploration will ultimately lead to an understanding of the "moral texture" of the Los Alamites' authoritative representations of their experiences, in which literary representation plays a dominant role. We will also come to recognize that our sense of the propriety of Oppenheimer's utterance likewise stems from its situation within a network of similar allusions that insist on a conception of nuclear weapons that is deeply, and perhaps alarmingly, literary.

Oppenheimer's quotation of the *Bhagavad Gita*, for instance, is it-self often quoted by individual's attempting to "explain" the meaning of nuclear weapons. Yet Vishnu's words—"Now I am become Death, the destroyer of worlds"—are most often cited out of the context of Oppenheimer's "own" words, to the extent that they are quoted in translations that differ from Oppenheimer's.[3] This serves to dislocate them even further from their original historical context, turning them into disembodied utterances appropriated as an expression of any given individual's sense of the significance of nuclear weapons. But is it possi-ble to avoid this appropriation entirely, or have these words already been transformed by quotation beyond any possible return to their proper context? And what is their proper context? I have quoted them from *The Making of the Atomic Bomb* quoting *The Decision to Drop the Bomb* quoting a documentary film quoting an interview film quoting Oppen-heimer quoting a translation (possibly his own) quoting the *Bhagavad Gita* quoting Vishnu. Which of these contexts is the true one? At what point do these words refer to a direct apprehension of the real world rather than to another individual's conception of yet other individuals' apprehensions of some ambiguous referent?

Clearly, Oppenheimer entangles his audience in a peculiarly literary conception of nuclear weapons—a conception which, through its his-torical air and religious provenance, contextualizes our understanding of the bomb within the tradition of human encounters with the divine and thereby leads us inescapably to questions of morality. Ultimately, Oppenheimer's invocation of this literary model simultaneously sharp-ens our awareness of the remarkable power and responsibility of the individual scientist in the creation of nuclear weapons and induces us to accept the inevitability of these bombs as yet another manifestation of an inhuman and inscrutable divinity.

But surely there are alternatives to this intensely textual representa-tion of nuclear weapons? Norris Bradbury, Oppenheimer's colleague and later his successor at Los Alamos, offers a pointed contrast when he takes exception to such "meaningful" literary interpretations of the Trinity test: "The Trinity shot worked. What was the reaction? Every-body and his brother asked you that question. 'What did you think when the bomb went off?' And you're supposed to have great . . . Hell, you just say, 'Thank Heaven the damned thing worked!' or words to that effect."[4] Bradbury appears to have remained stoically unmoved during the Trinity test, but this is not entirely the case, as a remark in another context makes clear: "For that first fifteen seconds the sight was so incredible that the spectators could only gape at it in dumb amazement. I don't believe at that moment anyone said to himself, 'What have we done to civilization?' Feelings of conscience may have come later."[5] Bradbury's response centers instead around an insistence on the difficulty of rendering the experience in a linguistic form: "The spectators could only gape in *dumb* amazement." Indeed, Bradbury's own verbal rendering is full of lacunae and blustery glosses that emphasize or perhaps create the illusion of its expressive paucity. Bradbury fosters the impression that he is all business and common sense—he refuses to waste time on words or indulge in moral reflections. In fact, he seems to connect the two, denying the possibility of moral examination by identifying it with verbal dexterity. In his view, the raw experience of the bomb strips away both: no one at the time could have *said* "What have we done," and so *"feelings* of conscience" might occur only later, if at all.

The radical difference between the reactions of these two collegial scientists comes into perspective when we recall their respective roles in the ongoing development of atomic weapons. Oppenheimer left the Manhattan Project immediately after the war and devoted himself to the cause of international control of atomic energy and to opposing the construction of hydrogen bombs. Bradbury, on the other hand, became director of the Los Alamos Laboratory for the twenty-five years following Oppenheimer's departure. Each reaction clearly reflects the individual's practical relationship to the nuclear arms industry following the end of World War II. Bradbury alludes directly to his own continuing involvement in an implicit rejection of what he saw as Oppenheimer's highhanded moral stance: "Look, it wasn't any of those deep moral convictions that people seem to have had when they saw the first bomb at Trinity, 'Now is Armageddon.' It was a very personal, very selfish sort of other things. 'If I once get into the thing, I'll never get out of it.' That turned out to be true."[6] Bradbury strives to appear down-to-earth. His acknowledgment of the personal, even selfish concerns at the root of the Los Alamites' responses to the Trinity test is disarming. "You can trust me," his rhetoric says without coming right out and saying it: "I'm giving it to you straight." Yet his language is hardly as simple and direct as he wants it to appear. If Oppenheimer is highhanded, close analysis of Bradbury's words might tempt one to conclude that he was being underhanded.

Ironically, Bradbury proves unable to avoid morally tinged language himself: "Hell, you just say, 'Thank Heaven the damned thing worked!' or words to that effect." Even more interestingly, Bradbury's verbal accounts depend as much on quotation as does Oppenheimer's. He seems almost unable to complete a sentence without invoking a fictional speaker and thus constituting each of his own utterances as a quotation of someone else. This phenomenon, I think, reflects the peculiar pressures of Bradbury's involvement with nuclear weapons, pressures quite different from those experienced by Oppenheimer, which, nonetheless, involve him in a similarly literary process of response. Given the strong antiweapons bias of many former Los Alamites, those scientists, like Bradbury, who continued on in that work after the war faced an implicit need to justify their actions. One of the strongest and most "natural" defenses lay in the ideal of scientific objectivity itself. The postwar Los Alamites could cite their commitment to scientific knowledge and in this way partially defuse potential questions regarding their morality. Bradbury, therefore, adopts a distanced voice in rendering his experience of the Trinity test, puts his own words in the mouths of others, and describes the spectators at Trinity in the third person, dismissing their ability to speak in justification of what he has to say himself. So Bradbury's comments become most expressive precisely when they appear most detached and objective, and yet this appearance of objectivity is itself the product of a complex and highly literary use of idiolect and quotation.

Both Oppenheimer and Bradbury attempt to constitute their particular accounts as universal, from the gentle but insinuating hypothesis of the former, "I suppose we all thought that in one way or another," to the latter's bombastic certainty. Yet the two directors contradict one another, and their accounts seem largely irreconcilable. What finally binds them together is their reliance on preexisting texts and the modes of expression those texts make available to them. This shared reliance demands that we question the apparent contradictions and come to an understanding of the two conceptions of the Trinity test in relation to one another. Only by studying these scientists' representations of their scientific productions in the context of their specific uses of literary models and techniques can we fully appreciate what those products mean—to the scientists, to us, and to society—and, furthermore, how those meanings have been constructed.

Rabbits' Feet and Four-Leafed Clovers

As I have pointed out in previous chapters, a large proportion of the scientists who went to Los Alamos to work on the bomb were self-proclaimed pacifists, and a recurring question in histories of the project, and in discussions among the scientists themselves, concerns their willingness to undertake military work. The most common explanation cites the scientists' fear of the Nazis and their desire to ensure that

Germany not develop atomic weapons before the Allies had them. This argument is compelling, particularly given the number of Los Alamites who were European refugees and who therefore knew firsthand the effects of Hitler's obsessive hatred. But this explanation does nothing to account for the fact that the Los Alamites did not stop their work when it became clear that Germany was nowhere near producing an atomic bomb. Only a few individuals left the project when Germany surrendered.[7] The rest of the scientists actually increased the pace of their efforts at around this time. Clearly, factors other than a fear of Nazi victory were at work in maintaining the dedication of these men and women to an undertaking that was, on the surface of it, abhorrent to them.

In response to this dilemma, Oppenheimer, Bradbury, and their colleagues turned to literature and its representational techniques for the tools with which to manage the moral ambiguity of their work at Los Alamos. In particular, they turned to religious literature, from the *Bhagavad Gita* to the Bible. Although one important function of religious allusions is often to assert the moral rectitude of the speaker, references such as Oppenheimer's and Bradbury's do not function as a kind of moral sop. Although it is often a factor in their representations, the Los Alamites did not, in general, turn to religious texts primarily for direct moral *justification* of their work.[8] They did not seek out comforting passages of scripture to reassure themselves of their righteousness. Instead, their religious references tend to emphasize the moral ambiguity and the dire consequences of their efforts. How, then, did such allusions serve them?

The answer to this question has to do with the ways in which such allusions allow Oppenheimer and his colleagues to position themselves in relation to the powerful and conflicting aspects of their experience designing and constructing these terrifying weapons. Oppenheimer's reference to the *Bhagavad Gita*, for example, provides him with the narrative materials to represent forcefully crucial elements of the scientists' experience: the feeling of being in control of unlimited power; an awareness that the exercise of this power will result in death and destruction on a vast scale; a sense of personal submission to these forces; and a belief that it all must have a meaning or moral. Second, the embodiment of these forces in the character of Vishnu gives them a voice and agency of their own. This has the potent effect of mitigating the scientists' responsibility for the bomb by reassigning that responsibility to the bomb itself—a dynamic reminiscent of Joseph McKibben's attribution of responsibility for the Los Alamites' work to nature.[9]

Even more, however, the embodiment of the bomb in the form of a divine entity allows Oppenheimer's voice, like Bradbury's, to be transformed through the power of quotation. When Oppenheimer speaks Vishnu's words, whose voice are we hearing: Oppenheimer's, Vishnu's, or the bomb's? As the speaker, Oppenheimer occupies all three roles simultaneously, and therefore he is bound to none of them. In this way, Oppenheimer is able to engage deeply with the scientists' conflicting emotional and intellectual perceptions, to embody them in a dramatic situation, to speak for them; at the same time, by virtue of his ambiguous positioning, he manages to avoid fixing himself in any specific relation to the forces he invokes. He lets the voices of the *Bhagavad Gita* speak through him in a kind of reverse ventriloquism.[10] So Oppenheimer's allusion allows him to balance a sense of power with a feeling of helplessness by constructing himself in a multivocal relation to the bomb: either speaker or auditor, both author of and mere witness to "the forces heretofore reserved to The Almighty."[11] As director of Los Alamos, he assumes the role of Vishnu, a representative of the power of modern science. As witness, he enters the role of Krishna and so frames the experience as an argument in favor of doing one's duty.[12] Ultimately, both combine to give the reader an impression of descriptive power, as if Oppenheimer's words accurately contained and transmitted the experience of the bomb itself. And, to cap this extraordinary performance, Oppenheimer at once undercuts his own authority and imposes it on his colleagues, along with his entire complex representation, as if it were a natural, even inevitable, conclusion, with the almost offhand comment: "I suppose we all thought that, one way or another."

Of course, not all scientists were willing to buy Oppenheimer's particular formulation of their experiences, or even his overt recognition of a moral dimension. But even the most hardheaded, practical-minded physicists, like Bradbury, found themselves turning in moments of stress to similar language. Bradbury's memorandum on the "TR Hot Run," which outlined the schedule for final assembly of the bomb in preparation for the Trinity (TR) test, reads in part:

Tuesday, 10 July, 1730	TR and Cruetz charges ready for delivery. Start papering. Arrange for night shift if necessary to paper charges. Additional personnel will be furnished as required....
Thursday, 12 July, 1500	Assembly of TR charge complete....
Friday, 13 July, 0001	TR charge starts on its way to TR. G-2 escort cars fore and aft. G. B. Kistiakowsky to ride in fore car....
Friday, 13 July, 1300	Assembly starts at this time....

"Taking the Cloth"

Saturday, 14 July, 0800	Turn over with main hoist and place on special cradle. . . . Lift to tower top. . . . Bring up G Engineer footstool. . . .
Saturday, 14 July, 1700	Gadget complete
Sunday, 15 July, all day	Look for rabbit's feet and four leafed clovers. Should we have the Chaplain down there? Period for inspection available from 0900–1000
Monday, 16 July, 0400	BANG![13]

For Bradbury, the chaplain seems to serve a function similar to that of "rabbits' feet and four-leafed clovers": even if his question is purely rhetorical, its very utterance acts as a kind of talisman or lucky charm. This, after all, is the chaplain's task: to shape words into a protective benediction, to circumscribe an event in language and cast it in the context of the familiar meanings of an established textual tradition. But Bradbury, unlike Oppenheimer, refuses to turn overtly to traditions outside science. Like Oppenheimer, however, Bradbury does manipulate voices here, juxtaposing the voice of superstition and belief with the practical voice of the technician. Perhaps in the tension between them Bradbury found a space in which he could express fear in the protective guise of gentle self-parody. Or perhaps by invoking the chaplain in the company of rabbits' feet and four-leafed clovers, on the one hand, and of a technical timetable, on the other, Bradbury used the mild humor of poking fun at superstition to constitute by contrast an expression of faith in the certitude of science.

Certainly, in the midst of all the practical considerations and attention to technical details necessary to the task at hand, Bradbury's invocation of a minister of God's Word stands out in sharp relief. Yet it does not seem entirely out of place; rather, it subtly alters the character of the step-by-step procedure in which it occurs. Bradbury's outline begins to assume a slightly ritual flavor: it becomes a litany of sorts, the recitation of an authorized version of events, which in itself insists that experience, no matter how momentous or unfamiliar, can in fact be prescribed and controlled. Ironically, in inscribing these events within a familiar, unitary order, Bradbury makes use of a multivocal strategy similar to, though less pronounced than, those employed by Oppenheimer.

Most strikingly, in this regard, the "BANG!" that concludes Bradbury's checklist gives the bomb a kind of speaking part of its own. Though less articulate than Oppenheimer's bomb, Bradbury's version nonetheless gives a voice to the thing they have created. In Bradbury's case, however, his responsibility for the creation of the bomb figures even more prominently, for it is this very document which brings the bomb into being in both representational and practical terms. Bradbury thus manages an especially effective rhetorical feat: through a conflation of these two voices, the bomb's and his own, he manages to express the potential horror of the bomb's imminent articulation while containing that horror within the framework of a humorous onomatopoetic representation.

Many Los Alamites followed Oppenheimer's and Bradbury's different leads across the apparent boundary between the amoral discipline of science and the moral sphere of religion. Joseph Hirschfelder, for example, refers to the Los Alamites' achievement as overtly miraculous: "I believe in scientific-technological miracles since I saw one performed at Los Alamos during World War II."[14] Hirschfelder's language demonstrates one of the most common effects of the Los Alamites' various religious borrowings: linking their work to an existing religious framework tended to give it what Robert Wilson has called "the verisimilitude of high moral purpose."[15] It is striking, however, that this "verisimilitude" occurs through a very unrealistic use of language. Indeed, this effect does not result from an actual belief in the divinity of the bomb or the holiness of their work—it is instead a literary effect. By playing on a metaphorical sense of their words, like Hirschfelder's "miracles," by constructing their experience as a narrative in the "high style" of the Bible, and by giving the bomb a speaking part in that narrative, the Los Alamites ultimately pay tribute to the power of literary language to shape their experience in a way that makes it seem true to a "high moral purpose."

Furthermore, Hirschfelder's words do not imply a simple moral justification, as I suggested before. Indeed, many of the Los Alamites' responses use biblical language to represent the *immorality* of the weapons they were building. So Edward Teller wrote to Szilard: "The things we are working on are so terrible that no amount of protesting or fiddling with politics will save our souls."[16] Yet Teller did not leave the project; in fact, his remark appears as a rejection of Szilard's request that he sign a petition urging the United States government to refrain from military use of atomic weapons. Clearly, Teller's conception of his work in moral terms did not discourage him from involvement with such "terrible things." In fact, his use of the language of salvation seems to have provided an excuse to avoid dealing with the consequences of his work. Casting his work in the context of a fixed morality, for good or ill, removed it from his hands and portrayed the Los Alamites as predestined to a particular fate, whether at the hands of God, nature, or their own narratives. Even in cases in which the Los Alamites used religious representation to cast their work in negative terms, a crucial effect of such representation seems to have been the translation of that work into terms of high moral purpose. The verisimilitude of this move subtly shifted the focus of many Los Alamites' reflections on the consequences of the bomb project from its victims to themselves, from the slaughter of hundreds of thousands of civilians to the salvation or damnation of individual souls.

Such representation facilitates a conception of working on the atomic bomb in personal terms as the narrative of an individual's journey through a figurative landscape replete with the linguistic resources of confession and absolution. But at the same time, ironically, the effect of religious analogy is often a complete *de*personalization of these weapons through their representation in the context of an epic and immemorial struggle between the forces of good and evil:

> I can think of no one who refused to participate in the project because of a conviction that our great science would be demeaned by serving in the manufacture of the means of death and destruction. We were all acutely aware that the whole civilized world was under attack by a force of the greatest evil. Still, the question loomed in our minds whether it was moral to use such a devastatingly destructive weapon even to defeat an enemy as undeniably evil as the Nazi's. But this was an old question, one humankind had had to face many times during its history.[17]

Here Victor Weisskopf uses the language of good and evil to represent atomic weapons in terms that give them "the verisimilitude of high moral purpose" and, at the same time, allow him to express his awareness of how terrible they are. The tension between the two conceptions is apparent in the twists and turns of Weisskopf's reasoning, which moves from its opening assertion through doubt ("still") to a final, rather ambiguous affirmation ("but"). This last turn depends on Weisskopf making explicit what each of the examples I have examined so far implicitly asserts: that atomic weapons may be represented within existing symbolic structures as merely a new manifestation of the venerable complications "humankind [has] had to face many times during its history."

Rather than trying to resolve the complications associated with atomic weapons through grounding them in religious rhetoric, however, Weisskopf seems to turn with relief to the ultimate unresolvability of the questions they raise. Indeed, the complications inherent in such representations play a number of crucial roles in helping the Los Alamites carry on with their work. They provide a moral context in which to locate the construction of atomic weapons, thus potentially defusing any qualms the scientists might have felt on that score. They offer individual scientists the shelter of introspection, depicting their work through narratives of personal salvation, or damnation. They situate the bomb project within the breadth and width of human history and, in particular, within the legitimizing structures of the Judeo-Christian tradition. And they justify the Los Alamites' participation in war by associating it with an epic and immemorial opposition to "a force of the greatest evil." In the process, however, the complexities involved in the scientists' use of religious rhetoric complicate their understanding of not only the bomb, but also the science behind it.

"The Last Great Mystical Religion"

The Los Alamites apply religious metaphors to physics almost as often as to the nuclear weapons it produced. Wilson, for example, recalls that when he joined the field, "Going into physics was not all that different from taking the cloth."[18] Isador Rabi, likewise, remarks, "I think my interest in science came more from religion, more as God, the Creator, rather than God, the Administrator or the Preacher—not the moral side, more the wonder of the universe."[19] Bohr spoke of physics in similar terms, as Sandro Petruccioli noted: "At bottom, according to Bohr, the difficulties that scientists had met with in the world of atoms were not all that different from those encountered by the prophets when they had sought 'to describe the nature of God on the basis of our human concepts.' "[20] None of these men intends his analogy of physics and religion as a comment on the moral status of his discipline; for each it expresses a conception of the position of physics in the hierarchy of social forms of knowledge. Wilson's comment, for instance, embodies a tension between physicists' attempts to constitute an independent and therefore internally coherent symbolic order and the inevitable involvement of that order in a surrounding network of social meanings: "taking the cloth" implies the scientist's investment in a separate order, complete with its own rules and habits, while the analogy to a religious community binds that order back into the fabric of society at large.

In a similar sense, Louis Ridenour cites "a remark made to me by a distinguished mathematical physicist about ten years ago": " 'Science,' he said, 'is the last great mystical religion.' He meant that science is a regimen with an informed priesthood who are its practitioners, and a great mass of adherents who do not understand at all the aims, methods, or tenets of science, but are convinced of its value and power."[21] The metaphor used by Ridenour's distinguished physicist is echoed by other Los Alamites, like Oppenheimer, who wrote: "I have sometimes asked myself whether we can find any analogy to [Los Alamos] in the practice of the monastic orders that devote a part of their attention and derive part of their sustenance from the making of their private liqueurs."[22] Such references describe physics as a form of social organization centered around a closed set of intellectual premises. What may strike a contemporary reader, however, is the incongruity of comparing the modern and rational discipline of physics with the medieval and mystical form of monasticism. Yet that same reader can hardly avoid sensing the relevance of the comparison. And, in fact, it suggests a continuity which historical study bears out: Medieval monasticism evolved a closed, communal, tightly knit, international, textually based set of interpretive practices, and these in turn provided science with an essential model when it emerged in its modern form at the end of the Middle Ages.

The Los Alamos physicists' use of religious metaphors leads them at times to striking claims for their discipline, and these in turn reveal some of their more deep-seated assumptions about it. Oppenheimer, for instance, goes so far as to suggest that "science in being research, may be to the liberal education, not an accident, not an ancillary or secondary or convenient thing to be held in balance—it may be the scripture itself."[23] Philip Morrison describes Bohr's atomic model in similar language:

Of course it was not right. It resembles the atom no more than a quick pencil sketch resembles a living face, as O. R. Frisch put it. The real Jacob, quantum mechanics, appeared only in the mid-twenties. How much Bohr meant to this second coming, even more as a personal focus of understanding than in published papers, is the next high theme of [*Niels Bohr: A Centenary Volume*].[24]

Perhaps it is only logical that if we assume science can be described as a kind of religious order, it will produce work of a scriptural significance and authority. That initial assumption is, of course, rather large; but whether or not we accept it at face value, it says a great deal about the way scientists conceive of the insight that science allows them into nature.

Of what does this conception consist? Perhaps most obviously, the representation of science as a kind of scripture equates nature, the source and subject of its revelation, with God. Nature in this analogy becomes uppercase; it is divine, beyond us, in a separate realm. Yet, in the view handed down by medieval scholastics, Nature is also a divinely produced linguistic entity—the Book of Nature—which provides a means of glimpsing the divine order that underlies it. We are able to access this Book of Nature because we have been blessed with Reason, a platonic shadow of the natural order, in conjunction with language, a dim reflection of God's Word. This constitutes one important basis on which science has traditionally claimed its authority: as Nature is the Book of the Word (God), science asserts its status as the book of the Book. In this way, it offers us access to Nature and speaks with the authority of Nature. Individual scientists, then, become merely inspired vehicles, priests interpreting scriptures, and in their interpretations conveying a transcendent order which predates them and exists absolutely and independently.

I may seem to overstate the case somewhat; but the only excess in my description of this common assumption of the authority of science is the degree to which I make it explicit. My depiction of modern science as a divinely authorized exploration into the mystical workings of a transcendental order barely matches what many scientists would claim, more elliptically, for their own discipline. Oppenheimer, for example, describes quantum physicists in such oracular terms:

To what appeared to be the simplest questions, we will tend to give either no answer or an answer which will at first sight be reminiscent more of a strange catechism than of the straightforward affirmations of physical science. If we ask, for instance, whether the position of the electron remains the same, we must say "no"; if we ask whether the electron's position changes with time, we must say "no"; if we ask whether the electron is at rest, we must say "no"; if we ask whether it is in motion, we must say "no." The Buddha has given such answers when interrogated as to the conditions of a man's self after his death.[25]

Oppenheimer's words take on a startling resonance given that it was in the context of this kind of science that the development of atomic weapons took place. So Oppenheimer's "strange catechism" invokes Hirschfelder's "miracle"—an unusual, incredible, and disturbing event, yet one that confirms rather than disrupts the order that makes it possible. Likewise, William Higginbotham describes his response to the Trinity test by remarking: "That's where I got the Gospel."[26] Once again what the scientists "got" from their work was a bomb figured as a form of divine revelation, along with a conception of their discipline as a "Gospel" which authorized their work, including the development of atomic weapons.

It is fascinating that as physics evolves into an increasingly complex and sophisticated discipline, as it seems to leave its roots in the medieval exegetical tradition further and further behind, and to distance itself increasingly from superstition and faith, on one level at least it comes to resemble a kind of religious practice more and more, even to the extent of self-consciously adopting those practices as metaphorical descriptions of itself.[27] This does not mean, however, that its practitioners have become entirely comfortable with the comparison, or the role in which it casts them. We have already seen, for example, that Bradbury takes exception to Oppenheimer's language. Even Weisskopf, whose temperament corresponds more closely to his director's, admits that he feels troubled by the symbolic associations that occur to him in response to the Trinity test:

When the brightness subsided, we saw a blue halo surrounding the yellow and orange sphere, an aureole of bluish light around the ball. This effect of the radioactive radiation on the adjacent air was a totally unexpected phenomenon, although it would have been easy to predict. The appearance of this uncanny blue light made a deep impression on me. It reminded me, in spite of an inner resistance to such an analogy, of a painting by the medieval master Matthias Grünewald. Part of the altar piece at Colmar, the painting depicts Jesus in the middle of a bright yellow ascending sphere surrounded by a blue halo. The explosion of an atomic bomb and the resurrection of Christ—what a paradoxical and disturbing association![28]

Weisskopf's discomfort stems in part precisely from the kind of associations I have been examining. He reminds us not to assume that such metaphor-making is always safe or entirely comfortable, for sometimes it can disrupt rather than facilitate our conceptual control, as in this case in which it leads to a paradoxical, disturbing connection between destruction and redemption.

Ironically, the representational function that Weisskopf reluctantly imagines for the Isenheim Altarpiece in relation to a technological artifact is essentially the same work it was originally meant to do in a religious context: to render the unknown and unknowable in symbolic terms and thus to embody it in a social space that links the artist (or Weisskopf) and the viewer (or his reader). In the process, such symbolic representation yokes together disparate, even antithetical materials in a way that leads us toward particular interpretations of those materials. These interpretations may, for example, help the Los Alamites (and us) "make sense" of their experiences, but they may also challenge our own established internal texts associated with the vehicles they employ— in this case, narratives of the crucifixion.[29] So Weisskopf writes that his representation of a nuclear explosion in terms of a religious icon is "disturbing." What it disturbs is his existing understanding of the crucifixion. Such disturbance does not necessarily imply a representational failure, however; rather, it is an inherent part of the metaphorical extension of meaning that characterizes art, just as it is a part of the human hopes and fears that art represents. In its simultaneous depiction of extreme human cruelty and the redemption of mankind, for instance, the Isenheim Altarpiece itself involves associations no less "paradoxical and disturbing" than Weisskopf's link between that work of art and the explosion of an atomic bomb.

In broad terms, this dynamic is implicit in the work of science as well as that of art. Los Alamite Cyril Smith puts it this way: "Both art and science are basically symbol-making activities, and both have the quality of yielding metaphors that match far more than their creators intended."[30] An essential component of this conceptual expansiveness is the fact that metaphors are not unidirectional. As Weisskopf's discomfort illustrates, metaphors make meaning in two directions, and in more than one sense. Although it is fair to describe their primary function as a mapping of meaning from the vehicle (Isenheim Altarpiece) onto the tenor (atomic bomb), in practice the tenor also shapes our understanding of and response to the vehicle.[31] Likewise, while a metaphor ostensibly conveys meaning from an author (like Weisskopf) to the reader, it also shapes the author's understanding, sometimes dramatically. The resultant unpredictability (or "undecidability," if you prefer) can be productive, in either discipline. In physics, for example, the metaphors of wave and particle stimulated over several centuries an expanding and deepening understanding of the behavior of light, and finally of matter as well, precisely because the physical phenomena in question (the tenor) repeatedly challenged existing notions of the metaphorical vehicles of light and wave, requiring repeated reexamination of both the metaphorical tenor and vehicle. In literature, likewise, unforeseen associations provide an important basis of the longevity of any given work.

Despite this similarity, however, when the two traditions mix overtly, as in the Los Alamites' uses of literature to describe their work on nuclear weapons, the associations can proliferate to the point of discomfort. The essence of this discomfort has to do with the blurring of a key distinction between the representational goals of each tradition: scientists strive to produce static representations, whereas literary authors struggle to create dynamic ones. Put another way, scientific representations are designed to mean the same thing to every reader at all times; literary representations cater to the eye of the beholder. When the representational criteria of one discipline intrude on the other, we find ourselves on shaky ground, uncertain how to judge our own representations, doubting their truth, unsure even of their meanings. Most often this will result in little more than, say, a physicist's annoyance over the "misuse" of a scientific theory, such as relativity, in a work of literature or an author's frustration with a physicist's literal-minded rejection of a work of magic realism. But in other instances, the consequences can be more disturbing, as when Weisskopf finds himself drawing connections between a technological artifact and a religious icon. Such instances suggest that the conventional boundaries by which we categorize and delimit our experiences are more permeable and ethereal than we might like to think, leaving us with less control over either their consequences or their meanings than we would like.[32]

"Batter My Heart": The Bomb as a Vehicle of Transcendence

Most of the Los Alamites who have left us accounts of their experiences express a considerable degree of discomfort, but few demonstrate much inclination toward introspection regarding its sources. They tend to assume their discomfort is associated with the bomb itself rather than with the representational resources they mobilize to describe it. By and large, consciously at least, most Los Alamites were simply groping with varying degrees of subtlety and skill for a language commensurate with their experience. So Glenn Price turned to the biblical tradition for a vivid image to describe his impression of the Trinity test: "It felt like you were looking into the bowels of Hell."[33] Likewise, Teller portrayed the mass departure of scientists from Los Alamos after the war as an "Exodus."[34]

Though we may feel uncomfortable in the presence of such rhetoric, this discomfort seems so appropriate to the subject that it rarely elicits comment. But in failing to explore the source of our discomfort, we allow these representations to fix nuclear weapons in a web of associations that have profound consequences for how we understand and respond to them. Thus, whatever Teller's intentions or his degree of consciousness regarding the effects of his allusion, his apparently simple analogy figures him as a member of a tribe chosen by God and leaving a desert country where all had shared in a common affliction—in this case the inescapable need to work on such "terrible" weapons. Similarly, Price's image, although fearsome, conveys his experience in terms of a moral geography which predates him and which, therefore, constitutes atomic weapons as an embodiment of an inevitable—though infernal—aspect of the order underlying our universe.

If religious literature provided the Los Alamites with images, metaphors, and diction that seemed commensurate with their experience, however, it also shaped that experience to be commensurate with traditional representations. In effect, the Los Alamites' use of religious language translated their somatic experiences into symbolic entities according to literary conventions. Even particular technical apparatuses were translated in this way, as when subcritical assemblies of uranium blocks became "Jezebel" or "Lady Godiva."[35] The test of the first plutonium implosion bomb similarly turned into "Trinity." Underlying each of these names is a deep rhetorical structure which, by constituting somatic experience in symbolic terms, ultimately transforms not only specific conceptions of scientific artifacts but the very means by which an individual can conceive of them and, therefore, what can be known about them and how they can be used.

Consider, for instance, the "inspiration" behind Oppenheimer's naming of the Trinity test. In a letter to Groves written in 1962, Oppenheimer explains that he had two poems by John Donne in mind when he named the test: "Hymne to God My God, in My Sicknesse" and the Holy Sonnet which beings "Batter my heart, three person'd God. . . ."[36] In the latter poem, the speaker calls on the Trinity, asking to be battered, besieged, divorced, imprisoned, enslaved, and raped.

> Batter my heart, three-personed God; for You
> As yet but knock, breathe, shine, and seek to mend;
> That I may rise and stand, o'erthrow me, and bend
> Your force, to breake, blow, burn, and make me new.
> I, like an usurped town, to another due,
> Labor to admit You, but Oh, to no end!
> Reason, Your viceroy in me, me should defend,
> But is captived, and proves weak or untrue.
> Yet dearly I love You, and would be loved fain,
> But am betrothed unto Your enemy:
> Divorce me, untie or break that knot again,
> Take me to You, imprison me, for I,
> Except You enthrall me, never shall be free,
> Nor ever chaste, except You ravish me.[37]

This is hardly a model of rational behavior; yet it offered what to Oppenheimer seemed the most fitting name for the moment in which the Los Alamites would come face to face with the product of their scientific labors. In Oppenheimer's act of naming, therefore, we may glimpse the dynamics at work in the incorporation of atomic weapons into the preexisting structure of religious rhetoric.[38]

In Donne's poem, there are three points of particular importance for my argument. First, the speaker calls for a stripping away of earthly forms and illusions as a way to achieve a transcendent union with God. This level dramatizes the conscious recognition that somatic experience constitutes a barrier between the self and a true experience of God; and it uses poetic conventions to create the representation of an autonomous speaker struggling to construct a rhetorical utterance capable of breaking through that barrier. Second, Donne structures the poem around pairs of paradoxical metaphors: rise / o'erthrow, betrothed / divorce, enthrall / free, chaste / ravish. This level works toward unsettling the logical structures of everyday thought which keep poet, speaker, and reader alike from apprehending God. Third, the poem employs convoluted, confusing, and contradictory forms of syntax. This level acts to break the received linguistic forms which tend to surround and obscure truth and which finally replace it with formulaic expression and conventional understanding.

On these three levels, then, speaker and poem fight against established modes of perception, including their own. Yet this drama of self-abnegation proves to be the means by which Donne invests his speaker with representational substance. For by convincingly representing thematic, metaphoric, and linguistic self-consumption, the poem leads its reader by implication to accept the existence of the self being consumed. If the poem manages to be the means of its own undoing, it does so as a palpable enactment of the speaker's desire to escape the bonds that imprison him. Yet the poem itself is a symptom of those bonds: it embodies the speaker's physical voice; it constitutes through particular metaphors and images his immersion in an earthly context; and it manifests the imperfect medium of language—whether prayer, poetry, or both—to which his transcendental efforts are confined. In the poem's self-consumption, then, the reader witnesses the dissolution of those bonds. What remains is a substantiation of the speaker's desire: a symbol of the creation of self through self-destruction.

When the time came for Oppenheimer to name the first test of an atomic bomb, the Los Alamites had already chosen a site: the Jornada del Muerto desert of southern New Mexico. In this appropriately (or ominously) named desert, the scientists planned to stage the culmination of years of work by more than a hundred thousand people and perhaps, as Isidor Rabi once suggested, of three hundred years of physics as well.[39] As we have seen in previous chapters, the United States government had poured two billion dollars into the project. Scientists had given up university jobs and posts in proven fields such as radar research; had uprooted themselves and their families to live in what seemed to many of them a kind of moonscape; had struggled to master unfamiliar branches of learning, including metallurgy, ballistics, explosives, and chemistry; had pushed themselves to the edge of exhaustion and nervous collapse again and again, fighting against their apparent helplessness as they watched the war kill relatives and destroy the homes many had left behind in Europe. The pressure to bring their work to a successful conclusion was intense; and yet, what if they did succeed? Theoreticians had repeatedly been called upon to determine whether the bomb might ignite the earth's atmosphere. The potential that its effects would be so much greater than anything mankind had ever experienced made them difficult if not impossible to calculate ahead of time. A pool on the bomb's yield held in the days immediately preceding the test included bets ranging from "a dud" to "will incinerate the state of New Mexico." It was in this context that Oppenheimer chose a name for the test.

As director of Los Alamos, Oppenheimer felt the pressure of the scientists' collective uncertainty more than anyone. Donne's poem would therefore attract Oppenheimer as a means of defining and fixing the significance of the first test of an atomic weapon for several reasons, some obvious, others less so. The relevance of its language of battering, breaking, and burning, for instance, should be clear. Further, the poem's optimistic attitude toward such destructive power expressed the scientists' hope that their weapon would function properly. Somewhat less obviously, the situation of the speaker in the poem reflected the scientists' own position confronting an unknown, indescribable, unimaginable force—one that threatened to destroy them but which they nonetheless chose to invoke. Likewise, the poem dramatized the struggle to find symbolic terms adequate for the invocation of such an unearthly force. In the poem, these two levels are inseparable: physical confrontation and symbolic representation blend into one another in a world of appearances, of hidden significance, of meaning.

These are the conceptual consequences of Oppenheimer's act of naming. By trying to delimit its meaning in particular symbolic terms, Oppenheimer situates the bomb in an interpretive context. Such a context bifurcates the bomb into a dual-level phenomenon: a physical surface and an ideational substrate. Furthermore, the particular interpretive context which Oppenheimer applies—that of religious symbolism—privileges the ideational level. So Christ was man and God; the Eucharist is bread and wine on the one hand and transubstantiated body and blood on the other; the Bible is history and spiritual revelation; but in each of these pairings, the second element is dominant. Religious rhetoric, in general, is predicated on a rejection of the physical world in favor of a higher spiritual existence. As a result, Oppenheimer's specific reference to "Batter My Heart" invokes a general prejudice inherent, as we have seen, in that poem's use of language—a prejudice against the phenomenal world and in favor of stripping away physical experience in a search for the truth that was hidden.

What is that truth? Is it possible to say? Are such acts of naming, such uses of literary precedents, a form of revelation or obfuscation? The

Los Alamites' accounts of their experiences seem to exhort the reader toward certain conceptions and away from others. Yet their layering of literary references, allusions, and echoes invites active interpretation on our part. Unless we are passive recipients of these texts, they will inspire in us a mixture of revelation and discomfort comparable to that felt by the Los Alamites themselves. We can neither accept them uncritically nor reject them outright. Instead, we must analyze not only the overt meanings they make, but the ways in which they make those meanings—a process in which their interactions with our own internal texts will play a crucial role.

Conclusion

Oppenheimer's naming of the test "Trinity," like the other uses of religious rhetoric I have examined, asserts that the bomb's "meaning" should be as important to its scientific observers as its destructive power. This interpretive position is a particularly privileged one, as should be clear if we contrast it to the position of Hiroshima and Nagasaki survivors, for whom the somatic element effectively excluded all other considerations. By situating their "immediate" reactions in this way, the Los Alamites' use of religious literature took advantage of their ability to remove themselves from a potentially debilitating awareness of the physical "terror" of their work into a more abstract consideration of its metaphorical terrors. Their reactions came to dwell on a sense of metaphysical awe in the presence of the bomb rather than on a fear of its awful, earthly destructive power.

The Trinity test represents, in fact, a remarkable demonstration of the Los Alamites' ability to control the forces they intended to unleash, in conceptual as well as physical terms. In determining where official observers should stand or crouch or lie in relation to the Trinity test, for instance, the scientists sought to structure their physical involvement with the bomb in very precise ways. Their use of religious metaphors, like the name "Trinity," further structured their involvement, in intellectual terms, positioning its witnesses in a conceptual frame that emphasized their role as interpreters of a shifting, multivocal, "three personed" meaning inherent in the somatic experience of "the bomb." In doing so, such exercises of literary contextualization stacked the interpretive deck, influencing which meanings were likely to turn up and situating those meanings in existing conceptual structures, often of great antiquity, as evident in the platonic assumptions inherent in Donne's poem. So the Los Alamites located themselves as observers of the bomb not in the role of guinea pigs offering up their physical reactions as evidence of its terrible powers but as interpreters of the event's meanings, carefully cloaked and protected within established ways of "knowing" what they observed. We, of course, have inherited the Los Alamites' representations, and at every level they permeate not only our understanding of nuclear weapons but also the ways in which we use them. The consequences—indeed serious, perhaps terrifying— are the subject of the next chapter.

Norman Ramsey signing the Fat Man bomb. (Courtesy National Archives.)

8 "BEGGARED DESCRIPTION"

WRITING NUCLEAR WEAPONS

In the third of his Reith Lectures broadcast by the BBC in 1953, Robert Oppenheimer looked from his position as "Father of the Atomic Bomb" back over the short history of subatomic physics to "its origins at the turn of the century and its great synthesis and resolutions in the nineteen-twenties." This was for Oppenheimer "a heroic time," a period of high creativity which comes rarely to any discipline but which, when it does occur, offers us a glimpse of "a great adventure in human understanding. . . . So men listen to accounts of soldiers returning from a campaign of unparalleled hardship and heroism, or of explorers from the high Himalayas, or of tales of deep illness, or of a mystic's communion with God." Such stories, however, while they offer gripping narrative material and perhaps even unusual insight, also challenge the resources of would-be storytellers. In the development of subatomic physics, for instance, "Its re-creation would call for an art as high as the story of Oedipus or the story of Cromwell, yet in a realm of action so remote from our common experience that it is unlikely to be known to any poet or any historian."[1]

Although the extension of modern physics into the subatomic realm certainly ranks among the great intellectual exploits of modern times, most of Oppenheimer's listeners probably would not have felt that in itself it warranted comparison to heroic deeds and adventures. Even today, the general public has little interest in reading about Niels Bohr delivering a lecture to a group of colleagues or Werner Heisenberg scrawling equations on a blackboard. But Oppenheimer's assertion of the dramatic significance of subatomic physics does make sense even to a layperson in the context of events in the 1940s through which this new branch of physics produced obviously spectacular results. Oppenheimer knew the story well, of course, having played a leading role himself. Indeed, despite the intellectual excitement among physicists during the first quarter of the twentieth century, without the development of nuclear weapons and his participation in it there would have been little interest among general listeners to the BBC in either Oppenheimer or his subject.

"Beggared Description"

In 1947, David Hawkins wrote an insider's history of the construction of the first nuclear weapons at Los Alamos, in which he aspired to Oppenheimer's "high art" by attempting to construct a satisfying narrative of the heroic time he had shared with his colleagues. The book seems to have succeeded in presenting an accurate portrait of its subject, for government officials quickly classified the work; even its author was denied access for years. But despite this measure of "success," Hawkins remained dissatisfied with his account. In the introduction to a 1983 reissue of *Project Y: The Los Alamos Story*, he reflects on the shortcomings of his own efforts to portray "a development which would, in one way or another, alter the whole pattern of world affairs."

I well remember my first reading of [my book] after declassification, early in 1962, and some of the reactions it provoked . . . a sense that of such extraordinary people, events, and developments, I had produced a record so limited by the style and restraint of an official military history. Could I not have emulated, say, the style of Sir Thomas Malory, or that of a Bernal Díaz in his chronicle of the conquest of Mexico?[2]

Hawkins uses language very similar to Oppenheimer's in trying to describe the social importance of the work done by the scientists at Los Alamos, and he similarly emphasizes the difficulties involved in such a descriptive act. He also expresses a conviction that in order to overcome those difficulties an essentially literary approach is required, one that boasts "the style of Sir Thomas Malory, or that of a Bernal Díaz."

Oppenheimer and Hawkins are not alone in this conviction. The last three chapters have shown that many veterans of Los Alamos turned to literature in their descriptions of the work of designing and constructing the first nuclear weapons. When we consider a domain of literary language wider than that associated with narratives of exploration and discovery and of religious revelation, examples multiply. After only a few months at Site Y, for instance, Robert Wilson wrote to H. D. Smyth, a colleague at Princeton University who would write the first official government report on the Manhattan Project: "Life is not at all hard on this 'magic mesa.' "[3] Nearly fifty years later, Wilson would still report that *"The Magic Mountain* of Thomas Mann seemed particularly relevant to me, even though it was about the period before W.W.I. I recently read it again, as he had recommended, and it still seems to be relevant."[4] Another Los Alamite found Shakespeare similarly apropos. "One evening the Oppenheimers gave a party. Edward U. Condon picked up a copy of *The Tempest* and sat in a corner reading aloud passages appropriate to intellectuals in exotic isolation."[5]

These examples only begin to give a sense of the hundreds of similar allusions to literature and uses of literary metaphors, analogies, and rhetoric by Los Alamos scientists in their attempts to account for their experience of the new science of nuclear physics and the construction of the first nuclear weapons. Other references range from Arthur Conan Doyle's *Lost World* to H. G. Wells's *The World Set Free*; from Mary Shelley's *Frankenstein* to Isak Dinesen's *Gothic Tales*; from Thucydides to Lewis Carroll; from the Buddha's teachings to *Babes in the Woods*. These references make it clear that Oppenheimer's comparison of subatomic physics to the "high art" of literature does not stem from an aesthete's rarefied perceptions; it occurs throughout the Los Alamites' accounts, if not often in the context of a self-reflective examination of their own descriptive modes.

But how closely do such narratives fit the actual experiences of scientists in the New Mexican desert during wartime? Would not a great deal of rewriting be required to adapt "the story of Oedipus" or "that of a Bernal Díaz" to the Tale of Los Alamos? At first glance there does indeed appear to be a wide gap between these literary vehicles and the tenor of the Los Alamites' experiences. My analysis in the last few chapters, however, suggests two important qualifications of this observation. First, the distance between vehicle and tenor is an essential feature of the expressive dynamic of such metaphorical representation, for it is precisely this sort of distance that separates our common experience from what the Los Alamites are trying to tell us. Second, the apparent disparity between the historical facts of the Manhattan Project and the narrative elements of these literary models is not as great in practice as it appears in theory. We have seen the expressive power Oppenheimer achieves through the unlikely means of representing the test of the first plutonium bomb in terms of a two thousand-year-old Hindu text, on the one hand, and the devotional writings of a Renaissance poet, on the other. In light of the many examples we have already encountered, how can we reasonably maintain that differences in subject matter, historical provenance, or rhetorical approach constitute any real impediment to the Los Alamites' metaphorical use of literary precedents?

In the last few chapters I have focused on the Los Alamites' uses of language associated with a couple of specific literary genres. I have also focused primarily on what these representations meant to the Los Alamites themselves. In this chapter I will extend my consideration in two ways: I will look more broadly at the dynamic involved in their use of literary precedents in general; and I will examine what this dynamic means to those of us who depend on it for our primary knowledge of nuclear weapons—including both the political leaders responsible for determining their initial uses and the rest of us who must live with these weapons without, seemingly, the least power to influence their role in our lives. In particular, I will explore the pivotal function performed by literary rhetoric in transforming the bomb from a scientific artifact into a social construct. As I argued at the end of the last chapter, this process imposed on the bomb a peculiar and powerful textuality, which prepared the way for its wide dissemination throughout society and its constant utility as a military-political weapon without the need for its regular physical use. This peculiarly literary conception of "the bomb" continues to be a defining feature of nuclear weapons even now, fifty years after they first exploded into our social consciousness.

The Los Alamites' Dynamic Metaphors

Before moving on to examine the social influence of the Los Alamites' figurative accounts, it is worth considering in more detail the general motivation behind their use of literature and literary language, as well as the justification for our own examination of the texts they produced. There are several important points to be made here. Most obviously, by invoking an existing work of literature, the Los Alamites make use of a prefabricated representational framework that helps them to represent their individual experiences with relative ease and in an economical fashion. It is as if preexisting literary narratives allowed the Los Alamites to express themselves in a kind of shorthand. Years after he left Los Alamos, for example, when asked what literary work seemed most relevant to his experience at Los Alamos, Robert Serber answered, *Alice in Wonderland*.[6] By means of this single allusion, Serber conveys an impression of the simultaneous disorientation, excitement, and sense of discovery inherent in his experience "on the Hill." The utility of this literary shorthand depends, of course, on the assumption that the majority of Serber's readers would be familiar with *Alice*—as with the stories of Oedipus, King Arthur, and so on. Like Compton's "extemporaneous code," the success of the Los Alamites' metaphorical descriptions depends on their audiences' familiarity with their literary vehicles. Given that familiarity, a basic understanding would be almost immediate, as it was for Conant.

Representation by means of existing literary narratives does more than communicate quickly, however. It also inscribes the events and relations that are its primary concern within the secondary set of events and relations that are in turn the primary subject of the invoked text. The effects of this are numerous and complex. For the moment, I will merely point out a few that are most relevant to this study. First, an ostensible purpose of any metaphorical representation is to bridge a gap between our experience and the author's and thereby to simplify the process by which we gain access to the latter; but in the case of a metaphorical connection between two extended narratives, our interpretation of the author's experience depends on how we interpret her narrative vehicle as well. We are therefore caught in a doubled act of reading that can more than double the complexity of the interpretive process. Second, this process introduces meanings that may be extraneous to the author's experience of the original events—and which therefore divert our understanding—or, if pertinent, may have been too easily obtained and therefore insufficiently considered. Third, another central function of metaphor is to limit and direct our interpretation of an author's meaning. While there is some expansion of meaning in any dynamic metaphor, the author's ability to shape meaning usually outweighs any coincident slippage.[7] In metaphorical uses of literary precedents, however, the resonances between the primary and secondary narratives almost inevitably introduce contradictions and emphasize the semiotic slipperiness of their comparison. Therefore, though such metaphorical codes may facilitate a quick initial understanding, they will also tend to resist our efforts to achieve a complete or static interpretation.

We do not, however, tend to feel these interpretive difficulties acutely—except in unusual circumstances, such as those examined in Chapters 1 through 3. In the case of the Los Alamites' descriptions of their work, for instance, the vast conceptual distance crossed by their metaphors obscures much of the attendant slippage. This conceptual distance is twofold. As Oppenheimer insists, physics constitutes "a realm of action so remote from our common experience" that it has been thought of as a different culture, if not a different world. When physics concerns itself with the perihelion of Mercury's orbit around the sun, or the measurable curvature of the path of light from a distant star as it passes the sun during a solar eclipse, we are not likely to object to the remoteness of this esoteric branch of science. But when it leads to the construction of a worldwide nuclear arsenal, its relevance suddenly becomes pressing and its remoteness an obstacle to be overcome. In this context, literature provides a medium through which physicists can anchor their forays into the remote realms of the marvelous by means of a shared and well-established medium of cultural representation. Therefore, though we do not hear scientists quoting literature every day, the development of nuclear weapons foregrounds the dynamic role of literature in mediating between specialized scientific practices and our common social understanding.

"Beggared Description"

The Los Alamites' work is distant from our common experience in a second sense as well, for the scale of the Manhattan Project and the effects of nuclear weapons were so immense and so unfamiliar that, in the words of one participant, they "beggared description."[8] Indeed, as should be apparent by now, the variety of the Los Alamites' attempts to describe their experience is enormous. The "atomic bomb" seems to inspire a procession of metaphorical descriptions, each more extravagant than the last, as if the only way to represent the bomb was to overload a reader's imagination. Even the Los Alamites themselves complain of their own (and each other's) descriptive excesses.[9] Yet there seems to be no alternative: even considered from a "purely" scientific point of view, these new weapons span physical scales from the subatomic to the stellar, confronting us with apparent incongruities of size and power, matter and energy.

Is it possible, then, for us to know what this "gadget" is "like"? "A red-hot elephant standing balanced on its trunk," thought Otto Frisch, as he writes, "incongruously."[10] But is any description better? Most seem to hide behind a screen of literary allusion, as if to shift representational responsibility onto someone else's words, or else they construct a dramatic context that implicitly identifies the speaker as one in a community of voices. Such descriptions present us with exceptionally thick surfaces. They claim the authority of eyewitness accounts, even as they speak with the voices of texts written before nuclear weapons existed. At the same time, these familiar voices and well-known narratives lull us into a dangerous sense of the security of our understanding. They distract us (and in many cases their authors as well) from a rigorous examination of the dynamic metaphors that underlie them. Indeed, their very inconsistencies and excesses encourage us to believe that their authors have engaged their own representational failures—and that these accounts are, therefore, trustworthy.

Despite the complexities involved in the Los Alamites' attempts to represent their experience and the difficulties we face in our efforts to interpret them, we cannot simply reject their more literary descriptions as subjective fictions or the products of overheated imaginations. For one thing, the Los Alamites' descriptions are an indispensable source of knowledge about nuclear weapons. Any description or analysis of these weapons must ultimately refer to accounts written by one or more of the following groups: the Los Alamites, the Hibakusha,[11] or postwar developers (including the soldiers involved in combat-simulation tests). Of these three groups, the Los Alamites had the greatest impact on our society's general understanding of nuclear weapons both because their accounts were the first to be widely disseminated and because they claim the respect due to the authors of the bomb. For better or worse, an understanding of the meaning of nuclear weapons in our society requires an engagement with the Los Alamites' descriptions of their experiences.

Yet must we depend on their figurative fabrications? Why not consider only their more literal accounts? Indeed, why not acknowledge that all other description falls short of the objective, scientific representations that accumulated in locked safes in the offices of the Tech Area at Los Alamos? These documents, after all, offer anyone with the appropriate security clearance a literal description sufficient to reproduce a working copy of an atomic bomb. Of course, most people have no means of accessing these accounts; despite an ongoing process of declassification, many of these documents retain their original, restrictive ratings, and most of the rest remain in archives that enforce their own rules to limit access. Yet I do not mean this question to be merely rhetorical: Given that such powerful practical descriptions exist, what makes the Los Alamites' figurative representations useful enough to warrant extended attention?

One practical consideration is the impossibility of consistently and absolutely distinguishing between figurative and literal language, given that no inviolable line separates them. Most of the Los Alamites' accounts—even their most technical documents—employ both modes, as we have seen in the case of *The Los Alamos Primer*. In a more theoretical vein, the reasons that led the Los Alamites to turn to metaphorical language and literary models in the first place likewise compel us to pay close attention to such representations. Furthermore, they are, in my experience, the most emotionally powerful and personally influential of the Los Alamites' utterances. If figurative language lacks the ability to convey a static, experimentally verifiable conception of nuclear weapons, literal descriptions are inadequate in another sense: they exclude human emotions, personal significance, subjective experience— and because of this, they require interpretation just as much as literary descriptions, though they discourage it even more than the literary. For most of us, this means that literal descriptions of nuclear weapons are less valuable than figurative accounts, since a technical knowledge of these weapons is superfluous for us, while an understanding of their human meaning is of the greatest importance.

The Los Alamites' figurative descriptions, therefore, offer us a particular kind of insight. On the surface, they are narratives recounting the experiences of the individuals most immediately involved in and responsible for the development of weapons that have had an enormous impact on our social development, not least in having given us the capacity to exterminate ourselves. These narratives contain a tremendous amount of historical information, and they continue to be mined by historians. But they are less interesting to me as sources of historical "fact" than as interpretive acts in themselves, for at a deeper level they embody the means by which these individuals tried to make sense of the weapons they had built and of themselves as the builders. The construction of these accounts, therefore, mirrors our own interpretations of them, and in doing so they offer us an unusually rich opportunity. Precisely because of their dense, figurative textures, they contain not only narratives that show us nuclear weapons as directly as we are ever likely to know them, but also enactments of the process through which such knowledge is socially constituted.

"The Second Coming in Wrath"

In this section, I will examine the impact of the Los Alamites' eyewitness descriptions of the Trinity test on the first major audience for such accounts: Harry Truman and Winston Churchill. As hundreds of scientists and technicians made final preparations for the test of the first plutonium bomb, code-named Trinity, Truman and Churchill arrived in Germany for their meeting with Joseph Stalin at Potsdam. The success or failure of the test would, they believed, influence the United States's and Britain's ability to hold in check the Soviet Union's expansionist drive. On the evening of July 16, 1945, Truman received a coded cable announcing the successful detonation that morning of the first atomic bomb. At lunch the next day, Secretary of War Henry Stimson shared the information with Churchill. Both leaders were, naturally, encouraged by the news, which potentially meant a quick end to the war with Japan as well as a stronger negotiating position with Stalin.

Ironically, neither wanted the Soviet leader to know about the bomb until it was used in combat to end the war. They were concerned that Stalin's territorial ambitions extended to the Pacific, and they felt that he would have little claim in the region if the Soviet Union was unable to join the war there before it ended. Both men foresaw that if Stalin realized the full potential of an atomic bomb, he would rush to declare war on Japan before the new weapon could be used to force a surrender. Yet at that point neither Truman nor Churchill had much more sense of what their weapon could do than Stalin did.[12] Four more days of meetings went by before Truman received, on the afternoon of July 21, General Leslie Groves's memorandum outlining in some detail the results of the Trinity test.

A full third of Groves's memorandum consists of the impressions of his deputy at Los Alamos, Brigadier General Thomas Farrell, who was present at the test. Farrell's account contains the document's most detailed description of the explosion and its effect on those who witnessed it:

The scene inside the shelter was dramatic beyond words. . . .

Everyone in that room knew the awful potentialities of the thing that they thought was about to happen. . . . The feeling of many could be expressed by "Lord, I believe; help Thou mine unbelief." We were reaching into the unknown and we did not know what might come of it. It can be safely said that most of those present—Christian, Jew and Atheist—were praying and praying harder than they had ever prayed before. . . .

For the last few seconds, [Oppenheimer] stared directly ahead and then when the announcer shouted "Now!" and there came this tremendous burst of light followed shortly thereafter by the deep growling roar of the explosion, his face relaxed into an expression of tremendous relief. Several of the observers standing back of the shelter to watch the lighting effects were knocked flat by the blast.

. . . No matter what might happen now all knew that the impossible scientific job had been done. Atomic fission would no longer be hidden in the cloisters of the theoretical physicists' dreams. It was almost full grown at birth. It was a great new force to be used for good or for evil. There was a feeling in that shelter that those concerned with its nativity should dedicate their lives to the mission that it would always be used for good and never for evil. . . .

The effects could well be called unprecedented, magnificent, beautiful, stupendous and terrifying. No man-made phenomenon of such tremendous power had ever occurred before. The lighting effects beggared description. The whole country was lighted by a searing light with the intensity many times that of the midday sun. It was golden, purple, violet, gray and blue. It lighted every peak, crevasse and ridge of the nearby mountain range with a clarity and beauty that cannot be described but must be seen to be imagined. It was that beauty the great poets dream about but describe most poorly and inadequately. Thirty seconds after the explosion came first, the air blast pressing hard against the people and things, to be followed almost immediately by the strong, sustained, awesome roar which warned of doomsday and made us feel that we puny things were blasphemous to dare tamper with the forces heretofore reserved to The Almighty. Words are inadequate tools for the job of acquainting those not present with the physical, mental and psychological effects. It had to be witnessed to be realized.[13]

I have quoted from Farrell's account at length because it introduces a broad range of issues and rhetorical techniques which are also important elements of the scientists' responses to the bomb. His account represents an instance, and a particularly influential one, of the complex and subtle interplay of metaphor, biblical allusion, and self-conscious rhetorical positioning that characterizes the responses of the individuals most closely associated with the development of atomic weapons. Although it would be easy to criticize, or indeed parody, Farrell's purple prose and mixed metaphors, they are far from being simply the naïve effusions of a histrionic individual. As we have seen, the scientists themselves turned frequently to similar rhetorical strategies in their efforts to convey the significance of what they had witnessed. Joseph Hirschfelder, for example, insists that "There weren't any agnostics watching this stupendous demonstration. Each, in his own way, knew that God had spoken."[14] If we do not allow the roughness of Farrell's technique to obscure the effectiveness of his formulations, this awkwardness itself may offer us an opportunity to see through the apparent naturalness of the scientists' more polished uses of similar strategies.

Farrell begins by implying that he is attempting to do the impossible: the "scene" of which Truman and Churchill wish to hear is "beyond words." "The lighting effects beggared description." "It was that beauty the great poets dream about but describe most poorly and inadequately." "Words are inadequate tools for the job. . . . It had to be witnessed to be realized." In effect, he tells his readers that he cannot tell them anything; if they were not present themselves, they will never know what the bomb is like. Farrell portrays the experience as dependent on its physical dimensions, its overwhelming sensory scale. He seems to insist that the atomic bomb can be known only in a somatic mode; the symbolic medium of language is inadequate, even in the hands of the "great poets," its putative masters.

Yet Farrell employs precisely this medium in claiming its inadequacy. Of course, he is bound to it, as we all are, as even Truman was by his need to know what was happening six thousand miles away in the desert of southern New Mexico while he toured the ruins of Berlin. To meet this need, therefore, Farrell invokes what he feels to be among the most powerful linguistic resources available to him: that of biblical language. The biblical tradition offers an array of verbal gestures, attitudes, and techniques, all of proven efficacy and potent associations. It provides an established language of transcendental experience, which would seem to be exactly what Farrell requires. Biblical language carries with it an implication of the great significance of its subjects. Since it represents the word of God, it is by definition authoritative. Furthermore, since God alone possesses the power to speak through things, by means of physical objects in the sensory world, His language, the language of the scriptures, enjoys a special status as regards the representation of the physical world.

In short, biblical language claims an ability to signify what lies under its subjects' surfaces, to say what God "means" by them. Many of the assumptions underlying the interpretive practices of the Western analytical tradition, whether in the form of literary exegesis or scientific hypothesis, derive from medieval efforts, beginning with St. Augustine, to reconcile the variety of literary representations of earthly experience in the scriptures with a neoplatonic conception of the physical world as symbolic of a transcendent Ideal. In this context, Farrell's simultaneous attempts to insist on the essentially somatic nature of the atomic bomb and to represent it by means of biblical language as an archetypal symbol of "forces heretofore reserved to The Almighty" lose their contradictory appearance. Farrell's account is, in fact, an example of the interpretive assumptions and methods that underlie the Western analytical traditional in general, though here they are in a more breathy and jumbled form than we are used to finding them.

So we should not be surprised that Farrell seems to have so little difficulty going on and on talking about what he says he cannot talk about. As Hirschfelder's comment suggests, despite the experience being "beyond words," many of those present felt it to be precisely a matter of words—God's words. Furthermore, Farrell is, ultimately, compelled by his circumstances to report to his superiors as exactly as possible what "can be safely said" or "well be called" and not be satisfied with simply impressing upon his readers the transcendent nature of his experience that makes such saying and calling problematic. What he can say is that "those present—Christian, Jew and Atheist" responded to a scene "beyond words" with words, by "praying and praying harder than they had ever prayed." Farrell constructs the significance of his experience in the same way: symbolizing it as being beyond symbolizing; invoking a language that helps his reader know the unknowable, God, the bomb; bridging the distance between Potsdam and Alamogordo, or between the divine and the human, by emphasizing the barrier that separates them.

In the end, Farrell turns his impossible task of representation itself into a metaphor for the construction of an atomic bomb. "No matter what might happen now all knew that the impossible scientific job had been done." Just as he faces the challenge of describing something beyond words, he points out that the physicists likewise confronted the need to achieve the "impossible." Farrell's account constructs the two tasks as parallel. As the scientists labored to turn the symbolic materials of their discipline into a physical entity, Farrell works to translate that "thing" back into a symbolic form. In this way, his own struggle—to make words convey the culmination of the scientists' three-year struggle with stubborn natural facts—does double duty. By emphasizing the difficulty of his own descriptive task, he portrays the immensity of his ostensible subject. So Farrell describes what he can describe—his own representational dilemma—and in the process manages to describe indirectly the very thing that resists direct description but that it is his responsibility to describe: the bomb itself.

Groves's memorandum, reinforced by Farrell's account, seems to have had a strong effect on its recipients. Churchill said of Truman, "When he got to the meeting after having read this report, he was a changed man. He told the Russians just where they got on and off and generally bossed the whole meeting."[15] Truman even adopted Farrell's language in his own attempt to express an understanding of what this new "thing" meant: "We have discovered the most terrible bomb in the history of the world. It may be the fire destruction prophesied in the Euphrates Valley Era, after Noah and his fabulous Ark."[16] Churchill's response likewise echoed Farrell: "What was gunpowder? Trivial. What was electricity? Meaningless. This atomic bomb is the Second Coming in Wrath."[17]

By taking over Farrell's descriptive approach, Truman and Churchill were not simply borrowing a convenient metaphorical base. Their words betray a dependence on a complex set of assumptions regarding the authority of Farrell's account. On the one hand, it purported to represent the observations of an eyewitness; on the other, it actually offered little original observation but instead presented a hash of biblical images and rhetorical flourishes. But while one might argue that the former would have been more useful, the latter was not a failure on Farrell's part. Indeed, this hash was precisely what Truman and Churchill needed, for it offered them the materials of social utterance. Compare this account, for example, with these more "objective" official descriptions submitted by scientists who observed the test:

I looked at the explosion through the dark glass. . . . I saw flames and smoke of an estimated diameter of 1000 yds. which was slowly decreasing in brightness seemingly due to more smoke development. At the same time it rose slightly above the surface. After about three seconds its intensity was so low I could remove the dark glass and look at it directly. Then I saw a reddish blowing smoke ball rising with a thick stem of dark brown color. This smoke ball was surrounded by a blue glow which clearly indicated a strong radioactivity and was certainly due to the gamma rays emitted by the cloud into the surrounding air. At that moment the cloud had about 1000 billions of curies of radioactivity whose radiation must have produced the blue glow.[18]

Turned on Leet meter—1 sec approx. At t_0 sky lit up white.
At $t + 1$ sec may have shaken floor ducking due to being blinded.
Sky turned to brilliant red and faded in about 4 sec. 2 smoke puffs blew up at about 4–5 sec. rapidly into sky—then more slowly rose fiery smoke cloud which faded to pink in several seconds.

At about 10 sec. (maybe 15) there were 2 lightning flashes, sort of white, illuminated the cloud which was rising all the time.
At 2 min 38 seconds air shock arrived. . . . [19]

About 40 seconds after the explosion the air blast reached me. I tried to estimate its strength by dropping from about six feet small pieces of paper before, during and after the passage of the blast wave. Since, at the time, there was no wind I could observe very distinctly and actually measure the displacement of the pieces of paper that were in the process of falling while the blast was passing. The shift was about 2½ meters, which, at the time, I estimated to correspond to the blast that would be produced by ten thousand tons of T.N.T.[20]

Farrell's words offer the reader a terrifying weapon; the scientists' restrained, unimpassioned accounts suggest a large experiment. In a time of war, and in the midst of laying the foundations of another, colder war, the Allied leaders needed just what Farrell gave them: a rhetorical weapon.[21]

The irony here, of course, is that by co-opting the rhetorical power of Farrell's account, Churchill and Truman were accepting a whole range of associations and conceptual baggage over which they had no control. Biblical rhetoric resonates powerfully in the Western ear as a function of its historical pedigree. But such rhetoric is far from empty. Hand in hand with its descriptive efficacy goes conceptual commitment. Rational thought is only as good as the words that express it.[22] By accepting Farrell's rhetoric and employing it for their political advantage, Truman and Churchill were perpetuating its conceptual underpinnings as well, situating atomic weapons in our culture within a framework of biblical reasoning—of an eye for an eye and a tooth for a tooth, for example. As a result, while atomic weapons transformed the world around them, the men who were apparently responsible for leading the way into a new age seemed to be helplessly attached to texts of the distant past.

"I Heard Another Voice—My Own"

They were not alone in their dependence on familiar "modes of thinking." When the existence of atomic weapons was announced to the world less than three weeks later with the destruction of Hiroshima, the general public's first conception of these weapons depended almost exclusively on the written descriptions of another witness to the Trinity test. Well before the first fission bombs were completed, General Groves had recognized the importance of how they would be perceived by the public. He knew that when these bombs were finally used (and he had no doubt that they would be used) the public would demand information; but he also knew that the conventions of military secrecy would give him a great deal of control over how this information was initially disseminated. He saw that he had an opportunity to shape the public's understanding of this two billion dollar project, for which he had assumed responsibility, and to convince them that it was a justifiable, even an inevitable, undertaking.

So Groves set out to assemble materials with which to glut the world's news media. He placed William Laurence, a science reporter for the *New York Times*, at the heart of this effort, arranging for him to take a leave of absence from the *Times* in order to tour the entire Manhattan Project and to be present at the Trinity test itself. Laurence was to be Groves's ace in the hole: a man of established credibility (he had won a Pulitzer Prize) and prestigious connections (through his position at the *Times*), he had already shown himself to be a proponent of nuclear energy in prewar paeans published in the *Times*. Groves's strategy proved to be an effective one. During the course of "several months of labor," Laurence produced "pounds of official reports and bales of War Department 'handouts.' "[23] After Little Boy fell on Hiroshima, reporters from all over the world scrambled for information about these strange, new weapons. But there were only a few places to turn: Laurence's work made up the bulk of available material, and his writings, along with Farrell's account quoted above, and official statements from Truman, Churchill, and Stimson (which also relied on Laurence's and Farrell's accounts), formed the basis for these reporters' "own" narratives and analysis.

On August 7, 1945, the existence of nuclear weapons at last became a matter of public knowledge in the West. The news dominated the front pages of papers around the world, and Truman's voice could be heard on the radio warning over and over of "a rain of ruin from the air, the like of which has never been seen on this earth."[24] Reporters did what they could to flesh out the few sources available to them: one *Times* writer, for example, asserted that "Graphic word pictures of the test were given by eye-witnesses, who were awed by the mysterious and gigantic power of the bomb,"[25] but offered as evidence only Farrell's account, chopped up and sprinkled through a long article. As a result, the news coverage invariably echoes the Los Alamites' descriptions of their experience, as reporters tried to evoke "the New Mexico desert lands" in which "a group of eminent scientists gathered, frankly fearful to witness the results of the invention, which might turn out to be either the salvation or the Frankenstein's monster of the world."[26]

After the war, as the Los Alamites emerged from their "secret laboratory," they began to tell their stories for themselves, in contexts ranging from impromptu remarks at garden parties to formal testimony before Congress. But in practical terms, Laurence had already spilled the beans—skilled as a popularizer, he had managed to distill the Los Alamites' experiences, and he disseminated them to the world in a series of bite-sized pieces that firmly anchored the public's understanding of nuclear weapons in the same metaphorical contexts we have seen in the Los Alamites' own accounts. In fact, Laurence continued for years to be one of the most energetic spokesmen for "atomic power"—continuing to do Groves proud as a kind of cheerleader and ultimately capitalizing on his privileged position as a witness to the "birth of the atomic age" with two volumes of reminiscences—*Men and Atoms* and *Dawn over Zero: The Story of the Atomic Bomb.*

Laurence's reminiscences epitomize the dynamic that is the central focus of this chapter: the ways in which "witnesses" transformed nuclear weapons into literary icons. For example, he describes his experience returning to Los Alamos immediately after the Trinity test in these terms:

On arriving at Los Alamos I called on Dr. Oppenheimer. He looked tired and preoccupied. I asked him how he felt at the moment of the flash.

"At that moment," I heard him say, "there flashed into my mind a passage from the Bhagavad-Gita, the sacred book of the Hindus: 'I am become Death, the Shatterer of Worlds!' "

. . . Later that Monday morning, at the breakfast table in the pleasant dining room of the Los Alamos Lodge, the silence was broken by Dr. George B. Kistiakowsky of Harvard. Though he was seated next to me, his voice seemed to come from a great distance. And what I heard has been haunting me ever since.

"This was the nearest to doomsday one can possibly imagine," he said. "I am sure," he added after a pause, as though speaking to no one in particular, "that at the end of the world—in the last millisecond of the earth's existence—the last man will see something very similar to what we have seen."

And out of the silence that ensued I heard another voice—my own—which also sounded as though it came from a distance.

"Possibly so," I said, "but it is also possible that if the first man could have been present at the moment of Creation when God said, 'Let there be light,' he might have seen something very similar to what we have seen."[27]

Both Laurence and Kistiakowsky share Farrell's sense of the propriety of biblical imagery and dramatic description. Laurence, however, clearly has the advantage over his dining partner as a propagandist: where Kistiakowsky thinks of endings, Laurence thinks of beginnings; where the former pictures doomsday, the latter imagines the Creation.

Clearly Laurence revels in the opportunity to act as a medium between his readers and the experience he describes. He asserts the authority of his privileged position as eyewitness by taking care to locate himself, literally, in the scene he describes and by making sure we recognize the pedigree of his confreres: "*Dr.* George B. Kistiakowsky of *Harvard* . . . was seated next to me. . . ." Laurence depicts Dr. George in such a way that he begins to sound almost oracular. In the silence, "his voice seemed to come from a great distance," and his words—as Laurence reconstructs them—are prophetic and "haunting." In such company, Laurence finds himself being transformed. His own voice takes on a similar power; it, too, wells up "out of the silence . . . as though it came from a distance." It hardly sounds like his voice at all—to the degree that he must identify it for us as his own. And this voice portrays itself in even more exalted company than that of the doctors who so recently delivered the atomic bomb; now Laurence is with the Almighty Himself, present at the Creation, able to quote God as if he had heard Him with his own ears. Like Farrell, Laurence characterizes the bomb as a manifestation of God's power, and his direct experience of it allows him to speak with a biblical authority. Through his narrative, Laurence turns himself into a kind of prophet coming down from the mountain, or in this case the Los Alamos mesa, and as readers we have no opportunity to contradict him because we have not had any such authorizing experiences.

In this passage, Laurence struts his stuff with a facility that fully justifies Groves's faith in him. His narrative is complex, and far more layered and nuanced than its surface naïveté would lead us to believe. Although he quotes God to justify his version of what happened at Trinity, he is not content to rest his presentation on these biblical underpinnings. Instead, he draws us into the action by offering us two opposing versions of what occurred that July morning, in the form of a dramatic debate between two fallible individuals: Kistiakowsky and himself. And though he allows himself the last word, we may be able to overlook this bit of authorial legerdemain if we notice that it is the debate itself, and not any particular conclusion, through which he tries to legitimize his authorship. Laurence creates the illusion that he is submerging his own voice within a multivocal exchange—his is, of course, the only voice we hear, though fragmented into a narrator and three characters, two of whom seem to be engaged in a dialogue or at least to be declaiming in one another's presence. Through this illusion, he constitutes his readers as witnesses themselves, not dependent on his words alone but able to "sit in" on the scene and listen to the evidence of their own ears. He deemphasizes his own authority and sets it in the context of a number of even more authoritative voices: those who not only witnessed the bomb but built it. Yet, as we have seen, his proximity to such authority converts him into one of the chosen as well, and so through submission to dialogue and debate, his voice reemerges even more strongly and authoritatively.[28]

There is a strong dramatic component to many accounts of the Trinity test. Farrell describes it as "dramatic beyond words" and refers repeatedly to "the lighting effects." Laurence actually constructs his description as a kind of drama. And he reports that a soldier briefing his group before the test cautioned them, "If the first flash is viewed, a 'blind spot' may prevent your seeing the rest of the show."[29] Newspaper reports, likewise, dutifully reproduce these representations, referring to the Trinity test site, for instance, as "The scene of the great drama."[30] Indeed, responses to the test tend to demonstrate a tension between the revelatory and the dramatic qualities of the experience. As Ernest Lawrence, the director of the Berkeley Radiation Laboratory and a colleague of Oppenheimer's, remembers, after the blast "There was a restrained applause, but more a hushed murmuring bordering on reverence in manner as the event was commented upon."[31] Many witnesses did not seem to know whether they should laugh or cry, respond as if they had just seen a "show" or "the Second Coming in wrath." And so most eyewitness accounts, like Laurence's and Farrell's, in attempting to represent the bomb accurately and vividly, ironically call attention to the literary character of their representations.

Autographing the Bomb: Atomic Weapons as Literature

Although most readers will, I hope, find the literary representations of nuclear weapons that we have inherited from the Los Alamites a worthwhile scholarly topic in their own right, there is a crucial sense in which they are of far more than academic interest. In conjunction with the destructive power of atomic weapons, these representations should be understood as matters of life and death. At the heart of this understanding lies the question, formulated by Jacques Derrida, of whether there exists any "radically new predicate in the situation known as 'the nuclear age.'" Derrida himself offers an optimistic response to his own question: "a precipitous assertion, a *belief*," that there is not any such "new predicate." Yet the fear lingers that "the critical zeal that leads us to recognize precedents, continuities, and repetitions at every turn can make us look like suicidal sleepwalkers, blind and deaf *alongside the unheard-of*."[32] Derrida identifies this critical zeal with the putative "nuclear critic," but I believe it may characterize anyone who thinks, speaks, or writes about nuclear weapons. It is, at its root, the source of the terrible danger that Einstein describes when he says that "the unleashed power of the atom has changed everything save our modes of thinking, and we thus drift toward unparalleled catastrophe."[33] Because we have inherited the Los Alamites' conceptions of nuclear weapons, and because these conceptions are based on preexisting literary models, it is very difficult, perhaps impossible, for us to determine whether or not these weapons introduce any "radically new predicate." We are, in effect, wrapped in the protective covering of long-established "ways of thinking," and as a result we may have constructed nuclear weapons in a potentially devastating role in our society.

That role is, in Derrida's terms, "textual," and he describes nuclear weapons as

a phenomenon whose essential feature is that of being *fabulously textual*, through and through. Nuclear weaponry depends, more than any weaponry in the past, it seems, upon structures of information and communication, structures of language, including non-vocalizable language, structures of codes and graphics decoding. But the phenomenon is fabulously textual also to the extent that, for the moment, a nuclear war has not taken place: one can only talk and write about it.[34]

Here Derrida offers an important insight, but he undercuts the power of his argument by failing to acknowledge that nuclear weapons exist as solid, physical objects, in far greater numbers than most of us might like to imagine. The residents of Hiroshima and Nagasaki in 1945 might well argue with some bitterness that a nuclear war *has* taken place. Yet the essence of Derrida's point is on target: To virtually everyone on the planet, nuclear weapons remain a purely literary phenomenon in that they exist for us in solid form only on paper, in our writings about them. Few people have actually seen or touched a nuclear weapon, much less experienced one in action, and therefore our own accounts of them must remain essentially textual.

We can, however, go even further than Derrida. Based on my examination of the Los Alamites' attempts to describe their direct experience of nuclear weapons, and of the dissemination of those descriptions through Farrell's and Laurence's accounts, I would argue that nuclear weapons have been constructed in our society not only as *textual* entities but more specifically as *literary* ones. It is not merely their primary existence as linguistic constructs that is crucial to our understanding and treatment of them; it is that they do not exist for us except insofar as we are able to imagine in language a set of experiences we have never had and which (we hope) will never be tested in comparison to physical fact. What's more, the Los Alamites' own accounts of these weapons deliver them to us preformed as fictions, for in our first encounter with them, they are already construed as literary entities. Even if we were to handle them at some future point, to witness for ourselves a nuclear explosion, we would see it through the veil of its current literary configuration.

From their inception, nuclear weapons, generally assumed to be the physical products of particular scientific practices, have existed for most of us as evolving metaphoric entities. Despite their physical substance, since World War II nuclear weapons have exercised their power in the purely literary form of their fictional use in the future. The nuclear powers have not built atomic weapons for the primary purpose of employing them in combat. Instead, they have continued to develop, construct, and maintain these bombs to perform first (and, we hope, solely) a symbolic purpose: by representing the massive death and destruction they might cause, they are meant to render their physical use superfluous. In effect, nuclear weapons as scientific artifacts have little function except through the stories people (like the Los Alamites) tell about them.

Even when the United States dropped nuclear weapons on Hiroshima and Nagasaki, the intent was in part symbolic. These bombs were nicknamed "Little Boy" and "Fat Man" and "autographed with all sorts of ribald messages to the Emperor."[35] Their purpose was not to cause more damage than had previously been achieved using conventional weapons, and, in fact, they did not do so; rather, they were meant to stun the Japanese with a single blow into a perception of the massive superiority of Allied forces.[36] The Nagasaki bomb conveyed even more particularly focused messages: the first, to the Japanese, implied that the United States had a limitless supply of such weapons, although it did not; the second, to the Soviet Union, suggested that the Americans would be formidable enemies. Of course, I do not mean to downplay the horrific physical effects of these weapons. Even a cursory glance at accounts written by survivors of Hiroshima and Nagasaki, or the reports of observers, or even the technical summaries compiled years after those bombings, will leave a reader sickened and fearful.[37] But I do mean to insist on the centrality of the literary treatment of nuclear weapons examined here to our willingness to deploy them against Japan in the first place, and even more to the policies that have governed their uses since that time.

Curiously, this reliance on literary representations of atomic weapons goes hand in hand with a widespread mistrust of such representations in our culture. We continue to crave the authority of direct experience, though we have great reason to fear it in this case; and so we turn to the scientists who built these weapons. In doing so, we defer not only to the details of their accounts but to the assumption that physical experience constitutes the truest form of knowledge. So the scientists' representations assert their authority in an additional sense, for they borrow the aura of a direct involvement in physical experience that characterizes science itself. Ironically, however, in turning to the Los Alamites' accounts, we are gaining access not to physical experience but to more texts. And as we have seen, these texts, and even the scientific practices to which they refer, are themselves full of the very literary qualities we mistrust. A prejudice against literary representations is, therefore, not only counterproductive but dangerous. Since we cannot escape our dependence on these representations by turning to scientists' accounts, or even, as we have seen in preceding chapters, to actual scientific texts, by continuing to privilege literal representation over figurative we are deluding ourselves. Instead, it would be more helpful to acknowledge and attempt to analyze the particular ways in which literary practices, within science as without, facilitate and complicate our efforts to understand and represent nuclear weapons.

Conclusion

This analysis has many practical implications, for it contradicts the efforts of policymakers, military officials, and all who belong to the secret cabal of those with direct experience of atomic weapons. These individuals tend to work hard to consolidate their power and exclude others with different "interpretations" of these weapons. In fact, the secrecy surrounding nuclear armaments functions effectively precisely because it constructs a rigid distinction between "symbolic," literary knowledge and "experiential," scientific knowledge. By privileging the latter and keeping most of us confined to a "merely" metaphorical understanding, the powers that be maintain their powers, limit debate and dissension, and even manage to police their own ranks. The utility of this dynamic appears perhaps most strikingly in the case of Oppenheimer himself. As I described in Chapter 5, following the war, he occupied a position of immense power and influence; but his opposition to the development of hydrogen weapons earned him many enemies within military-political circles, and in 1953, immediately following his lectures on the BBC with which I began this chapter, the Atomic Energy Commission revoked his security clearance and denied him access to his files, even though a large portion of them consisted of his own writings.[38] Without access to "direct," scientific knowledge of the weapons he had helped to build, Oppenheimer believed that it was inappropriate for him to claim further authority in the debate over their proper use.

If Oppenheimer was right, then the general public has no role to play in shaping nuclear weapons policy; indeed, many of the people who "defrocked" him would insist on this. Yet Oppenheimer's own rhetorical practices contradict his belief that science offers a superior and separate access to knowledge about atomic weapons. As we have seen, such rigid distinctions between literary and scientific representations are always misleading and often illusory. In fact, literature and physics echo and reinforce one another to a remarkable extent. Literature, for example, routinely depends on an acute attention to physical detail in the creation of its effects. Physics, likewise, particularly in the twentieth century, recognizes and incorporates the vagaries of human perception into its understandings of the phenomenal world; with increasing frequency, scientific theories describe a world that contradicts our untutored observations. Indeed, the most highly marked differences between the conceptual tools of physics and literature result from tendencies in the ways their practitioners make use of them rather than from any absolute incompatibility of cognitive approach. Neither discipline exists in a vacuum, and even to the extent that physics and literature constitute an opposition, they also participate in the larger continuity of the Western intellectual tradition.

All this suggests that literary analysis can play an important role in our understanding of atomic weapons and even in our decisions regarding their proper and improper uses. It can offer a means of breaking the experts' stranglehold over policy decisions and granting to the general public a greater measure of understanding and control of their own lives. Literary criticism, of course, is itself a specialized discipline; yet, unlike subatomic physics, it is a discipline to which all schoolchildren receive at least some exposure. The curricular emphasis in secondary schools on the techniques of analyzing literary texts demonstrates the high degree of importance our culture accords these skills, though their practical benefits are rarely clear in that context. Here we see a dramatic example of those potential benefits. In this chapter I have argued that the use of literary rhetoric is not limited to overtly literary texts but in fact pervades the thinking and writing even of individuals who specialize in "a realm of action so remote from our common experience." And I have tried to demonstrate the interdisciplinary power of literary criticism by applying it in an analysis of the Los Alamites' rhetorical responses to the new weapons they had built. The ways in which they describe the results of their work have constituted nuclear weapons as a literary force in our culture with vast practical consequences. Literary criticism can help us understand the structure of that force and thereby give us potentially useful tools in confronting its consequences.

Hiroshima, January 1946, signed August 5, 1990, by Lieutenant Colonel Paul Tibbets, Major Thomas Ferebee, Captain Theodore J. "Dutch" Van Kirk, the pilot, bombardier, and navigator of the *Enola Gay*. (Photo by Corporal Bill Jones, courtesy Bill Jones.)

PHYSICS IN FICTION

"THE VOICE OF THE DOLPHINS"

AND *RIDDLEY WALKER*

*That the bomb would pose a novel problem to the world was
clear as early as 1946. . . . Why, then, one may ask, did
scientists in general, and the President's Science Advisory
Committee in particular, fail to advance a solution of this
problem during the Eisenhower adminsitration?*
—Leo Szilard, The Voice of the Dolphins and Other Stories

*Words! Theywl move things you know theywl
do things. Theywl fetch. Put a name to some thing
and youre beckoning. Iwl write a message if I have
to but I wunt word nothing moren that on paper.
Eusa been fetcht by words on paper you know.*
—*Russell Hoban,* Riddley Walker

In 1896, in the midst of his research into fluorescence,
Antoine Henri Becquerel, a Nobel Prize–winning physicist, identified a
new phenomenon in uranium when he noticed that a sample of potas-
sium uranyl sulfate had caused dark spots to appear on a photographic
plate. The discovery was partly accidental—the choice of which fluo-
rescent material to subject to x-rays; the placement of the uranium salt
in a drawer that also contained a photographic plate wrapped in dark
paper—but it set off an explosion in the growth of atomic science that
would continue in its as yet unborn nuclear offspring. As the historian J.
D. Bernal put it, "Once radioactivity was discovered scientific progress
was fast—faster, indeed, than in any earlier period in the history of
science."[1] Soon Marie Curie, who would go on to win two Nobel Prizes
for her research, had coined the word "radioactivity" to describe this
phenomenon, based on the fact that the radiation emitted by these
substances could be heard as static on a radio. She and her husband,
Pierre, conducted an extensive examination of pitchblende, one of the
primary ores containing uranium, and in 1898 their researches led them

to discover two new elements, both products of the radioactive decay of uranium: radium and polonium (named for Marie's native Poland). To some, it seemed as if the dreams of medieval alchemists might prove to have been prophetic after all. What might not be possible with this new source of energy? In 1908, in an effort to summarize the short but eventful history of the most promising of these new substances, and to anticipate its apparently limitless uses in the future, the British chemist Sir Frederick Soddy delivered a series of six popular lectures at the University of Glasgow, which were then published as a monograph in both Britain and the United States.[2]

Four years later, H. G. Wells published *The World Set Free*, the novel that Leo Szilard credits as inspiring his investigation of the possibility that radioactive substances might be exploited as a means of releasing huge amounts of energy—whether in the form of bombs or in more controlled industrial applications. This was not simply a case of literature influencing physics, however, for Wells's novel itself drew heavily on Soddy's *Interpretation of Radium*. Indeed, Soddy's influence was great enough to lead Wells to the curious expedient of dedicating his text to that earlier text:

TO
FREDERICK SODDY'S
INTERPRETATION OF RADIUM
THIS STORY
WHICH OWES LONG PASSAGES
TO HIS ELEVENTH CHAPTER
ACKNOWLEDGES AND INSCRIBES ITSELF[3]

The first nuclear weapons were in an important sense, therefore, a scientific interpretation of a fictional interpretation of a scientific interpretation of radioactive substances. Furthermore, our own knowledge of these weapons, based on the kind of descriptions examined in Chapters 5 through 8, adds a layer of literary interpretation on top of this *mélange*.

So far in *The Nuclear Muse*, I have explored this *mélange* from two general perspectives: the uses of literature and literary techniques within scientific practices (Chapters 1 through 4) and the encoding of scientific practices within fragments borrowed from existing literary texts (Chapters 5 through 8). These explorations might be broken down more specifically according to the following:

Chapters 1 and 2   The use of literary techniques as a means of practicing physics, considering physics as an abstract intellectual enterprise.

Chapters 3 and 4   The use of literature and literary techniques as a means of practicing physics, considering physics as a social enterprise.

Chapter 5	The use of literature and literary techniques as a means of encoding physicists' conceptions of their involvement in the social enterprise of physics at Los Alamos.
Chapters 6 and 7	The use of literature and literary techniques as a means of encoding the Los Alamos physicists' conceptions of their discipline in general and their work on nuclear weapons in particular.
Chapter 8	The use of literature and literary techniques as a means of encoding and distributing their conceptions of physics and nuclear weapons to society at large.

What remains is to round out this study by investigating the ways in which entire works of literature, and more particularly those created in direct response to the work of atomic physics, struggle to represent and explore the meanings of that science and the weapons it created. My first example will be the prewar novel with which this study began.

The World Set Free and the Limits of Language

Wells's novel describes a future that is now our past in which scientists solve "the problem of inducing radio-activity in the heavier elements and so tapping the internal energy of atoms" (40). Yet this context is not immediately clear, for Wells begins the novel in the mode of historical prose with his narrator looking back over the millennia of human history to its earliest conscious roots:

Man began to think . . . he blinked at the sun and dreamt that perhaps he might snare it and spear it as it went down to its resting-place amidst the distant hills. Then he was roused to convey to his brother that once indeed he had done so—at least that someone had done so—he mixed that perhaps with another dream almost as daring, that one day a mammoth had been beset; and therewith began fiction—pointing a way to achievement—and the august, prophetic procession of tales. . . . And that first glimmering of speculation, that first story of achievement, that story-teller, bright-eyed and flushed under his matted hair, gesticulating to his gaping, incredulous listener, gripping his wrist to keep him attentive, was the most marvellous beginning this world has ever seen. It doomed the mammoths, and it began the setting of that snare that shall catch the sun. (14–15)

Although the tone here is panegyric, the stance is that of a historical survey of human development. Wells never overtly identifies his work as "a novel" or "a work of fiction"; the subtitle tells us only that it is "A Story of Mankind," and only later is one able to state confidently that this is a fiction of a historical narrative. Yet the author's prejudice on behalf of "fiction—pointing the way to achievement" is apparent almost at once: he describes its genesis as "the most marvellous beginning this world has ever seen."

Indeed, Wells seems to identify storytelling with our most elemental imaginative powers, as though it were the source of all human productivity. For example, he extends his narrative of the Stone Age birth of fiction to the Middle Ages and the implicit emergence of science out of the creative processes of the storyteller:

Yet the dreamer, the story-teller, was there still, waiting for his opportunity amidst the busy preoccupations, the comings and goings, the wars and processions, the castle building and cathedral building. . . . Whenever there was a certain leisure for thought throughout these times, then men were to be found dissatisfied with the appearances of things, dissatisfied with the assurances of orthodox belief, uneasy with a sense of unread symbols in the world about them. . . . Hitherto Power had come to men by chance, but now there were these seekers, seeking, seeking among rare and curious and perplexing objects, sometimes finding some odd utilisable thing, sometimes deceiving themselves with fancied discovery, sometimes pretending to find. (20–21)

So the storyteller begets the seeker-scientist as Wells, the author, would beget Szilard, the nuclear physicist, and Wells' novel becomes a fictional narrative of a historical narrative of how fictional narratives inspire scientific narratives. Slowly and subtly, Wells enfolds his reader in a "story of mankind" in which it is increasingly difficult to identify the narrative voice.

Over the next twenty pages, Wells introduces additional elements to his narrative voice, including descriptions of scientific experiments— "He set up atomic disintegration in a minute particle of bismuth, and it exploded with great violence into a heavy gas of extreme radio-activity, which disintegrated in its turn in the course of seven days" (40)—and third-person accounts of the actions of particular individuals, both fictional and historical. Sometimes he even combines both of these elements in a single sentence: "The problem which was already being mooted by such scientific men as Ramsay, Rutherford, and Soddy, in the very beginning of the twentieth century, the problem of inducing radio-activity in the heavier elements and so tapping the internal energy of atoms, was solved by a wonderful combination of induction, intuition and luck by Holsten so soon as the year 1933" (40). Only here, in this sentence, after the reader has ventured forty pages into the book and become acclimatized, as it were, to the layering of narrative elements, does Wells implicitly admit that his story is, in fact, a novel rather than an impressionistic history of humanity; and only then does he introduce the overarching conceit of his novel—that it is an account of an imaginary future narrated from a point even further into that future.

Thus, central to Wells's tale of the development of nuclear weapons are the lengths to which he went to create its curious narrative voice: a hybrid containing elements of historical, scientific, and literary narration. I see two features of this hybrid narration as particularly important in the context of this study. First, and most obviously, it constructs the reader's perspective on the story as that of historical retrospect. This is an intriguing point of view in its own right, at least in part because it locates the reader in a context that is completely unknowable at first—a distant, invisible future. Only gradually does the story bring the reader closer and closer to her own implicit observational location, slowly revealing the contours of the point of view the reader has inhabited throughout the narrative. This encourages a sense of tension and personal investment on the reader's part, for the course of the story will determine the shape of the space the reader has occupied in it throughout its unfolding.

A second important feature of Wells's hybrid narration is that, in mixing different narrative modes, it invokes their various representational conventions, expectations, and standards of interpretation. One might expect that the result would be a hodgepodge: an inconsistent, perhaps even incoherent tale of one man's quirky vision of the future. Wells is a skillful writer, however, and if the novel is, at first, somehow unsatisfying, this is less a product of any lack of control on the author's part than a necessary side effect of his desire to unsettle the assumptions we would associate with any single narrative mode. Wells associates these assumptions with a conceptual stasis that in his view had trapped humanity in a savage and self-destructive ignorance. In this respect, his novel is an accurate forecast not only of the possibility of nuclear weapons but also of what Einstein called the static "modes of thinking" that make them so dangerous. In *The World Set Free*, Wells foresaw the need to get beyond the limitations of our existing, partisan perspectives, and therefore he wrote a book that was not "merely" a novel, a history, or a scientific memoir. Instead, he obliges us to see it from many narrative perspectives at once, hoping that in this way we may, perhaps, be able to avoid the mistakes made by the inhabitants of his future world.

Whether or not it is merely coincidental, the popular, philosophical, and autobiographical writings of many twentieth-century physicists evince a similar dissatisfaction with existing representational conventions—in particular, the failure of language to express the insights of physics—and likewise call for new modes of expression. Richard Feynman, for example, insisted: "Now we know how the electrons and light behave. But what can I call it? If I say they behave like particles I give the wrong impression; also if I say they behave like waves. They behave in their own inimitable way."[4] One might easily assume that he was reacting here against the inadequacy of figurative language. Yet he was far from eschewing such language, even in its most blatant forms, as his own subsequent uses of simile and metaphor attest. He was, rather, reacting against the assumption, championed in our culture by science itself, that his words had to (or even could) correspond directly and consistently to the phenomena they described. So, throughout his life, he repeatedly flaunted the conventions of scientific language to communicate his insights more forcibly.[5] Niels Bohr's work on complementarity, likewise, grew out of his awareness of the representational difficulties foregrounded by quantum mechanics; in it he called for a more relational, metaphorical use of language.[6] More recently, David Bohm has suggested that physics requires a new form of language (the rheomode) based on verbs rather than nouns.[7]

This language already exists: it is literary language. Throughout this study we have seen physicists turning to it in a variety of ways as they struggled to represent their insights, their representations of those insights, and the products of those insights as well. This does not, of course, mean that the representations these scientists were producing were what we would commonly call "literature." The use of literary language is only one of the characteristics of literature, just as the use of scientific language is only one of the features of science. But the quantum physicists' use of literary language does establish a greater common ground between literature and physics than the obvious differences between the disciplines would lead us to expect. It opens up quantum theory to the application of literary and cultural criticism—without, naturally, guaranteeing that most of it will be any good, any more than *Moby Dick*'s use of literary language guarantees the quality of its critics' readings.

This same common ground tempts individuals involved in the humanities to believe that quantum physics offers insight into their own activities. Some literary and cultural critics focus on quantum theory not because they are especially interested in the science itself, but because they sense a deep relevance to the work they know best: aesthetic production. That relevance may exist; but it is not possible to understand it simply by interpreting the quantum physicists' more literary remarks out of context as though they were, in fact, literature. Indeed, what some critics intuit as a mysterious force—a kind of cultural "black box"— underlying and unifying all the diverse productions of our culture may be no more than a transference through the medium of literary language of their own concerns onto the development of a new mechanics in the early years of the twentieth-century—a transference that these critics then perceive as an echo. Therefore, if quantum physics and postmodernism *are* related—and surely they must be, if only by virtue of the fact that they cohabit the same general social space—the relationship is devilishly intricate and subtle.

At the same time, it is surely appropriate that nuclear physicists' uses of literary language unsettle literary authors' notions of what constitutes satisfactory representation. For one thing, physicists do often have keen insights into the limitations and potential of language—this can hardly be surprising given the difficult representational work they are called on to do on a regular basis in their work. For another thing, nuclear physics has, throughout this century, pushed the envelope of our understanding of the phenomenological world—a world in which literary authors are, by default, also interested and of which adequate representation is no easier in literature than in physics. As a result (and of course for a wide variety of other reasons as well), many literary authors in this century—like their contemporaries in physics—have found themselves at a loss for words, deeply suspicious of the linguistic medium on which they depend, and eager to find new representational modes with which to inscribe their insights.

The existence of nuclear weapons only compounds this problem, for two reasons: first, these weapons introduce a whole new range of representational difficulties; second, they exist in our culture, as I explained in Chapter 8, primarily as literary entities themselves, and this necessarily involves any effort to represent them in considerable reflexive complexities. To illustrate this dynamic, I will turn now to consider two very different postwar works of literature, the first by a nuclear physicist—none other than Szilard himself—and the second by a literary author.

"The Voice of the Dolphins"

Szilard's career provides a particularly clear instance of the circularity I have tried to point out in the relationship between literature and science. Over the years, he moved from a belief that science was the best way to respond to a literary representation of atomic bombs to an active faith that literature might be the best way to deal with their scientific reality. As a physicist, his writings on the subject initially took ostensibly nonliterary forms: innumerable letters (including the one signed by Einstein), patent applications, memoranda, articles. Gradually, however, his orientation toward atomic weapons began to change. As the threat from Nazi Germany abated, he felt the need for atomic weapons had also decreased. Reading Wells's novel left Szilard with a powerful sense of the potential horror of these weapons' destructive capabilities. He tried to exert his influence on the weapons program once again—this time to slow its pace—by writing letters and circulating petitions among his colleagues. But the monster he had helped set in motion proved too powerful to stop. He met with blank indifference on the part of the military and political leaders he addressed and an apparent political naïveté on the part of the scientists most closely involved in the actual construction of nuclear weapons. Szilard was unable to stop the Allied bombings of Hiroshima and Nagasaki.

After the war, Szilard became disillusioned with the social influence of his discipline, in much the same way W. H. Auden lost faith in the social efficacy of poetry in the 1930s.[8] Szilard's response was less breezily pessimistic, however: atomic weapons made all too clear just how much science could make happen. But he also grew increasingly aware how little room the impersonal institutions of science left for the moral or ethical concerns of individuals. In the end, his own discipline's recalcitrance led him to hope that literature might prove to be effective precisely where science had failed him: as a medium through which to voice his concerns and shape the world's understanding and, perhaps, use of nuclear weapons. So he turned his hand to writing fiction and, in 1961, published a collection of stories called *The Voice of the Dolphins*.

Szilard begins the long title story on a grim note: "On several occasions between 1960 and 1985, the world narrowly escaped an all-out atomic war. In each case, the escape was due more to fortuitous circumstances than to the wisdom of the policies pursued by statesmen."[9] This opening paragraph reveals a great deal about Szilard's literary ambitions. He is deadly serious about his subject and wastes no time naming it: the threat of "all-out atomic war." Yet his narrative is also tinged with humor, as we see in his satiric reflection on the wisdom of politicians. The story quickly reveals that the narrator can afford such flashes of wry wit because he writes from the safe haven of a future in which the "problem" of atomic weapons has been solved: "That the bomb would pose a novel problem to the world was clear as early as 1946. It was not clearly recognized, however, that the solution of this problem would involve political and technical considerations in an inseparable fashion" (19). In an obvious bow to Wells, "The Voice of the Dolphins" imitates the detached, analytical voice of historical narrative that we have seen in *The World Set Free*. Indeed, Szilard draws heavily on Wells's novel throughout his own literary effort, not least in his narrator's distanced position of superior knowledge from which he describes our current predicament and its successful resolution.

In short, "The Voice of the Dolphins" offers the reader a modern-day version of Thomas More's *Utopia*—though Szilard's utopian dreams extend no further than "the solution of this problem" of atomic weapons. The solution, in the story's terms, stems from a recommendation made by the President's Science Advisory Committee "that there be set up, at the opportune time, a major joint Russian-American research project having no relevance to the national defense or to any politically controversial issues" (20). The "opportune" time turns out to be 1963, the place Vienna, and the project the "Biological Research Institute." The Vienna Institute immediately draws in the majority of the world's most distinguished scientists, its director "having played the role of the Pied Piper" (21). The narrative here echoes in an eerie way the beginnings of the Los Alamos Laboratory—in particular the way in which Robert Oppenheimer convinced a majority of the world's best physicists to leave established careers and join him in a secret scientific project. But Szilard does not pursue the comparison. Instead, the Vienna Institute immediately embarks on a course of research that at first appears in no way related to atomic weapons: an attempt to communicate with dolphins.

The institute's efforts are quickly rewarded. The scientists learn to speak with the dolphins and discover that "their intelligence far surpassed that of man. However, on account of their submerged mode of life, the dolphins were ignorant of facts and thus they had not been able to put their intelligence to good use in the past" (22). The scientists set about rectifying this situation, teaching them "first mathematics, next chemistry and physics, and subsequently biology" (22). The dolphins soon turn their newfound knowledge of "facts" to good use, earning "each of the next five Nobel prizes for physiology and medicine" (23). Of course the dolphins "derived much prestige from these awards, and their prestige was to increase further in the years to come, until it reached almost fabulous proportions" (23). The rest of the story is probably obvious by now: Under the leadership of the dolphins, and trading on their "prestige," the Vienna Institute is able to influence the international policies of the superpowers sufficiently to ensure a gradual decrease in the world's nuclear stockpiles and, eventually, complete disarmament.

It is curious that in turning to fiction Szilard adopts such an insistently nonfictional stance. His tone is bland and flat, his narrative imitates that of a historical text, and he seems less concerned with telling a good story than with defending science against the very shortcomings that drove him to fiction in the first place. Early in the story, for example, the narrator engages the question "Why . . . did scientists in general, and the President's Science Advisory Committee in particular, fail to advance a solution of this problem" (20) of atomic weapons? The answer, for the narrator, lies in the oddly playful expression, " 'Scientists should be on tap but not on top' " (20), which summarizes an attitude among policymakers that keeps scientists from being as helpful as they could and would like to be: "Scientists must not concern themselves with devising and proposing policies; they ought to limit themselves to answering such technical questions as they may be asked. Thus, it may well be that the scientists gave the wrong answers because they were asked the wrong questions" (20). The issue here centers on the scientists' lack of control over their discourse with politicians. Just as scientists use a specialized discourse to control who can contribute to their discipline, the politicians use that same discursive separation to contain scientists within their self-proclaimed field of specialization. Although this effectively muzzles the scientists, it does have the advantage of relieving them from responsibility for "the problem posed by the bomb" (20).

Ironically, in an effort to circumvent their exclusion from politics, the scientists apparently remove themselves even further from the political arena, retreating behind the closed doors of the Vienna Institute. In that idealization of the detached scientific community, they engage in a line of research that involves a further submission of their discursive practices, in this case to "the voice of the dolphins." By assuming a subservient role as spokespeople for the ostensibly more intelligent dolphins, the scientists succeed in gaining the ear of policymakers and the general populace as well. In being trained by the Vienna Institute fellows in the physical sciences, the dolphins learn enough about human society to conduct, through the medium of the scientists, a successful campaign toward disarmament.

In two respects, however, the scientists' submission is a fiction. First, while ostensibly bowing before the dolphins' superior intelligence, the scientists actually construct the thing to which they submit by training the dolphins in mathematics and the natural sciences. Without this training, the dolphins' intelligence would be (as it has been) inconsequential. Nor do the scientists apparently feel it necessary to include any of the humanities in the dolphins' education. What the scientists really want to hear—and what apparently makes them willing to listen to the dolphins—are their own disciplines echoed back to them by reputedly greater intellects. Yet the second irony is that, as some readers will have guessed, the dolphins' intelligence is itself a fiction concocted by the Vienna scientists. Thus it is the scientists themselves who mastermind and implement international disarmament. Yet in their own persons—in the voices of human scientists—their insights and intelligence were insufficient. The key to their success lies in the fictional act of ventriloquism by which they cast their utterances into "the voice of the dolphins." In the end, it is only through a combination of fictional and scientific modes that the scientists make themselves heard and affect a solution to the atomic problem.

Szilard's narrative closely parallels his own experience. As a representative scientist, he had felt excluded from the corridors of political power. So he looked to fiction for a more influential voice. Like the scientists in his story, he submerges his voice within the fiction of "The Voice of the Dolphins" as a way of making his own voice heard more loudly.[10] This tactic will probably strike most of us as absurd, since we are likely to share Auden's sense that "art makes nothing happen." And Szilard's point is not to suggest that fiction can by itself change anything—for we must remember that within the context of Szilard's metafiction, the voices of the dolphins are fictional, but the content of what they say is portrayed as scientific fact. Yet he does seem to insist, and I think rightly, that literary issues such as rhetorical stance, narrative voice, and the ways we shape stories about our experiences *do* matter in a social arena. Without a thoughtful application of literary techniques, therefore, the knowledge of facts claimed by scientists can seem useless, even destructive. Having introduced atomic weapons into society, science can feel all too powerless to shape their uses.

In Szilard's story, the dolphins' voice describes a detailed plan for disarmament. Should we read this plan as a serious proposal? I think not. Ultimately, like any work of fiction, Szilard's story undermines any prescriptive message it might seem to convey. While scientific writing privileges a literal mode that attempts to constrain its symbolic utterances within a linear, one-to-one correspondence to their meanings, literature revels in a metaphorical proliferation of meanings. Therefore, despite the nonfictional narrative voice, and notwithstanding the story's title, Szilard's dolphins do not speak with a single voice. They perform instead like a collective dummy, saying nothing themselves, but providing a distraction and locus for the projection of the scientists' own voices. This is an echo of "The Voice of the Dolphins" itself, for it serves as a medium for Szilard's own attempt at ventriloquism. It allows him to say without saying, to prescribe without committing him to any particular diagnosis. Thus, despite the inability of fiction to solve the problem of atomic weapons, I think Szilard does mean for his readers to come away from his story with a sense of the power of literature.[11] The bomb poses "a novel problem," and Szilard's story demonstrates that novels (or novellas) can help us find voices in which to break out of our discursive isolation in order to explore the range of its possible meanings.

Riddley Walker

In 1980 Russell Hoban published a stunning experimental novel entitled *Riddley Walker*. Of course any novel worthy of the name breaks new ground of some sort, whether aesthetic or epistemological, and might therefore be called "experimental"; but Hoban's novel is even more adventurous than most. Like *The World Set Free* and "The Voice of the Dolphins," it takes up the theme of nuclear weapons. Like those works, it engages in a similar struggle to construct a narrative perspective sufficiently removed from our own circumstances to offer us fresh insight without being so distant as to diminish its relevance. And like Wells and Szilard, Hoban sets his novel in the future. Yet in several respects he goes much further than either of his predecessors, taking greater aesthetic risks that ultimately produce a far more successful work of art.

As we have seen, Wells and Szilard each sets his work in an indefinite future from which a narrator looks back in time to trace a course of events that begin in the past, relative to both the author and the narrator, and lead to a middle ground that is in the author's near future and the narrator's recent past. Hoban's narrator, likewise, speaks to us from an indefinite point in the future and through his words we learn about some of the events leading from our time to his. But while Wells's and Szilard's narrators look back from a point perhaps a hundred years beyond the publication dates of their respective works, Hoban's narrator, the Riddley Walker of the title, lives some two and a half thousand years into our future. Furthermore, where the former are disembodied voices of third-person historical narrative, Riddley's voice is an emphatically bodied first person. Consequently, his story is firmly rooted in his present, in his experiences, and is not an objective unfolding of the events that separate his time from ours; it is a highly subjective account of a brief period in Riddley's life—indeed, all but the last couple of chapters describe the events of just nine days.

There is, in short, a radical disjunction between Riddley's present and ours that makes it impossible for him to relate what went on in between. He is only dimly aware of what our world was like, for where Wells and Szilard write of futures in which nuclear weapons have been tamed— have, in fact, been instrumental in the construction of beneficent new world orders—Hoban depicts a time in which nuclear weapons do not exist except in the apparently vague and imprecise form of myths. At some point after 1997, a nuclear war crippled human civilization, to the extent that 2347 years after they began to keep track of time once again, the society in which Riddley lives—a few dozen small communities surrounding the abandoned city of Canterbury, England—is only now emerging from a hunting-gathering phase and remains well shy of Greek or Roman civilization. Nuclear weapons have destroyed nearly everything we know, including themselves.

Only a few vestiges of our world have survived: the buried, rotting hulks of machines; a few stone structures, mostly in ruins; the outlines of some roads; a tourist guide to a mural depicting the life of St. Eustace. Even the land itself has been dramatically altered: a new coastline, the barren area surrounding Canterbury's ground zero. Undoubtedly, the greatest resource retained from our time by Riddley's contemporaries is the English language, and it, too, has undergone a metamorphosis:

Erny said, 'It bint the 1 Big 1 it ben the 1 Littl 1. Which youre looking at Riddley Walker but it bint him ternt it luce it were a farring seakert tryer from other side and looking to goatch the wayt he wer looking to bargam a seakert gready mint for Nos. of the mixter. Which 1ce his boat gratit on the shingel that 1 Littl 1 were luce in Inland it were on the road to blow up some 1 and you cud be sure some 1 wer roading fas to be there when it come.'[12]

This quirky, difficult, apparently primitive language is the heart of Hoban's achievement: a reconstruction of English that in itself communicates the reality of nuclear weapons more forcefully and fully—though not necessarily more clearly—than anything we can say through it, because (in the world of the novel) this language was shaped by nuclear weapons. It is a language that works by means of its limitations and failures, not despite them. Every neologism, every bastardized spelling, every corrupt echo of a familiar phrase resonates in our ears and helps us feel in our guts the power of nuclear weapons to "change everything," even our modes of speaking and, ultimately, of thinking. One of the novel's great questions, therefore, is: Can the imaginative manipulation of language match the power of nuclear weapons—can it help us change "our modes of thinking" before the bomb does it for us?

Change is, not surprisingly, a major theme throughout the novel. Its characters, for example, go through an endless cycle of "Chaynjis" that ends only when "Aunty," an embodiment of the Grim Reaper, rides up on her big, red-eyed rat, ready to "do the juicy" with her "stoan boans and iron tits and teef be twean her legs plus she has a iron willy for the ladys it gets red hot" (90–91). As these images suggest, the changes that disrupt and ultimately end these characters' lives are largely unpleasant.

They provide the pattern of life in Riddley's world—a pattern that he and his contemporaries trace to "time back way back" when "the 1 Big 1 in barms" set off "Bad Tym" when

> Peapl din no if they wud be alyv 1 day tu the nex. Din even no if thayd be alyv 1 min tu the nex. Sum stuk tu gether sum din. Sum tyms thay dru lots. Sum got et so uthers cud liv. Cudn be shur uv nuthing din no wut wuz sayf tu eat or drink & tryin tu keap wyd uv uther forajers & dogs it wuz nuthing onle Luck if enne 1 stayd alyv. (33)

One of the great achievements of this novel is that it can indulge in such an obsessive focus on the effects of nuclear weapons without ever making us feel that Hoban wants to preach at us. Where Wells and Szilard structure their fictions around overt political doctrines, Hoban uses his novel as a medium through which to explore possible meanings and, even more, the process of interpretation itself. The preceding passage is typical of Hoban's artfulness: it strives for grim, visceral representation, yet it is not shrill. It achieves its effect not by telling us how awful nuclear war is, but by enacting the "Chaynjis" brought on by "the 1 Big 1 in barms" in the physical substance of Riddley's voice. We feel their effects in every bump and hollow of Riddley's language.

Like all his contemporaries, Riddley sees his life, with all its discomfort and suffering, as a direct consequence of a cataclysm he does not fully understand but which dominates his conscious and unconscious life. Their efforts to understand this predicament focus on a single ancient text, known as "The Eusa Story." This text, which comprises an entire chapter of *Riddley Walker*, begins with a description of the efforts of a man named Eusa to harness nuclear energy for use in bombs. This task requires that he look in "the hart uv the stoan hart uv the dans" where "Evere thing blippin & bleapin & movin in the shiftin uv thay Nos" (31) in order to find the "Littl Man the Addom" who knows "the No. uv thay Master Chaynjis" (32) which will give Eusa control over the "1 Big 1." He was set this task by a character named "Mr Clevver," who then took the fruits of Eusa's labor and

> droppit so much barms thay kilt as menne uv thear oan as thay kilt enemes. Thay wun the Warr but the lan wuz poyzen frum it the ayr & water as well. Peapl din jus dy in the Warr thay kep dyin after it wuz over. Mr Clevver din cayr it wuz aul the saym tu him poyzen wuz meat & drink tu him he wuz that hard. (33)

With ironic understatement, "The Eusa Story" goes on to report that "Eusa with his wyf & 2 litl suns gon lukin for a nuther plays tu liv" (33). The rest of the story narrates Eusa's experiences in the "Bad Tym" that followed, including the loss of his wife and children and a second confrontation with the "Littl Man the Addom," who tells Eusa: " . . . yu wantit thay Master Chaynjis & this is 1 uv them. In the wud in the hart uv the stoan yu pult me in 2 yu opent me lyk a chikken. Yu let thay Nos. uv thay master Chaynjis owt. Now yu mus go thru them aul" (35).

"The Eusa Story" figures as centrally in *Riddley Walker* as the Bible did in medieval Europe, and its characters spend a similar amount of time and effort struggling to interpret it. Obviously there is a great deal of room for interpretation: the images are rich and densely interwoven, and the language is probably supposed to present almost as much of a challenge to Riddley and his contemporaries as it does to us, since "The Eusa Story" is "all ways wrote down in the old spel." Its language is, in fact, noticeably different from the rest of *Riddley Walker*, and it would probably appear to Riddley as foreign as Shakespeare's language seems to most of us. This is not, however, the greatest obstacle faced by would-be exegetes:

Every body knows bits and peaces of it but the connexion men and the Eusa show men they all have the woal thing wrote down the same and they have to know all of it by hart. You wunt have seen the woal thing wrote out without you ben a Eusa show man or connexion man or in the Mincery. No 1 else is allowit to have it wrote down the same which that dont make no odds becaws no 1 else knows how to read. (29)

Again like the Bible in medieval society, "The Eusa Story" is a carefully controlled text, for access to it is limited both by social station and by literacy. Just as, in the Middle Ages, most people's experience of the Bible was filtered through their priest's representations of it, most people in *Riddley Walker* depend for their knowledge of "The Eusa Story" on puppet shows produced by traveling "Eusa show men" and commented on by "connexion men" in their own community; and every member of each of these groups is vetted and officially sanctioned by the "Mincery" (Ministry)—a cabal loosely modeled on England's parliamentary system and led by a "Pry Mincer" and "Wes" (or "Shadder") "Mincer."

The transformation of familiar terms such as these—and there are many in *Riddley Walker*—contributes to an important dynamic. Complementing the theme of "change" is that of "connection," already alluded to in the persons of the "connexion men" who interpret the Eusa shows. The two themes form a dynamic pair characterized by the strange mixture of difference and similarity, transformation and continuity that both the novel's characters and its readers feel in the contrast between Riddley's world and our own. This is expressed perhaps most poignantly by Riddley, as he and his moon brother, Lissener, wander through an underground room full of giant, well-preserved machines from our own time:

> Tears begun streaming down my face and my froat akit.
> Lissener hispert, "Whats the matter?"
> I hispert back, "O what we ben! And what we come to!" Boath of us were sniffling and snuffling then. (100)

These are words that will strike most readers powerfully at this point in the story. We have been encouraged to identify with Riddley's situation and perspective throughout the novel—indeed we have nothing other than his words—and it is easy to share the wonder and loss he feels in response to a glimpse of those gleaming but motionless machines. They manifest so evocatively the "time back way back" that he is torn between a tantalizing identification with the grandeur of the past ("O what *we* ben!") and an overwhelming awareness of how unapproachable it has become.

A similar dynamic is at work in our own apprehension of Riddley and his world. At the same time that we share Riddley's emotions, we are always conscious at some level of our differences. His language never lets us forget them, for one thing; and during moments in which we identify most intensely with Riddley, Hoban seems to undercut that identification deliberately, forcing us to remain aware of our distance. In the passage quoted above, for example, Riddley follows his heartfelt expostulation with the observation that "Boath of us were sniffling and snuffling then." The language in this sentence is just absurd enough— to our ears—to pull us back from Riddley's feelings, to make us self-conscious about our identification with him, without quite destroying the power or the poignancy of the moment.

As the passages I have quoted suggest, Riddley's efforts to decipher the "chemistery" and "fizzics" of the "1 Big 1" involve him—along with his contemporaries—in the construction of an elaborate mythology that combines elements ranging from Adam to Christ, St. Eustace to Punch and Judy shows, the Devil to the "fizzics" of "party cools" (particles). In addition to "The Eusa Story," there is a second, even more carefully controlled text at the center of these efforts. It is a text that actually dates from our own time: "The Legend of St. Eustace," a twentieth-century informational leaflet describing a fifteenth-century wall painting of St. Eustace's life. Like the grocery list in Walter Miller, Jr.'s, *A Canticle for Leibowitz*, "The Legend of St. Eustace" is an unremarkable object from our own time transformed into a kind of holy relic by the passage of time and its changing context. And like the grocery list, "The Legend of St.

Eustace" provides a concrete manifestation of how different Riddley's perspective is from our own, for what is obscure and mysterious to him is clear and prosaic to us: "1. At the bottom of the painting St. Eustace is seen on his knees before his quarry, a stag, between whose antlers appears, on a cross of radiant light, the figure of the crucified Savior" (123). Yet despite our confidence in our ability to interpret this text, when Abel Goodparley, the Pry Mincer, shares it with Riddley (who reproduces it for us), it has the effect of a revelation for us no less than for Riddley. We feel simultaneous shocks of recognition— suddenly we can interpret with new confidence many of the references in "The Eusa Story" that had seemed mysterious to us ("Ah, so Eusa is St. Eustace!")—and discomfort, for we see the fragility of all acts of interpretation, including the thousands of basic, unspoken assumptions on which our lives depend. In Riddley's world, most of these assumptions no longer exist; they have been destroyed or fragmented by nuclear war, and for the duration of the novel we have to make our way through a hostile landscape in which little is certain and less is secure.

As a result, we learn to see the world through Riddley's eyes, as we are obliged to learn to read it through his words. From this perspective, words from our own time come to seem less stable and their meanings more fluid than we are probably comfortable imagining. Even words associated with the objective disciplines of science mutate and resonate with new, mysterious significance: "trants mission" (transmission), "pirntow" (assert or determine, from "printout"), "vantsit theary" (advanced theory), "tryl narrer" (trial and error), "catwl twis" (catalyst), "res and due" (residue), "dyergam" (diagram). In this world, everything is open to interpretation, everything full of possible significance and hidden meaning (even "chemistery"). Following Riddley, we learn to be quick on our metaphorical feet, to pursue meaning in unlikely places, and to forgo the "foolish consistency" that Emerson called "the hobgloblin of little minds."[13]

Consider, for example, the obvious conjunction of the passage from "The Legend of St. Eustace" quote previously with the following excerpt from "The Eusa Story," in which Eusa finds what he has been looking for: "8. In the dark wud Eusa seen a trak uv lyt he follert it. He cum tu the Hart uv the Wud it wuz the Stag uv the Wud it wuz the 12 Poynt Stag stud tu fays him & stampin its feat. On the stags hed stud the Littl Shynin Man the Addom in be twean thay horns with arms owt strecht & each han holdin tu a horn" (31). Goodparley, who for much of the book is most active in his efforts to recapture the lost knowledge of the "1 Big 1," gives Riddley a lesson in interpretation:

I dint know nothing of chemistery nor fizzics then I hadnt payd no tension to it. Any how I wer reading over this here Legend like I use to do some times and I come to *"the figure of the crucified Saviour"*. Number of the crucified Saviour and wunnering how that be come the Littl Shyning Man the Addom. Suddn it jumpt in to my mynd "A littl salting and no saver". I dint have no idear what *crucified* myt be nor up to then I hadnt give *Saviour* much thot I thot it myt mean some 1 as saves only that dint connect with nothing. Id never put it to gether with saver like in *savery*. Not sweet. Salty. A salt crucified. I gone to the chemistery working I askit 1 Stoan Phist that were Belnots dad what *crucified* myt be nor he wernt cern but he thot itwd be some thing you done in a cruciboal. 1st time Id heard the word. Thats a hard firet boal they use it doing a chemistery try out which you cud call that crucifrying or crucifying. Which that crucified Saviour or crucifryd salts thats our Little Shyning Man him as got pult in 2 by Eusa. So *"the figure of the crucified Saviour"* is the number of the salt de vydit in 2 parts in the cruciboal and radiating lite coming across it. The salt and the saver. 1ce youve got that salt youre on your way to the woal chemistery and fizzics of it. . . . But thats all tecker knowledging realy you wunt hardly unner stan it nor I wont wear you out with it. (128–129)

I have quoted this lengthy passage (still only a small fraction of Goodparley's larger reading of "The Legend of St. Eustace") in order to convey, if it is possible to do so in an excerpt, the logic of this mode of interpretation. Goodparley identifies it as "tecker knowledging," and clearly to him, and to Riddley, it represents a highly specialized knowledge with very practical applications.

Readers in our time would, of course, be inclined to laugh at the naïveté of Goodparley's interpretations. Lacking the appropriate background in either physics or Christian doctrine, many of his readings are "wrong"—as when he abandons his understanding of Saviour as "some 1 as saves" in favor of reading it as a technical term for "salt." But this exegetic capriciousness is hardly surprising given that his method seems to be a hodgepodge, including elements of superstition, on the one hand, and of scholastic reasoning (a forerunner of both literary and scientific representation), on the other. We should, however, beware of dismissing out of hand either his interpretive strategy or the conclusions he draws from it. Our wish to do so is presumptuous and may eventually redound on our own heads. The average person in our time does not have a significantly "better" understanding of the "tecker knowledging" behind nuclear weapons than either Goodparley or Riddley. He or she may know a few more "uncorrupted" terms, but this does not translate into useful knowledge.

What, then, does constitute "useful knowledge"? Is there any sense in which Goodparley's perambulations (and their kind) might qualify?

To answer these questions, we should begin with the recognition that our common notions of "useful" have been deeply influenced by the assumptions of the scientific tradition. We tend to associate "usefulness" with knowledge that allows us to manipulate the world around us. Based on this assumption, auto mechanics, plumbers, carpenters, electricians, computer technicians, chemists, doctors, physicists all possess "useful" knowledge; professors of literature do not. But in the case of nuclear weapons, would it really be useful for the average citizen to know how to make one? It would, on the contrary, be either entirely useless or profoundly dangerous. Where nuclear weapons are concerned, some other kind of knowledge is needed.

If we bear in mind the character of the general conception of nuclear weapons that prevails in our society, as discussed in the last chapter, the utility of a rather different, nontechnical kind of knowledge will eventually assert itself. Since these weapons exist for most of us primarily as literary entities, it would make sense for us to think of them as such. Yet because of the common preconception that literature is largely irrelevant where power or utility are concerned, it is difficult to avoid the temptation to dismiss the literary character of our knowledge of nuclear weapons as just so much window-dressing and assume instead that we should strive to know them in a more literal sense. This assumption, like the scientific model on which it is based, has the effect of rendering static the metaphors through which we conceive of these weapons. But this assumption is false, and the understanding it encourages is not only false but dangerous, for it fosters complacency in an illusion of real knowledge.

Goodparley's understanding, by contrast, strikes us as false. And so it is, to the extent that he imagines it amounts to technological knowledge. Yet in this respect it reflects the most common conceptions in our own society, and in doing so it offers us useful knowledge. Goodparley's interpretations of "The Eusa Story" and "The Legend of St. Eustace" as representations of nuclear power are no better or worse than our readings of nuclear bombs in terms of the Isenheim Altarpiece or "the Second Coming in wrath." Indeed, they are mirror processes. Our society possesses these weapons, and we want ways of describing them. Goodparley's society possesses texts that echo our descriptions, and he wants the weapons. The mistake in both cases is assuming that description and object are equivalent or even causally related. Yet each mistake can illuminate the other by revealing its static assumptions in the face of these bombs' essential dynamism. Just as a glimpse of our society might give Goodparley a chance to recognize how mistaken he is to assume that his interpretations constitute a stable,

Physics in Fiction

accurate description of nuclear weapons, our reading of *Riddley Walker* allows us the opportunity to see how mistaken we are to assume that our descriptions constitute "realistic" interpretations.

In the end, it is not Goodparley's metaphorical style of reading that is at fault—it is his failure to recognize the difference between scientific and literary knowledge. The same may be said of our own readings of nuclear weapons. This does not mean, however, that we should discard our literary understanding. As this study has shown, nuclear weapons do not exist solely as scientific artifacts; nor does science itself constitute a separate world. Even the most technical aspects of physics make use of resources more commonly associated with literature, and its artifacts inhabit a social sphere in which the average individual does not possess sufficient technical knowledge to repair, let alone reproduce, those artifacts. In this context, it would be wise to pay attention to the character of the knowledge we do have. Goodparley's interpretive activity can be useful to us in this regard in two ways. First, his way of understanding reveals a great deal about our own, as I have suggested. Second, *Riddley Walker* allows us to read our own readings of nuclear weapons through several, layered filters, including those of a different time, an alien but largely comprehensible language, and Goodparley's and Riddley's own subjective readings. Each of these contributes to the distanced perspective necessary for self-reflection.

Finally, of course, *Riddley Walker* does not offer us an objective or literal distance, any more than does *The World Set Free* or "The Voice of the Dolphins." But where these latter works of fiction valorize science, place scientists in central roles as saviors of human society, and even counterfeit the relative objectivity of historical narrative, *Riddley Walker* privileges literature and provides us with an overtly, indeed an emphatically literary distance. Goodparley's interpretive methods as we have seen them are particular manifestations of Hoban's more general methods. They are subjective, mythical, metaphorical, and dynamic. Unlike *The World Set Free* and "The Voice of the Dolphins," *Riddley Walker* does not preach a static solution to the social crisis precipitated by nuclear weapons. Ironically, that is precisely its strength: as desirable as Wells's and Szilard's utopian visions may be, they are ultimately dead because they cannot cope with the dynamism inherent in human social relations and the symbolic and interpretive processes that underlie them. Hoban's fiction recognizes this dynamism and responds to it with the dynamic resources of literature. If the vision of our future it presents in the process is not as appealing as those set forth in *The World Set Free* and "The Voice of the Dolphins," it is at least more useful in our present circumstances.

Conclusion

A few paragraphs back I suggested that—like Good-parley—most of us fail to understand the differences between scientific and literary forms of knowledge. Few readers would deny Goodparley's failure; but the assertion that we share in it will strike many readers as nonsensical, given that the distinction between "science" and "literature" is largely accepted as a truism in our society. Most of us believe the differences between these disciplines are so pronounced that they can be felt even (or perhaps particularly) by a casual observer. Yet no matter how strongly they are felt, one cannot understand the real differences between science and literature without also understanding their similarities—and this latter understanding is clearly lacking in our society. Therefore I have been working throughout this book not to disprove the reigning belief in the differences between science and literature but to sharpen and refine our understanding of their relationship though an exploration of the circular pattern of interaction between physics and literature manifest in the development of the first atomic bombs.

Despite my emphasis throughout this study on their points of contact, it may be useful here at the end to consider some of the divergences between literature and physics, in order to avoid misunderstandings (whether real or pretended) of the claims I am making in this study. The kind of deep and pervasive interactions between literature and physics that I have described in these pages would not be possible if there were not also considerable differences between them. Neither claims of essential identity nor claims of complete incompatibility can adequately describe the relationship. Among the differences that seem (to me) most significant are the following:

Physics focuses on natural phenomena, literature on human phenomena. The purview of physics is the external world of physical processes. Although human phenomena are a category of natural phenomena, and although physics is, in principle, applicable to the human realm—through its contributions to the biological sciences, for example—the phenomena of human consciousness, desire, identity, and social interactions remain largely inaccessible to physicists. Even the less "hard" sciences have only begun to examine the tip of the human iceberg, as it were. Yet human consciousness, actions, and interactions are the primary foci of literature. Works of literature do, of course, often describe the natural world, but those descriptions tend to be interesting largely to the extent that they bear on human consciousness, whether intellectual or emotional, rather than because of any insight

Physics in Fiction

they offer into natural processes. Caveat: it is not possible to define an *absolute* distinction between physics and literature based upon subject matter. Physics blends into biology and the science of artificial intelligence, which merge with psychology, which has exerted a strong influence on literature. Likewise, a significant overlap exists between literature and physics in the genre of nature writing, which combines characteristic concerns from each discipline and appeals to readers of both orientations.

Physics quantifies, literature qualifies. It is no surprise that physics is most successful when applied to the non-human world, given that it seeks to render the phenomena it studies in quantifiable form. A central feature of the practice of physics involves reduction and simplification, eliminating details that can be considered superfluous and focusing on the remaining "essential" details of any given object of study. Physics requires the isolation of individual variables; and in its taxonomic categories, we can read the lineaments of this desire: to bind the individual into an overarching framework of related phenomena in order to define permissible behavior for that individual and account for all possible outcomes of its interactions. Literature, on the other hand, revels in the extravagant. It seeks out the unique qualities in individuals and their interactions. Its subjects are composites: the totality of an individual, including desires and fears, limitations and abilities, physical and social circumstances. From a literary perspective, reducing a subject to isolated fragments would deprive a representation of the greater part of its value, or perhaps even render it meaningless.

Physics strives for objectivity, literature for subjectivity. Physicists struggle to construct dispassionate, verifiable, and universal descriptions of the phenomena they study. As a consequence, representations in physics suppress their relationships to human individuals. This is manifest on three levels in most physics papers. (1) Physics papers do not cite their human authors but the impersonal authority of experiments and previously published papers in justifying their particular claims. (2) Physics papers favor the impersonal language of scientific prose that asserts its objectivity and that elides the subjectivity of its authors and readers. (3) Physics papers shy away from any consideration of what specific findings might mean to particular human beings or how they might be used by those individuals and focus instead on how those findings relate to or revise other scientific representations. Literature, on the other hand, is all about the subjective experiences of its authors, characters, and readers. Literists strive to represent human subjectivity, both as a subject (in the persons represented) and as a process (in the language of the representation itself). A work of literature makes meanings that are overtly tied to particular human points of view, and therefore it cannot refer to any external agent for its authority but must be justified over and over again, in each act of reading, by the subjective intuitions of each of its readers.

Clearly, literature and physics are beasts of different stripes. In trying to master the representations of each, I have felt their differences on a visceral level, as have other critics as diverse as C. P. Snow and Norman Levitt. Yet despite these differences, I resist the easy conclusion that they constitute separate cultures, for I have consistently found evidence that these disciplines are both complementary and interconnected. In this study I have considered some of the evidence that may be found in the context of a specific "episode" in our recent history. This evidence suggests that it would not have been possible for Wells to fictionalize Soddy's scientific understanding of radium; for Szilard to nurse Wells's fiction on toward scientific fact; for the Los Alamites to represent their work on nuclear weapons in terms of literary metaphors and allusions; or for Hoban to meld myth, textual exegesis, and scientific method in a work of literature, without considerable and enduring common ground between the disciplines. If we truly wish to understand either literature or physics, or more generally how knowledge is constructed and circulated in our society, we must extend the explorations undertaken in this study to other disciplines in the arts and sciences, being careful always to examine the differences between them in the context of a thorough familiarity with their subtle and pervasive interactions.

NOTES

BIBLIOGRAPHY

INDEX

NOTES

Introduction

1. Spencer Weart and Gertrud Weiss Szilard, eds., *Leo Szilard: His Version of the Facts: Selected Recollections and Correspondence* (Cambridge, Mass.: MIT Press, 1978), p. 16.

2. Ibid.

3. Ibid.

4. Ibid., p. 17, n. 23. The phrases I have quoted are from a summary of Rutherford's speech published in *Nature* 132 (16 September 1933): 432–433.

5. Ibid., Szilard to Hirst (17 March 1934), p. 38.

6. See the next section for a detailed consideration of Einstein's assertion.

7. Weart and Szilard, *Leo Szilard*, p. 17.

8. H. G. Wells, *The Word Set Free: A Story of Mankind* (New York: E. P. Dutton & Company, 1914), p. 46.

9. Weart and Szilard, *Leo Szilard*, p. 18.

10. Ibid., p. 18, n. 28.

11. Ibid., p. 53.

12. Fermi's atomic pile was constructed in Chicago, underneath the University of Chicago's Stagg Field, under the auspices of the Manhattan Project. It first went critical on December 2, 1942. Fermi later joined his colleagues in the Theoretical Division at Los Alamos. See Chapter 5 for more details.

13. Weart and Szilard, *Leo Szilard*, Szilard to Frédéric Jolit-Curie (2 February 1939), p. 69.

14. Ibid., Einstein to Roosevelt (2 August 1939), p. 95.

15. Note that whenever I use the word "science" in this study, I am referring specifically to modern, Western science. I do not intend any of my remarks to apply to ancient or Eastern forms of science.

16. I consider the issue of the symbolic nature of nuclear weapons in more depth in Chapter 8.

17. Albert Einstein, *New York Times*, 25 May 1946, p. 13, col. 5.

18. W. H. Auden, "The Prolific and the Devourer," in *The English Auden*, ed. Edward Mendelson (London: Faber and Faber, 1977), p. 406.

19. Michael Hart, *One Hundred: A Ranking of the Most Influential Persons in History* (New York: Carol Publishing Group, 1992).

20. Paul R. Gross and Norman Levitt, *Higher Superstition: The Academic Left and Its Quarrels with Science* (Baltimore: Johns Hopkins University Press, 1994), p. 12. N.B.: I am not sure which folklore the authors envision as administering this "epistemological sweepstakes."

21. Ibid. I leave it to the reader to imagine what Gross and Levitt might mean by "hard scientists."

22. Robert Oppenheimer, *Uncommon Sense* (Boston: Birkhäuser, 1984), p. 38. See Chapter 7 for a more detailed consideration of Oppenheimer's remark.

23. M. A. K. Halliday and J. R. Martin, *Writing Science: Literacy and Discursive Power* (Pittsburgh: University of Pittsburgh Press, 1993), p. 11.

24. Niels Bohr, "The Quantum Postulate and the Recent Development of Atomic Theory," *Nature* 121 (14 April 1928): 580–590. See Chapter 2 for a detailed discussion of this essay.

25. Of course, literary criticism rarely pauses before considering texts of this type, and this further illustrates the practical difficulty of distinguishing precisely between texts of different types.

26. For an extended discussion of this latter kind of cross-disciplinary borrowing, see Chapters 5 through 8.

27. See, for example, Charles Bazerman, *Shaping Written Knowledge: The Genre and Activity of the Experimental Article in Science* (Madison: University of Wisconsin Press, 1988); Bruce Gregory, *Inventing Reality: Physics as Language* (New York: Wiley, 1988); Alan Gross, *The Rhetoric of Science* (Cambridge, Mass.: Harvard University Press, 1996); M. A. K. Halliday and J. R. Martin, *Writing Science: Literacy and Discursive Power* (Pittsburgh: University of Pittsburgh Press, 1987); Bruno Latour, *Science in Action* (Cambridge, Mass.: Harvard University Press, 1987); Michael Lynch and Steve Woolgar, eds., *Representation in Scientific Practice* (Cambridge, Mass.: MIT Press, 1990); and Greg Myers, *Writing Biology: Texts in the Social Construction of Scientific Knowledge* (Madison: University of Wisconsin Press, 1990).

28. See, for example, Gillian Beer, *Darwin's Plots: Evolutionary Narrative in Darwin, George Eliot, and Nineteenth-Century Fiction* (London: Routledge and Keegan Paul, 1983).

29. Literary-critical treatments of art and science include Leo Marx, *The Machine in the Garden: Technology and the Pastoral Ideal in America* (Oxford: Oxford University Press, 1964); Hyatt Waggoner, *The Heel of Elohim: Science and Values in Modern American Poetry* (Norman: University of Oklahoma Press, 1950); I. A. Richards, *Poetries and Sciences* (London: Routledge, 1970); N. Katherine Hayles, *The Cosmic Web: Scientific Field Models and Literary Strategies in the 20th Century* (Ithaca, N.Y.: Cornell University Press, 1984) and *Chaos Bound: Orderly Disorder in Contemporary Literature and Science* (Ithaca, N.Y.: Cornell University Press, 1990); and George Levine, ed., *One Culture: Essays in Science and Literature* (Madison: University of Wisconsin Press, 1987). Historical studies include Stephen Kern, *The Culture of Time and Space, 1880–1918* (Cambridge, Mass.: Harvard University Press, 1983); Douglas Hofstadter, *Gödel, Escher, Bach: An Eternal Golden Braid* (New York: Basic Books, 1979); Paul Boyer, *By the Bomb's Early Light: American Thought and Culture at the Dawn of the Atomic Age* (New York: Pantheon, 1985); Spencer Weart, *Nuclear Fear: A History of Images* (Cambridge, Mass.: Harvard University Press, 1988). Studies in the history of science include Thomas Kuhn, *The Structure of Scientific Revolutions* (Chicago: University of Chicago Press, 1962); Gerald Holton, *The Advancement of Science, and Its Burdens* (Cambridge: Cambridge University Press, 1986) and *Thematic Origins of Scientific Thought*, rev.

ed. (Cambridge, Mass.: Harvard University Press, 1988); and Marcel LaFollette, *Making Science Our Own: Public Images of Science, 1910–1955* (Chicago: University of Chicago Press, 1990).

30. There are also, of course, studies that examine the relations between science and painting or science and music, such as Lawrence LeShan and Henry Margenau, *Einstein's Space and Van Gogh's Sky: Physical Reality and Beyond* (New York: Macmillan, 1982); Jamie James, *The Music of the Spheres: Music, Science, and the Natural Order of the Universe* (New York: Springer Verlag, 1995); or James Jeans, *Science and Music* (Cambridge: Cambridge University Press, 1937). These works are, however, beyond the scope of this study.

31. See George Levine, "Why Science Isn't Literature: The Importance of Differences," *Annals of Scholarship* 8, no. 3–4 (1991): 365–380.

32. I am of course referring here to C. P. Snow's famous (or infamous) construction of science and art as the "Two Cultures." Snow used the phrase for the first time publicly in the title of a 1956 *New Statesman* essay. He then expanded on his academic exposition of this popular prejudice in a monograph also entitled *The Two Cultures* (Cambridge: Cambridge University Press, 1959).

33. Ian Hacking, *Representing and Intervening: Introductory Topics in the Philosophy of Natural Science* (Cambridge: Cambridge University Press, 1983), pp. 154–155.

34. Peter Galison, *Image and Logic: A Material Culture of Microphysics* (Chicago: University of Chicago Press, 1997), p. 799.

35. Chapter 6, "Drawing Boundaries," in Barry Barnes, David Bloor, and John Henry, *Scientific Knowledge: A Sociological Analysis* (Chicago: University of Chicago Press, 1996) offers a detailed consideration of boundary-making both between science and other forms of knowledge and among the various scientific specializations. More narrowly, in "The Care of the Self and Blind Variation: The Disunity of Two Leading Sciences," in *The Disunity of Science: Boundaries, Contexts, and Power*, ed. Peter Galison and David J. Stump (Stanford, Calif.: Stanford University Press, 1996), Karin Knorr Cetina explores "the differences in the empirical procedures of experimental high-energy physics and molecular biology" (287).

36. Philippe Halsman describes taking his famous photographic portrait of Einstein in 1947: "Ordinarily, Einstein did not like photographers, whom he called *Lichtaffen* (light monkeys)." But on this occasion, Halsman was lucky: "Suddenly, looking into my camera, he started talking. He spoke about his despair that his formula $E = mc^2$ and his letter to President Roosevelt had made the atomic bomb possible, that his scientific search had resulted in the death of so many human beings. . . . He grew silent. His eyes had a look of immense sadness. There was a question and a reproach in them. . . . The spell of this moment almost paralysed me. Then, with an effort, I released the shutter of my camera." From Halsman's reminiscence in *Einstein: A Centenary Volume*, ed. A. P. French (Cambridge, Mass.: Harvard University Press, 1979), pp. 27–28.

37. Weart and Szilard, *Leo Szilard*, pp. 94–96.

38. There is some debate surrounding this assertion. One line of argument maintains that, since the true beginning of the Manhattan Project did not occur until mid-1942 with the creation of the Manhattan Engineer District under the overall direction of General Leslie Groves; since Einstein had nothing to do with the actual theorizing, design, or construction of atomic weapons; and since Einstein's letter simply stimulated President Roosevelt to appoint a three-person committee to investigate the feasibility of constructing atomic weapons, Einstein cannot be credited with (or blamed for) bringing the American bomb project into existence. Another argument points out that the letter was Leo Szilard's idea, that he convinced Einstein to send it, and that he played a major role in drafting it; therefore, some suggest, he should be held responsible for its effects. Both of these arguments raise important considerations. But the Manhattan Project did not result from any one person's efforts in any case. What matters more in our context than doling out blame or praise is understanding that, in the popular view as well as in his own mind, Einstein was closely associated with the atomic bomb. *Time* magazine, for instance, ran a cover story on Einstein not long after the existence of atomic weapons became public knowledge; the cover illustration showed a half-length portrait of Einstein side by side with a mushroom cloud on which was inscribed "$E = mc^2$."

39. For detailed analyses of the shifting social role of scientists, see Alice Kimball Smith, *A Peril and a Hope: The Scientists' Movement in America, 1945–1947* (Cambridge, Mass.: MIT Press, 1970); R. W. Reid, *Tongues of Conscience: War and the Scientists' Dilemma* (London: Constable, 1969); and Robert Gilpin, *American Scientists and Nuclear Weapons Policy* (Princeton, N.J.: Princeton University Press, 1962).

40. Samuel Allison, "The State of Physics; or the Perils of Being Important," *Bulletin of the Atomic Scientists* 6, no. 1 (January 1950): 2–4, 26–27.

41. Although the development of nuclear energy in World War II led to an explosion of public awareness of the social consequences of science, scientists themselves had begun struggling with the implications of their work long before. The development of relativity and quantum theories at the beginning of the century stimulated this self-consciousness among physicists; by the 1930s, they were already deeply engaged in a complex exploration of the social and moral dimensions of their work. In Chapter 3, I examine a case in which they used the Faust legend as a literary foundation for their explorations.

42. W. H. Auden, *Forewords and Afterwords* (New York: Random House, 1973), p. 497.

43. Auden, "Prolific," pp. 397–398.

44. Humphrey Carpenter, *W. H. Auden: A Biography* (Boston: Houghton Mifflin, 1981), pp. 52–53.

45. Auden, "Prolific," p. 398.

46. Carpenter, *Auden*, p. 5.

47. For a detailed account of Auden's trips to Spain and China, see Carpenter's biography or Charles Osborne, *W. H. Auden: The Life of a Poet* (New York: Harcourt Brace Jovanovich, 1979).

48. Carpenter, *Auden*, p. 256.

49. Ibid., p. 219.

50. Auden, *English Auden*, p. 211.

51. See Elizabeth Eisenstein, *The Printing Press as an Agent of Change* (Cambridge: Cambridge University Press, 1979).

52. There are many histories of the Manhattan Engineer District, written from a variety of perspectives. See the Bibliography for a listing. Henry Smyth, *Atomic Energy for Military Purposes* (Washington, D.C.: U.S. Government Printing Office, 1945) was the first history of the project. The most comprehensive are Richard Rhodes, *The Making of the Atomic Bomb* (New York: Simon and Schuster, 1986); and Richard Hewlett and Oscar Anderson, *The New World: A History of the United States Atomic Energy Commission, Vol. I 1939–1946* (University Park: Pennsylvania State University Press, 1962; rpt. ed., Berkeley: University of California Press, 1990). Among the histories that focus on Los Alamos itself, two stand out: David Hawkins, *Project Y: The Los Alamos Story* (Los Angeles: Tomash, 1983), was written by a mathematician and philosopher who served as Oppenheimer's administrative assistant on the project; and Lilliam Hoddeson et al., *Critical Assembly: A Technical History of Los Alamos during the Oppenheimer Years, 1943–1945* (Cambridge: Cambridge University Press, 1993), goes into the most technical detail. The most detailed history of the Trinity test is Ferenc Morton Szasz, *The Day the Sun Rose Twice: The Story of the Trinity Site Nuclear Explosion, July 16, 1945* (Albuquerque: University of New Mexico Press, 1984). Upon his retirement, Groves also wrote his own version of events—*Now It Can Be Told: The Story of the Manhattan Project* (New York: Harper, 1962).

53. Greg Myers in *Writing Biology: Texts in the Social Construction of Scientific Knowledge* (Madison: University of Wisconsin Press, 1990) examines what seems to me an interesting parallel to the dynamic I have been describing when he considers the unexpected role of narrative in E. O. Wilson's controversial work *Sociobiology: The New Synthesis* (Cambridge, Mass.: Harvard University Press, 1975). The appearance of narrative in a scientific work of this type seems unexpected because scientific prose in general seeks for ways to convey determinate meaning, and this has tended to lead it away from narrative traditions and techniques for the same reason that the Los Alamites' stories have proven to be unreliable vehicles for their overt political purposes. But in *Sociobiology*, Wilson's project is to connect biological evolution with the development of human societies, and to achieve this Wilson embeds mininarratives throughout his text. In part as a result of this, Wilson's work is open to a wide range of interpretations and to attack from many different points of view.

54. Quoted in Robert Jungk, *Brighter than a Thousand Suns* (New York: Penguin, 1958), p. 197. There is some confusion here, however, as Jungk names Robert Serber the winner of the pool and the author of this quote. But Serber was no part-time visitor to Los Alamos; in fact, he was one of the earliest inhabitants and personally delivered the orientation lectures to the rest of the incoming scientists. Therefore, I follow Richard Rhodes in identifying Rabi as the visitor, friend, and best guesser (Rhodes, *The Making of the Atomic Bomb*, p. 677). Rhodes,

however, asserts that Rabi chose this figure because by the time he arrived "the only bet left was for 18,000 tons" (p. 656).

55. The quotation runs from "It looked like a giant magnesium flare" to "40,000 feet above the ground." From an anonymously authored booklet called *Los Alamos: Beginning of an Era, 1943–1945* (Los Alamos, N.Mex.: Los Alamos National Laboratory, 1984), p. 53.

56. Sheldon Goldstein, "Quantum Philosophy: The Flight from Reason in Science," in *The Flight from Science and Reason*, ed. Paul R. Gross, Norman Levitt, and Martin Lewis (New York: New York Academy of Sciences, 1997), pp. 120–121.

57. Ibid., p. 120.

Chapter 1. "What We Can Say about Nature"

1. Otto Frisch, *What Little I Remember* (Cambridge: Cambridge University Press, 1979), p. 3.

2. Ibid., p. 114.

3. Ibid., p. 116.

4. Frisch writes, "I asked an American biologist who was working with [Hungarian chemist Georg] Hevesy what they call the process by which single cells divide in two; 'fission', he said, so I used the term 'nuclear fission' in that paper" (Frisch, *What Little I Remember*, p. 117). "That paper" was published in *Nature*.

5. Otto Frisch, *Working with Atoms* (New York: Basic Books, 1965), dust jacket copy.

6. Ibid., p. 7.

7. Ibid.

8. This is a line that scientists have struggled to draw, beginning in the late Middle Ages, when science and literature emerged in their modern forms, and continuing through the seventeenth and eighteenth centuries via such forums as the *Philosophical Transactions of the Royal Society of London*. Indeed, this line did not exist with much clarity until the nineteenth century, when amateur scientists ceased to exist in any meaningful form.

9. Such disclaiming is far from a trivial rhetorical ploy. Richard Feynman writes, for example: "Now we know how the electrons and light behave. But what can I call it? If I say they behave like particles I give the wrong impression; also if I say they behave like waves. They behave in their own inimitable way, which technically could be called a quantum mechanical way. They behave in a way that is like nothing that you have ever seen before" (*The Character of Physical Law* [Cambridge, Mass.: MIT Press, 1967], p. 128). The difficulty in casting their "technical" understanding of the "inimitable" behavior of sub-atomic phenomena in terms of what we have "seen before" is at the heart of the crisis precipitated by quantum mechanics. It has compelled physicists to a greater awareness of the indistinct borderland between the metaphorical and the literal, and it has highlighted the importance of narrative positioning,

such as Frisch's—even when the science in question is not of a "popular" variety.

10. See Chapter 6 for an examination of this relationship in action at Los Alamos. Chapter 7 offers a more detailed discussion of the metaphor of a priesthood as it applies to modern physics.

11. Frisch, *Working with Atoms*, pp. 7–8.

12. Francis Bacon used this analogy to frame his prescription for the development of a fully modern form of science in both his *Novum Organum* and his *Great Instauration*. For a more detailed discussion of scientists' application of the rhetoric of exploration and discovery to their own work, in the context of the Manhattan Project, see Chapters 5 and 6.

13. Chapter 2 offers an in-depth examination of one such structure in a scientific paper by Niels Bohr.

14. Such claims assume that naming is a powerful act: that words grant human beings a degree of control over the world, both in the form of an individual scientist's intellectual property rights and of the scientific tradition's ability to replace our jumbled experience of nature with a coherent representational structure. See Chapter 3 for a detailed instance of this, a conflict in which James Chadwick and Wolfgang Pauli each claimed the right to use the word "neutron" to describe a different particle.

15. Richard Boyd, "Metaphor and Theory Change: What Is 'Metaphor' a Metaphor For?" in *Metaphor and Thought*, 2nd ed., ed. Andrew Ortony (Cambridge: Cambridge University Press, 1993), p. 481.

16. See James Bono, "Science, Discourse, and Literature: The Role/Rule of Metaphor in Science," in *Literature and Science: Theory and Practice*, ed. Stuart Peterfreund (Boston: Northeastern University Press, 1990), for an overview of different takes on this issue.

17. There is an ongoing debate over whether the distinction between literal and metaphorical language is realistic or fanciful. Like many semantic debates, arguments on both sides range from extreme philosophical abstraction to hardheaded pragmatism, with no particular resolution in sight. The two terms, however, continue to serve as the demonstrable basis of widespread rhetorical practices in science and are therefore helpful in describing tendencies in our uses of language, though I have found no convincing description of any absolute distinction between them. Zenon Pylyshyn's "tentative" basis for a distinction seems to me a better starting point than most: "The difference between literal and metaphorical description lies primarily in such pragmatic considerations as (1) the stability, referential specificity, and general acceptance of terms; and (2) the perception, shared by those who use the terms, that the resulting description characterizes the world *as it really is*, rather than being a convenient way of talking about it, or a way of capturing superficial resemblances" ("Metaphorical Imprecision and the 'Top-Down' Research Strategy," in Ortony, *Metaphor and Thought*, p. 556).

18. Furthermore, by demonstrating their continuing deference to classical authority, the chemists remind us of the historical contingency of scientific

descriptions of nature, calling into question the efforts of most scientific texts to remain ahistorical and "objective."

19. For a detailed analysis of this paper, as well as the responses of Newton's contemporaries (including Huygens), see Charles Bazerman, *Shaping Written Knowledge: The Genre and Activity of the Experimental Article in Science* (Madison: University of Wisconsin Press, 1988), pp. 82–119.

20. Isaac Newton, *Opticks*, Book III, Querie 29 (New York: Dover, 1979), p. 370.

21. Christian Huygens, *Treatise on Light, In which are explained The causes of that which occurs In Reflexion, & in Refraction And particularly In the strange Refraction of Iceland Crystal*, trans. Silvanus P. Thompson (Chicago: University of Chicago Press, 1912), p. 4. Abraham Pais, *Niels Bohr's Times, in Physics, Philosophy, and Polity* (Oxford: Oxford University Press, 1991), quotes both Newton's and Huygens's remarks in the course of a brief but fascinating account of the wave-particle debate. See also Peter Achinstein, *Particles and Waves: Historical Essays in the Philosophy of Science* (Oxford: Oxford University Press, 1991).

22. The phrase is from Pais, *Niels Bohr's Times*, p. 85. The paper in question was entitled "Ueber das Gesetz der Energieverteilung im Normalspectrum" ("On the Law of Energy Distribution in the Normal Spectrum") and published in *Annalen der Physik* 4 (1901): 553–563. Edward MacKinnon, however, points out that "in the space of a few months Planck gave three different presentations of the same law. None of them were complete." The pivotal moment, therefore, is perhaps not quite as clear as some historians (such as Pais) describe it. It is a matter of debate, for instance, whether Planck attributed quantization to the physical oscillators of the blackbody, or whether that conceptual leap was first made by Einstein in 1905. (Edward M. MacKinnon, *Scientific Explanation and Atomic Physics* [Chicago: University of Chicago Press, 1982], p. 135.)

23. Quotations and equations in this paragraph from Planck, "Ueber das Gesetz der Energieverteilung," p. 561.

24. Ibid., p. 556. My translation.

25. Einstein, *Out of My Later Years* (New York: Philosophical Library, 1950), p. 229.

26. Bohr, quoted by Pais, *Niels Bohr's Times*, p. 87.

27. Werner Heisenberg, interviewed by Thomas Kuhn, 25 February 1963 (Archives of the Niels Bohr Library, The American Institute of Physics), pp. 7–8.

28. Alfred North Whitehead and Bertrand Russell, *Principia Mathematica*, 3 vols. (Cambridge: Cambridge University Press, 1927), p. vii.

29. *Monatshefte für Mathematik und Physik* 38 (1931): 173–198. Translated and reprinted as "On Formally Undecidable Propositions of *Principia Mathematica* and Related Systems I," in *Frege and Gödel: Two Fundamental Texts in Mathematical Logic*, ed. Jean van Heijenoort (Cambridge, Mass.: Harvard University Press, 1970), pp. 87–107.

30. A common example is the paradox in which a paper is inscribed with two statements: on one side, "The statement on the other side of this paper is

true," and on the other side, "The statement on the other side of this paper is false."

31. Niels Bohr, quoted by Aage Petersen, "The Philosophy of Niels Bohr," *Bulletin of the Atomic Scientists* 19, no. 7 (September 1963): 12.

32. Ibid.

33. There are, of course, a variety of factors responsible for the stability of modern physics. See, for example, Peter Galison's description of the intercalation of theoretical, experimental, and instrumental branches of physics: "The practice of experimental physics in the quantum mechanical revolution of 1926–27 was not violently dislocated despite the startling realignment of theory: spectroscopy continued unabated, as did measurements of specific heat and blackbody radiation. And practitioners of these experimental arts continued undaunted their dialogue with theorists on both sides of the great theoretical divide" (*Image and Logic: A Material Culture of Microphysics* [Chicago: University of Chicago Press, 1997], p. 798). In the pages that follow, I examine what I take to be the factors of greatest interest from a literary-critical point of view.

34. Boyd, "Metaphor and Theory Change," p. 483.

35. Ibid.

36. A "dynamic" metaphor is one in which the gap or dissimilarity between the tenor and vehicle remains an active feature in our use; a "static" metaphor is one in which the gap is not a feature of our use. Examples of the latter include the word "atom," as discussed above, or the phrase "the computer is running." A given metaphor may be either static or dynamic depending on either historical or individual use. In general, as discussed below, scientific use of metaphors privileges their static forms. There is, however, no absolute distinction between them. As Mary Hesse points out: "The interaction view [of metaphor, first propounded by Max Black in *Models and Metaphors* (Ithaca, N.Y.: Cornell University Press, 1962)] sees language as dynamic: an expression initially metaphoric may become literal (a 'dead' metaphor [what I call 'static' metaphors]), and what is at one time literal may become metaphoric (for example the Homeric 'he breathed forth his life,' originally literal, is now a metaphor for death). What is important is not to try to draw a line between the metaphoric and the literal, but rather to trace out the various mechanisms of meaning-shift and their interactions" (*Revolutions and Reconstructions in the Philosophy of Science* [Bloomington: Indiana University Press, 1980], pp. 116–117).

37. Thomas Kuhn, *The Structure of Scientific Revolutions*, 3rd ed. (Chicago: University of Chicago Press, 1996).

38. The dynamic I am describing can be interpreted as an interesting variation on the more clearly Kuhnian shift from metaphors—or *themata*, as Gerald Holton has called them—of continuity to those of discontinuity. See Holton, *Thematic Origins of Scientific Thought*, rev. ed. (Cambridge, Mass.: Harvard University Press, 1988), p. 102.

39. Petersen, "The Philosophy of Niels Bohr," p. 12. Emphasis in original.

40. Feynman, *The Character of Physical Law*, pp. 128–129. Emphasis in original.

41. Ibid., pp. 129–130

Chapter 2. "Wandering on New Paths"

1. Niels Bohr, "Introductory Survey," *The Philosophical Writings of Niels Bohr, Volume I: Atomic Theory and the Description of Nature* (Woodbridge, Conn.: Ox Bow Press, 1987), p. 9.

2. It is of course important to bear in mind that Einstein played a major role in the development of quantum theory. His reservations had to do with the epistemological status of the theory as it existed rather than the practical necessity of a quantum theory in some form.

3. Bohr's territory included, most notably, his work on the spectral lines of hydrogen, including the notion of stationary states, and the correspondence principle. Heisenberg's included the matrix mechanics of 1925.

4. Abraham Pais, *Niels Bohr's Times, in Physics, Philosophy, and Polity* (Oxford: Oxford University Press, 1991), p. 296.

5. Ibid., p. 304.

6. Werner Heisenberg, "Über den anschaulichen Inhalt der quantentheoretischen Kinematik und Mechanik," *Zeitschrift für Physik* 43 (1927): 172–198. Heisenberg sent the paper on March 22 (David Cassidy, *Uncertainty: The Life and Science of Werner Heisenberg* [New York: W. H. Freeman, 1992], p. 226) only a few days after Bohr's return on or around March 18 (Pais, *Niels Bohr's Times*, p. 308).

7. Cassidy, *Uncertainty*, p. 226. Heisenberg's uncertainty relations are $\Delta q \Delta p \geq h/2\pi$ and $\Delta E \Delta t \geq h/2\pi$. Based on these equations, the uncertainty principle states that the precision with which one can define the position q of a photon or material particle is inversely proportional to the accuracy with which one defines its momentum p; the precision with which one can define its energy E is also inversely proportional to the accuracy with which one records the time t of the measurement. Mathematically, this derives from the fact that the product of the uncertainty in a measurement of a particle's position in space and time—represented here by Δq (in three dimensions) and Δt respectively—times the uncertainty in a measurement of its energy ΔE and the corresponding momentum Δp must equal or exceed a factor $(1/2\pi)$ of Planck's constant.

8. Quoted in Pais, *Niels Bohr's Times*, p. 308.

9. A number of different sources examine Heisenberg's mistake in detail. See, for example, Pais, *Niels Bohr's Times*, or Cassidy, *Uncertainty*. Cassidy's description is particularly interesting, for it suggests a relation between Heisenberg's error and a mistake involving the same apparatus that Bohr himself made during his final oral examination for his Ph.D.

10. Mara Beller has argued that Bohr saw a greater opportunity for a reconciliation of quantum mechanics with the conventions of classical mechanics in Schrödinger's wave-packet formulation than Heisenberg's matrix mechanics, and that he therefore gave greater emphasis to the wave model in his initial presentation of the complementarity principle at Como; in subsequent drafts of this talk—e.g., the *Nature* article—he then shifted his argument to give more nearly equal weight to the two metaphors. See Beller, "The Birth of Bohr's Complementarity: The Context and the Dialogues," *Studies in History and Philosophy of Science* 23 (1992): 147–180.

11. In *Physics and Beyond: Encounters and Conversations* (New York: Harper & Row, 1971), Heisenberg suggests that Bohr "probably considered" the uncertainty principle "too special a case of the general rule of complementarity" (p. 79).

12. Heisenberg quoted in Cassidy, *Uncertainty*, p. 242.

13. From a letter written by Bohr to Einstein on 13 April 1927, quoted in Henry Folse, *The Philosophy of Niels Bohr: The Framework of Complementarity* (Amsterdam: North-Holland, 1985), p. 97.

14. Folse, in *Philosophy*, would take issue with my association of the term "principle" with complementarity, for good reason. As he writes:

Although Bohr's pupils and defenders are fond of referring to the *"principle* of complementarity" or the *"theory* of complementarity," in no place in Bohr's writings—including both published essays and private letters and manuscripts—have I ever found any reference to such an alleged "principle" or "theory," much less to an explicit statement of any such principle or theory. In fact, Bohr wisely avoided such terms, for speaking in this way would tend to produce misunderstandings regarding the sort of a thing he intended complementarity to be. "Complementarity" never labels any principle or theory, and searching for such merely obscures the fact that it is a "conceptual framework" from which to view physical principles or theories. (18–19)

I continue to refer to the "principle of complementarity," however, for two reasons. First, the phrase has earned the status of conventional usage. More important, however, though I find Folse's argument compelling, and though I agree that complementarity is more of a general conceptual orientation than a narrowly focused principle, in the end I reserve the phrase "conceptual framework" for even larger fish. A conceptual framework, such as that associated with classical physics, is in my view a concatenation of precedents, assumptions, and habits built up over time as the result of the actions of many individuals; as such, it is not something that can be created *ab ovo* by any one individual. Therefore, although I agree that complementarity was a cornerstone of the conceptual framework that oriented the work of quantum physics in the 1930s, I do not believe that in and of itself it constituted such a framework.

15. In response to objections that he was riding a hobbyhorse, he would laughingly compare himself to Socrates endlessly repeating his philosophy in the marketplace (Pais, *Niels Bohr's Times*, p. 422).

16. Beller, "The Birth of Bohr's Complementarity," p. 147.

17. Different versions of "The Quantum Postulate and the Recent Development of Atomic Theory" have been published in a variety of forums. Bohr's talk was first published (in its original English version) in *Atti del Congresso Internazionale dei Fisici 11–20 Settembre 1927, Como—Pavia—Roma*, vol. 2 (Bologna: Nicola Zanichelli, 1928). An emended version (with abbreviated introductory remarks and scattered amplifications throughout) was published as a special supplement to *Nature* 121 (14 April 1928): 580–590. Both of these texts have been reproduced in Niels Bohr, *Collected Works, Volume 6: Foundations of Quantum Physics I (1926–1932)*, ed. Jørgen Kalckar (Amsterdam: North-Holland, 1985). A hybrid version (retaining the original introductory remarks while incorporating

the amplifications of the *Nature* article) was published in Niels Bohr, *Atomic Theory and the Description of Nature* (Cambridge: Cambridge University Press, 1934) and subsequently reprinted in Niels Bohr, *The Philosophical Writings of Niels Bohr, Volume I: Atomic Theory and the Description of Nature* (Woodbridge, Conn.: Ox Bow Press, 1987). In addition, the lecture has been translated (both at the time and since) into various languages.

In the analysis that follows, most of the passages I consider can be found in all of these different versions. I do, however, look at some passages from Bohr's original introduction as well as several passages that include material added with the *Nature* article. For the convenience of readers who may wish to consult the context of passages excerpted in my analysis, I will refer for the introductory remarks to the version of Bohr's talk printed in *Atti del Congresso . . .* (hereafter cited as "Como paper") and for all other passages to the version published in *Nature* (hereafter cited parenthetically in the text, reprinted by permission from *Nature*, copyright 1928, Macmillan Magazines Ltd.). The reproductions in the *Collected Works* include the original page numbers of both these texts.)

This passage, from the opening remarks of the original lecture, is from the Como paper, p. 565.

18. Como paper, p. 565.

19. Dirac, Oppenheimer, and Wheeler, quoted in Ruth Moore, *Niels Bohr: The Man, His Science, and the World They Changed* (New York: Knopf, 1966), p. 156.

20. Quoted in Pais, *Niels Bohr's Times*, p. 315.

21. Moore, *Niels Bohr*, p. 164.

22. Gerald Holton, *Thematic Origins of Scientific Thought*, rev. ed. (Cambridge, Mass.: Harvard University Press, 1988).

23. These commentators include—in addition to Pais, Holton, Folse, and Beller—Edward M. MacKinnon, *Scientific Explanation and Atomic Physics* (Chicago: University of Chicago Press, 1982); Aage Petersen, "The Philosophy of Niels Bohr," *Bulletin of the Atomic Scientists* 19, no. 7 (September 1963); Sandro Petruccioli, *Atoms, Metaphors and Paradoxes: Niels Bohr and the Construction of a New Physics* (Cambridge: Cambridge University Press, 1993); Max Jammer, *The Conceptual Development of Quantum Mechanics*, 2nd ed. (Los Angeles: Tomash Publishers; Woodbury, N.Y.: American Institute of Physics, 1989); and Bruce Gregory, *Inventing Reality: Physics as Language* (New York: Wiley, 1988). In addition, of course, innumerable physicists have struggled to understand complementarity in the course of their professional lives. Carl von Weizsäcker, a young German physicist at the time of Bohr's Como address, for instance, made an "extensive effort to elucidate the original meaning of complementarity. However, when von Weizsäcker asked Bohr 'whether his interpretation accurately presents what Bohr had in mind, Bohr gave him a definitively negative answer'" (Beller, p. 148, quoting Jammer). The layering of references here will suggest how extensive commentary on complementarity has become.

24. Bohr, "Introductory Survey," p. 10. Bohr refers here to the observed quantization of electromagnetic radiation and of matter itself—the fact that the energy of photons and the momentum of material particles may only

assume certain discrete values—which Planck had codified as the quantum of action. Classical mechanics required these energy and momentum values to exist in a continuum such that any transition from one state to another would occur as a continuous increase or decrease. Such a gradual shift would allow a "causal mode of description" in accord with our sensory experience: when a car accelerates, for example, its passengers sense a continuous increase in velocity, without sudden leaps from lower to higher speeds. But experimental data gathered from observations of blackbody radiation and the behavior of subatomic particles insisted on the falsity of this interpretation. From 1900 on, it seemed that the acceleration of a material body could more accurately be described as a series of minute velocity "jumps."

25. See, for example, Paul R. Gross and Norman Levitt, *Higher Superstition: The Academic Left and Its Quarrels with Science* (Baltimore: Johns Hopkins University Press, 1994) or Paul R. Gross, Norman Levitt, and Martin W. Lewis, eds., *The Flight from Science and Reason* (New York: New York Academy of Sciences, 1997).

26. Moore, *Niels Bohr*, pp. 162–163. Schrödinger's response to the Como talk deserves consideration in the context of Beller's contention that Bohr was initially arguing for an interpretation of quantum phenomena that emphasized Schrödinger's wave method rather than a more balanced complementarity between the wave and particle models, as most commentators see it.

27. H. S. Allen, "New Problems in Quantum Theory," *Nature* 121 (14 April 1928): 579. [Reprinted in *Niels Bohr: A Centenary Volume*, ed. A. P. French and P. J. Kennedy (Cambridge, Mass.: Harvard University Press, 1985), p. 194.]

28. Quoted in Gregory, *Inventing Reality*, p. 85.

29. Pais, *Niels Bohr's Times*, p. 311.

30. Or "normal science," in Thomas Kuhn's phrase.

31. Note that Bohr continues to believe that "classical concepts" remain "necessary for the elucidation of phenomena." As we shall see, his radical program is both complicated and aided by his attempts to maintain the "classical point of view" as a working part of contemporary physics even as he overturns its domination of the discipline.

32. Pais, *Niels Bohr's Times*, pp. 311 and 316.

33. Como paper, p. 565.

34. Moore, *Niels Bohr*, p. 161.

35. Como paper, pp. 565–566. An anonymous reader of a draft of this chapter noted that it is worth pointing out that Bohr did not mean his metaphor of "wandering" to imply an aimless movement. Although it was not always clear in which direction they should move, quantum physicists generally, and Bohr in particular, were far from aimless.

36. See Chapters 5 and 6 for a detailed consideration of this rhetoric in the context of Los Alamos.

37. See Chapter 1.

38. Heisenberg recalled his debate with Bohr: "I would say, 'Well, waves and corpuscles are, certainly, a way in which we talk and we do come to these

concepts from classical physics. Classical physics has taught us to talk about particles and waves, but since classical physics is not true there, why should we stick so much to these concepts? Why should we not simply say that we cannot use these concepts with a very high precision, therefore the uncertainty relations, and therefore we have to abandon these concepts to a certain extent. When we get beyond this range of the classical theory, we must realize that our words don't fit. They don't really get a hold in the physical reality and therefore a new mathematical scheme is just as good as anything.' " Interview with Thomas Kuhn, 25 February 1963 (Archive for the History of Quantum Physics), typescript p. 18.

39. So Bohr says, "What is it that we human beings ultimately depend on? We depend on our words. We are suspended in language" (Petersen, "The Philosophy of Niels Bohr," p. 10), and Richard Feynman argues that "you have to have an understanding of the connection of words with the real world" (Richard Feynman, *The Character of Physical Law* [Cambridge, Mass.: MIT Press, 1967], p. 55). See Chapter 6 for a detailed consideration of Feynman's remark.

40. Bohr uses this phrase throughout his essay, with numbing regularity.

41. Quoted in Pais, *Niels Bohr's Times*, p. 312.

42. See, for example, Pais, *Niel Bohr's Times*, p. 315, or Beller, "The Birth of Bohr's Complementarity," p. 166.

43. Bohr calls his formulas "simple" and claims that their consequences are "immediately apparent." Yet for anyone not acquainted with mathematical reasoning of this kind, and especially for those unfamiliar with trigonometric and algebraic manipulations or physical quantities such as period, phase, and wavelength, Bohr's argument must appear virtually impenetrable. These readers are urged to bear in mind that his larger point, despite its dependence on mathematics, is not in itself mathematical. The following notes may also help elucidate Bohr's line of reasoning.

He begins with "the simple formulae which form the common foundation of the theory of light quanta and of the wave theory of material particles." In 1900, Planck derived the relation $E = h\nu$, in which E represents the energy of the atomic oscillators making up the walls of a blackbody cavity, h is Planck's constant, and ν stands for the frequency of the oscillators. Then in 1905, Einstein derived this same relation for the energy of a photon. Eighteen years later, in 1923, Arthur Compton discovered that the linear momentum of a light wave, like its energy, must be concentrated in a particlelike wave packet according to the relation $I = h/\lambda$, where I stands for the photon's momentum and λ refers to its wavelength. By simply substituting the period τ for the inverse of the frequency $(1/\nu)$ and solving each equation for Planck's constant, Bohr arrived at the triple relation that he labels equation (1): $E\tau = I\lambda = h$.

By invoking these equations, Bohr points out the centrality of both the particle and wave models even in the mathematics of modern physics. So he says, "In these formulae, the two notions of light and also of matter enter in sharp contrast." The "sharp contrast" here stems from the intimate manner in which the mathematical entities representing each model are related to one another through h, for the energy E and the momentum I are classical concepts associated with particles, while the period of vibration τ and the wavelength λ correspond, obviously, to a wave conception. Thus quantum theory relies on both the wave and particle models in a more obvious and inescapable manner than classical physics, in which proponents of either model could discount the necessity of the other; indeed the quantum of action seems to imply an essential connection between the two.

We should bear in mind that the quantities expressed in these quantum equations derive from classical mechanics. As mathematical entities they are free of any meaning whatsoever and exist as pure relational elements in the particular scheme described by the mathematical operations that join them. It is in the interpretation of the new relations into which mathematical manipulation places them that the question of their "meaning" has relevance. Only in this context, does Bohr differ from his quantum confederates. And, as we shall see, it is here that his mathematical argument bears fruit.

44. It is probably impossible to avoid confusion when the term "symbolic" crops up. As I will describe below, Bohr uses the term to contrast two types of interpretation, "literal" and "symbolic," though of course all interpretation is, by definition, "symbolic." Pragmatically, Bohr, like most of us, uses the two terms to denote relative degrees of symbolic activity, where literal implies a more stable, one-to-one correspondence between symbol and referent, and symbolic suggests a more slippery, multivalent relation. Scientists obviously prefer the former, though out of practical necessity they often engage in metaphorical descriptions.

45. Note his quiet use of the preposition "in" to maintain the relative positions of classical and quantum mechanics.

46. Such a situation would include that of the "stationary states" in which an electron in a stable relation to its nucleus is said to exist.

47. Heisenberg, "Quantum Theory and Its Interpretation," in *Niels Bohr: His Life and Work as Seen by His Friends and Colleagues*, ed. Stefan Rozental (New York: Wiley, 1967), p. 95.

48. Beller, "The Birth of Bohr's Complementarity," suggests that a potent source of motivation behind Bohr's development of complementarity was his desire to defend his earlier work, especially on the hydrogen atom and the correspondence principle.

49. Moore, *Niels Bohr*, p. 163.

50. Como paper, p. 565.

Chapter 3. "The Sense of Option in Knowledge"

1. George Gamow, *Thirty Years that Shook Physics: The Story of Quantum Theory* (New York: Dover, 1985), p. 167. Sadly, Gamow was not able to attend the 1932 Copenhagen conference himself, "the Soviet Russian Government having refused him a passport" (p. 168).

2. C. F. von Weizsäcker, "A Reminiscence from 1932," in *Niels Bohr: A Centenary Volume*, ed. A. P. French and P. J. Kennedy (Cambridge, Mass.: Harvard University Press, 1985), p. 186.

3. A photograph of the participants, along with a list of their names, was published in *Physics Today* 16, no. 10 (October 1963): 26–27.

4. Von Weizsäcker, "A Reminiscence," p. 186.

5. Robert Oppenheimer, "Tradition and Discovery," in *Uncommon Sense* (Boston: Birkhäuser, 1984), p. 109.

6. Paul Ehrenfest in a letter to Niels Bohr, Albert Einstein, James Franck, Gustav Herglotz, Abram Joffé, Philip Kohnstamm, and Richard Tolman, 14 August 1932. The letter is stored in the Niels Bohr Archive, Copenhagen, and quoted in Abraham Pais, *Niels Bohr's Times, in Physics, Philosophy, and Polity* (Oxford: Oxford University Press, 1991), p. 409. Pais reports that this letter was never sent. The emphasis is in the original.

7. As Karl von Meyenn writes, "Wie sehr man sich auch in Kopenhagen mit Paulis Neutronen befaßte"—people were very occupied with Pauli's neutron in Copenhagen. Meyenn, "Die Faustparodie," in *Niels Bohr, 1885–1962: Der Kopenhagener Geist in der Physik*, ed. Karl von Meyenn, Klaus Stolzenberg, and Roman U. Sexl, (Berlin: F. Vieweg, 1985), p. 309.

8. Gamow, *Thirty Years*, p. 167. Gamow had himself contributed a "stunt" to the previous year's conference (which coincided with a celebration of the institute's tenth anniversary) by drawing a cartoon history of quantum mechanics with Mickey Mouse as the protagonist.

9. My thanks to Felicity Pors and the Niels Bohr Archive in Copenhagen for help locating a copy of the original *Blegdamsvej Faust* and for providing a range of background information. In addition to the Bohr Archive, the original manuscript is also available as microfilm no. 66 of the Archive for the History of Quantum Physics (AHQP). Thanks also to Timothy Taylor, Beate Jahn, and Justin Rosenberg for their kind and painstaking reviews of my translations from the *Blegdamsvej Faust*. Any remaining flaws should be attributed to my stubbornness rather than a lapse in their diligence.

10. The only version of the *Blegdamsvej Faust* generally available to Anglophones is an English translation by George Gamow's second wife, Barbara, published as an appendix to *Thirty Years*, pp. 165–214. Throughout this chapter, I quote from the original German script. Parenthetical references are to page numbers in this text.

11. Meyenn, "Die Faustparodie," p. 308. In 1983, Weizsäcker revealed Delbrück's central role in the play's creation.

12. Ibid., pp. 312–313.

13. Unless otherwise noted, all emphases and ellipses in passages quoted from the *Blegdamsvej Faust* come from the original German text. The phrases marked with brackets are copied directly from Goethe by the authors of the *Blegdamsvej Faust*.

Any translation, of course, does some degree of disservice to its original. I have tried to offer a literal rendition while at the same time preserving what seem to me the most important metaphorical nuances of the original. I am indebted to Peter Salm's excellent translation of Goethe's *Faust*. As an antidote to my own bland, unrhymed, and arhythmic version, I would recommend Barbara Gamow's translation, though the reader should be aware that she took a number of liberties with the original in the process of turning it into an aesthetically rich English version.

14. Johann Wolfgang von Goethe, *Faust: First Part*, trans. Peter Salm (New York: Bantam, 1985), p. 16. This text is a dual-language edition; the translation here is mine.

15. This admission should be read within the context of the parody in which it appears; it was certainly not intended as a serious "confession" of ignorance but rather as a general spoof on the presumption of scientists in their reduction of vastly complex and mysterious processes to a limited number of symbolic "laws." Of course, some scientific theories do seem impenetrable at first, so it was said that only three people fully understood Einstein's Theory of Relativity when it was first published. This certainly overstates the case both ways. On the one hand, it would be a very poor theory that was accessible to only three people; although complicated, Einstein's theory was elegant and accessible to well-educated scientists. On the other hand, it is unlikely that even three scientists fully understood its implications, for, as in most powerful theories, they were numerous and far-reaching. Even the scientist who formulates a theory may well be unsure of its full meaning.

Cultural critics who examine scientific practices should be careful not to assume that scientists believe their theories represent some absolute Truth; most are well aware of their limitations, as the *Blegdamsvej Faust* demonstrates. Yet as it also suggests, science makes enormous claims for the truth value of its understanding of the natural world. These claims are generally well supported by experiment and technological application, and scientific disciplines demonstrate a remarkable level of achievement. Consequently, it is all too possible to caricature these achievements as divine, as the *Blegdamsvej Faust* does.

16. The *Blegdamsvej Faust* sometimes uses "Mephisto" and sometimes "Mephistopheles." I will use the former to refer to the character in the *Blegdamsvej Faust* and the latter to indicate Goethe's character.

17. The last line here copies the final line of Mephistopheles' opening speech in Goethe's original: "In jeden Quark begräbt er seine Nase." Salm translates this more idiomatically than I: "to rub his nose in imbecility!" (p. 18). Curiously, the physicists went on to prove Mephisto right: in 1963 Murray Gell-Mann and George Zweig proposed the name "quark" for the basic constituents of the most elementary subatomic particles. Physicists did indeed at last stick their noses into quarks. Ironically, however, the name was borrowed not from Goethe's *Faust* but from James Joyce's *Finnegans Wake*.

18. The phrases in angle brackets, < >, are in English in the original text.

19. The text as printed in Gamow here substitutes "Neutrino" for the *Blegdamsvej Faust*'s "Neutron." I retain the original word, though as Gamow argues it may lead to confusion with Chadwick's neutron. But I believe this confusion

was an important feature of the *Blegdamsvej Faust*—a way of engaging in the debate and uncertainty of the time. By replacing "neutron" with "neutrino," Gamow's version retroactively imposes an order that the scientific community was in the process of constructing in a time of debate and confusion, in part through the *Blegdamsvej Faust* itself.

20. Barbara Gamow makes the pun "an errin' Faust" in her translation of the *Blegdamsvej Faust*.

21. Just before their long back-and-forth exchange about Mass and Charge, the Lord asks Mephisto, "Kennst du den ehrenfesten?" ("Do you know Ehrenfest?"). To which Mephisto replies, "Schulmeister?" ("Schoolmaster?"), and the Lord counters, "Meinen Knecht!" ("My knight!"). *Blegdamsvej Faust*, pp. 4–5.

22. Goethe, p. 24. The ellipsis skips eight lines. The emphasis is mine.

23. Goethe, p. 25. Salm's translation. The emphasis is mine.

24. The ellipsis skips ten lines. The emphasis is mine.

25. For comparison's sake, I have used Salm's translation as the basis for mine, substituting my translation only where the *Blegdamsvej Faust* differs from Goethe.

26. Goethe, p. 104. Salm's translation, p. 105.

27. Ibid., p. 170. Salm's translation, p. 171.

28. Ibid., pp. 170, 172. My translations.

29. The song (to the tune of Schubert's "Gretchen at the Spinning Wheel") goes on for two more new verses and another repeat of the chorus.

30. "Mrs. Ann Arbor's Speak Easy (otherwise called 'Auerbachs Keller')" after Goethe, p. 128.

31. Werner Heisenberg's uncertainly principle is a case in point.

32. See Act III, Scene iii, line 58.

33. Note that he does not suggest the quantum mechanical approach itself should be thrown out, only the work of the past six years. The implication is that the effort should be begun again, not abandoned.

34. Note the echo here in the word "gerettet," the past participle of "retten," of Mephisto's lament, "nichts mehr zu retten ist," in his opening lines. The play has come full circle, and Mephisto retracts his earlier complaint.

35. Chapter 4 examines a case in point: the creation of the scientific community at Los Alamos.

36. Note that Pauli's theorized particle was ultimately validated by the same experimental authority that seems to defeat him here.

Chapter 4. *The Los Alamos Primer*

1. John H. Dudley, "Ranch School to Secret City," in *Reminiscences of Los Alamos, 1943–1945*, ed. Lawrence Badash et al. (Dordrecht, Holland: D. Reidel, 1980), pp. 3–4.

2. Ibid., p. 3.

3. The military members of the Manhattan Project often referred to their scientific colleagues by this and other equally disparaging terms.

4. Emilio Segrè, *Enrico Fermi: Physicist* (Chicago: University of Chicago Press, 1970), p. 135.

5. Robert Serber, preface to *The Los Alamos Primer: The First Lectures on How to Build an Atomic Bomb* (Berkeley: University of California Press, 1992), p. xxiii. This reprint of *The Los Alamos Primer* consists of four major parts: an Introduction by historian Richard Rhodes, a Preface by Robert Serber, Notes on the *Primer* written by Serber for the reprint edition, and the *Primer* text itself. Page references to the *Primer* itself will be given parenthetically in the text. Two drawings are reproduced courtesy Los Alamos National Laboratory Archives.

6. Richard Rhodes, *The Making of the Atomic Bomb* (New York: Simon and Schuster, 1986), p. 460.

7. Rhodes, Introduction, *Primer*, p. xi.

8. What was a rarity in 1943 became more common over the next fifty years. World War II marked a sudden and dramatic growth in military technologies, from radar and jet propulsion to computers and nuclear weapons. As a result, there is a large volume of writings on the relationship between science and the military, from which I have benefited. For works on nuclear science and the military (in addition to histories of the Manhattan Project) see, for example, Stanley Blumberg and Gwinn Owens, *Energy and Conflict: The Life and Times of Edward Teller* (New York: G. P. Putnam's Sons, 1976); Donald Brennan, ed., *Arms Control, Disarmament, and National Security* (New York: George Braziller, 1961); Brian Easlea, *Fathering the Unthinkable: Masculinity, Scientists and the Nuclear Arms Race* (London: Pluto Press, 1983); Daniel Ford, *Cult of the Atom: The Secret Papers of the Atomic Energy Commission* (New York: Touchstone, 1984); Robert Gilpin, *American Scientists and Nuclear Weapons Policy* (Princeton, N.J.: Princeton University Press, 1965); Len Giovannitti and Fred Freed, *The Decision to Drop the Bomb* (New York: Coward-McCann, 1965); Leslie Groves, *Now It Can Be Told: The Story of the Manhattan Project* (New York: Harper, 1962); Hugh Gusterson, *Nuclear Rites: A Weapons Laboratory at the End of the Cold War* (Berkeley: University of California Press, 1996); Stephen Hilgartner et al., *Nukespeak: The Selling of Nuclear Technology in America* (New York: Penguin, 1983); Alice Kimball Smith, *A Peril and a Hope: The Scientists' Movement in America, 1945–1947* (Cambridge, Mass.: MIT Press, 1970); Robert Williams and Philip Cantelon, eds., *The American Atom, 1939–1984* (Philadelphia: University of Pennsylvania Press, 1984); Robert Jay Lifton and Richard Falk, *Indefensible Weapons: The Political and Psychological Case against Nuclearism* (New York: Basic Books, 1982).

9. Serber, Preface, *Primer*, p. xi.

10. Rhodes, Introduction, *Primer*, p. xi.

11. I know of no work that addresses the issue of disciplinary conflict at Los Alamos, though it would make for a fascinating study.

12. At the center of this inner circle sat Oppenheimer, as the laboratory's director, with Serber, his former student turned colleague, close beside him.

13. For examinations of what constitutes "traditional scientific discourse" see Bazerman, *Shaping Written Knowledge: The Genre and Activity of the Experimental Article in Science* (Madison: University of Wisconsin Press, 1988); Alan Gross,

The Rhetoric of Science (Cambridge, Mass.: Harvard University Press, 1996); M. A. K. Halliday and J. R. Martin, *Writing Science: Literacy and Discursive Power* (Pittsburgh: University of Pittsburgh Press, 1993); Bruno Latour and Steve Woolgar, *Laboratory Life: The Construction of Scientific Facts* (Princeton, N.J.: Princeton University Press, 1986); and Greg Myers, *Writing Biology: Texts in the Social Construction of Scientific Knowledge* (Madison: University of Wisconsin Press, 1990).

14. Were it possible, sociological quantification of the Los Alamites' sense of the influence of the *Primer* might be desirable. Unfortunately, there is an insufficient statistical pool for such analysis.

15. Serber, for one, had a keen sense of the absurdity of the Los Alamos enterprise, citing *Alice in Wonderland* as the literary work most relevant to his experience there (correspondence with the author, 8 March 1993).

16. See, for example, Francis Bacon's *New Atlantis* (1627). In a chapter on "The Emergence of a Social Norm" of science in *The Rhetoric of Science*, Gross discusses the *New Atlantis* and the development of communal science in England.

17. "Indoctrination" is, of course, a standard term in military training. Since the Los Alamos scientists were joining a project run by the military, one could argue that they were, de facto, agreeing to be indoctrinated. But I believe there is also a deeper reason for their willingness to submit to the *Primer's* "indoctrination course."

18. See, for example, Latour and Woolgar, *Laboratory Life*.

19. Of course, as I have already suggested, complete consensus even within a tightly knit research community is rare and not necessarily advantageous.

20. As Halliday and Martin have shown in *Writing Science*, scientific language has developed a number of recognizable and consistent features. In large measure these features center on a process of nominalization in which complex noun groups compact process in three primary ways: (1) by transforming actions and processes into things (verbs into nouns); (2) by allowing for a shorthand referencing of taxonomic entities and their relations; and (3) by permitting further grouping of these entities across abstract, relational verbs. A characteristic scientific sentence, therefore, consists of two such noun groups— an initial group that restates an established set of relations and a secondary group that introduces a new element—joined by a simple verb that tends to avoid referring to particular processes in favor of establishing a causal or logical relation between the noun groups.

21. As Serber recalls: "I started talking about the 'bomb.' After a couple of minutes Oppie [Robert Oppenheimer] sent John Manley up to tell me not to use that word. Too many workmen around, Manley said. They were worried about security." Serber, Notes, *Primer*, p. 4.

22. Ibid., pp. 10–11.

23. This number code, used sporadically by Serber throughout the *Primer*, referred to fissionable elements by the second digit of their atomic number and the third digit of their atomic mass. So "25" meant the isotope of uranium (element 92) with 235 protons and neutrons.

24. Serber, Notes, *Primer*, p. 14.

25. Serber's use of fictions in the *Primer* requires its readers to engage in

something very like a "willing suspension of disbelief."

26. Historians and cultural critics of science generally recognize that varying degrees of uncertainty are involved in the practice of science, whether they view that practice as the "discovery" or the "construction" of scientific facts. Latour and Woolgar's identification in *Laboratory Life* of "statement types" commonly found in scientific prose, for example, maps in some detail five levels of certainty and their representative syntactic forms. None of these levels, however, engages a degree of uncertainty greater than that of a speculation believed by its author likely to be true. I know of no study that directly treats the role of what I am calling overt "fictions" in science.

27. Serber, Preface, *Primer*, pp. xxx–xxxi.

28. Teller, a superlative scientist, in addition to his own work on the Super, continued to make significant contributions to the efforts of his colleagues in other branches of the project.

29. Albert Einstein, "On the Method of Theoretical Physics," in *Ideas and Opinions* (New York: Dell, 1954), p. 266.

30. Ibid.

31. Ibid.

32. Ibid., pp. 266–267.

33. Ibid., p. 267.

34. Ibid., pp. 265–266.

35. I consider this issue in even greater depth in Chapter 9.

Chapter 5. A City on "The Hill"

1. The epigraph is from a coded telephone call from Arthur Compton to James Conant, chairman of the National Defense Research Council, announcing the critical achievement of the first sustained, manmade nuclear chain reaction on December 2, 1942, in the graphite pile built by Enrico Fermi's team in a squash court under the west stands at the University of Chicago's Stagg Field. Arthur Holly Compton, *The Cosmos of Arthur Holly Compton*, ed. Marjorie Johnston (New York: Knopf, 1967), p. 248.

2. Richard Rhodes, *The Making of the Atomic Bomb* (New York: Simon and Schuster, 1986), p. 436.

3. Herbert Anderson, quoted in Rhodes, *The Making of the Atomic Bomb*, p. 440.

4. Compton, *Cosmos*, p. 248.

5. Richard G. Hewlett and Oscar E. Anderson, Jr., *The New World, 1939–1946*, vol. 1, *A History of the United States Atomic Energy Commission*, (University Park: Pennsylvania State University Press, 1962; rpt. ed., Berkeley: University of California Press, 1990).

6. Chapter Four, "Secrecy," of Hugh Gusterson's *Nuclear Rites: A Weapons Laboratory at the End of the Cold War* (Berkeley: University of California Press, 1996), drawing on the work of contemporary anthropologists, offers an in-depth look at the effects of the culture of secrecy on employees of a modern weapons

laboratory. He writes, for example, that "practices of secrecy should be analyzed not just as ways of preventing other countries from imitating America's weapons programs but also as, in their own right, symbolic practices with social, as well as military, functions and consequences" (p. 80).

7. Ruth Marshak, "Secret City," in *Standing By and Making Do: Women of Wartime Los Alamos*, ed. Jane Wilson and Charlotte Serber (Los Alamos, N.Mex.: Los Alamos Historical Society, 1988), p. 2.

8. Hayden White, *Tropics of Discourse: Essays in Cultural Criticism* (Baltimore: Johns Hopkins University Press, 1978), pp. 85–86.

9. In the past, of course, a few scientists, such as Niels Bohr or Ernest Rutherford, wore an administrative hat in addition to their other work, generally as directors of institutes or laboratories. But Oppenheimer's role was new in that his duties were entirely administrative.

10. In some respects, all this resembles a return to the late Middle Ages. Many of the disciplinary boundaries that had been carefully constructed since the scientific revolution were broken down. Once again, political considerations could dictate how individual scientists practiced their discipline. Scientists were again subject to witch hunts such as McCarthyism. The possibility of technical applications had a renewed importance in determining the course of a scientist's research and career.

11. Leslie Groves, *Now It Can Be Told: The Story of the Manhattan Project* (New York: Harper, 1962), p. 151.

12. Victor Weisskopf, *The Joy of Insight: Passions of a Physicist* (New York: Basic Books, 1991), p. 142.

13. Peter Bacon Hales, *Atomic Spaces: Living on the Manhattan Project* (Urbana: University of Illinois Press, 1997), p. 74. Although the construction of Los Alamos may be called "violent," the Corps of Engineers, the contractors, and the laborers would probably object, rightly, that this was not one of their intentional goals.

14. David Hawkins. *Project Y: The Los Alamos Story* (Los Angeles: Tomash, 1983), pp. xi–xii.

15. Emilio Segrè, *A Mind Always in Motion: The Autobiography of Emilio Segrè* (Berkeley: University of California Press, 1993), p. 190. There is more than a passing resemblance here to the way the governments that funded the voyages of Renaissance explorers claimed their discoveries.

16. Hales, *Atomic Spaces*, p. 78.

17. Charlotte Serber, "Labor Pains," in *Standing By and Making Do: Women of Wartime Los Alamos*, ed. Jane Wilson and Charlotte Serber (Los Alamos, N.Mex.: Los Alamos Historical Society, 1988), p. 57.

18. John Manley, "A New Laboratory Is Born," in *Reminiscences of Los Alamos, 1943–1945*, ed. Lawrence Badash, Joseph Hirschfelder, and Herbert Broida (Dordrecht, Holland: D. Reidel, 1980), pp. 29–31.

19. Kathleen Mark, "A Roof Over Our Heads," in *Standing By and Making Do: Women of Wartime Los Alamos*, ed. Jane Wilson and Charlotte Serber (Los Alamos, N.Mex.: Los Alamos Historical Society, 1988), p. 32.

20. Ibid., p. 33.

21. Jane Wilson, "Not Quite Eden," in *Standing By and Making Do: Women of Wartime Los Alamos,* ed. Jane Wilson and Charlotte Serber (Los Alamos, N.Mex.: Los Alamos Historical Society, 1988), p. 43.

22. Marshak, "Secret City," p. 2.

23. Weisskopf, *Joy of Insight,* p. 122.

24. Bebe Caldes, personal interview, 10 June 1993. Note the conjunction of religious and geographical metaphors; this apparent coincidence turns up with remarkable frequency, as we shall see.

25. Hawkins, *Project Y,* p. xi.

26. Mark, "Over Our Heads," p. 29.

27. Manley, "A New Laboratory," p. 32.

28. Marshak, "Secret City," p. 3.

29. Phyllis Fisher, *Los Alamos Experience* (Tokyo: Japan Publications, 1985), p. 87.

30. As a result, they cast about for "extemporaneous" substitutes: "gadget," "fizzler," "stinker." Jane Wilson recalls: "A friend in the Tech Area, seeking the Chemistry Office, once asked a janitor, 'Where is the Stinker's Office located?' He led her up the stairs and down a long hallway, then ceremoniously opened a door and ushered her in. She was embarrassed to find herself in the Ladies Room." "Not Quite Eden," p. 46.

31. Weisskopf, *Joy of Insight,* p. 140.

32. Serber, "Labor Pains," p. 69.

33. Elsie McMillan, "Outside the Inner Fence," in *Reminiscences of Los Alamos, 1943–1945,* ed. Lawrence Badash, Joseph Hirschfelder and Herbert Broida (Dordrecht, Holland: D. Reidel, 1980), p. 44.

34. Bernice Brode, *Tales of Los Alamos: Life on the Mesa, 1943–1945* (Los Alamos, N.Mex.: Los Alamos Historical Society, 1997), pp. 114–115.

35. Ibid., p. 111.

36. Ibid.

37. Charlie Masters, "Going Native," in *Standing By and Making Do: Women of Wartime Los Alamos,* ed. Jane Wilson and Charlotte Serber (Los Alamos, N.Mex.: Los Alamos Historical Society, 1988), p. 124.

38. Hales, *Atomic Spaces,* contains the only scholarly account of this issue I have seen. Masters, "Going Native," is perhaps the most detailed single contemporary account of the Los Alamites' relations with the Native Americans, though both Brode, *Tales,* and Fisher, *Los Alamos Experience,* contain considerable information, scattered throughout.

39. Segrè, *A Mind Always in Motion,* p. 192.

40. Weisskopf, *Joy of Insight,* p. 150.

Chapter 6. New Worlds, Old Words

1. Edward Teller, Berkeley Interview, Los Alamos Historical Society Archives, (M) 4559g/82.652: p. 2.

2. Elsie McMillan, "Outside the Inner Fence," in *Reminiscences of Los Alamos,*

1943–1945, ed. Lawrence Badash, Joseph Hirschfelder, and Herbert Broida (Dordrecht, Holland: D. Reidel, 1980), p. 45. Note the use in McMillan's title of a geographical metaphor to describe her own relationship to the work being done at Los Alamos.

3. Robert Oppenheimer, *General Magazine and Historical Chronicle*, 1946, quoted in Richard Rhodes, *The Making of the Atomic Bomb* (New York: Simon and Schuster, 1986), p. 676.

4. From Einstein's letter to Franklin Roosevelt (2 August 1939), in Spencer Weart and Gertrud Weiss Szilard, eds., *Leo Szilard: His Version of the Facts: Selected Recollections and Correspondence* (Cambridge, Mass.: MIT Press, 1978), p. 95.

5. I am referring here to Einstein's assertion that "The unleashed power of the atom has changed everything save our modes of thinking, and we thus drift toward unparalleled catastrophe." See the Introduction for a discussion of Einstein's claim.

6. Of course such platitudes can and should undergo periodic revision, as the Columbus narrative has in recent years. Such revision often has the effect of destabilizing our relations—to the past, to our social institutions, even to our sense of self—but it occurs within an order shaped by the very narratives and the conceptual framework being revised. In this "revision from within" there exists an inevitable tension between stability and change, each relying on the other for its existence. In this dynamic, stability provides the foothold and leverage of change, and change maintains the vitality of cultural forms on which any stability depends.

7. Kenneth Bainbridge, "Orchestrating the Test," in *All in Our Time*, ed. Jane Wilson (Chicago: Bulletin of the Atomic Scientists, 1975), p. 230.

8. Quoted in Robert Locke, "Los Alamos Scientists Discuss the Legacy of Trinity," *Los Alamos Monitor*, 16 July 1975, p. 6.

9. William Wordsworth, "Lines Composed a Few Miles above Tintern Abbey, on Revisiting the Banks of the Wye during a Tour, July 13, 1798," in *Selected Poems and Prefaces by William Wordsworth*, ed. Jack Stillinger (Boston: Houghton Mifflin, 1965), p. 110.

10. Robert Oppenheimer, "Tradition and Discovery," in *Uncommon Sense* (Boston: Birkhäuser, 1984), p. 103.

11. The terror in this instance was real enough that Columbus felt the need to maintain two logbooks: one version for the crew in which he understated the expedition's distance from Europe and a private record of the actual distance they had traveled.

12. In another context, Oppenheimer asserted that the development of subatomic physics calls "for an art as high as the story of Oedipus or the story of Cromwell. . . ." See Chapter 8.

13. Oppenheimer, "Tradition and Discovery," p. 105.

14. Werner Heisenberg, "Fresh Fields," in *Physics and Beyond: Encounters and Conversations* (New York: Harper & Row, 1971), p. 70.

15. Richard Feynman, *The Character of Physical Law* (Cambridge, Mass.: MIT Press, 1967), p. 173.

16. Ralph Waldo Emerson, "The American Scholar," in *Emerson: Essays and Lectures*, ed. Joel Porte (New York: Library of America, 1983), p. 55.

17. Heisenberg, "Fresh Fields," pp. 80–81.

18. Feynman, *Character of Physical Law*, p. 56.

19. Aage Petersen, "The Philosophy of Niels Bohr," *Bulletin of the Atomic Scientists* 19, no. 7 (September 1963), p. 11.

20. Ibid., p. 12. Emphasis in original.

21. Feynman, *Character of Physical Law*, p. 128. See Chapter 1 for the full context of this quote.

22. Ibid., p. 129.

Chapter 7. "Taking the Cloth"

1. Quoted in Ferenc Morton Szasz, *The Day the Sun Rose Twice: The Story of the Trinity Site Nuclear Explosion, July 16, 1945* (Albuquerque: University of New Mexico Press, 1984), p. 85.

2. This passage comes from a portion of a film interview of Oppenheimer included in the biographical documentary *The Day after Trinity*. Also involved in my citation (as will become clear) are Richard Rhodes, *The Making of the Atomic Bomb* (New York: Simon and Schuster, 1986), p. 676; and Len Giovannitti and Fred Freed, *The Decision to Drop the Bomb* (New York: Coward-McCann, 1965), p. 197.

3. There are many examples of this. Indeed, it is easier to find a "misquotation" of Oppenheimer than one that catches his precise phrasing. We need look no further than the title of Peter Goodchild's biography, *J. Robert Oppenheimer: Shatterer of Worlds* (Boston: Houghton Mifflin, 1980).

4. Interview with Arthur Norberg (11 February 1976) Bancroft Library, University of California, Berkeley. Ellipsis in the original transcript.

5. Quoted in the Los Alamos National Laboratory publication, *Los Alamos 1943–1945: The Beginning of an Era*, p. 54.

6. Interview with Arthur Norberg.

7. R. W. Reid, *Tongues of Conscience: War and the Scientists' Dilemma* (London: Constable, 1970), p. 181.

8. Hugh Gusterson found a similar dynamic at work at the Lawrence Livermore weapons laboratory in California. As he writes: "Rather than ignore the ethical dilemmas of their work, weapons scientists learn to resolve these dilemmas in particular socially patterned ways" (*Nuclear Rites: A Weapons Laboratory at the End of the Cold War* [Berkeley: University of California Press, 1996], p. 42).

9. See Chapter 6.

10. It is a pleasure to acknowledge Robert Frost (a thoughtful reader of an earlier draft of this study) for pointing out the usefulness of the metaphor of ventriloquism in this context.

11. Thomas Farrell, quoted in Leslie Groves, "Memorandum for the Secretary of War," July 18, 1945. The original is stored in Groves's files, part of the

Manhattan Engineer District Records at the National Archives, Washington, D.C. It is reproduced in full or in part in numerous secondary sources. See, for example, Martin Sherwin, *A World Destroyed: The Atomic Bomb and the Grand Alliance* (New York: Vintage, 1977) where it appears in full (without accompanying "inclosures" [*sic*]) as Appendix P, pp. 308–314.

12. To a group of intellectuals in Edenic isolation during wartime, subject to accusations of cowardice and avoidance of military service, this could be quite a compelling argument.

13. Los Alamos National Laboratory Archives (A-84–019/22–7).

14. Joseph Hirschfelder, "The Scientific and Technological Miracle at Los Alamos," in *Reminiscences of Los Alamos, 1943–1945*, ed. Lawrence Badash, Joseph Hirschfelder, and Herbert Broida (Dordrecht, Holland: D. Reidel, 1980), p. 67.

15. Robert Wilson, "The Conscience of a Physicist," in *Alamogordo Plus Twenty-Five Years*, ed. Richard Lewis and Jane Wilson (New York: Viking, 1970), p. 71.

16. From a letter written on 2 July 1945, and reprinted in Spencer Weart and Gertrud Weiss Szilard, eds., *Leo Szilard: His Version of the Facts: Selected Recollections and Correspondence* (Cambridge, Mass.: MIT Press, 1978), p. 208.

17. Victor Weisskopf, *The Joy of Insight: Passions of a Physicist* (New York: Basic Books, 1991), p. 128.

18. Robert Wilson, "The Conscience of a Physicist," in *All in Our Time*, ed. Jane Wilson (Chicago: Bulletin of Atomic Scientists, 1975), p. 160.

19. Isidor Rabi, Berkeley Interview, Los Alamos Historical Society Archives (M) 4559e/82.652, p. 17.

20. Petruccioli is quoting a letter from Bohr to his Swedish colleague Carl Oseen, in *Atoms, Metaphors and Paradoxes: Niels Bohr and the Construction of a New Physics* (Cambridge: Cambridge University Press, 1993), p. 26.

21. *Los Alamos Newsletter*, 13 November 1945.

22. Robert Oppenheimer, *Uncommon Sense* (Boston: Birkhäuser, 1984), p. 30. It is worth noting here that Oppenheimer's implicit depiction of the atomic bomb as one of the Los Alamites' "private liqueurs" is chilling. It recalls another phrase Oppenheimer used to describe working on the bomb: he described it as a "technically sweet" project. This "sweetness" was one reason the project built up such momentum, he explains, and why so few of the participants stopped to question the morality of what they were doing once they had become initiates in the Los Alamos cloisters. Their "private liqueurs" seem to have been intoxicating and to have perpetuated the illusion that they might remain hidden from the rest of the world.

23. Ibid., p. 38.

24. Philip Morrison, *Philip Morrison's Long Look at the Literature* (New York: W. H. Freeman, 1990), pp. 81–82.

25. Robert Oppenheimer, *Atom and Void: Essays on Science and Community* (Princeton, N.J.: Princeton University Press, 1989), pp. 31–32.

26. William Higginbotham, interview with the author, 7 June 1993.

27. We should bear in mind how aggressively early modern scientists sought

to distance themselves and their practices from precisely these sorts of comparisons in order to stake out a distinct set of claims to knowledge.

28. Weisskopf, *The Joy of Insight*, p. 152.

29. "Internal texts" here refers to the patterns of language and narrative that collect in our memories as products of the external texts and conversations we encounter as well as our own language-based thought processes. These internal texts are different for every individual, though within a given milieu they are likely to share a wide range of similarities. Writers (both literary and scientific) shape their work to take advantage of these similarities—whether invoking them subliminally or challenging them overtly.

30. Cyril Stanley Smith, "Art, Technology, and Science: Notes on Their Historical Interaction," in *A Search for Structure: Selected Essays on Science, Art, and History* (Cambridge, Mass.: MIT Press, 1981), p. 227.

31. The dynamic I am describing here corresponds to what Max Black (in *Models and Metaphors* [Ithaca: Cornell University Press, 1962]) has characterized as the interaction view of metaphor. As Mary Hesse puts it:

Metaphor works by transferring the associated ideas and implications of the secondary to the primary system. These select, emphasize, or suppress features of the primary; new slants on the primary are illuminated; the primary is "seen through" the frame of the secondary. In accordance with the doctrine that even literal expressions are understood partly in terms of the set of associated ideas carried by the system they describe, it follows that the associated ideas of the primary are changed to some extent by the use of the metaphor, and that therefore even its original literal description is shifted in meaning. The same applies to the secondary system, for its associations, to be affected by assimilation to the primary; the two systems are seen as more like each other; they seemed to interact and adapt to one another, even to the point of invalidating their original literal descriptions if these are understood in the new, post-metaphoric sense. Men are seen to be more like wolves after the wolf-metaphor is used, and wolves seemed to be more human. Nature becomes more like a machine in the mechanical philosophy, and actual, concrete machines themselves are seen as if stripped down to their essential qualities of mass in motion. (*Revolutions and Reconstructions in the Philosophy of Science* [Bloomington: Indiana University Press, 1980], pp. 114–115)

32. Sometimes scientists seek to avoid these issues by enforcing the traditional but artificial separation between the disciplines, as seems to be frequently the case with cloning. Many scientists are choosing to ignore the ethical and social implications of such work by conceiving of it solely within the relatively narrow boundaries of their discipline, refusing to engage in the kind of cross-disciplinary metaphorical thinking that Weisskopf is bold enough to undertake despite its discomforts.

33. Glenn Price, interview with the author, 7 June 1993.

34. Interview. Los Alamos Historical Society Archives, (M)4559g/82.652, p. 8.

35. Otto Frisch describes the Lady Godiva assembly in *What Little I Remember* (Cambridge: Cambridge University Press, 1979), p. 161. Jezebel is mentioned in Paul Sperling's "Jews of Early Los Alamos: A Memoir," *Western States Jewish*

Notes to Pages 199–200

History 18, no. 4 (July 1986): 361. Thanks to Jon Hunner for bringing this article to my attention.

36. Rhodes, *The Making of the Atomic Bomb*, pp. 571–572.

37. A. L. Clements, ed., *John Donne's Poetry: Authoritative Texts, Criticism* (New York: Norton, 1966), p. 86.

38. For the purposes of the following discussion, it is helpful to locate Donne's poem in its particular representational tradition. In *Self-Consuming Artifacts*, Stanley Fish identifies Donne's method in the context of two broad rhetorical approaches, which he exemplifies through the traditions of Puritan and Anglican sermons:

Here, then, is the fundamental difference between the two sermon traditions; in one the faculties are put in good working order and made answerable to the task of comprehending truth; in the other the faculties are first broken and then replaced by the object of their comprehension, "a kind of saving by undoing"; one makes linguistic forms serviceable by making them unobtrusive; the other thrusts the forms of language before us so that we may better know their insufficiency, and our own; one claims to convey the truth and therefore claims everything; the other begins by claiming everything and then presides over the gradual disallowing of all its claims; one invites us to carry the truth away, the other to be carried away by the truth. (Stanley Fish, *Self-Consuming Artifacts: The Experience of Seventeenth-Century Literature* [Berkeley: University of California Press, 1972], p. 75)

Among other things, the "plain style," associated with the Puritans, influenced, as Robert Merton might suspect, the foundation of scientific prose. (See Robert Merton, *Science, Technology and Society in Seventeenth-Century England* [New York: Harper, 1970], particularly Chapters 4 through 6). This use of language assumes, first, its solidity and sufficiency as a medium for representing natural facts and, second, the sufficiency and solidity of natural facts as a medium for truth—whether because the natural world constitutes the author's interest and end, or because the author conceives of the natural world as itself luminous in some way (e.g., nature as the Word of God), or through a mixture of both assumptions. In this tradition, language serves as a more or less transparent vehicle for truth. The Anglican style, on the other hand, developed from platonic assumptions as filtered through St. Augustine. This tradition assumes that both words and natural facts are, in effect, shadows flitting across the inconceivable and trascendent face of God. But because words do mirror the unreliability and transitory character of earthly life, to the Christian author—and here we see a distinct recasting in Christian terms of Plato's attitude toward language—they offer an opportunity to capture and undo the toils of mere appearance in which we labor day to day.

Fish associates Donne in his sermons with the second tradition, and "Batter my heart" likewise functions according to this paradigm, on several levels.

39. Quoted in a letter from Oppenheimer to Rabi included in Alice Kimball Smith and Charles Weiner, eds., *Robert Oppenheimer: Letters and Recollections* (Cambridge, Mass.: Harvard University Press, 1980), p. 250.

Chapter 8. "Beggared Description"

1. Robert Oppenheimer, *Science and the Common Understanding* (London: Oxford University Press, 1954), pp. 37, 37–38, 38–39.

2. David Hawkins, *Project Y: The Los Alamos Story* (Los Angeles: Tomash, 1983), pp. xi, xiv.

3. Robert Wilson to Professor H. D. Smyth, 27 November 1943. Los Alamos National Laboratory Archives, A 84–019, 7–7. Smyth was a former professor of Wilson's and author of *Atomic Energy for Military Purposes* (Washington, D.C.: U.S. Government Printing Office, 1945).

4. Robert Wilson, from a letter to the author, 4 April 1992.

5. Alice Kimball Smith and Charles Weiner, eds., *Robert Oppenheimer: Letters and Recollections* (Cambridge, Mass.: Harvard University Press, 1980), p. 253.

6. Correspondence with the author, 8 March 1993.

7. See Chapter 1 for a discussion of dynamic versus static metaphors.

8. Thomas Farrell, "Memorandum for the Secretary of War," 18 July 1945. I examine the context of Farrell's remark in the next section.

9. See, for example, Bradbury's response to moral readings of the Trinity test and Weisskopf's remarks on the Isenheim Altarpiece, both considered in Chapter 7.

10. Otto Frisch, *What Little I Remember* (Cambridge: Cambridge University Press, 1979), p. 164.

11. Survivors of the Hiroshima and Nagasaki bombings.

12. In fact, Stalin had a much more complete knowledge of atomic weapons than Churchill and Truman imagined, thanks to the espionage of Klaus Fuchs and Harry Gold at Los Alamos.

13. Thomas Farrell, quoted in Leslie Groves, "Memorandum for the Secretary of War," 18 July 1945. The original is stored in Groves's files, part of the Manhattan Engineer District Records at the National Archives, Washington, D.C. It is reproduced in full or in part in numerous secondary sources. I have relied on Martin Sherwin, *A World Destroyed: The Atomic Bomb and the Grand Alliance* (New York: Vintage, 1977), where it appears in full (without accompanying "inclosures" [sic]) as Appendix P, pp. 308–314.

14. Joseph Hirschfelder, "The Scientific and Technological Miracle at Los Alamos," in *Reminiscences of Los Alamos, 1943–1945*, ed. Lawrence Badash, Joseph Hirschfelder, and Herbert Broida (Dordrecht, Holland: D. Reidel, 1980), pp. 76–77.

15. Quoted by Charles Mee, Jr., *Meeting at Potsdam* (New York: M. Evans and Co., 1975), p. 164.

16. From Truman's diary, quoted by Farrell, "Truman at Potsdam," *American Heritage*, June–July, 1980, p. 42.

17. Quoted in Mee, *Meeting at Potsdam*, p. 164.

18. Victor Weisskopf, "Eye Witness Account," 24 July 1945 (Los Alamos National Laboratory Archives, VFA 470: A-84–019/10–7).

19. E. R. Graves, "Notes, written at t_0 + approximately 2 hours, on visual observations of the gadget shot from Carrizozo" (Los Alamos National Laboratory

Archives, VFA 470: A-84–019/53–10).

20. Enrico Fermi, "My Observations during the Explosion at Trinity on July 16, 1945" (Los Alamos National Laboratory Archives, VFA 470).

21. As we shall see, following Hiroshima and Nagasaki the primary function of nuclear weapons has been precisely that of a rhetorical agent.

22. This assertion, of course, expresses a central (conscious) tenet in the development of the current style of scientific discourse.

23. From an unsigned article in *New York Times*, 7 August 1945, p. 5, col. 2.

24. "Text of Statements by Truman, Stimson on Development of Atomic Bomb," *New York Times*, 7 August 1945, p. 4, col. 2.

25. Lewis Wood, "Steel Tower 'Vaporized' in Trial of Mighty Bomb," *New York Times*, 7 August 1945, p. 1, col. 6.

26. Sidney Shalett, "First Atomic Bomb Dropped on Japan," *New York Times*, 7 August 1945, p. 1, col. 8.

27. William Laurence, *Men and Atoms* (New York: Simon and Schuster, 1959), p. 118.

28. It might be useful to point out that this is not simply a device peculiar to dramatic writings; a similar submission to the larger scientific community likewise authorizes the writings of individual scientists.

29. William Laurence, *Dawn over Zero: The Story of the Atomic Bomb* (London: Museum Press, 1947), p. 6.

30. Wood, "Steel Tower 'Varporized.' "

31. Quoted by Fletcher Knebel and Charles Bailey, *No High Ground: The Secret History of the Hiroshima Bomb* (London: Weidenfeld and Nicolson, 1960), p. 118.

32. Jacques Derrida, "No Apocalypse, Not Now (full speed ahead, seven missiles, seven missives)," *Diacritics* 14, no. 2 (Summer 1984): 22.

33. *New York Times*, 25 May 1946, p. 13, col. 5. See the Introduction for a detailed consideration of Einstein's assertion.

34. Derrida, "No Apocalypse," p. 23.

35. Laurence, *Dawn over Zero*, p. 172.

36. The military use of atomic weapons was further intended by those responsible for their development as a justification of the billions of dollars and hundreds of thousands of worker-years expended in their construction.

37. For survivors accounts, see *Hibakusha: Survivors of Hiroshima and Nagasaki* (Tokyo: Kosei Publishing, 1986); *Children of Hiroshima* (Tokyo: Publishing Committee for "Children of Hiroshima," 1980); Takashi Nagai, *We of Nagasaki* (London: Victor Gollancz, 1951) and *The Bells of Nagasaki* (Tokyo: Kodansha International, 1984); Michihiko Hachiya, *Hiroshima Diary* (Chapel Hill: University of North Carolina Press, 1955); Mikio Kanda, ed., *Widows of Hiroshima* (New York: St. Martin's Press, 1989); Nagasaki Appeal Committee, *Living beneath the Atomic Cloud: The Testimony of the Children of Nagasaki* (Tokyo: San-Yu-Sha, 1979); and Hitoshi Takayama, ed., *Hiroshima in Memoriam and Today* (Hiroshima: Society for the Publication of "Hiroshima in Memoriam and Today," 1973). For observers accounts, see John Hersey, *Hiroshima* (New York: Knopf, 1946); Naomi Shohno, *The Legacy of Hiroshima: Its Past, Our Future* (Tokyo: Kosei Publishing, 1986);

Rafael Steinberg, *Postscript from Hiroshima* (New York: Random House, 1965); Edita Morris, *The Seeds of Hiroshima* (Berlin: Seven Seas Books, 1966); Wilfred Burchett, *Shadows of Hiroshima* (London: Verso, 1983); and Robert Jay Lifton, *Death in Life: Survivors of Hiroshima* (New York: Random House, 1967). For technical summaries, see Samuel Glasstone, ed., *The Effects of Nuclear Weapons* (Washington, D.C.: U.S. Atomic Energy Commission, 1962) and The Committee for the Compilation of Materials on Damage Caused by the Atomic Bombs in Hiroshima and Nagasaki, *Hiroshima and Nagasaki: The Physical, Medical, and Social Effects of the Atomic Bombings* (New York: Basic Books, 1981).

38. Denying individuals access to their writings implies a belief that separating writers from their texts amounts to separating them from what they know—as if the physical embodiment of an idea in a text were the only "real" form in which it could exist. This reflects the common scientific assumption that the literal representations of scientific discourse are congruent to the things they represent. In the end, this grants an almost divine authority to scientific texts, modeling them on a vision of the world as an embodiment of God's Word, and effectively polices the scientific community by controlling the access of its individual members to their scriptures in much the same way the medieval Catholic Church controlled the laity's access to the Latin Bible.

Chapter 9. Physics in Fiction

1. J. D. Bernal, *Science in History, Volume 3: The Natural Sciences in Our Time* (Cambridge, Mass.: MIT Press, 1971), p. 735.

2. Frederick Soddy, *The Interpretation of Radium: Being the Substance of Six Free Popular Experimental Lectures Delivered at the University of Glasgow, 1908* (London: John Murray; New York: G. P. Putnam's Sons, 1909).

3. H. G. Wells, *The World Set Free: A Study of Mankind* (New York: E. P. Dutton, 1914). (Further page references will be given parenthetically in the text.) The first (British) edition of Wells's novel was published in 1913. Note how Wells constructs this inscription as an interaction between two books, attributing an unusual degree of agency to them. This presents us with a view very different from W. H. Auden's assertion(s) that "art (like poetry) makes nothing happen," considered in the Introduction.

4. Richard Feynman, *The Character of Physical Law* (Cambridge, Mass.: MIT Press, 1967), p. 129. Emphasis in original.

5. I discuss Feynman's remarks in more detail in Chapter 1.

6. Chapter 2 offers an extended consideration of Bohr's complementarity principle.

7. David Bohm, *Wholeness and the Implicate Order* (London: Routledge, 1980).

8. As we saw in the Introduction.

9. Leo Szilard, *The Voice of the Dolphins and Other Stories* (New York: Simon and Schuster, 1961), p. 19. (Further page references will be given parenthetically in the text.)

10. I should point out here that this is a common device throughout Western

literature. As science and literature emerged in their modern forms at the end of the Middle Ages, each adopted different techniques of authorizing their own utterances. Scientific writing tended to deemphasize the individual writer's authority in favor of the "things" of the material world about which the individual wrote. Since God created those things in the first place, scientists thereby claimed a kind of divine imprimatur. Literature, on the other hand, emphasized a distinction between the author's voice and that of the narrator. By downplaying the authority of the latter—"I'm just a simple man telling a simple story"—literary authors gained a wide latitude in the representation of human society and other less than divine subjects.

11. As I have shown in the last few chapters, the stories we tell ourselves about atomic weapons have a direct and dramatic effect on the ways in which we as a society integrate them into our lives.

12. Russel Hoban, *Riddley Walker* (New York: Summit Books, 1980), pp. 209–210. (Further page references will be given parenthetically in the text.) Perhaps a paraphrase would be useful here for the reader encountering this language for the first time—although we should beware of relying on such devices. As Hoban has pointed out, *Riddley Walker* "couldn't be translated. . . . It's not just the meaning, but the language itself" (from excerpts of a talk at San Diego State University published in *Poets & Writers Magazine* 20, no. 4 [July/August, 1992]: 35). The passage reads, roughly, "Erny said, 'It wasn't nuclear power, it was gunpowder. You're looking at Riddley Walker, but it wasn't he who turned gunpowder loose [among us], it was a wayfaring agent from the other side of the English Channel who was looking to negotiate, who wanted to bargain for a secret ingredient needed to complete the gunpowder mixture. Once his boat grated on the shingle [on the English shore where Riddley found it], gunpowder was loose in England, and it was going to blow someone up, and you can be sure someone was headed eagerly in that direction."

13. Ralph Waldo Emerson, "Self-Reliance," in *Emerson: Essays and Lectures*, ed. Joel Porte (New York: Library of American, 1983), p. 265.

BIBLIOGRAPHY

In addition to the texts listed below, this study drew on the following archival resources:

The Archive for the History of Quantum Physics.
The Bancroft Library, University of California, Berkeley.
The Los Alamos Historical Society Archives.
The Los Alamos National Laboratory Archives.
The National Archives and Records Administration, Washington, D.C.
The Niels Bohr Archive of the Niels Bohr Institute, University of Copenhagen.
The Niels Bohr Library of the American Institute of Physics.

I would like to acknowledge again my gratitude to the archivists and other employees of these institutions for their prompt and knowledgeable assistance.

Achinstein, Peter. *Particles and Waves: Historical Essays in the Philosophy of Science.* Oxford: Oxford University Press, 1991.
Ackland, Len, and Steven McGuire. *Assessing the Nuclear Age.* Chicago: Educational Foundation for Nuclear Science, 1986.
Akizuki, Tasuichiro. *Nagasaki 1945.* Trans. Keiichi Nagata. Ed. Gordon Honeycombe. London: Quartet Books, 1981.
Allison, Samuel K. "The State of Physics; or The Perils of Being Important." *Bulletin of the Atomic Scientists* 6, no. 1 (January 1950): 2–4, 26–27.
Alvarez, Luis. *Alvarez: Adventures of a Physicist.* New York: Basic Books, 1987.
Alvarez, Luis. *Discovering Alvarez: Selected Works of Luis W. Alvarez with Commentary by His Students and Colleagues.* Ed. Peter Trower. Chicago: University of Chicago Press, 1987.
Anders, Günther. Untitled essay. In *A Matter of Life.* Ed. Clara Urquhart. Boston: Little, Brown, 1963.
Auden, W. H. *Forewords and Afterwords.* New York: Random House, 1973.
Auden, W. H. *The English Auden.* Ed. Edward Mendelson. London: Faber and Faber, 1977.
Bacon, Francis. *The New Organon and Related Writings.* Ed. Fulton Anderson. New York: Bobbs-Merrill, 1960.
Badash, Lawrence, Joseph Hirschfelder, and Herbert Broida, eds. *Reminiscences of Los Alamos, 1943–1945.* Dordrecht, Holland: D. Reidel, 1980.
Bainbridge, Kenneth. *Trinity.* Los Alamos, N.Mex.: Los Alamos Scientific Laboratory, 1976.
Barber, Bernard. *Science and the Social Order.* New York: Collier, 1962.
Barnes, Barry, David Bloor, and John Henry. *Scientific Knowledge: A Sociological Analysis.* Chicago: University of Chicago Press, 1996.

286

Bibliography

Bartter, Martha A. *The Way to Ground Zero: The Atomic Bomb in American Science Fiction*. New York: Greenwood Press, 1988.

Bazerman, Charles. "Emerging Perspectives on the Many Dimensions of Scientific Discourse." In *Reading Science: Critical and Functional Perspectives on Discourses of Science*. Ed. J. R. Martin and Robert Veel. London: Routledge, 1998.

Bazerman, Charles. *Shaping Written Knowledge: The Genre and Activity of the Experimental Article in Science*. Madison: University of Wisconsin Press, 1988.

Beer, Gillian. *Darwin's Plots: Evolutionary Narrative in Darwin, George Eliot, and Nineteenth-Century Fiction*. London: Routledge and Keegan Paul, 1983.

Beller, Mara. "The Birth of Bohr's Complementarity: The Context and the Dialogues." *Studies in History and Philosophy of Science* 23 (1992): 147–180.

Beller, Mara. "Einstein and Bohr's Rhetoric of Complementarity." *Science in Context* 6 (1993): 241–255.

Bernstein, Barton, ed. *The Atomic Bomb: The Critical Issues*. Boston: Little, Brown, 1976.

Bernstein, Jeremy. *Prophet of Energy: Hans Bethe*. New York: E. P. Dutton, 1981.

Bethe, Hans. "Negotiations and Atomic Bombs." *Bulletin of the Atomic Scientists* 10, no. 1 (January 1954): 9–10.

Bethe, Hans. *The Road from Los Alamos*. New York: Simon and Schuster, 1991.

Bethe, Hans. "The Story of the Los Alamos Laboratory." *Los Alamos Scientific Laboratory Community News*, 30 June 1960, 4, 12; 14 July 1960, 5–6, 13.

Bethe, Hans. Interview with Thomas Kuhn. 17 January 1964. Archive for the History of Quantum Physics.

Bethe, Hans. Interview with Charles Weiner. 27 October 1966. Archive for the History of Quantum Physics.

Bethe, Hans. Interview with Charles Weiner. 8–9 May 1972. Archive for the History of Quantum Physics.

Bethe, Hans, and Philip Morrison. *Elementary Nuclear Theory*. New York: John Wiley and Sons, 1947.

The Bhagavad Gita. Trans. Franklin Edgerton. Cambridge, Mass.: Harvard University Press, 1944.

Blake, William. *The Complete Poetry and Prose of William Blake*. Rev. ed. Ed. David Erdman. Berkeley: University of California Press, 1982.

Bloch, Felix. Interview with Charles Weiner. 15 August 1968. Archive for the History of Quantum Physics.

Bloor, David. *Knowledge and Social Imagery*. 2nd ed. Chicago: University of Chicago Press, 1991.

Blumberg, Stanley, and Gwinn Owens. *Energy and Conflict: The Life and Times of Edward Teller*. New York: G. P. Putnam's Sons, 1976.

Bohm, David. *Wholeness and the Implicate Order*. London: Routledge, 1980.

Bohr, Niels. *Atomic Theory and the Description of Nature*. Cambridge: Cambridge University Press, 1934.

Bohr, Niels. *Collected Works, Volume 6: Foundations of Quantum Physics I (1926–1932)*. Ed. Jørgen Kalckar. Amsterdam: North-Holland, 1985.

Bohr, Niels. *The Philosophical Writings of Niels Bohr, Volume I: Atomic Theory and the Description of Nature*. Woodbridge, Conn.: Ox Bow Press, 1987.

Bohr, Niels. "The Quantum Postulate and the Recent Development of Atomic Theory." In *Atti del Congresso Internazionale dei Fisici 11–20 Settembre 1927, Como–Pavia–Roma*. Vol. 2. Bologna: Nicola Zanichelli, 1928.

Bohr, Niels. "The Quantum Postulate and the Recent Development of Atomic Theory." *Nature* 121 (14 April 1928): 580–590.

Bohr, Niels. Interviews with Thomas Kuhn. October–November 1962. Archive for the History of Quantum Physics.

Bono, James. "Science, Discourse, and Literature: The Role/Rule of Metaphor in Science." In *Literature and Science: Theory and Practice*. Ed. Stuart Peterfreund. Boston: Northeastern University Press, 1990.

Boyarin, Jonathan. *The Ethnography of Reading*. Berkeley: University of California Press, 1982.

Boyd, Richard. "Metaphor and Theory Change: What Is 'Metaphor' a Metaphor For?" In *Metaphor and Thought*. 2nd ed. Ed. Andrew Ortony. Cambridge: Cambridge University Press, 1993.

Boyer, Paul. *By the Bomb's Early Light: American Thought and Culture at the Dawn of the Atomic Age*. New York: Pantheon, 1985.

Bradbury, Norris. "The Los Alamos Laboratory." *Bulletin of the Atomic Scientists* 10, no. 9 (November 1954): 358–359.

Bradbury, Norris. Interview with Arthur Norberg. 11 February 1976. Bancroft Library, University of California, Berkeley.

Brennan, Donald, ed. *Arms Control, Disarmament, and National Security*. New York: George Braziller, 1961.

Brode, Bernice. "Tales of Los Alamos." *Los Alamos Scientific Laboratory Community News*, 2 June 1960, 5–8; 16 June 1960, 5–8; 30 June 1960, 5–8; 14 July 1960, 7–10; 28 July 1960, 5–8; 11 August 1960, 5–8; 25 August 1960, 5–8; 8 September 1960, 5–8; 22 September 1960, 5–7.

Brode, Bernice. *Tales of Los Alamos: Life on the Mesa, 1943–1945*. Los Alamos, N.Mex.: Los Alamos Historical Society, 1997.

Brooke, John Hedley. *Science and Religion: Some Historical Perspectives*. Cambridge: Cambridge University Press, 1991.

Burchett, Wilfred. *Shadows of Hiroshima*. London: Verso, 1983.

Bush, Vannevar. *Modern Arms and Free Men*. New York: Simon and Schuster, 1949.

Bush, Vannevar. *Science Is Not Enough*. New York: William Morrow, 1967.

Carpenter, Humphrey. *W. H. Auden: A Biography*. Boston: Houghton Mifflin, 1981.

Carroll, Lewis. *The Complete Works of Lewis Carroll*. New York: Modern Library, 1936.

Cassidy, David. *Uncertainty: The Life and Science of Werner Heisenberg*. New York: W. H. Freeman, 1992.

Chevalier, Haakon. *Oppenheimer: The Story of a Friendship*. London: Andre Deutsch, 1968.

Bibliography

Chevalier, Haakon. *The Man Who Would Be God*. New York: G. P. Putnam's Sons, 1959.

Church, Fermor, and Peggy Pond Church. *When Los Alamos Was a Ranch School*. Los Alamos, N.Mex.: Los Alamos Historical Society, 1974.

Church, Peggy Pond. *The House at Otowi Bridge: The Story of Edith Warner and Los Alamos*. Albuquerque: University of New Mexico Press, 1960.

Clark, Ronald W. *Einstein: The Life and Times*. New York: World, 1971.

Cohen, I. Bernard. *Revolution in Science*. Cambridge, Mass.: Harvard University Press, 1985.

Cohen, I. Bernard, ed. *Puritanism and the Rise of Modern Science: The Merton Thesis*. New Brunswick, N.J.: Rutgers University Press, 1990.

Cohn, Carol. "Sex and Death in the Rational World of Defense Intellectuals." *Signs: Journal of Women in Culture and Society* 12, no. 4 (1987): 687–718.

Columbus, Christopher. *Four Voyages to the New World*. Trans. and ed. R. H. Major. Gloucester, Mass.: Peter Smith, 1978.

Columbus, Christopher. *The Log of Christopher Columbus*. Trans. Robert H. Fuson, Camden, Maine: International Marine, 1992.

Committee for the Compilation of Materials on Damage Caused by the Atomic Bombs in Hiroshima and Nagasaki. *Hiroshima and Nagasaki: The Physical, Medical, and Social Effects of the Atomic Bombings*. New York: Basic Books, 1981.

Compton, Arthur Holly. *The Cosmos of Arthur Holly Compton*. Ed. Marjorie Johnston. New York: Knopf, 1967.

Crombie, A. C. *Medieval and Early Modern Science*. 2nd ed. 2 vols. Garden City, N.Y.: Doubleday, 1959.

Dampier, William, and Margaret Dampier, eds. *Readings in the Literature of Science*. New York: Harper, 1959.

Danin, D. *The Friendly Atom*. Trans. A. Shkarovsky. Moscow: Foreign Languages Publishing House, 1960.

Darrigol, Olivier. *From c-Numbers to q-Numbers: The Classical Analogy in the History of Quantum Theory*. Berkeley: University of California Press, 1992.

Davis, Nuel Pharr. *Lawrence and Oppenheimer*. New York: Simon and Schuster, 1968.

Dear, Peter. *The Literary Structure of Scientific Argument: Historical Studies*. Philadelphia: University of Pennsylvania Press, 1991.

De Kerckhove, Derrick. "On Nuclear Communication." *Diacritics* 14, no. 2 (1984): 72–81.

Derrida, Jacques. "No Apocalypse, Not Now (full speed ahead, seven missiles, seven missives)." Trans. Catherine Porter and Philip Lewis. *Diacritics* 14, no. 2 (1984): 20–31.

Dewey, Joseph. *In a Dark Time: The Apocalyptic Temper in the American Novel of the Nuclear Age*. West Lafayette, Ind.: Purdue University Press, 1990.

Doggett, Rachel, ed. *New World of Wonders: European Images of the Americas, 1492–1700*. Washington, D.C.: Folger Shakespeare Library, 1992.

Donne, John. *The Complete English Poems*. Ed. David Campbell. London: Everyman's, 1991.

Doorman, S. J., ed. *Images of Science: Scientific Practice and the Public*. Aldershot, England: Gower, 1989.

Dyson, Freeman. *Disturbing the Universe*. New York: Harper & Row, 1979.

Easlea, Brian. *Fathering the Unthinkable: Masculinity, Scientists and the Nuclear Arms Race*. London: Pluto Press, 1983.

Editors of Scientific American. *Atomic Power*. New York: Simon and Schuster, 1955.

Einstein, Albert. "Autobiography." In *Albert Einstein: Philosopher-Scientist*. La Salle, Ill.: Open Court, 1970.

Einstein, Albert. *Ideas and Opinions*. New York: Dell, 1954.

Einstein, Albert. *Out of My Later Years*. New York: Philosophical Library, 1950.

Eisenstein, Elizabeth. *The Printing Press as an Agent of Change*. Cambridge: Cambridge University Press, 1979.

Emerson, Ralph Waldo. *Emerson: Essays and Lectures*. Ed. Joel Porte. New York: Library of America, 1983.

Febvre, Lucien, and Henri-Jean Martin. *The Coming of the Book: The Impact of Printing, 1450–1800*. London: Verso, 1990.

Ferguson, Frances. "The Nuclear Sublime." *Diacritics* 14, no. 2 (1984): 4–10.

Fermi, Laura. *Atoms in the Family*. Chicago: University of Chicago Press, 1954.

Feynman, Richard. *The Character of Physical Law*. Cambridge, Mass.: MIT Press, 1967.

Feynman, Richard. *QED: The Strange Theory of Light and Matter*. Princeton, N.J.: Princeton University Press, 1985.

Feynman, Richard. *Six Easy Pieces: Essentials of Physics Explained by Its Most Brilliant Teacher*. Reading, Mass.: Addison-Wesley, 1995.

Feynman, Richard. *Surely You're Joking, Mr. Feynman!* New York: Norton, 1985.

Feymnan, Richard. *What Do You Care What Other People Think?* New York: Norton, 1988.

Fish, Stanley. *Self-Consuming Artifacts: The Experience of Seventeenth-Century Literature*. Berkeley: University of California Press, 1972.

Fisher, Phyllis. *Los Alamos Experience*. Tokyo: Japan Publications, 1985.

Folse, Henry. *The Philosophy of Niels Bohr: The Framework of Complementarity*. Amsterdam: North-Holland, 1985.

Ford, Daniel. *Cult of the Atom: The Secret Papers of the Atomic Energy Commission*. New York: Touchstone, 1984.

Franklin, Wayne. *Discoverers, Explorers, Settlers: The Diligent Writers of Early America*. Chicago: University of Chicago Press, 1979.

French, A. P., ed. *Einstein: A Centenary Volume*. Cambridge, Mass.: Harvard University Press, 1979.

French, A. P., and P. J. Kennedy, eds. *Niels Bohr: A Centenary Volume*. Cambridge, Mass.: Harvard University Press, 1985.

Friedman, Alan J., and Carol C. Donley. *Einstein as Myth and Muse*. Cambridge: Cambridge University Press, 1985.

Frisch, Otto. *Atomic Physics Today*. New York: Basic Books, 1961.

Frisch, Otto. *What Little I Remember*. Cambridge: Cambridge University Press, 1979.

Bibliography

Frisch, Otto. *Working with Atoms*. New York: Basic Books, 1965.

Funkenstein, Amos. *Theology and the Scientific Imagination*. Princeton, N.J.: Princeton University Press, 1986.

Galison, Peter. *Image and Logic: A Material Culture of Microphysics*. Chicago: University of Chicago Press, 1997.

Galison, Peter, and David J. Stump, eds. *The Disunity of Science: Boundaries, Contexts, and Power*. Stanford, Calif.: Stanford University Press, 1996.

Gamow, George. *Biography of Physics*. New York: Harper, 1961.

Gamow, George. *Mr. Tompkins in Paperback*. Cambridge: Cambridge University Press, 1965.

Gamow, George. *Mr. Tompkins in Wonderland*. New York: Macmillan, 1940.

Gamow, Geoge. *Thirty Years that Shook Physics*. New York: Dover, 1985.

Geddes, Donald, et al., eds. *The Atomic Age Opens*. New York: Pocket Books, 1945.

Geertz, Clifford. *The Interpretation of Cultures*. New York: Basic Books, 1973.

Gibbins, Peter. *Particles and Paradoxes: The Limits of Quantum Logic*. Cambridge: Cambridge University Press, 1987.

Giglioli, Pier Paolo, ed. *Language and Social Context*. New York: Penguin, 1972.

Gilpin, Robert. *American Scientists and Nuclear Weapons Policy*. Princeton, N.J.: Princeton University Press, 1962.

Gimpel, Jean. *The Medieval Machine: The Industrial Revolution of the Middle Ages*. New York: Penguin, 1976.

Giovannitti, Len, and Fred Freed. *The Decision to Drop the Bomb*. New York: Coward-McCann, 1965.

Glasstone, Samuel, ed. *The Effects of Nuclear Weapons*. Washington, D.C.: U.S. Atomic Energy Commission, 1962.

Gleick, James. *Genius: The Life and Science of Richard Feynman*. New York: Vintage, 1992.

Gödel, Kurt. "On Formally Undecidable Propositions of *Principia Mathematica* and Related Systems I." In *Frege and Gödel: Two Fundamental Texts in Mathematical Logic*. Ed. Jean van Heijenoort. Cambridge, Mass.: Harvard University Press, 1970.

Goethe, Johann Wolfgang von. *Faust: First Part*. Dual-language ed. Trans. Peter Salm. New York: Bantam, 1985.

Goldstein, Sheldon. "Quantum Philosophy: The Flight from Reason in Science." In *The Flight from Science and Reason*. Ed. Paul R. Gross, Normal Levitt, and Martin Lewis. New York: New York Academy of Sciences, 1997.

Goodchild, Peter. *J. Robert Oppenheimer: Shatterer of Worlds*. Boston: Houghton Mifflin, 1980.

Greenblatt, Stephen. *Marvelous Possessions: The Wonder of the New World*. Chicago: University of Chicago Press, 1991.

Greenblatt, Stephen. *Renaissance Self-Fashioning from Moore to Shakespeare*. Chicago: University of Chicago Press, 1980.

Gregory, Bruce. *Inventing Reality: Physics as Language*. New York: Wiley, 1988.

Grodzins, Morton, and Eugene Rabinowitch, eds. *The Atomic Age*. New York: Basic Books, 1963.

Gross, Alan. *The Rhetoric of Science*. Cambridge, Mass.: Harvard University Press, 1996.

Gross, Paul R., and Norman Levitt. *Higher Superstition: The Academic Left and Its Quarrels with Science*. Baltimore: Johns Hopkins University Press, 1994.

Gross, Paul R., Norman Levitt, and Martin W. Lewis, eds. *The Flight from Science and Reason*. New York: New York Academy of Sciences, 1997.

Groueffe, Stephane. *Manhattan Project*. Boston: Little, Brown, 1967.

Groves, Leslie. *Now It Can Be Told: The Story of the Manhattan Project*. New York: Harper, 1962.

Gusterson, Hugh. *Nuclear Rites: A Weapons Laboratory at the End of the Cold War*. Berkeley: University of California Press, 1996.

Haber, Heinz. *The Walt Disney Story of Our Friend the Atom*. New York: Simon and Schuster, 1956.

Hachiya, Michihiko. *Hiroshima Diary*. Chapel Hill: University of North Carolina Press, 1955.

Hacking, Ian. *Representing and Intervening: Introductory Topics in the Philosophy of Natural Science*. Cambridge: Cambridge University Press, 1983.

Hales, Peter Bacon. *Atomic Spaces: Living on the Manhattan Project*. Urbana: University of Illinois Press, 1997.

Hall, A. R. *The Scientific Revolution, 1500–1800: The Formation of the Modern Scientific Attitude*. Boston: Beacon Press, 1954.

Halliday, M. A. K., and J. R. Martin. *Writing Science: Literacy and Discursive Power*. Pittsburgh: University of Pittsburgh Press, 1993.

Harré, Rom. *The Principles of Scientific Thinking*. Chicago: University of Chicago Press, 1970.

Hawkins, David. *Project Y: The Los Alamos Story*. Los Angeles: Tomash, 1983.

Hayles, N. Katherine. *Chaos Bound: Orderly Disorder in Contemporary Literature and Science*. Ithaca, N.Y.: Cornell University Press, 1990.

Hayles, N. Katherine. *The Cosmic Web: Scientific Field Models and Literary Strategies in the 20th Century*. Ithaca, N.Y.: Cornell University Press, 1984.

Hayles, N. Katherine. "Self-Reflexive Metaphors in Maxwell's Demon and Shannon's Choice." In *Literature and Science: Theory and Practice*. Ed. Stuart Peterfreund. Boston: Northeastern University Press, 1990.

Heisenberg, Werner. *Across the Frontiers*. New York: Harper & Row, 1974.

Heisenberg, Werner. *Philosophic Problems of Nuclear Science*. New York: Pantheon, 1952.

Heisenberg, Werner. *Physics and Beyond: Encounters and Conversations*. New York: Harper & Row, 1971.

Heisenberg, Werner. *Physics and Philosophy*. New York: Harper & Row, 1958.

Heisenberg, Werner. "Quantum Theory and Its Interpretation." In *Niels Bohr: His Life and Work as Seen by His Friends and Colleagues*. Ed. Stefan Rozental. New York: Wiley, 1967.

Bibliography

Heisenberg, Werner. "Über den anschaulichen Inhalt der quantentheoretischen Kinematik und Mechanik." *Zeitschrift für Physik* 43 (1927): 172–198.

Heisenberg, Werner. Interview with Thomas Kuhn. 25 February 1963. Archive for the History of Quantum Physics.

Hersey, John. *Hiroshima*. New York: Knopf, 1946.

Hersey, John. "Hiroshima: The Aftermath." *New Yorker*, 15 July 1985, 37–63.

Hesse, Mary. *Revolutions and Reconstructions in the Philosophy of Science*. Bloomington: Indiana University Press, 1980.

Hewlett, Richard, and Oscar Anderson. *The New World: A History of the United States Atomic Energy Commission, Vol. I 1939–1946*. University Park: Pennsylvania State University Press, 1962. Reprint, Berkeley: University of California Press, 1990.

Hilgartner, Stephen, et al. *Nukespeak: The Selling of Nuclear Technology in America*. New York: Penguin, 1983.

Hoban, Russell. *Riddley Walker*. New York: Summit Books, 1980.

Hoddeson, Lillian, Paul Henriksen, Roger Meade, and Catherine Westfall. *Critical Assembly: A Technical History of Los Alamos during the Oppenheimer Years, 1943–1945*. Cambridge: Cambridge University Press, 1993.

Hofstadter, Douglas. *Gödel, Escher, Bach: An Eternal Golden Braid*. New York: Basic Books, 1979.

Holmes, Frederic L. "Argument and Narrative in Scientific Writing." In *The Literary Structure of Scientific Argument: Historical Studies*. Ed. Peter Dear. Philadelphia: University of Pennsylvania Press, 1991.

Holton, Gerald. *The Advancement of Science, and Its Burdens*. Cambridge: Cambridge University Press, 1986.

Holton, Gerald. "Quanta, Relativity, and Rhetoric." In *Persuading Science: The Art of Scientific Rhetoric*. Ed. Marcello Pera and William R. Shea. Canton, Mass.: Science History Publications, 1991.

Holton, Gerald. *Thematic Origins of Scientific Thought*. Rev. ed. Cambridge, Mass.: Harvard University Press, 1988.

Huie, William Bradford. *The Hiroshima Pilot*. New York: G. P. Putnam's Sons, 1964.

Huygens, Christian. *Treatise on Light, In which are explained The causes of that which occurs In Reflexion, & in Refraction And particularly In the strange Refraction of Iceland Crystal*. Trans. Silvanus P. Thompson. Chicago: University of Chicago Press, 1912.

Hyde, Montgomery H. *The Atom Bomb Spies*. London: Sphere Books, 1980.

James, William. *Psychology: The Briefer Course*. Ed. Gordon Allport. Notre Dame, Ind.: University of Notre Dame Press, 1985.

Jameson, Fredric. *The Political Unconscious: Narrative as a Socially Symbolic Act*. Ithaca, N.Y.: Cornell University Press, 1981.

Jammer, Max. *The Conceptual Development of Quantum Mechanics*. 2nd ed. Los Angeles: Tomash Publishers; Woodbury, N.Y.: American Institute of Physics, 1989.

Japan Broadcasting Corp., ed. *Unforgettable Fire: Pictures Drawn by Atomic Bomb Survivors.* New York: Pantheon, 1977.

Jehlen, Myra. *American Incarnation.* Cambridge, Mass.: Harvard University Press, 1986.

Jette, Eleanor. *Inside Box 1662.* Los Alamos, N.Mex.: Los Alamos Historical Society, 1977.

Jungk, Robert. *Brighter than a Thosuand Suns.* New York: Penguin, 1958.

Jungk, Robert. *Children of the Ashes: The Story of a Rebirth.* Trans. Constantine Fitzgibbon. London: Heinemann, 1961.

Kanda, Mikio, ed. *Widows of Hiroshima.* New York: St. Martin's Press, 1989.

Kern, Stephen. *The Culture of Time and Space, 1880–1918.* Cambridge, Mass.: Harvard University Press, 1983.

Kitcher, Philip. "Persuasion." In *Persuading Science: The Art of Scientific Rhetoric.* Ed. Marcello Pera and William R. Shea. Canton, Mass.: Science History Publications, 1991.

Knebel, Fletcher, and Charles Bailey. *No High Ground: The Secret History of the Hiroshima Bomb.* London: Weidenfeld and Nicolson, 1960.

Knorr Cetina, Karin. "The Care of the Self and Blind Variation: The Disunity of Two Leading Sciences." In *The Disunity of Science: Boundaries, Contexts, and Power.* Ed. Peter Galison and David J. Stump. Stanford, Calif.: Stanford University Press, 1996.

Koestler, Arthur. *Darkness at Noon.* New York: Time, 1962.

Kolodny, Annette. *The Lay of the Land: Metaphor as Experience and History in American Literature.* Chapel Hill: University of North Carolina Press, 1975.

Kuhn, Thomas. *The Essential Tension: Selected Studies in Scientific Tradition and Change.* Chicago: University of Chicago Press, 1977.

Kuhn, Thomas. "Metaphor in Science." In *Metaphor and Thought.* 2nd ed. Ed. Andrew Ortony. Cambridge: Cambridge University Press, 1993, pp. 533–542.

Kuhn, Thomas. *The Structure of Scientific Revolutions.* 3rd ed. Chicago: University of Chicago Press, 1996.

Kunetka, James. *City of Fire.* Albuquerque: University of New Mexico Press, 1979.

Kunetka, James. *Oppenheimer: The Years of Risk.* Englewood Cliffs, N.J.: Prentice-Hall, 1982.

Kurzman, Dan. *Day of the Bomb.* London: Weidenfeld and Nicolson, 1986.

LaFollette, Marcel. *Making Science Our Own: Public Images of Science, 1910–1955.* Chicago: University of Chicago Press, 1990.

Lamont, Lansing. *Day of Trinity.* New York: Atheneum, 1965.

Larsen, Rebecca. *Oppenheimer and the Atomic Bomb.* New York: Franklin Watts, 1988.

Latour, Bruno, and Steve Woolgar. *Laboratory Life: The Construction of Scientific Facts.* Princeton, N.J.: Princeton University Press, 1986.

Latour, Bruno. *Science in Action.* Cambridge, Mass.: Harvard University Press, 1987.

Bibliography

Laurence, William. *Dawn over Zero: The Story of the Atomic Bomb*. London: Museum Press, 1947.

Laurence, William. *Men and Atoms*. New York: Simon and Schuster, 1959.

Leiss, William. *Under Technology's Thumb*. Montreal: McGill-Queens University Press, 1990.

Levine, George. "Why Science Isn't Literature: The Importance of Differences. *Annals of Scholarship* 8, no. 3–4 (1991): 365–380.

Levine, George, ed. *One Culture: Essays in Science and Literature*. Madison: University of Wisconsin Press, 1987.

Levine, George, and Owen Thomas, eds. *The Scientist vs. the Humanist*. New York: Norton, 1963.

Lewis, Richard, and Jane Wilson, eds. *Alamogordo Plus Twenty-Five Years*. New York: Viking, 1970.

Libby, Leona Marshall. *The Uranium People*. New York: Crane Russak and Charles Scribner's Sons, 1979.

Liebow, Averill A. *Encounter with Disaster: A Medical Diary of Hiroshima, 1945*. New York: Norton, 1970.

Lifton, Robert Jay. *Death in Life: Survivors of Hiroshima*. New York: Random House, 1967.

Lifton, Robert Jay, and Richard Falk. *Indefensible Weapons: The Political and Psychological Case against Nuclearism*. New York: Basic Books, 1982.

Lindberg, David. *The Beginnings of Western Science*. Chicago: University of Chicago Press, 1992.

Lindberg, David, ed. *Science in the Middle Ages*. Chicago: University of Chicago Press, 1978.

Locke, Robert. "Los Alamos Scientists Discuss the Legacy of Trinity." *Los Alamos Monitor*, 16 July 1975.

Los Alamos: Beginning of an Era, 1943–1945. Los Alamos, N.Mex.: Los Alamos National Laboratory, 1984.

Lynch, Michael, and Steven Woolgar, eds. *Representation in Scientific Practice*. Cambridge, Mass.: MIT Press, 1990.

MacKinnon, Edward M. *Scientific Explanation and Atomic Physics*. Chicago: University of Chicago Press, 1982.

Mann, Thomas. *The Magic Mountain*. New York: Vintage, 1955.

Marlowe, Christopher. *Doctor Faustus*. Ed. Sylvan Barnet. New York: New American Library, 1969.

Martin, J. R., and Robert Veel, eds. *Reading Science: Critical and Functional Perspectives on Discourses of Science*. London: Routledge, 1998.

Marx, Joseph. *Seven Hours to Zero*. New York: McFadden-Bartell, 1969.

Marx, Leo. *The Machine in the Garden: Technology and the Pastoral Ideal in America*. Oxford: Oxford University Press, 1964.

Masters, Dexter, and Katherine Way, eds. *One World or None*. London: Latimer House, 1947.

Mayer, Richard E. "The Instructive Metaphor: Metaphoric Aids to Students' Understanding of Science." In *Metaphor and Thought*. 2nd ed. Ed. Andrew Ortony. Cambridge: Cambridge University Press, 1993.

McColley, Grant, ed. *Literature and Science*. Chicago: Packard, 1940.

McKibbin, Dorothy. Interview. 13 January 1982. Los Alamos National Laboratory Archives.

McPhillips, Martin. *Hiroshima*. Morristown, N.J.: Silver Burdett, 1985.

Mee, Charles L., Jr. *Meeting at Potsdam*. New York: M. Evans, 1975.

Mehra, Jagdish. *The Beat of a Different Drum: The Life and Science of Richard Feynman*. Oxford: Oxford University Press, 1994.

Meitner, Lise, and Otto Frisch. "Disintegration of Uranium by Neutrons: A New Type of Nuclear Reaction." *Nature* 143 (1939): 239.

Merton, Robert. *Science, Technology and Society in Seventeenth-Century England*. New York: Harper, 1970.

Merton, Robert. *The Sociology of Science: Theoretical and Empirical Investigations*. Ed. Norman Storer. Chicago: University of Chicago Press, 1973.

Meyenn, Karl von, Klaus Stolzenberg, and Roman U. Sexl, eds. *Niels Bohr, 1885–1962: Der Kopenhagener Geist in der Physik*. Berlin: F. Vieweg, 1985.

Michelmore, Peter. *The Robert Oppenheimer Story*. New York: Dodd, Mead, 1969.

Miller, Arthur. *Imagery in Scientific Thought*. Cambridge, Mass.: MIT Press, 1986.

Moore, Ruth. *Niels Bohr: The Man, His Science, and the World They Changed*. New York: Knopf, 1966.

Morris, Colin. *The Discovery of the Individual, 1050–1200*. New York: Harper Torchbooks, 1972.

Morris, Edita. *The Seeds of Hiroshima*. Berlin: Seven Seas Books, 1966.

Morrison, Philip. *Philip Morrison's Long Look at the Literature*. New York: W. H. Freeman, 1990.

Morrison, Philip. Interview with Charles Weiner. 7 February 1967. Archive for the History of Quantum Physics.

Myers, Greg. *Writing Biology: Texts in the Social Construction of Scientific Knowledge*. Madison: University of Wisconsin Press, 1990.

Nagai, Takashi. *The Bells of Nagasaki*. Tokyo: Kodansha International, 1984.

Nagai, Takashi. *We of Nagasaki*. London: Victor Gollancz, 1951.

Nagasaki Appeal Committee. *Living beneath the Atomic Cloud: The Testimony of the Children of Nagasaki*. Tokyo: San-Yu-Sha, 1979.

Nagasaki Prefecture Hibakusha Teachers Association. *In the Sky over Nagasaki: An A-Bomb Reader for Children*. Trans. Cheryl Green Lammers. Wilmington, Ohio: Wilmington College, 1977.

Oe, Kenzaburo. *Hiroshima Notes*. Trans. Toshi Yonezawa, ed. David Swain. Tokyo: YMCA Press, 1981.

Ong, Walter. *Orality and Literacy*. London: Methuen, 1982.

Oppenheimer, Frank. Interview with Charles Weiner. 9 February 1973. Archive for the History of Quantum Physics.

Oppenheimer, Frank. Interview. (M)4559(d)/82.652. Los Alamos National Laboratory Archives.

Oppenheimer, Robert. "Analogy in Science." *Centennial Review* 2, no. 4 (Fall 1958): 351–373.

Oppenheimer, Robert. *Atom and Void: Essays on Science and Community*. Princeton, N.J.: Princeton University Press, 1989.

Oppenheimer, Robert. *Letters and Recollections.* Ed. Alice Kimball Smith and Charles Weiner. Cambridge, Mass.: Harvard University Press, 1980.

Oppenheimer, Robert. *The Open Mind.* New York: Simon and Schuster, 1955.

Oppenheimer, Robert. *Science and the Common Understanding.* London: Oxford University Press, 1954.

Oppenheimer, Robert. *Uncommon Sense.* Boston: Birkhäuser, 1984.

Oppenheimer, Robert. Interview with Thomas Kuhn. 18 November 1963. Archive for the History of Quantum Physics.

Ortony, Andrew, ed. *Metaphor and Thought.* 2nd ed. Cambridge: Cambridge University Press, 1993.

Osborne, Charles. *W. H. Auden: The Life of a Poet.* New York: Harcourt Brace Jovanovich, 1979.

Pacey, Arnold. *The Culture of Technology.* Cambridge, Mass.: MIT Press, 1983.

Pacific War Research Society. *The Day Man Lost: Hiroshima, 6 August 1945.* Tokyo: Kodansha, 1981.

Pais, Abraham. *Niels Bohr's Times, in Physics, Philosophy, and Polity.* Oxford: Oxford University Press, 1991.

Pais, Abraham. *"Subtle Is the Lord . . .": The Science and the Life of Albert Einstein.* New York: Oxford University Press, 1982.

Pearl, Carleton. *The Tenth Wonder: Atomic Energy.* Boston: Little, Brown, 1956.

Peattie, Lisa. "Normalizing the Unthinkable." *Bulletin of the Atomic Scientists* 40, no. 3 (March 1984): 32–36.

Peierls, Rudolph. *Bird of Passage.* Princeton, N.J.: Princeton University Press, 1985.

Peierls, Rudolph. *The Laws of Nature.* New York: Charles Scribner's Sons, n.d.

Peierls, Rudolph. "The Uncertain Scientist." *New York Review of Books,* 23 April 1992, 43–45.

Pera, Marcello, and William R. Shea, eds. *Persuading Science: The Art of Scientific Rhetoric.* Canton, Mass.: Science History Publications, 1991.

Petersen, Aage. "The Philosophy of Niels Bohr." *Bulletin of the Atomic Scientists* 19, no. 7 (1963): 8–14.

Petruccioli, Sandro. *Atoms, Metaphors and Paradoxes: Niels Bohr and the Construction of a New Physics.* Cambridge: Cambridge University Press, 1993.

Pettit, Roland A. *Los Alamos before the Dawn.* Los Alamos, N.Mex.: Pajarito Publications, 1972.

Planck, Max. "Ueber das Gesetz der Energieverteilung im Normalspectrum." *Annalen der Physik* 4 (1901): 553–563.

Poirier, Richard. *A World Elsewhere: The Place of Style in American Literature.* New York: Oxford University Press, 1966.

Prelli, Lawrence J. *A Rhetoric of Science: Inventing Scientific Discourse.* Columbia: University of South Carolina Press, 1989.

Publishing Committee for "Children of Hiroshima." *Children of Hiroshima.* Tokyo: Author, 1980.

Purcell, John. *The Best-Kept Secret: The Story of the Atomic Bomb.* New York: Vanguard, 1963.

Pylyshyn, Zenon W. "Metaphorical Imprecision and the 'Top-Down' Research Strategy." In *Metaphor and Thought*. 2nd ed. Ed. Andrew Ortony. Cambridge: Cambridge University Press, 1993.

Rabi, I. I. *Science: The Center of Culture*. New York: World, 1970.

Rabi, I. I., et al. *Oppenheimer*. New York: Charles Scribner's Sons, 1969.

Reid, R. W. *Tongues of Conscience: War and the Scientists' Dilemma*. London: Constable, 1970.

Rhodes, Richard. *The Making of the Atomic Bomb*. New York: Simon and Schuster, 1986.

Richards, I. A. *Poetries and Sciences*. London: Routledge, 1970.

Rigden, John S. *Rabi: Scientist and Citizen*. New York: Basic Books, 1987.

Rosenfeld, Léon. "Niels Bohr's Contribution to Epistemology." *Physics Today* 16, no. 10 (October 1963): 47–54.

Rosenthal, Debra. *At the Heart of the Bomb: The Dangerous Allure of Weapons Work*. Reading, Mass.: Addison-Wesley, 1990.

Ross, Andrew, ed. *Science Wars*. Durham, N.C.: Duke University Press, 1996.

Rouse, Joseph. *Knowledge and Power: Toward a Political Philosophy of Science*. Ithaca, N.Y.: Cornell University Press, 1987.

Rozental, Stefan, ed. *Niels Bohr: His Life and Work as Seen by His Friends and Colleagues*. New York: Wiley, 1967.

Sayle, Murray. "Did the Bomb End the War?" *New Yorker*, 31 July 1995, 40–64.

Schwenger, Peter. *Letter Bomb: Nuclear Holocaust and the Exploding Word*. Baltimore: Johns Hopkins University Press, 1992.

Schwenger, Peter. "Writing the Unthinkable." *Critical Inquiry* 13 (1986): 33–48.

Seaborg, Glenn T. *Nuclear Milestones*. San Francisco: W. H. Freeman, 1972.

Segrè, Emilio. *Enrico Fermi: Physicist*. Chicago: University of Chicago Press, 1970.

Segrè, Emilio. *From X-rays to Quarks: Modern Physicists and Their Discoveries*. Berkeley: University of California Press, 1980.

Segrè, Emilio. *A Mind Always in Motion: The Autobiography of Emilio Segrè*. Berkeley: University of California Press, 1993.

Segrè, Emilio. Interview with Charles Weiner. 13 February 1967. Archive for the History of Quantum Physics.

Sekimori, Gaynor, trans. *Hibakusha: Survivors of Hiroshima and Nagasaki*. Tokyo: Kosei Publishing, 1986.

Serber, Robert. *The Los Alamos Primer: The First Lectures on How to Build an Atomic Bomb*. Ed. Richard Rhodes. Berkeley: University of California Press, 1992.

Sherwin, Martin. *A World Destroyed: The Atomic Bomb and the Grand Alliance*. New York: Vintage, 1977.

Shimony, Abner. "Role of the Observer in Quantum Theory." *American Journal of Physics* 31 (1963): 755–773.

Shohno, Naomi. *The Legacy of Hiroshima: Its Past, Our Future*. Tokyo: Kosei Publishing, 1986.

Shroyer, Jo Ann. *Secret Mesa: Inside Los Alamos National Laboratory*. New York: Wiley, 1998.

Slotkin, Richard. *Regeneration through Violence: The Mythology of the American*

Bibliography

Frontier, 1600–1860. Middletown, Conn.: Wesleyan University Press, 1973.
Smith, Alice Kimball. *A Peril and a Hope: The Scientists' Movement in America, 1945–1947.* Cambridge, Mass.: MIT Press, 1970.
Smith, Cyril Stanley. *A Search for Structure: Selected Essays on Science, Art, and History.* Cambridge, Mass.: MIT Press, 1981.
Smith, Henry Nash. *Virgin Land: The American West as Symbol and Myth.* Cambridge, Mass.: Harvard University Press, 1970.
Smith, Jeff. *Unthinking the Unthinkable: Nuclear Weapons and Western Culture.* Bloomington: Indiana University Press, 1989.
Smyth, Henry. *Atomic Energy for Military Purposes.* Washington, D.C.: U.S. Government Printing Office, 1945.
Snow, C. P. *The Physicists: A Generation that Changed the World.* London: Macmillan, 1981.
Snow, C. P. "The Two Cultures." *New Statesman and Nation,* 6 October 1956, pp. 413–414.
Snow, C. P. *The Two Cultures; and A Second Look.* Cambridge: Cambridge University Press, 1964.
Soddy, Frederick. *The Interpretation of Radium: Being the Substance of Six Free Popular Experimental Lectures Delivered at the University of Glasgow, 1908.* London: John Murray; New York: G. P. Putnam's Sons, 1909.
Solomon, J. Fisher. *Discourse and Reference in the Nuclear Age.* Norman: University of Oklahoma Press, 1988.
Sperling, Paul. "Jews of Early Los Alamos: A Memoir." *Western States Jewish History* 18, no. 4 (1986): 355–361.
Steinberg, Rafael. *Postscript from Hiroshima.* New York: Random House, 1965.
Stock, Brian. *The Implications of Literacy: Written Language and Models of Interpretation in the Eleventh and Twelfth Centuries.* Princeton, N.J.: Princeton University Press, 1983.
Stout, Wesley. *Secret.* Detroit: Chrysler Corp., 1947.
Sykes, Christopher. *No Ordinary Genius: The Illustrated Richard Feynman.* New York: Norton, 1994.
Szasz, Ferenc Morton. *The Day the Sun Rose Twice: The Story of the Trinity Site Nuclear Explosion, July 16, 1945.* Albuquerque: University of New Mexico Press, 1984.
Szilard, Leo. *The Voice of the Dolphins and Other Stories.* New York: Simon and Schuster, 1961.
Takayama, Hitoshi, ed. *Hiroshima in Memoriam and Today.* Hiroshima: Society for the Publication of "Hiroshima in Memoriam and Today," 1973.
Taylor, Bryan. "Make Bomb, Save World: Reflections on Dialogic Nuclear Ethnography." *Journal of Contemporary Ethnography* 25, no. 1 (1996): 120–143.
Taylor, Bryan. "The Politics of the Nuclear Text: Reading Oppenheimer's *Letters and Recollections.*" *Quarterly Journal of Speech* 78 (1992): 429–449.
Taylor, Bryan. "Reminiscences of Los Alamos: Narrative, Critical Theory and the Organizational Subject." In *Critical Questions: Invention, Creativity, and the Criticism of Discourse and Media.* Ed. William Nothstine, Carole Blair, and Gary Copeland. New York: St. Martin's Press, 1994, pp. 423–448.

Teller, Edward. *The Legacy of Hiroshima*. New York: Doubleday, 1962.

Teller, Edward. Interview with Mario Balibrera. 25 August 1979. Los Alamos National Laboratory Archives.

Thomas, Gordon, and Max Morgan Witts. *Enola Gay*. New York: Stein and Day, 1977.

Thomas, Gordon, and Max Morgan Witts. *Ruin from the Air: The Atomic Mission to Hiroshima*. London: Hamish Hamilton, 1977.

Townsend, Peter. *The Postman of Nagasaki: The True Story of a Nuclear Survivor*. New York: Penguin, 1985.

Truslow, Edith. *Manhattan District History: Nonscientific Aspects of Los Alamos Project Y, 1942–1946*. No publisher or date.

Ulam, Stanislaw. *Adventures of a Mathematician*. New York: Scribners, 1976.

U.S. Department of Energy. *Trinity Site*. Washington, D.C.: U.S. Department of Energy, 1992.

Urquhart, Clara. *A Matter of Life*. Boston: Little, Brown, 1963.

Weart, Spencer. *Nuclear Fear: A History of Images*. Cambridge, Mass.: Harvard University Press, 1988.

Weart, Spencer, and Gertrud Weiss Szilard, eds. *Leo Szilard: His Version of the Facts: Selected Recollections and Correspondence*. Cambridge, Mass.: MIT Press, 1978.

Weaver, Warren. *The Scientists Speak*. New York: Boni & Gaer, 1947.

Weisskopf, Victor. *The Joy of Insight: Passions of a Physicist*. New York: Basic Books, 1991.

Weisskopf, Victor. *Knowledge and Wonder: The Natural World as Man Knows It*. Rev. ed. Garden City, N.Y.: Anchor Books, 1966.

Weisskopf, Victor. *Physics in the Twentieth Century: Selected Essays*. Cambridge, Mass.: MIT Press, 1972.

Weisskopf, Victor. *The Privilege of Being a Physicist*. New York: W. H. Freeman, 1989.

Wells, H. G. *The World Set Free: A Story of Mankind*. New York: E. P. Dutton, 1914.

Wheaton, Bruce R. *The Tiger and the Shark: Empirical Roots of Wave-Particle Dualism*. Cambridge: Cambridge University Press, 1991.

White, Hayden. *Tropics of Discourse: Essays in Cultural Criticism*. Baltimore: Johns Hopkins University Press, 1978.

Whitehead, Alfred North, and Bertrand Russell. *Principia Mathematica*. 3 vols. Cambridge: Cambridge University Press, 1927.

Williams, Robert, and Philip Cantelon, eds. *The American Atom, 1939–1984*. Philadelphia: University of Pennsylvania Press, 1984.

Wilson, Jane, ed. *All in Our Time*. Chicago: Bulletin of Atomic Scientists, 1975.

Wilson, Jane, and Charlotte Serber, eds. *Standing By and Making Do: Women of Wartime Los Alamos*. Los Alamos, N.Mex.: Los Alamos Historical Society, 1988.

Wilson, Robert. Interview with Spencer Weart. 19 May 1977. Archive for the History of Quantum Physics.

Wyden, Peter. *Day One: Before Hiroshima and After*. New York: Simon and Schuster, 1984.

INDEX

Alice in Wonderland, 208, 272n15
Allen, H. S.: quoted, 61
Allison, Samuel: quoted, 14
Anderson, Herbert: quoted, 139
Art: "makes nothing happen," 7, 15–18, 237; popular conceptions of, 7–9; and science, 7–9, 10, 11, 15; and metaphor, 196–99
Atomic bomb, *frontispiece, 182, 204;* and Szilard, 3, 5, 134, 228, 233–37, 238, 240, 246; literature about, 3, 5, 234–46; and Wells, 3, 134, 228, 231, 238, 240, 246; as literary entity, 3, 221–23, 233, 245; and Einstein, 6, 12, 13; and science, 6, 83, 109, 113, 135, 209, 224; as symbolic entity, 6, 184–85, 221–23; as focus of this book, 18, 25–26; described, 21, 22–23, 210–12, 213–19; scientists' responses to, 21, 145, 155, 163–64, 184, 197, 203, 210–12, 221; and literary criticism, 24, 225, 245–46; and *Primer*, 111, 114–15, 117–18, 125–26; scientific knowledge of, 111, 117–18, 119–23, 125–31, 210–11, 216–17, 224–25, 237; morality of, 120, 184; use of term "bomb," 120, 272n21; interpreting, 145, 163–64, 185, 201–2, 210–11, 224, 228; in Germany, 171–72, 188; and religious rhetoric, 183–87, 192, 196–202, 213–15; existing literature used to describe, 183–87, 198–202, 206–8, 245–46; literary knowledge of, 185–87, 201–2, 210–11, 224–25, 228, 233, 237, 238–40, 245–46; literal vs. metaphorical description of, 196–97, 210–12, 223–24, 237, 244–46; and art, 196–99; and Churchill, 212, 216; and Truman, 212, 216, 218; and Hoban, 238–40, 245–46; and Riddley's English, 239, 240
Atomic power: as "moonshine," 3; and fiction, 4, 205, 207, 218, 229, 230; and Einstein, 6, 12, 13, 221–22; and scientists' authority, 14, 32, 128

Atoms: fission of, 21, 31, 127, 213; scientific knowledge of, 31, 34, 39–40, 47–48, 75–76, 122–24, 127–28, 173–74, 227–28; and metaphors, 35–36, 39–40, 61, 72–76, 102, 131, 193; origin and meaning of term, 40; Bohr's model of, 56, 61, 75, 194; and observers, 67, 73, 95, 131
Auden, George, 15
Auden, W. H.: and Blake, 7; and Einstein, 7; "In Memory of W. B. Yeats," 7, 15–17; "art makes nothing happen," 7, 15–18, 237; and his father, 15; and science and literature, 15; and Spain, 15, 16–17; and social responsibility of poets, 15–18; and China, 16; "Spain, 1937," 16–17; and Szilard, 234, 237

Babes in the Woods, 206
Bacon, Francis, 135, 145
Barium, 31
"Batter My Heart," 199–203; quoted, 199
Bazerman, Charles: quoted, 109, 114
BBC (Oppenheimer lectures), 205
Becquerel, Antoine Henri, 227
Beller, Mara, 58, 59, 262n10, 264n23; quoted, 58, 264n23
Bethe, Hans: quoted, 22–23
Bhagavad Gita, 20, 183–85, 188–90, 219; quoted, 183–84, 219
Bible, 20, 188, 201; and atomic bomb, 191–92; and Eusa story, 241
Black, Max, 261n36, 279n31
Blake, William, 7
Blegdamsvej Faust, 25, *80*, 84–107; and physicists' bargains, 82, 83, 85, 90–91, 104–7; authorship of, 84; characters in, 84; use of comedy in, 88; epigraph of, 90; and Ehrenfest's view of physics, 91; compared with Goethe's *Faust*, 91–94; role of Gretchen in, 95–96; conclusion of, 103–6; and Los Alamos, 146; quoted, 86–105 *passim*

301

SCIENCE AND LITERATURE
A series edited by George Levine